Teamsters and Turtles?

People, Passions, and Power
*Social Movements, Interest Organizations,
and the Political Process*
Series Editor: John C. Green

Titles in the Series

After the Boom: The Politics of Generation X edited by Stephen C. Craig and Stephen Earl Bennett

American Labor Unions in the Electoral Arena by Herbert B. Asher, Eric S. Heberlig, Randall B. Ripley, and Karen Snyder

Citizen Democracy: Political Activists in a Cynical Age by Stephen E. Frantzich

Cyberpolitics: Citizen Activism in the Age of the Internet by Kevin A. Hill and John E. Hughes

Democracy's Moment: Reforming the American Political System for the 21st Century edited by Ron Hayduk and Kevin Mattson

Gaia's Wager: Environmental Movements and the Challenge of Sustainability by Gary C. Bryner

Multiparty Politics in America edited by Paul S. Herrnson and John C. Green

Multiparty Politics in America, 2nd ed., edited by Paul S. Herrnson and John C. Green

Social Movements and American Political Institutions edited by Anne N. Costain and Andrew S. McFarland

Teamsters and Turtles?: U. S. Progressive Political Movements in the 21st Century edited by John C. Berg

The Social Movement Society: Contentious Politics for a New Century edited by David S. Meyer and Sidney Tarrow

The State of the Parties: The Changing Role of Contemporary American Parties, 3rd ed., edited by John C. Green and Daniel M. Shea

Waves of Protest: Social Movements since the Sixties edited by Jo Freeman and Victoria Johnson

Forthcoming

Chimes of Freedom: Student Protest and the American University by Christine Kelly

Rage on the Right: The American Militia Movement from Ruby Ridge to September 11th by Lane Crothers

Rethinking Social Movements: Structure, Meaning, and Emotion edited by Jeff Goodwin and James M. Jasper

The Art and Craft of Lobbying: Political Engagement in American Politics by Ronald G. Shaiko

The Gay and Lesbian Rights Movement: Changing Policies! Changing Minds? by Steven H. Haeberle

The State of the Parties, 4th ed., edited by John C. Green and Rick D. Farmer

The U.S. Women's Movement in Global Perspective edited by Lee Ann Banaszak

Teamsters and Turtles?

U.S. Progressive Political Movements in the 21st Century

Edited by
John C. Berg

ROWMAN & LITTLEFIELD PUBLISHERS, INC.
Lanham • Boulder • New York • Oxford

ROWMAN & LITTLEFIELD PUBLISHERS, INC.

Published in the United States of America
by Rowman & Littlefield Publishers, Inc.
A Member of the Rowman & Littlefield Publishing Group
4720 Boston Way, Lanham, Maryland 20706
www.rowmanlittlefield.com

PO Box 317, Oxford, OX2 9RU, United Kingdom

British Library Cataloguing in Publication Information Available

Library of Congress Cataloging-in-Publication Data

Teamsters and Turtles? : U.S. progressive political movements in the 21st century /
    edited by John C. Berg.
        p.   cm. — (People, passions, and power)
    Includes bibliographical references and index.
    ISBN 0-7425-0191-4 (cloth : alk. paper) — ISBN 0-7425-0192-2 (pbk. : alk.
paper)
        1. New Left—United States.   2. Social movements—United
States.   3. United States—Politics and government—2001– .   I. Berg, John C.
II. Title: U.S. progressive political movements in the 21st century.   III. Series.
HN90.R3T4   2003
322.4'0973—dc21   2002009706

Printed in the United States of America

 ⊗ ™ The paper used in this publication meets the minimum requirements of
American National Standard for Information Sciences—Permanence of Paper for
Printed Library Materials, ANSI/NISO Z39.48-1992.

Contents

Acknowledgments   vii

1   Introduction   1
     John C. Berg

2   From Anti-Globalization to Global Justice: A Twenty-First-
     Century Movement   17
     Ronald Hayduk

Part I: Movements Based on Material Needs

3   Unions and American Workers: Whither the Labor
     Movement?   53
     Immanuel Ness

4   Mass-Membership Senior Interest Groups and the Politics of
     Aging   65
     Laura Katz Olson and Frank L. Davis

5   Radical and Pragmatic: United Students against Sweatshops   83
     Christine Kelly and Joel Lefkowitz

Part II: Movements Based on Postmaterialist Identities

6   From Women's Survival to New Directions: WAND and
     Anti-Militarism   101
     Melissa Haussman

7   The AIDS Coalition to Unleash Power: A Brief
     Reconsideration   133
     Benjamin Shepard

8   The Disability Movement: Ubiquitous but Unknown   159
     David Pfeiffer

Part III: Altruistic Movements

9 Growing Green: Can It Happen Here?   187
   James R. Simmons and Solon J. Simmons

10 Human Rights Watch: American Liberal Values in the Global
   Arena   211
   Claude E. Welch, Jr.

11 The Peace Movement: Voices in the Wilderness   229
   Meredith Reid Sarkees

Index   265

About the Contributors   281

Acknowledgments

Many people have contributed to this book, most of all the chapter authors, to whom I am deeply grateful, both for their work and for the patience they have shown me as I failed time after time to send them my introduction by the promised deadline. I would also like to thank R. Claire Snyder for providing an opportunity, in her capacity as program chair for the Caucus for a New Political Science, for several of the chapter authors to meet at a mini-conference in August 2000. Jennifer Knerr of Rowman & Littlefield and John C. Green, series editor of "People, Passions, and Politics" have been wonderfully supportive throughout. The librarians at Suffolk University's Sawyer Library have been invariably cheerful and cooperative as they obtained yet another interlibrary loan; and my research assistants during the time of writing, Aine Cryts and Jason Devine, were indispensable. The Rothermere American Institute at Oxford University and its assistant director, Andrea Beighton, made it possible to correct the proofs while far from home. Needless to say, any errors are my own responsibility.

1

Introduction

JOHN C. BERG

TEAMSTERS AND TURTLES . . . TOGETHER AT LAST! This sign, carried by Tacoma longshoreman Brad Spannon at the 1999 Seattle protests, captures the hope felt by many that those protests marked a promising new turn in the U.S. left. That hope was twofold. First, the protests united a broad range of constituencies that had often opposed each other in recent years, such as some of the more conservative labor unions (Teamsters) and radical environmentalists (Turtles—the Earth Island Institute had brought five hundred sea turtle costumes to the demonstration) in a movement for global justice. Just as important, the protesters managed to maintain a sense of quirkiness, optimism, and fun in the face of tear gas, police clubs, and jail.[1]

Seattle was exciting, but the unity of progressive political movements remains a goal, not an accomplishment. The movements that were represented in the Seattle protests—and those that were not, but might have been—are divided by their histories, their organizational needs, their visions of the future, and their strategies for achieving those visions. In this book we examine the global justice movement itself and then look at nine other movements that might be part of a future coalition to see where they are today, how they got there, where they might be going in the future, and how they fit in to the broader social movement picture. In doing so, we hope to provide some insight into the future of left protest politics in America. Before we do, however, we need to define our terms and examine some theoretical issues that will frame our analysis.

DEFINING OUR TERMS

It was hard to choose the subtitle for this book. The publisher's idea was to have a book on liberal movements paired with another book on conservative movements; but they said from the beginning that they knew "liberal" was not the right word. The trouble is that liberal means different

1

things in different contexts. Sometimes liberal and conservative are opposed in the sense of left *versus* right, but sometimes liberal means support for the freedom of capitalist businesses against state regulation. The causes of this confusion are too involved to discuss here;[2] but the result is that the "liberal" label would be rejected by many of the participants in the movements discussed in this book.

My own preference was to refer to "left" movements. This soon led to debate about whether a given movement or organization was or was not truly part of the left. For purposes of the subtitle we turned to "progressive" as a more amorphous and, therefore, inclusive term. The intention was to signal our use of an inclusive approach. However, "left" is used in the following paragraphs in order to make use of the considerable literature (mostly not American) that attempts to answer the question What is left?

In fact, if we want to discuss left political movements, we need to define all three terms. The meanings of left and political are subject to considerable controversy; while movements are a common focus of study, it is far from clear how the phenomena known as movements are to be distinguished from those known as interest groups or political parties.

What Is Left?

A vast body of literature debates the meaning of left and right. Some question whether the words still mean anything at all; Anthony Giddens, for example, maintains that while the distinction is useful for practical politics, it is meaningful "only on a very general plane."[3] The meaning of left is clouded by decades of confused usages arising from the Cold War and the Civil Rights movement. The Cold War tended to divide left and right by their attitude toward the Soviet Union, whereas the use of "states' rights" to justify racial segregation led to the idea that left and right could be divided by their support for or opposition to a larger role for the federal government.

Neither of these criteria made any theoretical sense. Internationally, left and right alike found themselves supporting governments that were hostile to their basic values, simply because of those governments' foreign policy alliances, whereas in domestic politics federal preemption of public policy has just as often protected giant corporations from proconsumer regulation as it has guaranteed the rights of the oppressed.[4] In practice, though, these convenient rules of thumb accurately predicted political alignments in the United States in the 1960s and 1970s. It is in good part the declining validity of these rules, in their British variant, that leads Giddens to question the usefulness of the basic terms. Can we find a more logical criterion?

Equality as a Criterion

Many Marxists would argue that left and right are matters of class position. From this point of view the left position corresponds to the interest of the industrial working class, while the right position corresponds to that of capital. There is much to say for this approach, and we can dismiss one of the common objections to it, that the industrial working class is no longer with us. As Michael Zweig shows, the working class still constitutes a majority of the American population, even if a smaller fraction of it is organized into labor unions than had been previously.[5] However, to insist that all social movements can be reduced to a class essence excludes those movements that do not define themselves that way. Faced with the movement for reproductive freedom, analysts must either give up class as the basis for classification or develop convoluted chains of reasoning to show that, for example, abortion is really beneficial for workers but bad for capitalists.

Free-market conservatives like to define left and right as adherents of the competing principles of equality and liberty.[6] The problem with this distinction, as Norberto Bobbio shows, is that there are many authoritarian rightists and just as many libertarian leftists.[7] Bobbio argues, convincingly, that the real dividing principle is equality *tout court.*

> We can then correctly define as egalitarians those who, while not ignoring the fact that people are both equal and unequal, believe that what they have in common has greater value in the formation of a good community. Conversely, those who are not egalitarian, while starting from the same premise, believe that their diversity has greater value in the formation of a good community.
>
> It is very difficult to know the complex origin of this fundamental choice. But it is precisely this conflict between fundamental choices which, in my opinion, characterizes so well the opposing camps which for a long time we have been in the habit of calling left and right: on the one hand, people who believe that human beings are more equal than unequal, and on the other, people who believe that we are more unequal than equal.[8]

Left positions on gender, race, and class can thus be seen as instances of the basic support for equality. Similarly, sympathy for the Soviet Union during the Cold War and support for the federalization of U.S. public policy during the New Deal originated in the application of egalitarian principles to particular circumstances.

Postmaterialism and New Social Movements

This definition of the left, and others like it, has been challenged by Ronald Inglehart, who argues that the attainment of prosperity in the industrialized countries has made the left's concern with material equality irrelevant, and that a new "postmaterialist" left, which values belonging, self-esteem, and self-realization, is replacing it.[9] In Inglehart's view, such postmaterialist values are the basis for what have been called "new social movements."[10] I have argued elsewhere that Inglehart's distinction between material and postmaterial values lacks rigor. Inglehart considers environmentalists to be postmaterialist, but environmentalist opposition to toxic waste dumping and the growing of genetically modified foods are rooted in people's concern for physical safety, which Inglehart considers to be a material need.[11] There is also room for debate about the degree to which "new" and "old" social movements really differ. For Offe, that difference lies both in a movement's social basis and in its goals; new social movements, in his view, are not based on "collective contractual position" (e.g., wage-laborer), but on "some sense of collective identity," which may be ascriptive or "naturalistic"—"age, gender, 'nation' or 'mankind'" and seek not "representation" but "autonomy"—to stop state action, not to use it.[12] These criteria are hard to uphold in practice. Offe considers tenants' movements and ecology to be "new," yet both aim at least sometimes to use state action, while a sense of common identity is often vital to the growth of workers' movements.[13] Moreover, "contractual" and "ascriptive" identities cannot always be separated, as C. L. R. James shows in his analysis of the Haitian revolution, or Georgakas and Surkin in their study of the League of Revolutionary Black Workers in Detroit.[14]

In Inglehart's view, postmaterialist values are associated with peace and prosperity, with a generational time lag (because values are established in childhood). Theoretically, then, postmaterialism should rise or fall as it trails these two variables. However, Inglehart assumes that peace and prosperity are here to stay, and therefore predicts a "new postmaterialist left."[15] This premise seems increasingly shaky.

The fundamental questions about the theories of postmaterialism and new social movements are empirical. Are "new" and "old" social movements on the left divided by their conflicting approaches to material values, or does a common desire for greater equality have the potential to unite them? If Inglehart is right, the prospects for a "Teamsters and Turtles" coalition are dim.

What Is Political?

Leo Strauss claimed that "political science requires clarification of what distinguishes political things from things which are not political; it requires that the question 'what is political?' be raised and answered" and added, "This question cannot be dealt with scientifically but only dialectically. And dialectical treatment necessarily begins from pre-scientific knowledge and takes it most seriously."[16] Strauss's assertion reifies and exaggerates the distinctions between disciplines. After inquiry, we might well decide that the differences between the political, the economic, the social, and the cultural are superficial and serve only to make us approach the challenges of changing the world half-armed.

However, we face the practical question of what to include in this book. The choice to limit our scope to left *political* movements is not drawn from the belief that politics is different in essence from other parts of life; it is meant to help us focus our attention on forms of struggle that share certain methods. As long as we remember the contingency of this choice, we can usefully ask how *political* should be defined.

We can define *politics* by distinguishing it from *economics* and *ideology* (or perhaps from *culture*) as that which is concerned with the state. This distinction is useful as long as it is not essentialized. When the Nature Conservancy seeks to preserve wilderness by buying and owning wilderness land, instead of by seeking the creation of more national parks, it makes sense to say that it has chosen an economic strategy rather than a political one. Similarly, feminist campaigns to get men to share more equally in housework and childcare can be described as cultural rather than political.

For the purposes of this book, following this distinction has been applied loosely, for two reasons. First, nonpolitical movements are likely to have political effects. Nature Conservancy contributors, once organized, may support the creation of national parks as well, and feminists concerned with domestic responsibilities may be convinced of the need for a family leave law. More important, the choice of a political, economic, or cultural strategy is often debated *within* a movement; if we looked only at those movements and organizations that have already chosen politics, we would not see this debate. Such a debate is political, even if the result of the debate is to forgo politics. We have therefore leaned toward an inclusive interpretation of what politics is.

What Is a Movement?

The concept of a "movement" possesses its own complexity. A *movement* consists of people in motion—if it is a political movement, motion toward a political goal, however broadly defined (e.g., saving the environment or liberating women). Groups of people in motion for political goals can also be called *interest groups* or *parties*. Before proceeding, we need to decide whether these are three names for the same thing or three different things. If we choose the latter, we also need to decide how to distinguish among the three.

Movements and Interest Groups

Are movements different from interest groups, or are the two concepts interchangeable? In Sidney Tarrow's definition, social movements consist of people engaged in "contentious politics" who are "backed by dense social networks and galvanized by culturally resonant, action-oriented symbols," leading to "sustained interaction with opponents."[17] Movements are thus more inclusive and less organized than interest groups. An interest group is a single organization, which can be broad or narrow in its composition; but a movement can include several different organizations, together with individuals who are not members of any organization but who identify with the movement, support its goals, and participate in some of its activities. Can we then say that a movement includes interest groups among its component parts? Many scholars prefer to speak of "social movement organizations" (sometimes SMOs) rather than interest groups, believing that the two types of organization are qualitatively distinct.[18] Movement organizations are likely to be short-lived, low in resources, and driven by a demand for justice; interest groups more permanent, with budgets and staffs, and concerned with the material interests of their members.[19] Interest groups are rational; social movement organizations are passionate.

The distinction is clear; moreover, it is intuitively plausible. Those who marched with Martin Luther King, Jr., in Selma and Birmingham do not seem to have much in common with the members of the American Trial Lawyers Association. The former drew strength from their numbers and moral commitment, the latter from their ability to raise money. Yet if it is easy to imagine a spectrum running from social movement organization to interest group, it is more difficult to decide where on such a spectrum to place the cutting point, and impossible to place it in such a way that all organizations on one side have only the characteristics of social movement organizations and those on the other side only the characteristics of interest groups. The lack of such a cutting point leads Burstein to conclude that "the distinction between 'SMOs' and 'interest groups,' which seems so obvious initially, *does not exist*." Burstein proposes that we speak instead of "interest organizations."[20]

Burstein's logic is sound, and it helps us to notice that social movement organizations sometimes lobby, while interest groups sometimes protest. The distinction between "interest" and "justice" is similarly fuzzy since there are now public interest groups and nongovernmental organizations that use conventional lobbying techniques to pursue social justice.[21] At the same time, we do not want to lose sight of the difference between lobbying and protest as types of political action, nor deny that some organizations are prone to one and some to the other.

To some extent we can see a process of historic succession at work: social movements arise, social movement organizations spring up in their midst, these organizations then evolve into interest groups and perhaps continue to function after the movement has faded away. Jack Walker estimates that, as of the mid-1980s, 20 percent of U.S. interest groups arose "in the wake of broad social movements," and suggests that such groups are more likely than others to use "an 'outside' strategy of influence." Walker defines such an "outside" strategy as "appeals to the public through the mass media and effort at the broad-scale mobilization of citizens at the 'grass roots.' "[22] It is difficult to see what distinguishes such an interest group from a social movement organization. Douglas and Anne Costain leave out social movement organizations altogether and refer to the way that "movements institutionalize as interest groups."[23]

The authors of this book deal with a spectrum of organizations which differ in their respective proclivities to lobby or to protest. What these organizations have in common is their situation within a broader movement, characterized by its social networks, its mobilizing symbols, and its systematic contention with those in power.

Movements and Parties

The distinction between interest groups and parties seems clear. Parties try to gain control of the state, or a share of it, in their own right; interest groups seek instead to influence the actions of those in control of the state. From this perspective, instances where interest groups as such hold a share of power are seen as a corruption of the system.[24]

However, the distinction tends to blur in practice. The fundamentalist Christian movement seeks to elect its members to local school boards and affiliates with the Republican party nationally. The AFL-CIO has become almost a constituent part of the Democratic party. The Greens split for a while into two rival organizations, partly over the question of how the movement and party aspects of their work should be related.[25] And the Association of Community Organizations for Reform Now (ACORN), a social movement organization of low-income people, helped launch the New Party in order to give itself its own electoral vehicle.

Thus, party organizations and electoral campaigns may be included in movements. The important distinction is not the organizational form, but the orientation toward mobilization from outside for social change. For this reason we have not excluded parties from the analyses that follow.

THEORETICAL CONTROVERSIES

This is not a book about social movement theory. Nonetheless, in the past few years new theories of social movements have sprouted like wild flowers in spring, while theorists have plunged into debate as to which are the flowers and which the noxious weeds, and the reader may benefit from some awareness of these theories. Mark Lichbach has argued that the contemporary debate can be organized around the distinction between what he has felicitously labeled CARP—the Collective Action Research Program—and structural explanations.[26] A third, cultural, approach has now faded away, he claims. We will consider all three approaches here. The first two share the belief that the success or failure of movements is explained externally, by social structures or preexisting individual incentives, with little room left for the initiative of movement participants. Such explanations contrast strongly with the experience of organizers, who tend to feel that their efforts make a difference. Cultural explanations may help account for these feelings of efficacy.

Rational Choice

For those who work within the collective action paradigm, the central task is to explain why rational individuals would join a movement. Mancur Olson's definitive statement of this problem inspired a vast amount of subsequent research.[27] The problem, briefly, is twofold. First, the costs to an individual of participating in a movement are often greater than the benefits to that individual if the movement succeeds. Second, in what has become known as the "free rider" problem, in many cases the individual will share in the benefits (peace, clean air, racial equality) whether or not he or she participates.

Anyone who *has* participated in a movement knows the answer to this problem. People join a movement because they enjoy it, because they feel it as a duty, or for some other benefit that comes from participation itself, and thus is not available to free riders. Rational choice theorists account for such motives as nonmaterial incentives; their problem is how to account for such nonmaterial incentives without reducing the theory to circularity. From the viewpoint of movement organizers, the problem is how to get more people to respond to such incentives.

Structural Determinism

Rational choice theorists seek to explain individuals' decisions to get involved in movements. Structuralists seek to explain the rise or fall of movements by such external determinants as the availability of resources, the strength of constraints, and the possibilities for action offered by changing political circumstances. Since the outcome of an individual's cost-benefit calculations will be affected by these environmental considerations, the two approaches are complementary, although that has not always been clear to their respective proponents.[28]

As with rational choice, such variants of structuralism as "resource mobilization" and "political opportunity structure" attribute the success or failure of a movement to factors beyond the control of that movement's leaders and participants. They provide useful theoretical guidance for the leaders of individual organizations struggling with one another to fill a particular ecological niche, but do not answer the more basic question of what can be done to get a movement launched.

Cultural Hegemony

The basic premise of cultural and ideological approaches is that people will join a movement when they feel that it is right to do so. Such feelings come from the ways in which people understand the physical and social world, both ethically and materially. In principle, cultural explanations are compatible with rational choice. For example, where one person might see participation in a large demonstration as a cost because of the time and energy required, another might think it a benefit because of the feelings of solidarity, efficacy, and moral virtue produced by the experience. Thus, the outcome of a rational cost-benefit analysis depends upon the individual's set of values about what is desirable (utility function). The same calculation will depend as well on his or her assessment of the probability that the movement will attain its goals. However, all the explanatory work for such a combination is accomplished through the cultural part of the theory. Rational choice provides only a means of computing the relationship between cause and effect.

Similarly, cultural approaches can be harmonized with structural ones by seeing a culture of resistance as an additional resource available for potential movements. Such cultural resources are sometimes called social capital, although the metaphor is awkward for movements that may be anti-capitalist in their purposes. From the activist point of view, culture differs qualitatively from other possible resources in that it can be created within the movement. Money, splits in the ruling class, and other such conditions are there or they are not. If they are relied on, they force a movement to bend its purposes to fit those of potential donors or allies. But movement leaders can try to create and spread a culture of resistance without relying on external aid and, therefore, can remain true to their own goals. This emphasis on values is one of the features that makes an organization more movement and less interest group in its character.

PROBLEMS AND PROSPECTS

The theoretical questions discussed above have to do with how we are to *interpret* social movements; the point, though, is to change the world. To say this is not to reject theory as useless,[29] but to propose a criterion by which theories can be judged: Do they help us change the world? This book poses a more focused question: How can the progressive social movements that came together in Seattle unite more firmly and continue to grow in the future?

Movement Disagreements

Today's progressive movements differ in their constituencies, their goals, and their strategies. The first two factors tend to differentiate one movement from another, the third to differentiate organizations or factions within each of the movements. Such *differences* can, but need not, be *divisive* as well. One way of thinking about unity is to ask how important differences can be maintained without leading to divisiveness. Let us look at each of the three factors separately.

Constituency

The movements discussed in this book are united, first of all, by the sense that they have a common enemy. They are less united about how that enemy should be defined—"capitalism," "the corporations," "imperialism," or "the power structure," for example—but they have more or less the same social forces in mind, whatever the term. However, some movements would add other forces—"patriarchy," "white supremacy," "compulsory heterosexuality," for example—that refer to something different. For a long time this potential problem was handled through the language of primary and secondary contradictions. The idea was that everyone should unite around the primary contradiction, generally seen as that between the capitalists and the workers; meanwhile, various secondary contradictions—between men and women, white and black, able-bodied and disabled, as examples—should be resolved in order to preserve unity.

Sometime in the late 1960s members of various constituencies began to realize that any contradiction called secondary tended to be resolved in favor of the side that was already dominant. Just as A. Philip Randolph was persuaded to postpone his planned 1941 March on Washington for the sake of unity against Hitler,[30] women, African Americans, and others have been asked to downplay their particular concerns for the sake of the struggle. That degree of movement self-effacement became unacceptable to many, and the explosion of newly differentiated militant caucuses and groups that was eventually to become known as "identity politics" began.[31]

Many now agree that these identity-based movements should unite, but there is less agreement about how such unity can be obtained. The conflict can be intense. For example, some see the abandonment of demands for "affirmative action" as a necessary and desirable step that should be taken to promote unity, while others would see that same step as legitimizing continued discrimination, and thus an obstacle to unity.[32] The suppression of particular demands in favor of a broad class unity, in the style of the 1950s, is no longer acceptable to those whose concerns would be suppressed. Some of the most creative contemporary thinking has been devoted to new ways to resolve this dilemma.

Goals

All political movements have goals; but for constituency-based movements those goals are seen as the interests of a socially ascribed identity. For other movements, the goals are the result of conscious choice. This distinction should not be overstated, as there is some degree of choice in the acceptance or alteration of ascribed identities as well.[33] It is important to remember that identities are never fixed; nevertheless, since they are relatively stable in everyday life, this distinction is a useful one.

One might see this as a distinction between universalism (clean air, peace) and particularism (women's rights, racial equality), but such a criterion would be misleading. Racial justice and gender equality are just as universal as peace and ought to be supported, respectively, by white people and men.

However, goals need to be prioritized, and it is here that dissension may arise. Regulations designed to bring cleaner air and water and protect wilderness may be seen as raising prices, destroying jobs, or restricting recreational opportunities for poor people. Movement unity requires the successful propagation of the vision that such regulations are part of a broad anti-capitalist struggle, rather than a "jobs *versus* owls" conflict.

As with the growth of identity politics, the multiplication of single-issue groups was partially a response to perceived failures of the movements of the 1960s; in this case, to the tendency of those movements to erupt into bitter factional struggles among small revolutionary groups. Activists learned that they could avoid such struggles as long as they stuck to the specifics of the issue they were working on. The question today is whether these single-issue movements can be brought together without rekindling the fires of factionalism.

Strategy

In some times and places it is possible to speak of a "revolutionary movement." In the United States at the turn of the twenty-first century, however, movements identify themselves by goals and constituencies, not by their choice of strategy. Some activists want to form a broad progressive coalition to pressure the system for change, while others are convinced that the system will have to be overthrown before change can come; but the question of reform or revolution arises within each movement, not between them.

As movements unite, though, there is a tendency for reformists (or revolutionaries) in different movements to see one another as allies and to begin to form strategy-oriented coalitions. Moreover, some groups do define themselves by their strategy, and where that strategy is opposed by others their participation may generate controversy; that was the case with those the press labeled "anarchists from Eugene" at the Seattle protests. The numbers and destructiveness of these anarchists were greatly exaggerated; nevertheless, the question of how to avoid divisiveness inspired by anarchist tactics weighed heavily on the minds of some movement leaders in the ensuing months.

Movements for a New Millennium

The Seattle protests were followed by a series of actions in Washington, Prague, Philadelphia, Los Angeles, and elsewhere. These actions shared several characteristics: they targeted a powerful institution of global capital (the World Trade Organization, the International Monetary Fund, the Democratic and Republican national conventions); they combined a number of actions spread over several days; they included peaceful protest, nonviolent civil disobedience, and in some cases more militant forms of struggle; they included events focused on the education and enjoyment of participants together with more traditional public-oriented actions; and, perhaps most important, they mobilized groups with different constituencies, goals, and strategies who did not find it necessary to achieve agreement on a common policy or a common set of demands before taking action.

Then came the terrorist attacks of September 2001 and the subsequent war on Afghanistan. These events have demoralized progressive movements, probably temporarily but certainly profoundly. What had seemed to be one of the right's more ridiculous arguments, that Americans were threatened by Third World terrorism, had proven to be correct; moreover there was some public feeling—encouraged by conservative politicians—that to criticize the killing of innocent civilians in Afghanistan was morally equivalent to justifying terrorism. In these circumstances the next planned international demonstration for global justice was cancelled. Meanwhile the Bush administration did not hesitate to advance such disparate parts of its agenda as Alaskan oil drilling, "Star Wars" missile defense, and tax cuts that were presented as anti-terrorist policies.

As the war continued and Bush began to threaten attacks on additional countries, left movements began to regroup and find their voice. Most of this book was written before September 2001, but each author was asked to add a brief discussion of how the anti-terrorist campaign and the war in Afghanistan have affected the movements discussed in each chapter.

The demonstrations of the third millennium C.E. will probably follow the pattern whereby multiple groups make multiple demands in multiple separate actions, legal and illegal, militant and orderly, with loose coordination of time and place. Is this what democracy will look like? Perhaps. The following chapters may help answer this question. But first, a few words about the book's plan are in order.

THE PLAN OF THIS BOOK

The following chapters cover both the global anti-corporate movement itself, and nine of the movements that constitute possible constituencies for a larger movement in the future. Authors were asked to choose a particular movement organization for more detailed description, but to include some discussion of the movement as a whole. To the extent feasible, authors were also asked to touch on some of the theoretical issues raised in this introduction.

Chapter authors were chosen for their scholarly credentials, but also for their personal involvement in the movements they write about. These chapters are objective, in that they base their conclusions firmly on evidence; but they are not neutral, and some show passionate commitment to their cause. We hope this combination of analysis and commitment will give readers a fuller sense of what these movements are about.

For organizational purposes, we have classified movements by their constituencies. Chapter 2 treats the global justice movement itself, following which the chapters in part I describe movements—labor, the elderly, and students—that traditionally have been considered based on materialist interests. Part II covers movements around identities—women, gay-lesbian-bisexual-transgendered, and disability—that are often placed in the "new social movement" category. Finally, part III includes movements—for the environment, human rights, and peace—that focus on a view of universal justice, rather than on the interests or identities of movement participants. As will be clear from the earlier discussion, such a classification is problematic; the disabled have material interests, and industrial workers desire recognition. The fuzziness of the distinction will become even clearer as the individual chapters are read. The classification is for convenience only.

NOTES

1. Facts about the protest are taken from Jeffrey St. Clair, "Seattle Diary: It's a Gas, Gas, Gas," *New Left Review*, no. 238 (November–December 1999): 81–96.

2. See John Dewey, *Liberalism and Social Action* (New York: Putnam, 1935).

3. Anthony Giddens, *Beyond Left and Right: The Future of Radical Politics* (Stanford, Calif.: Stanford University Press, 1994), 251.

4. Gabriel Kolko, *The Triumph of Conservatism: A Reinterpretation of American History, 1900–1916* (Chicago: Quadrangle, 1967).

5. Michael Zweig, *The Working Class Majority: America's Best Kept Secret* (Ithaca, N.Y.: ILR Press, 2000).

6. Milton Friedman, *Capitalism and Freedom* (Chicago: University of Chicago Press, 1962).

7. Norberto Bobbio, *Left and Right: The Significance of a Political Distinction*, translated by Allan Cameron (Chicago: University of Chicago Press, 1996), 72–79.

8. Bobbio, *Left and Right*, 66–67.

9. Ronald Inglehart, *Culture Shift in Advanced Industrial Society* (Princeton, N.J.: Princeton University Press, 1990), 5, 367; the idea of higher needs that become relevant once material needs have been provided for comes, of course, from Abraham Harold Maslow, *Motivation and Personality* (New York: Harper & Row, 1970).

10. Jürgen Habermas, "New Social Movements," *Telos*, no. 49 (Fall 1981): 33–37.

11. John C. Berg, "State Green Parties in the USA: New Postmaterialist Wine or Old Wine in New Bottles?" Paper presented at the annual meeting of the American Politics Group, Keele, UK (January 2000), 6–12.

12. Claus Offe, *Contradictions of the Welfare State*, ed. John Keane (London: Hutchinson, 1984), 189–190.

13. See, for example, E. P. Thompson, *The Making of the English Working Class* (New York: Vintage, 1963). Cecelia Lynch makes a similar criticism of attempts to distinguish new from old social movements by whether they are universalistic or particularistic in outlook. See Cecelia Lynch, "Social Movements and the Problem of Globalization," *Alternatives* 23 (1998): 162, n. 43.

14. C. L. R. James, *Black Jacobins* (New York: Vintage, 1938); Dan Georgakas and Marvin Surkin, *Detroit: I Do Mind Dying* (New York: St. Martin's, 1975). See also Cedric Robinson, *Black Marxism: The Making of the Black Radical Tradition* (London: Zed, 1983).

15. See, for example, Terry Nichols Clark and Ronald Inglehart, "The New Political Culture: Changing Dynamics of Support for the Welfare State and Other Policies in Postindustrial Societies," in *The New Political Culture*, ed. Terry N. Clark and Vincent Hoffmann-Martinot, assisted by Mark Gromala (Boulder, Colo.: Westview, 1998).

16. Leo Strauss, *What Is Political Philosophy? and Other Studies* (Glencoe, Ill.: Free Press, 1959), 24–25, cited in David Fott, *John Dewey: America's Philosopher of Democracy* (Lanham, Md.: Rowman & Littlefield, 1998), 146.

17. Sidney G. Tarrow, *Power in Movement: Social Movements, Collective Action, and Politics* (Cambridge: Cambridge University Press, 1994), 2.

18. Tarrow contrasts "mass movement organizations" with "parties and interest groups with a movement vocation." Tarrow, *Power in Movement*, 206.

19. On the lifespan of movement organizations see Frances Fox Piven and Richard A. Cloward, *Poor People's Movements: Why They Succeed, How They Fail* (New York: Vintage, 1979); on the contrasting motivations, see Iris Marion Young, *Justice and the Politics of Difference* (Princeton, N.J.: Princeton University Press, 1990), 72.

20. Paul Burstein, "Interest Organizations, Political Parties, and the Study of Democratic Politics," in *Social Movements and American Political Institutions*, ed. Anne N. Costain and Andrew S. McFarland (Lanham, Md.: Rowman & Littlefield, 1998), 45.

21. Jeffrey M. Berry, *Lobbying for the People* (Princeton, N.J.: Princeton University Press, 1977). See chapter 10 of this book for a different view of this distinction.

22. Jack L. Walker, Jr., *Mobilizing Interest Groups in America: Patrons, Professions, and Social Movements*, prepared for publication by Joel D. Aberbach et al. (Ann Arbor: University of Michigan Press, 1991), 11–12, 9.

23. W. Douglas Costain and Anne N. Costain, "The Political Strategies of Social Movements: A Comparison of the Women's and Environmental Movements," *Congress & the Presidency* 19 (1991): 1.

24. This argument is made forcefully by Theodore Lowi in *The End of Liberalism: The Second Republic of the United States*, 2d ed. (New York: Norton, 1979).

25. Tarrow suggests that the relations of the German Greens to the movement are functionally the same as those of public interest groups "with a movement vocation" in the United States, with the differences in organizational structure due to the differences between the two countries' electoral systems. Tarrow, *Power in Movement*, 206.

26. Mark I. Lichbach, "Contending Theories of Contentious Politics and the Structure-Action Problem of Social Order," *Annual Review of Political Science* 1 (1998): 405; see also Mark I. Lichbach, *The Rebel's Dilemma* (Ann Arbor: University of Michigan Press, 1995).

27. Mancur Olson, Jr., *The Logic of Collective Action: Public Goods and the Theory of Groups*, 2d ed. (Cambridge: Harvard University Press, 1971). Lichbach, "Contending Theories," offers a review of attempts to fit social movements into Olson's framework.

28. John D. McCarthy and Mayer Zald, *The Trend of Social Movements in America: Professionalization and Resource Mobilization* (Morristown, N.J.: General Learning, 1973); John D. McCarthy and Mayer Zald, "Resource Mobilization and Social Movements: A Partial Theory," *American Journal of Sociology* 82 (1977): 1212–1241; Tarrow, *Power in Movement*, 16.

29. Nor was that Marx's intention in the eleventh thesis on Feuerbach, paraphrased here.

30. John C. Berg, "A. Philip Randolph (1889–1979)," in *Political Parties & Elections in the United States: An Encyclopedia*, ed. L. Sandy Maisel (New York: Garland, 1991), 906–907.

31. John Anner, *Beyond Identity Politics: Emerging Social Justice Movements in Communities of Color*, ed. John Anner (Boston: South End, 1996), 6–8. See, for example, Stokeley Carmichael and Charles V. Hamilton, *Black Power* (New York: Random House, 1967) or Marge Piercy, *The Grand Coolie Damn* (Boston: New England Free Press, 1969).

32. I place "affirmative action" in quotation marks to alert the reader to the wide variation in the meaning ascribed to this term, a lack of precision that has proven useful to affirmative action's opponents. See, on the one hand, Joel Rogers, "How Divided Progressives Might Unite," *New Left Review*, no. 210 (March–April 1995): 27n; and Paul Sniderman and Thomas Piazza, *The Scar of Race* (Cambridge, Mass.: Harvard University Press, 1993); on the other, Howie Hawkins, "The Greens after the Nader Campaign," *Synthesis/Regeneration*, no. 12 (Winter 1997): 16; and Young, *Justice and the Politics of Difference*, 195–200; or for an overview, Nijole V. Benokraitis and Joe R. Feagin, *Affirmative Action and Equal Opportunity: Action, Inaction, Reaction*, Westview Special Studies in Contemporary Social Issues (Boulder, Colo.: Westview, 1978).

33. For an insightful discussion of the interplay of social construction and personal choice in determining an individual's "race," see F. James Davis, *Who Is Black? One Nation's Definition* (University Park: Pennsylvania State University Press, 1991).

2

From Anti-Globalization to Global Justice: A Twenty-First-Century Movement

RONALD HAYDUK

Modern industry has established the world market. All old established national industries have been destroyed. They are dislodged by new industries whose products are consumed in every corner of the globe. In place of old wants, we find new wants, requiring for their satisfaction the products of distant lands and climes. . . . All fixed, fast frozen relations are swept away; all new-formed ones become antiquated before they can ossify. All that is solid melts into air.

—Karl Marx and Frederick Engels, *The Communist Manifesto*

This is what democracy looks like!

—Protest chant in Seattle at the meetings of the World Trade Organization

It's about Seattle. Since November 1999, any reference to Seattle immediately conjures up images of protestors who shut down meetings of the World Trade Organization (WTO). Today, Seattle is shorthand for a new social movement. Prior to the events in Seattle—if media coverage was a gauge that measured activism in the 1990s, at least in the United States—then signs of movements for social and economic justice appeared all but dead. But the anti-globalization movement that Seattle gave voice to helped expose a dirty secret: Capitalism is a global system that benefits the rich and keeps the majority of the world's population mired in poverty and pain. Seattle indisputably politicized capitalism and "globalization," the slippery term used to describe a wide range of phenomena, including, but not limited to, the rapid spread of the market into nearly every corner of the globe, the communications technology revolution, wrenching demographic changes (urbanization, migration, immigration), increased integration of economies and cultures, and environmental degradation.[1]

Global capitalism, movement activists contend, is mauling the public: the "commons" are being turned into private malls; genes and seeds are being altered and patented; water is being dammed, bought, and sold as an increasingly scarce and valuable commodity; health problems soar as ecological destruction escalates at exponential rates; economic pressures reduce wages and standards of living and increase poverty, unemployment, and underemployment; masses of people are dislocated; politicians and whole governments are routinely bribed and bent to capital's will; children are targeted and tracked at birth, then fed advertisements and slogans in place of needed nourishment.[2] In response to what it sees as the privatization and commodification of nearly every aspect of life, the movement aims to reverse or at least blunt capitalism's sharp edges.

Anti-globalization protestors challenge the assumption that this global free market system is inevitable or even desirable. Indeed, they seek to make capitalism untenable. The anti-globalization movement disputes the corporate-led version of globalization by exposing how it pits people and places against one another in a race to the bottom. As the movement gains public attention, it tears the veil away from the pretense that unregulated markets will be the rising tide that lifts all boats. The global justice movement counters the prevailing philosophy that governments should make way for the market's invisible hand. Members of the movement argue that free trade is not fair trade.

Seattle marked a high point in a decade of growing activism around the world that seeks to expose global capitalism's seamy side. Seattle sparked subsequent protests in dozens of cities on every continent among activists working to build a different kind of "global village"—one that prioritizes human need and the environment over corporate profits. In place of corporate-dominated capitalism, the movement seeks to forge sustainable and equitable development reached through democratic means. The anti-globalization movement boldly proclaims, "democratize globalization!" Or, as the title of one of the movement's manifestos reads, "Globalize This!"[3]

Comprised of a wide range of disparate groups and organizations from many countries—from revolutionary movements and radical anarchist collectives of direct action-oriented groups to longtime, well-established unions and nongovernmental organizations (NGOs), loosely associated in an uneasy coalition, anti-globalization activists may not have a well-formulated program, but they certainly know their opposition. The movement aims to reveal how a handful of powerful institutions, elites, and developed regions have constructed a system that, whether by design or default, maintains and exacerbates grueling inequalities. Their principal targets are the policies of such international institutions as the World Bank and the International Monetary Fund (IMF) and the myriad corporations and governments these agencies serve. They contend that these entities—and capitalism itself—are inherently and profoundly undemocratic and inhumane. For the first time in decades, thanks to this movement, mainstream discourse includes discussion of the need to regulate relations of production and consumption.

But there is more. Somewhere along the line—from protests in Seattle to Washington, D.C., to Genoa—the movement has matured. It is not just a movement against the ravages of globalization; it is also now a movement for global justice.[4] The global justice movement claims a better future is possible. It strives to create a radically egalitarian, multi-issue, community-controlled system that meets human needs through environmentally sustainable development worldwide. In many ways the movement itself models this vision. Made up of tens of thousands of participants with few leaders—including labor union members, anti-sweatshop activists, environmentalists, human rights advocates, and anarchists—the movement's goals embrace reform and revolution. Moreover, the movement crosses boarders and continents, comprising participants from both the developing and developed worlds.[5] Its tactics range from grassroots establishment of independent and environmentally sustainable production and consumption models of development, to lobbying, to nonviolent protest, to militant rebellion. Although the movement appears to be new—manifesting itself on a mass scale in periodic protests at meetings of the WTO, World Bank, and IMF—it has deep roots, and it is gaining momentum in many quarters of the world. The movement is popularizing notions about what a better "global village" would look like and ways it might be achieved, two crucial steps that may eventually lead to significant change. Equally important, it has not only put elites on the defensive, it has led to concrete changes in institutional policies and practices.[6] The anti-globalization movement reflects a mass mobilization and optimism about the possibility for progressive social change not seen for nearly thirty years.

This chapter seeks to explore the anti-globalization movement by examining its origins, members, goals and practices, targets and tactics, impacts, and challenges and prospects. While no survey of this worldwide, fragmented mobilization could be exhaustive, a detailed analysis of key elements and organizations of this nascent movement will serve to demonstrate its potential—and the potential of comparable movements—for progressive politics. In order to situate and compare the differing methods of the diverse elements of the movement, the human rights NGO Global Exchange is discussed as one established group working to further the cause of anti-globalization.[7]

ORIGINS: FROM BRETTON WOODS
TO THE NEW WORLD ORDER

Following World War II, the foundations for the current global economy were laid in Bretton Woods with the creation of the World Bank and the IMF.[8] Most Western industrial nations were rebuilt and adopted Keynesian economic and social welfare policies. But, as the postwar economic prosperity began to sputter in the 1970s—with rising inflation, oil shocks, and currency crises—older laissez-faire notions and practices began to reemerge. Corporations restructured and shifted operations to developing countries. Capital flowed more rapidly and freely through increasingly integrated economies and financial markets. Governments deregulated and privatized functions, reflecting a growing consensus that free markets work best, sometimes referred to as the Washington Consensus.[9] International trade organizations encouraged political regimes to reduce trade barriers and roll back state spending on social programs. They argued that "liberal market economics is the one and only economic hope for all countries, including poor countries."[10] Neoliberalism gained ideological currency as intense competition grew among nations and states to offer increasingly lucrative packages to entice private sector investment.[11]

During the 1980s, Margaret Thatcher and Ronald Reagan ushered in a notion that would dominate economic thinking and public policy for nearly two decades: "There Is No Alternative" (TINA) to globalization. Through political rhetoric and practice, TINA limited the use and scope of government authority. With the demise of the communist regimes of the former Soviet Union and Eastern Bloc countries, globalization became the dominant mantra, and the United States became the undisputed world power. As the chief cheerleader for free trade, the United States effectively pressed international organizations (the World Bank, IMF, and WTO) and other countries—often through these organizations—to adopt policies that furthered its own interests and the process of globalization. Globalizers actively worked for capitalism's institutionalization: to pry open markets, force governments to cut taxes and spending, privatize, and deregulate. Reagan and Thatcher, although neither was an egalitarian, stoked the ambitions of middle-class and working-class voters by presenting the free market as a vehicle of upward mobility. Indeed, globalization seemed beyond reproach. Within the United States, the influence of labor and environmentalists continued to decline, as reflected in their inability to stop the passage of either the North American Free Trade Agreement (NAFTA) or harmful amendments to the General Agreement on Tariffs and Trade (GATT), both of which were approved in the early 1990s by a Democratic Congress and president.

Instead of the widespread economic prosperity that these agreements and institutions promised, what occurred was the downsizing of the American Dream. The pace of deindustrialization hastened, and its impact exacerbated, economic and social inequalities.[12] These developments, in turn, spurred the growth of the low-wage service sector and contingent labor markets.[13] The concentration of wealth in the hands of the few reached heights not seen since the turn of the past century. Today, the United States has a greater degree of inequality than any other advanced nation.[14]

In the developing world, the effects were devastating. Financial crises in Thailand, Indonesia, Russia, Japan, and other countries ravaged millions of people's lives and threatened to drag the international economy into recession.[15] Globalization drastically changed people's material realities and their daily lived experience and activities worldwide: Mexicans make cars and sneakers; Brazilians produce paper and coffee; Nigerians pump oil and mine nickel, and so on. Yet, the regimes in these countries buckle under the weight of crippling debt, and the majority of their people remain mired in poverty.[16]

Globalization Breeds the Movement: Conditions of Movement Making

Not surprisingly, the ascendancy of globalizing forces spurred the growth of the anti-globalization movement. Conditions that gave rise to and/or limited the impact of earlier social protest movements substantially shifted in the past two decades, and some of these shifts provided fertile ground for the new social movements. Several developments are key to the anti-globalization movement.[17]

Profound economic changes in the past two decades established new political terrain—and identified new targets and coalition partners—for the fight for social justice. New technologies proliferated and facilitated the rapid mobility of capital and people across borders; waves of corporate mergers consolidated industries and market shares among fewer and more powerful multinational conglomerates; supra-national institutions and international trade agreements were established with new powers that usurped national and state sovereignty (such as NAFTA, the European Union, and the WTO). These changes provided identifiable targets for movement activists. These new macroforces and institutions highlighted the power of elites and the lack of available mechanisms for grassroots participation in decision making. Movement activists strategically focused attention on these institutions precisely because they have significant impact on local conditions.[18]

New communications technologies—the Internet, video, digital media transmission, cellular phones, desktop publishing, local pirate radio stations, and cable access public television—not only helped activists to communicate critical information (targets, issues, data, and organizing campaigns), but also made "do-it-yourself" organizing possible for a new generation of movement activists.[19]

In addition, long-established protest movement organizations have converged in the anti-globalization/global justice movement. Labor, civil rights, feminist, gay and lesbian, and traditional left movements—as well as national liberation movements in the developing world—not only were affected by corporate globalization, but also found common ground with anti-globalization activists. The new social motion that has been generated from this convergence gives this broader coalition greater force. New global justice movement activists acquire valuable resources from established institutions.[20] Grassroots organizations can gain legitimacy and funding, for example, from alliances with NGOs. Political tactics and skills of earlier social protest movements—from nonviolent civil disobedience to militant direct action strategies—are transferred and adapted by new activists. Similarly, moral and democratic arguments evident in earlier movements serve as models that new activists can draw upon for their own purposes. Indeed, as we shall see, global justice activists—both old and new—forged innovative strategies to battle a growing global behemoth.

Fissures among capitalists and nation-states also provided new political opportunities for anti-globalization activists.[21] The changes in the international political economy during the last quarter of the past century changed the economic and political interests of various segments of the business community and geopolitical world. For example, divisions between small and large producers of tradable goods (the former represented by the U.S. Business and Industrial Council and the latter by the U.S. Council for International Business) diverged further from the interests of financial investors.[22] Movement activists—in alliance with hundreds of NGOs—helped to defeat the Multilateral Agreement on Investment (MAI) in late 1998, in part, by exploiting such divisions as well as mobilizing popular support to pressure national and international institutions. NGOs successfully targeted Western governments at national and state levels (in the United States and the European Union) as well as the Organization for Economic Cooperation and Development (OECD).[23] In fact, the earlier struggle against NAFTA helped these groups increase coalition and network ties and facilitated refinement of tactics for their successful battle against the MAI. Thus, communication with, and emulation of, such protest successes serve to embolden activists to take on new actions and help to draw new members into the movement.[24]

Third World Roots of the Anti-Globalization Movement

Both the anti-apartheid movement and the Zapatista uprising were important precursors to the current anti-globalization movement. The Zapatistas explicitly challenged "neoliberalism" and NAFTA, launching their movement on January 1, 1994, the day NAFTA took effect. The Zapatistas articulated a sharp critique of the impact these policies had on indigenous peoples in Mexico and Mexican workers more generally. In response, they organized a powerful community-based and egalitarian revolt using innovative tactics and sophisticated communications technologies. The Zapatistas and other groups in the Global South convened meetings of organizations similarly opposed to globalization's policies and created People's Global Action (PGA), a network to facilitate ongoing organizing across borders.

PGA grew out of a 1998 meeting in Geneva of over four hundred representatives of grassroots organizations and NGOs from seventy-one countries to launch "a world-wide co-ordination of resistance against the global market."[25] PGA was the simultaneous counter party/protest to the fiftieth anniversary ball in Geneva that was thrown by those who set up the multilateral trade system that established the IMF and World Bank, and the second anniversary of the WTO. The self-described "hallmarks" of the PGA include a "confrontational attitude," a "clear rejection of the WTO and other trade liberalization agreements," a call for "non-violent civil disobedience and the construction of local alternatives by local peoples as answers to the action of governments and corporations" based on a philosophy of decentralization and autonomy, and a clear rejection of "patriarchy, racism, religious fundamentalism and all forms of discrimination and domination."[26]

This broad array of NGOs, human rights organizations, labor unions, direct action grassroots groups, anti-sweatshop activists, and environmentalists challenged corporate practices and government policies with varying degrees of success. Protests against similar policies—including GATT (which created the WTO) and the IMF and World Bank, which help manage global corporate capitalism, erupted in Indonesia, India, Brazil, Caracas, Geneva, London, Australia, Zimbabwe, and numerous other places.

These events indelibly changed the meaning of both globalization and the movement, positioning both on the larger political map, especially in the First World. The protests in Seattle were merely the next in an increasingly long string of actions.[27] Subsequent actions in Washington, D.C., Prague, Davos, and numerous other cities where the WTO, IMF, World Bank, World Economic Forum, and others met grew in force and impact. Increasingly, the anti-globalization movement put the international organizations on the defensive and began to affect their policies and practices.

MEMBER ORGANIZATIONS
AND CONSTITUENTS

The anti-globalization movement is made up of a broad array of groups, organizations, and individuals from the developed and developing worlds. Each group may focus on related but divergent issues, such as international human rights, sustainable economic development, environmentalism, labor rights, prison and incarceration growth, police brutality, or social rights and equal treatment issues across racial, gender, and sexual orientation lines. These highly variegated groups in the movement often hold different ideologies and posit different goals, target different institutions, and employ different tactics. Some of these differences can be quite divisive. The anti-globalization movement is far from a unified coalition of groups holding a common purpose and ideology, let alone engaging in similar activities. In fact, the movement is highly fragmented.

The movement appears to recede and almost disappear, and then reemerges en masse to protest a target, such as at a meeting of the WTO, IMF, or World Bank. These events may be the only times group members meet face to face, rather than over the Internet or in meetings of leaders. Even planned events often involve uneasy coalition at best; coordination is often fraught with infighting or unsustainable over time.

Nevertheless, several redeeming—if general—characteristics of the movement are discernable: it is decentralized, but coordinated; it acts spontaneously, but is well organized; it uses innovative protest tactics effectively; it is clever and witty; and it is democratic and optimistic. The movement—particularly its younger cohort—is developing new methods to address problems older movements failed to solve. According to some 1960s-generation-movement activists, "they are smarter."[28]

Many observers and movement activists see strength in the diverse nature of the movement. They embrace the multiplicity among themselves, often pointing to it as an example of the movement's democratic aspects. Others who seek a more unified or common program, however, argue that the varied nature of the movement is an obstacle to be overcome, especially if the movement is to become better coordinated and sustainable over the longer term. As some movement analysts have argued persuasively, coalitions are often strongest that focus on common targets, even if they may emphasize their differences among themselves and potential supporters.[29]

Self-identified member organizations range from standard NGOs—including environmental organizations such as the Sierra Club, consumer groups such as Public Citizen, labor unions such as the Teamsters, and faith-based organizations such as Jubilee 2000—to social movement organizations (SMOs), such as the Rainforest Action Network, the Direct

Action Network (DAN), and the Ruckus Society. The former are large, bureaucratic institutions that have many older members; the latter tend to be loose, decentralized networks, often of younger activists. The backbone of the movement is comprised of thousands of grassroots organizations that work in coalition with others who have "a movement vocation."[30] Some are fiercely independent and militant radical anarchist affinity groups (e.g., the Black Bloc), while others are collectives associated with one organization or a group of organizations.

Ideologically, some groups are self-identified "left" groups with more traditional Marxist orientations, while others are "left libertarians." Others identify themselves as "progressive" or even "liberal." NGOs such as Public Citizen and the Sierra Club fall into this category. Many identify themselves as "radicals." The youth-based, direct-action–oriented groups often identify themselves as "anarchists." Anarchism has become an attractive theoretical framework for movement members for two primary reasons: it is one of the only ideologies that has not been thoroughly discredited; and it lacks coherence or widespread agreement about what it is, which allows many different groups to shape its meaning. Anarchism also allows for the turn to postmodernism and postmaterialism that has pervaded our era and young people's education, as referred to in the introductory chapter of this volume. Nevertheless, old left and new left notions and groups are making a comeback in many organizations. In some countries, political parties have taken anti-globalization positions, and in a few instances joined protest actions. For example, in Brazil the Workers Party has been highly engaged; and communist-oriented parties, such as the Fuerzas Armadas Revolucionarias de Colombia (FARC) in Colombia, or the Farabundo Martí para la Liberación Nacional (FMLN) in El Salvador have championed anti-globalization programs.

Essentially the movement is a bunch of coalitions loosely linked together. These very different kinds of groups often show up at the same actions—whether through a coordinated effort or independently, sometimes participate in the same protest actions together and sometimes not, and are collectively referred to as "the movement."

GOALS AND PRACTICES

One of the most important goals and strategies of the anti-globalization movement was to reappropriate the meaning of the word "globalization." Anti-globalization groups expose the way in which globalization privileges economic values and priorities—as determined by capital and markets—and subordinates broader social, political, and ecological values, which comprise the interests of the vast majority of the world's population. The movement associated globalization with the wrenching social dislocation of hundreds of millions of people, increased poverty and social strife, widespread disease, rising incarceration rates, ecological destruction, cultural homogenization, sweatshops, layoffs, and the concentration of wealth among a small elite. Ironically, globalization destroys cultural "difference" at the same time it feeds the fires of ethnic strife. Global flows of capital contributed to the commercialization of land in agrarian societies, which, in turn, produced the greatest waves of mass migration since the turn of the past century, massive urbanization, deforestation, and desertification. When capital moves more rapidly and freely, people and resources are moved or move to follow it. As a result, social and economic inequalities are greater now than at any point in human history.[31]

Some movement activists explain the basic globalizing dynamic in a familiar model. They argue that investors direct their funds to developing nations or emerging markets only when they think they can draw a profit from their investments. Drawing on Marx's famous formula, $M \rightarrow C \rightarrow M'$ (in which M = money, C = commodity, and $M' = M + \Delta M$, value added from labor, which makes profit), Kevin Danaher of Global Exchange explains that capitalism is an extractive model, and the international trade organizations are mechanisms to ensure the process works to protect capital's interests; they provide access to cheap labor and raw materials, with no or few strings (i.e., environmental regulations, labor law, or taxation) attached. Indeed, elites in developing countries are more beholden to investors and lenders (private corporations, the World Bank, and IMF) than they are accountable to their own people.[32]

The anti-globalization movement moved to expose these nastier aspects of globalization. Through a broad range of innovative practices the movement has raised public awareness and political consciousness, key steps to achieving its goal of social transformation. As wages for the vast majority in the developed world have stagnated while the cost of living has increased, the touted "economic prosperity" rings increasingly hollow. The movement makes the human impacts generated by global capitalism less abstract and more concrete. High school students and sophomores in college in the First World may hear about, read about, see, or visit the harsh conditions in *maquiladoras* in Mexico, sweatshops in Indonesia, or mines in the Congo (perhaps on one of Global Exchange's "Reality Tours," which bring interested individuals to such places across the globe). Some have seen their fathers or mothers downsized by Verizon or Aetna. These sorts of exchanges and events connect the dots. According to one leader of Global Exchange's tours, many attending participants report, "so this is what a global economy looks like; there are devastating human consequences."[33] Such experiences provide life-transforming pathways to thousands of people who are drawn into movement activism. In other words, the many life-changing experiences of people in both developed and developing worlds—and the anti-globalization/global justice movement—both reflect and shape change in the "moral economy of the crowd."[34]

Many NGOs play an important role in disseminating information. Some are quite good at capturing media and public attention. Global Exchange, for example, produces educational materials that document and popularize the harsh realities of globalization. Wielding startling facts, Global Exchange and other NGOs—along with the broad range of grassroots groups and SMOs—help to mobilize people into action. From them, the public learns that fewer than five hundred billionaires possess a combined wealth greater than that of half the total population of the world; that Bill Gates is wealthier than the poorest 40 percent of the U.S. population combined, approximately 112 million people; that the ratio—or wealth gap—between the wealthiest and poorest nations was 30 to 1 in 1960 and by 1990 had doubled to 60 to 1; that the world's two hundred richest people saw their wealth more than double in just four years—from $440 billion to more than $1 trillion between 1994 and 1998.[35] The two hundred largest corporations in the world own as much wealth as 80 percent of the world's population. Half of the world's total population of six billion lives on less than $2 per day, and 1.2 billion, many of whom starve to death or die from preventable diseases, live in abject poverty. Twenty percent of the richest nations use between 70 and 90 percent of the world's food, energy, wood, metals, and raw materials, and account for about 75 percent of the world's environmental pollution.[36]

Corporate capitalist-led economic restructuring—and the rise of the anti-globalization movement—have helped to radicalize a broad range of liberal and progressive groups.[37] For example, environmental organizations founded during the 1970s may have been implicitly anti-corporate, but some are becoming explicitly anti-capitalist. Similarly, some labor unions—as well as a host of organizations that are descendants of the civil rights and feminist movements—have become more explicitly anti-capitalist in their orientation and work.[38] The rise of the anti-globalization movement has also contributed to the radicalization of many NGOs in recent years. NGOs proliferated in the 1970s following the lead of the world's poorest countries that formed the "G-77" in order to formulate a New International Economic Order in response to capital's New World Order. NGOs built networks and developed alternative agendas, including debt relief, increased aid to developing countries, technical assistance, and democratization of decision making in the IMF, World Bank, and the United Nations. In the vacuum left with the demise of the Soviet Union and Eastern Bloc, new political space opened up for such groups to ana-

lyze and critique the workings of capitalism. Today, many of these groups
more clearly and strongly point out capitalism's consequences, posit
stronger reforms and alternatives, and reach a greater audience. Thus,
globalization itself, in part, has generated this new and growing social
action: the anti-globalization/global justice movement. And greater
mobilization and collaboration among such groups make the movement
stronger.

When anti-globalization activists dramatically shut down the WTO
meetings in Seattle—continued to disrupt subsequent meetings of the
WTO, World Bank, and IMF whenever and wherever they met—they forever changed the meaning and direction of globalization. In Seattle, the
protestors' immediate target was the relatively new and unknown but
powerful and highly undemocratic WTO. Yet their larger target was the
undemocratic nature of global capitalism.[39] These unprecedented events
brought together local, regional, national, and international activists and
organizations—sometimes working independently, sometimes in coalition—that are able to affect the policies and practices of their targets,
albeit modestly. Some in the movement contend that their actions have
made globalization, as dictated by capital, untenable. While it remains to
be seen whether the movement can mount a sustained challenge that
brings significant transformation, there is no longer doubt about its
capacity to affect the process.[40]

The broad goal of the movement can be summed up as follows: to end
corporate rule over lives and the land and make people sovereign, especially at the local level; to radically equalize the vast disparities that currently exist; and to do so on an international scale. It is essentially a
radically democratic project. The global needs to be localized, and the
local needs to affect the global. It is not a single movement led by a group
of leaders or a party and does not desire to be (though some member
groups do). Rather, it is a diverse mix of many kinds of people striving
to reclaim control over the conditions of their lives. Equally important,
members of the movement are attempting explicitly to deal with critical
issues that have wracked earlier movements, including racism, sexism,
and homophobia.

TARGETS AND TACTICS

Some contend the main factor bonding the disparate elements of the anti-
globalization movement is less their common ground than a shared ani-
mus for their opponents. The movement has especially targeted private
and public institutions that support and manage global capitalism—
including the WTO, the IMF, and the World Bank—and also trade policy

agreements that help maintain the disparity between the rich and poor and North and South, such as NAFTA, MAI, GATT, and the pending Free Trade Area of the Americas (FTAA). Similarly, multinational corporations and their practices increasingly come under attack. Anti-sweatshop groups, for example, have effectively targeted Nike, the Gap, and Starbucks. Environmentalists have targeted Monsanto, which produces genetically altered food products. Finally, movement activists target national and subnational governments whose free trade policies undermine worker or environmental safeguards.

Yet because the influence of these key international financial institutions is so great—managing capitalism for banks and multinational corporations—they have become lightning rods for the movement. The World Bank and the IMF are the world's largest public lenders, or as Kevin Danaher of Global Exchange calls them, "the world's biggest loan sharks."[41] The World Bank manages over $200 billion and the IMF supplies member governments with short-term credit. The money they lend has thick strings attached—structural adjustment policies (SAPs). SAPs compel debtor governments to adopt free market policies that open their economies to penetration by multinational corporations. While done in the name of encouraging economic development, all too often these policies allow foreign capital to gain access to a country's workers and environment at bargain basement prices. Moreover, SAPs often require privatization of public utilities and publicly owned industries. They call for reducing government budgets, particularly in spending on health care and education, while encouraging governments to provide tax breaks and even subsidies to investors.

World Bank and IMF lending policies also encourage developing countries to focus their scarce resources on growing export crops (sugar, cotton, nuts, etc.) and extracting raw materials for export to advanced industrial countries, rather than fostering food production for local consumption or sustainable economic development. Sadly, the record shows that the imposition of SAPs in Latin America, Africa, and Asia has led to deeper inequality and environmental destruction.[42]

Tragically, given their need for loans and investment, the national elites of developing nations end up more accountable and responsive to the World Bank, IMF, and WTO than to their own people. A particularly disturbing example is the WTO's practice of finding local laws to be inimical to free trade and thus illegal. In this practice, the anti-globalization movement found a ripe target that represents how globalized capitalism systematically undermines local communities, working families, the environment, and political democracy around the world. In the five years it has existed, the WTO has ruled that many U.S. laws are "barriers to free trade," including clean air standards and laws protecting sea turtles and dolphins. Similarly, the WTO held that the European Union law banning hormone-treated beef is illegal. Laws passed by democratically elected public officials can thus be undermined. Further, unlike UN treaties, the WTO rulings can be enforced through sanctions. This gives the WTO more power than other international bodies and national governments. The movement has tried to portray the WTO as anti-consumer, anti-worker, anti-environment, and anti-democratic. When the WTO planned to launch its "Millennium Round" of trade talks in Seattle, which would have expanded the WTO's reach and privatization agenda into sensitive areas such as education and healthcare, a mass mobilization was launched and history was changed. The *Los Angeles Times* wrote, "On the tear gas shrouded streets of Seattle, the unruly forces of democracy collided with the elite world of trade policy. And when the meeting ended in failure on Friday the elitists had lost and the debate had changed forever."[43]

The tactics of the movement range from efforts to change consumption patterns, to lobbying, to organizing nonviolent civil disobedience actions, to militant acts. The anti-globalization movement has held events that use a mix of standard protest tactics—such as nonviolent civil disobedience and street marches—as well as a host of new and innovative practices, such as guerrilla street theater. The movement uses new technologies to coordinate the participants, including the Internet, cellular phones during actions, video recorders and video streaming, and "independent media centers" that bypass the corporate media to get the word out to the world. Some activism takes place solely on the Web, such as "virtual sit-ins" using a hacking tool called Floodnet, or hacking into websites to "steal" information or shut them down.

In addition, the movement has developed innovative forms of democratic decision making. One of the main mechanisms is a "spokescouncil" model, like the spokes of a wheel. Spokescouncils allow coalitions of groups to meet at "convergence centers" to strategize and coordinate actions, but with the close support and frequent input of members of each group. The spokespersons—or representatives—from each group attend meetings of coalition groups to exchange information and plans. In general, only the spokesperson is empowered to speak on behalf of a group, but members of each group may sit behind their representative spokesperson and communicate information back and forth to them. While joint plans may emerge, not all groups are bound by any "decision." Groups may choose to participate in a common action, turn out participants, endorse an action without participating, or take no part in an action. Thus, this model allows groups to collaborate while at the same time remaining autonomous. Spokescouncils may meet frequently to continue dialogue and communicate new information to groups, often by means of new communications technologies. This method produces decisions and plans with a great degree of input and support and facilitates rapid and effective action.[44] Unlike many of the consensus models of the 1960s and 1970s, the spokescouncil model is better designed to make quick consensus-like decisions during shifting protest conditions.

Beyond the thousands of people protesting international institutions in Seattle and Washington, D.C., the movement is also made up of countless individuals and groups in the developing world. The movement is landless peasants taking over golf courses and planting crops; workers taking over factories or forcing employers to pay living wages; young people trading music over the Internet or throwing street parties; independent media networks like Tao and Indymedia; Zapatistas demanding rights for indigenous people; environmentalists reclaiming privatized water systems; and NGOs seeking to reform or abolish international trade organizations.

IMPACTS OF THE ANTI-GLOBALIZATION MOVEMENT

The anti-globalization movement has had huge impacts and achieved many of its immediate goals. It has raised public consciousness about the nature of globalization and the institutions and policies that support it. Millions of people are at least aware of issues the movement has raised. The movement has exposed the interconnections and interdependence of the global village, infusing the perspective from the bottom up—not merely the top down model imposed by the world's elite. And increased awareness has generated important social mobilization.[45]

The movement has slowed the turn toward neoliberalism, put the world financial institutions and corporations on the defensive, and slowed the erosion of social democracy. The Washington Consensus—which argues for freer flows of capital, less regulated markets, and shrinking governments—which was dominant for the past twenty years under both Republicans and Democrats, is showing signs of breaking down.[46] Many quarters of the global elite now use rhetoric that a "new global financial infrastructure" is required to manage the problems and instabilities inherent in the New World Order. The World Bank, for example, speaks increasingly about addressing market failures and remedying increases in poverty rates in developing countries in its *World Development Reports*. The anti-globalization/global justice movement has changed the terms of the debate. The WTO moved a post-Seattle meeting to Doha, Qatar, far from easy protestor access.

More important, we witness changes, albeit moderate ones, in the poli-

cies and practices of the World Bank, the IMF, the WTO, corporate leaders, and heads of state. Even if changes are more symbolic than substantive, they still are, nevertheless, shifts in the right direction.[47] In late 1999, the World Bank adopted a new anti-poverty initiative that requires all debtor nations to submit "poverty reduction strategy papers," which must spell out how they will take steps to help their poorest citizens.[48] Representatives of the anti-globalization/global justice movement—including AFL-CIO President John Sweeney, environmentalist Jeremy Rifkin, and Lori Wallach of Ralph Nader's Global Trade Watch—were invited to join the otherwise usual list of corporate and government leaders at the meeting of the World Economic Forum in Davos, Switzerland, in 2001.

At the end of 2000, when more than 150 heads of state gathered at the United Nations for a Millennium Summit, "globalization" dominated the discussion. The heads of state were nearly unanimous in acknowledging the need to change the direction globalization has taken until now. Not surprisingly, the most pointed attacks came from leaders of the Global South. The United Nations established a forum and website[49] to bring nearly fifty multinational corporations and banks together with an assortment of labor federations and NGOs in order to work toward a "Global Compact" that better addresses human needs, labor rights, environmental conditions, and so on. In Europe, the Organization for Economic Cooperation and Development has revived its "Guidelines for Multinational Enterprises"; the World Bank and International Youth Foundation have set up a "Global Alliance for Workers and Communities." WTO director-general Michael Moore and U.S. Federal Reserve Chairman Alan Greenspan acknowledge that the protests have stalled discussion and progress on further trade agreements. The World Bank cancelled its planned meeting in Spain, expecting a crush of protestors and bad press, and instead will meet over the Internet.[50] All these developments are meant to rectify problems that have been highlighted by the anti-globalization/global justice movement.

In the United States, President Clinton launched the Fair Labor Association as a compromise between anti-sweatshop activists' demands and corporate responses in order to help U.S. firms clean up their act. One of Clinton's final acts as president was to secure from Congress approval of $435 million in foreign aid to help finance a debt-relief plan for forty-one of the poorest Third World nations.

In addition, six months after twenty thousand people descended on Washington in April 2000 to protest the policies of the IMF and the World Bank, Congress voted to require both to change some of the conditions they impose on borrowing countries. Both branches of Congress called for U.S. representatives to the World Bank and the IMF to oppose "user fees" that were being imposed on debtor countries. The ruling meant that the World Bank and IMF will no longer be able to force borrowing nations to charge their citizens for basic health and education services as they try to balance their budgets—making a huge difference in the lives of millions of people in the world's poorest countries. The user fee victory is an example of how protesters influenced legislators to make changes inside the institutions that run the global economy. The legislation was sponsored by Jesse Jackson, Jr. (D-Ill.) and Nancy Pelosi (D-Calif.), who saw the political opportunity opened up by the protests. For the first time, Congress ruled that the IMF and World Bank would lose their funding from the United States unless they changed their policies. With conservatives attacking the institutions from the other side, the IMF and World Bank had little defense inside Congress.

The user fees victory, while small in the scheme of the larger goals of the anti-globalization movement, nevertheless provides proof and direction for how the movement can affect policy. These victories also embolden anti-globalization activists for other campaigns, such as debt relief, which Jubilee 2000 helped win. The Rainforest Action Network changed Brazil's environmental policies; anti-sweatshop activists have changed labor conditions at Nike, Gap, and Starbucks around the world. Again, while insufficient in the aggregate—even symbolic in some cases—they spur on movement activists to struggle for greater gains. Indeed, the United Nations' Declaration of Human Rights, which includes the right to food, shelter, and an adequate standard of living, has yet to be signed by the G-7 nations (the largest and most powerful— Canada, France, Germany, Italy, Japan, the United Kingdom, and the United States), but is actively being pursued by some groups in this new political climate the anti-globalization movement has helped create. Similarly, the United Nations' World Court is being targeted as a place to bring governments and corporations to trial for violations of human, civil, political, and economic rights. Ultimately, it is in the court of world opinion that the movement must prevail. And, thus far, it is winning many more hearts and minds than the other side.

The July 2001 summit meeting of the G-8 (the G-7 plus Russia) in Genoa, where well over 100,000 global justice demonstrators converged to protest the ravages of the free trade policies of the world's largest economies, ended in violence with hundreds hurt and one protestor killed. Despite outer repression and inner division, this episode reaffirmed the coalition and commitment of a movement that appears to be growing in numbers and strength in its effort to remake the new global world order more democratic and just.

CHALLENGES AND PROSPECTS:
REFORM OR REVOLUTION?

Questions about whether the goals of the movement are to be accomplished through reform or revolution divide its members. Groups sharply debate the purpose and methods of the movement. Can the WTO, IMF, and World Bank be adequately reformed to meet the movement's goals, or must they be shut down and abolished? Can the movement infuse these institutions with greater labor and environmental standards, or must it instead establish a new global economic order and financial framework? These issues often mark the dividing line among key constituent members.

Significant tensions can emerge within the movement regarding goals, ideology, targets, and tactics. Too frequently conflicts among movement members occur along cultural, ethnic, racial, class, gender, or sexual orientation lines. The movement often looks more like several movements that are at odds with one another. Some group members are frankly bourgeois, while others are working-class and community-based activists. Similarly, the North/South divide is significant, and in the North, the movement often lacks participation by people of color.

Even recent efforts to forge unity—largely successfully—reveal deep divisions and tensions. For example, some 10,000 activists from 1,000 organizations and 120 countries met in Pôrto Alegre, Brazil, at the World Social Forum in February 2001. Pôrto Alegre itself is living proof that alternatives are possible. The city is governed by the Workers party, with substantial amounts of grassroots democratic participation; its budget-making sessions are radically participatory, using town halls of twenty thousand people. The World Social Forum posed these questions: What is the movement for? Can it formulate a common program, or at least achieve consensus on key issues? What does the movement perceive as critical targets and viable strategies? Is nonviolence an agreed upon method of protest? While not all of these questions were answered to everyone's satisfaction, progress was made, and part of progress is democratic dialogue. Many proposals were made—including calls for a manifesto—and healthy denunciations of the process and protests marked the five days activists met. The dominant slogan of the forum was "Another World Is Possible."[51]

While another world may be possible, there is no consensus within the anti-globalization movement on the direction or mode of transportation to that world. If the movement were to get the World Bank, IMF, and WTO to agree to one of many desired goals—a profoundly radical and sound environmental agenda that called for organic agricultural production and ecologically sustainable building using renewable energy; or debt forgiveness in developing countries; or the incorporation of a radical women's and labor agenda that included paid parental work and sharing childrearing activities, higher wages, benefits, and workers' control over labor conditions and investment of profits—would that be desirable?

Big structural problems would remain even if such a goal were reached, contend critics such as Global Exchange. In the first place, they argue, the prime imperative of these organizations is to keep their markets open to investors who are in the business of extracting profit. Soon developing countries would find themselves back in debt to the same corporate structures, whose other primary mandate is the repayment of those debts. Thus, the argument goes, the structure of capitalism—especially in the absence of a radical redistribution of wealth across the globe—would leave intact a system that would maintain and exacerbate these disparities. On the other hand, reformers argue, if the movement were able to achieve these and other far-reaching changes, there would be a revolutionary transformation.

Some have attempted to develop a "global program" or key planks for "globalization from below," which include equalizing labor, environmental, and social conditions; democratizing institutions at all levels by pushing decision making down as close as possible to those affected; leveling wealth and power; converting economic activity into environmental sustainability; and attaining prosperity by meeting human needs.[52] For some, such as some radical environmentalists, this project entails going back to simpler ways. Others, who criticize this philosophy as nostalgic backwardness, argue that technological advances can be retooled and harnessed to achieve socially productive ends.

These contending views raise critical questions for the movement: Which way forward, or, what is to be done? By whom? How?

GLOBAL EXCHANGE

Given the multitude of anti-globalization organizations and groups, the many constituencies, voices, orientations, why focus on an NGO called Global Exchange? NGOs are increasingly playing a larger role in the movement, both as organizers and spokespeople. The NGO "swarm" around anti-globalization themes, as it is sometimes referred to, has been given greater credibility and political influence by the growth of the movement itself. But tensions between such groups and radical grassroots organizations, which are smaller, more local, and more resource-poor, as well as divisions between the North and South, threaten to divide and derail the movement. Global Exchange offers an opportunity to examine these issues.

Global Exchange has been a leading voice in the anti-globalization movement long before, during, and after Seattle. Based in San Francisco, Global Exchange was one of the key coalition member groups that organized protests against the WTO in Seattle. Along with many other groups in between and since across the world, Global Exchange has helped organize protests against the World Bank and IMF in Washington, D.C., against the conventions of the Republican party in Philadelphia and the Democratic party in Los Angeles, against the meetings of the FTAA in Quebec, and against the G-8 meetings in Genoa.

Global Exchange engages effectively in different kinds of activities that represent key elements of the movement as a whole. With deep roots in social justice activism, the organization works for sustainable economic development at home and abroad and conducts research and educational activity. Global Exchange is generally well regarded among movement groups, even though some members find fault with the organization.

Global Exchange engages in many activities, including what its name suggests: It promotes exchanges across the globe. Acting as a liaison to others engaged in anti-globalization work, it brings together groups of people who engage in democracy-building across national boundaries. Global Exchange also recruits people into the movement and helps foster strong ties within the movement, with the goal of producing significant and lasting change. Moreover, it is effective at disseminating the movement's message, especially by garnering mainstream media attention.

Perhaps most important, Global Exchange sees itself as part of this movement with a purpose. As its co-founders—Medea Benjamin, Kevin Danaher, and Kirsten Moller—recently wrote:

All over the world we see signs of hope: democracy breaking forth, people recognizing their responsibility to be stewards of the earth, the growing consensus that military might is not the best road to peace and security, a new understanding that warehousing prisoners, especially for non-violent crimes, is a bankrupt strategy, unworthy of human creativity. Global Exchange is at the center of this new grassroots globalization—building international coalitions, shining a light on injustices, and working to expose the ways corporations and governments, under the guise of development or aid, thwart the will of people. At the beginning of a new century, we see a dying system's desperate efforts to survive. The "system" continues to foster destruction, but people everywhere are defying the old ways and taking it into their own hands to support their fellow human beings.[53]

Global Exchange articulates the anti-globalization message clearly and concisely: "Our movement is a profoundly humane response to a global economic system gone awry," says Medea Benjamin. The movement is about "democratic decision making, fair distribution of wealth, and environmental sustainability."[54] Because Global Exchange is highly effective at gaining access to mainstream media and adept at articulating the movement's messages, it popularizes the movement even as it promotes itself. Global Exchange does this through the use of a wide variety of written materials, videos, the Web, and individual contacts.

Global Exchange sees itself as embodying the kinds of programs and activities that can help bring about the goals and vision of the movement. It recruits, educates, facilitates, popularizes, politicizes, lobbies, and organizes. While the movement is comprised of disparate groups that sometimes have divergent interests, organizations like Global Exchange aim to expand and unify the strength of the whole by helping to articulate key common points, synthesize critical goals and strategies, and galvanize many elements of the movement and the public around a broad agenda. It acts as an incubator, clearinghouse, and facilitator of the movement. Global Exchange—along with a host of other groups—is actively transforming the corporate-led global agenda.

What Is Global Exchange and What Does It Do?

Global Exchange describes itself as "a human rights organization dedicated to promoting environmental, political and social justice around the world." Established in 1988, Global Exchange's roots go much farther back. The co-founders initially met in Food First, another Bay Area–based organization that works against hunger and environmental deterioration through research and educational materials. Danaher began his organizing in the anti-apartheid movement; Benjamin, trained as a nutritionist and economist, worked in Guatemala and Mozambique in the 1970s and 1980s before moving to Food First; Moller, born in Denmark and raised in Oregon, was a welder and millwright turned labor activist who also worked in Central America. They were all radicalized by their activism, particularly by their overseas experiences.

Danaher, now fifty years old, explains how, in the course of doing research for his Ph.D. in sociology (which he obtained from the University of California, Santa Cruz) and doing solidarity work in South Africa, he was told by members of the African National Congress (ANC) that the greatest impact he could have would be to change policy of the U.S. and international institutions. "We know how to dig ditches and build schools—the problem is we don't have the resources to do so," Danaher was told. But, by breaking the links between the national elite in South Africa and the global corporate elite—represented by the World Bank, IMF, and U.S. foreign policy—Danaher and other solidarity activists could weaken the apartheid regime and allow ANC activists to come to power on their own. At the same time, solidarity links could be built between anti-apartheid groups in the United States and elsewhere and with grassroots organizations and unions in South Africa. "Unite friends, divide enemies" is the task for the movement, Danaher explains. This means finding ways both to build linkages and solidarity and, at the same time, to weaken ties among powerful foes. The anti-apartheid movement's divestment strategy helped do just that. Building shantytowns on college campuses—among other effective tactics—made a difference. Danaher, now the author or co-author of eight books, took these lessons with him to Global Exchange.[55]

Global Exchange has grown from a staff of three in 1988 to a relatively sizable NGO today with about twelve thousand subscribing members, a $4.5 million budget, and a forty-member staff that engages in a mix of research, education, and organizing. It has five primary goals: to promote political and economic human rights; to educate the U.S. public about global issues; to encourage the U.S. government and international institutions to adopt policies that promote democratic and sustainable development; to link people in the developed and developing worlds who are working to achieve sustainable development; and to improve the lives of poor people by providing material and technical assistance.[56]

To achieve these goals, Global Exchange has seven main program areas. The first is "Global Economic Rights Campaigns," which aim to eliminate sweatshop conditions, monitor corporate behavior, and challenge global rule-makers, such as the WTO and IMF. It mobilizes members for the inclusion of labor and social rights in international trade agreements and mechanisms and encourages corporate responsibility to workers, local communities, and the environment. This program involves documenting and exposing corporate behavior that violates such rights and responsibilities and uses companies' own brand names against them via public campaigns that attempt to shame and embarrass the companies, ultimately threatening to hurt their sales and profits. These efforts to make corporations more accountable and responsive to social and environmental justice standards have had some success. For example, Global Exchange was able to help prevent Shell Oil from using the North Sea to dump oil from its vessels; to expose Chevron's links and complicity with the military government of Nigeria, whose human rights abuses became international news; and to force Home Depot to stop selling lumber obtained from old growth forests.[57]

A second area is "Human Rights Campaigns," which support pro-democracy movements in developing countries and monitor and report on human rights and elections in conflict areas. The project also works to improve relations among citizens in countries where the United States has been involved in conflicts (e.g., Cuba, Colombia, Mexico, or Brazil). A third area involves "Reality Tours," which aim to provide North Americans with an understanding of a developing country's internal dynamics through socially responsible travel. Participants from many walks of life examine contemporary political, economic, and social trends in a broad range of countries on nearly every continent. Reality Tours also serve as election monitoring and human rights delegations, observing and reporting on events in areas of conflict. A fourth area, the "Public Education Program," produces books, videos, articles, and editorials; organizes educational events and workshops; and works with the media to increase coverage of international issues from a grassroots, community perspective. The program also includes an International Speakers Bureau that brings community leaders from around the world to educate U.S. citizens on critical global issues.

A fifth program, related to the "Reality Tours," focuses on Global Exchange's home state. "Exploring California" offers travel seminars that explore critical issues facing Californians, including immigration, labor, and the environment, through solution-oriented dialogue. The seminars facilitate communication among a broad spectrum of Californians and encourage participants to become active citizens who will work to enrich community partners through contact with potential supporters.

The "Fair Trade Program," a sixth area, helps build economic justice through alternative trade stores in the San Francisco Bay area, and an online store that generates income for artisans in nearly forty countries. The artisans are paid for their products and earnings at a "fair" rate— usually more than double the market rate in that country—and the profits are reinvested in the United States and the host countries in community projects such as health clinics, childcare, education, and literacy training. These alternative microfinance programs also seek to educate First World consumers about conditions where the goods are made and about the importance of building a more just global economic order.

Finally, Global Exchange provides financial support to groups working for social change. Its "Grassroots Self-Help Project" provides material assistance—small seed grants and technical assistance—to community-initiated organizing, training, and development projects. Every year, Global Exchange provides approximately twenty projects with about $100,000 in direct grants and material aid.

Global Exchange promotes programs and models of democratic economic development. For example, they encourage citizens to make their cities "fair trade zones" by working with local and state governments to adopt policies and resolutions that support fair trade, human rights, environmental sustainability, and economic justice. Global Exchange has been an effective player in the anti-sweatshop movement, particularly against Nike.

Similarly, Global Exchange led a Fair Trade campaign against coffee retailers beginning in 1998. The "Fair Trade" coffee project sought to increase the share of profits that small farmers who grow the coffee receive, rather than the larger share middlemen siphon off, primarily by requiring a minimum of $1.26 per pound for beans to go directly to farmers, rather than the 30 to 50 cents they usually receive. Within a year, over one hundred retailers in the Bay Area were abiding by Fair Trade standards. As social movement research shows, a group may become emboldened by its successes, and Global Exchange took its campaign national against a highly visible target: Starbucks. After Starbucks refused Global Exchange's initial entreaty to carry Fair Trade coffee in all of its stores, Global Exchange brought greater pressure to bear through a series of demonstrations and a sustained public campaign beginning in the fall of 1999. By April 2000, Starbucks agreed to sell Fair Trade coffee at its outlets. "For the 550,000 farmers who are participating in the Fair Trade program," Danaher said, "they're getting twice as much for their coffee as Folgers or Nescafe is paying."[58]

Global Exchange has worked alongside hundreds of grassroots organizations, radical direct-action collectives, and other NGOs who have mobilized tens of thousands of people into a variety of actions. These anti-globalization/global justice movement activists now in motion are, in part, responsible for exposing the contemporary global crisis of capitalism. They have called into question the corporate paradigm of globalization.

The implementation of their projects and goals, however, cannot be accomplished unless some of the rifts in the movement can be mended. For this and other reasons, critics of NGOs and Global Exchange must be addressed.[59] Indeed, Danaher reminds his audiences—who are generally middle-class North Americans—to see themselves as part of the privileged few who benefit from the global economy, even as he exhorts them to ally themselves with poor masses in the South and work for change through one or more of Global Exchange's projects.

Global Exchange, NGOs, and Their Critics

The aforementioned fault lines among movement groups manifest in criticism of NGOs such as Global Exchange. Some who consider themselves more "grassroots" and "radical" in their politics and practices argue that NGOs are "reformist" and are "co-opting" the movement.[60] This ideological and material conflict became evident at certain moments during the Seattle protests and have left festering wounds among some coalition partners. For example, during the protests some anarchists broke windows of corporate franchises such as Starbucks, McDonald's, Niketown, and The Gap—chain stores that symbolize global capitalism. However, some NGO leaders—including Medea Benjamin of Global Exchange and

Lori Wallach of Public Citizen—publicly denounced such actions, recalling agreement among key organizers of the protests to adhere to nonviolent civil disobedience practices. In addition, according to critics, some NGO members turned in window-breakers to the police.[61] While some in the movement shared this outrage and sought to distance themselves from violent protestors, others reacted sharply to the condemnations, likening the NGO leaders to "red baiters."

Radical anarchist affinity groups—and other analysts of movements—contend movements are successful to the degree that they disrupt business as usual, recalling riots in the 1960s and labor strife in the 1930s,[62] or a host of revolutions historically in both the North and South. Moreover, they argue, the state is the primary agent using violence against the protestors and therefore the behavior of the authorities should be the focus of criticism, not the disruption of the activists. The movement must come to terms with such disagreements in order to achieve its goals.

Many direct action–oriented groups acknowledge that Global Exchange and other NGOs are important players in movement building. Still, critics contend, NGOs and union leaders have engaged in some revision of history. Some labor leaders and NGOs have claimed or implied that the Seattle victory was in large part due to their efforts, which downplays the critical role of direct action affinity groups (such as DAN and the Ruckus Society) who actually did much of the heavy lifting and placed their bodies on the line. Indeed, the mainstream media's focus on the disruption—even violence—of the protests in Seattle and elsewhere (by both protestors and police) certainly helped put the anti-globalization movement on the political map.

However well intentioned these NGOs are, their critics argue, some are "opportunistic." Critics assert that NGO leaders capture much of the media attention and often end up being the public face for what is a broader movement. NGOs thereby shape the movement's message, which of course does not always fully reflect the views of all participants. There are significant conflicts among groups, from contention around who can properly claim credit for various strategies and successes, to those who seek to distance themselves from other movement members or denounce one another. These fissures have made it difficult to forge ongoing and future working relationships.

Coalition work is always a tricky business. Practically speaking, NGOs possess valuable information and use their access to the mainstream media to popularize messages that radical movement activists often agree with and therefore cannot afford to ignore. In fact, many critics admit that Global Exchange mounts effective actions and gets important media attention.[63] Part of the tension among groups boils down to who gets credit for actions and who represents the movement, because credit and attention often lead to increases in resources and funding. Global Exchange has accumulated both political capital and increased funding. Due to its ability to play a prominent role in the anti-globalization movement, Global Exchange has been able to more than double its resources and staffing over the past several years. This has facilitated its capacity to organize activities and produce materials that have helped achieve important gains, as well as to become a leader within the anti-globalization movement.[64] Ideally, each side needs to negotiate with the other and create paths to present multiple voices, develop mutual respect, and distribute power, credit, and resources more equitably.

A related criticism of NGOs and Global Exchange is that some of their goals and programs are "reformist." The Fair Trade movement, for example, critics argue, may be a step in the right direction, but falls short of its goals and may end up co-opting movement activists and goals. When Global Exchange negotiated a deal with Starbucks—who agreed to improve working conditions and increase the pay of workers that produce coffee—critics argued that these workers still remain part of the exploited working class in the international division of labor where costs are merely passed on to consumers in the developed world who pay extra for fancy Italian-named coffee creations while the basic system remains intact. Although NGOs—including Global Exchange—acknowledge these facts, they contend nevertheless that such agreements are important incremental steps in the right direction. In fact, Global Exchange and others note that such companies now reach out to NGOs in order to negotiate similar settlements (even if only to avoid public criticism, further scrutiny, and pressure to change practices). From the vantage point of NGOs, this is testimony to their—and the movement's—impact and progress.

Yet, some of their critics see this "progress" as destructive; it amounts to deal-making with the enemy (Starbucks and Nike), and the deals are not even that great. The agreements are more symbolic than substantive, incrementalist at best. These agreements, critics argue, merely get companies to subscribe to a set of codes and practices that are voluntary, not compulsory; they have no teeth and serve only to help corporations clean up their tarnished images. The critics contend that true progress would be real regulations on corporate behavior and strong protections for people and the environment.

For example, Global Exchange's victory over Starbucks has severe limitations. Starbucks has, thus far, only agreed to sell Fair Trade coffee in whole bean form. All those fancy blends of mochacinos and lattes are made with free-trade, not Fair Trade, beans.[65] And the cost of the Fair Trade whole beans goes up nearly $2 from the house blend. Thus, Fair Trade coffee at Starbucks is only a minor portion of their total sales. Less than 1 percent of all the coffee sold in the United States carries the Fair Trade label. A handful of major companies, including Procter & Gamble, Philip Morris, Sara Lee, and Nestlé, control 60 percent of the U.S. market and 40 percent of the world market. Even in Europe, where this campaign is over a decade old, Fair Trade coffee accounts for approximately 5 percent of all sales.[66]

Still, others counter, even these gestures can eventually prove meaningful beyond what their strategists and consumers (or authors and subscribers) had in mind. Movement activists can use pledges to honor principles and codes to force them to do so, and thereby force more substantial changes.[67] Even harsh critics give NGOs credit for much of the work they do and things they have achieved.[68] Global Exchange launched a World Bank Bond boycott, for example, a campaign that many movement participants support. This boycott entails getting local governments to pledge not to buy World Bank Bonds, thus reducing the value of World Bank Bonds and hitting the Bank in its own pocket. Movement activists argue this concrete and targeted action has real prospects to leverage power to affect World Bank policies. In the end, many movement activists give Global Exchange kudos for most of their long list of programs.

Still, others contend, if global justice activists want to be effective at thwarting policies of the World Bank and other international institutions—and especially at blocking or reversing harmful international agreements like the FTAA or NAFTA—then greater focus should be placed on the member governments (national governments, especially of the G-8) who shape these institutions and their policies and make these agreements.[69]

A critical question for the movement is how to achieve desired change. Can reform and incremental change add up to structural change that movement activists strive to achieve? What is "success"? How does one gauge "effectiveness"? Might more than one path lead to producing impacts that reinforce different member organizations? These and other such issues are about overarching philosophical and tactical dividing lines among movement members. Should the movement articulate a common program and select representative leaders, or should it let a thousand flowers bloom? These need not be mutually exclusive positions, and some astute observers have presented ways for potentially mutually satisfying solutions.[70]

Nevertheless, it is clearly the combined efforts of all these movement organizations and activists that, in the end, made Seattle "happen." Similarly, subsequent protest actions in dozens of cities across the globe—and impacts on targeted institutions and policies—are the result of this broad range of divergent groups.

CONCLUSION

The anti-globalization/global justice movement, which crosses many borders and issue areas, already constitutes one of the numerically largest movements in human history. If the "free-rider" problem[71] can be effectively addressed—that is, if nonactive "members" who currently do not actively participate but gain benefits from the actions of active members can be drawn into the new social motion—the global justice movement has the potential to become a mass movement with considerable clout. If, however, the divisions among groups—of kind, program, and geography—remain or broaden, its potential will sputter and evaporate like many before it.

While the movement's potential is huge, its challenges and obstacles are formidable. The Internet has proven to be a useful tool for communicating and organizing, but the digital divide locks out the most aggrieved constituencies. Periodic street clashes with police at meetings of international institutions can produce battle fatigue and do not always lead to the development of ongoing relationships, common agendas, and real community building. Nevertheless, if movement organizations can broaden their constituency bases, if marginal groups and potential coalition partners can be brought into the movement, and if these groups can coalesce more effectively and regularly, the global justice movement has the potential to be one of the most transformative in human history.

In 2001 alone, increasing numbers of mass protests greeted elites in numerous cities across the globe, such as when financial ministers and government leaders met in Quebec during April to forge the FTAA. More dramatically, the explosive meetings in Genoa in July, where up to 100,000 protestors overwhelmed authorities (ending in the death of at least one protestor), left foreign ministers and heads of state of the G-8 scrambling to conduct public relations damage control.[72] These events fueled discussion on both sides of the barricades about what next steps global justice activists and elites might take.

But the events of September 11 altered the terrain on which this struggle is now playing out.[73] The ensuing war against terrorism has had a visible dampening effect on the movement by shifting the line activists had drawn in the sand.[74] The meetings of the IMF and World Bank scheduled for the fall 2001—and the planned protests against them—were both quickly cancelled. The war against terrorism portrayed activists fighting against world financial institutions and corporate dominated government policies as part of a larger enemy. The genuine pain and fear generated by September 11 permitted the United States and other world powers to rapidly shift to a wartime political economy and to renew their efforts to advance a New World Order, both of which make it difficult for activists to raise criticism or dissent about either the war or globalization without being accused of being unpatriotic.[75] Since September 11, global justice activists have been increasingly targeted for arrest and surveillance, including being restricted from international travel.[76]

Nevertheless, September 11 may ultimately aid the cause of global justice activists. Globalization's neoliberalist policies have reduced the scope of the state, particularly concerning protections for workers, the environment, and civil rights, through the IMF's and World Bank's structural adjustment policies, which have produced decreasing health, education, and living standards for so much of the world's population. Such devastation has created fertile ground for anyone who speaks to people's pain and suffering, including religious fundamentalists such as Osama bin Laden. Globalization's havoc hit home when the hijacked planes flew into the World Trade Center and the Pentagon. Once the flag waving dies down, the global justice movement may be more effective in making these connections.

Moreover, as recently suggested by Walden Bello, a Filipino economist and one of the leaders of the global justice movement, history recently handed activists a boon with the collapse of the Argentine economy and the Enron scandal.[77] In fact, the second mass gathering of the World Social Forum in Pôrto Alegre, Brazil, at the end of January 2002—a counter to the simultaneous meeting of the corporate World Economic Forum in New York City—provides proof that the global justice movement is alive and undeterred. "Another World Is Possible," the chant and song that marked the weeklong meetings in Pôrto Alegre, which opened to a crowd of 1.3 million, has become *the* theme of the movement. Comprised of over fifty thousand diverse activists from hundreds of countries on all continents—particularly the Global South—Pôrto Alegre holds out the promise that the movement may yet achieve its goals. Importantly, "a consensus seemed to emerge [from the Pôrto Alegre meetings] as to how and where to move the fight forward after the setback of September 11."[78] One of the planks of an emergent common agenda is the recognition that the movement must not be ambiguous about the use of violence—it must adopt a clear stance of nonviolence. As Lori Wallach of Public Citizen put it, "too often we get dragged into a swamp of debating what is euphemistically called 'diversity of tactics.'. . . Now we need to speak up and say clearly that violence, as a political tactic, just doesn't work either in the United States or in Europe."[79]

Ultimately, the power of the global justice movement may lie in its capacity to expose and exploit the contradictions that globalization itself generates and to develop and maintain viable alternatives. If staying power is any indication of future developments, then the sheer wherewithal and continued activity of the plethora of groups associated with the global justice movement suggest that the movement's power is vast. As Zapatista leader Subcommandante Marcos so eloquently stated, "The future's name is autonomy; its route is struggle; its engine is youth; its brain is experience; and, it has a heart with an indigenous history."[80]

NOTES

1. Manuel Castells, *The End of the Millennium* (Malden, Mass.: Blackwell, 1998); Saskia Sassen, *Globalization and Its Discontents: Essays on the New Mobility of People and Money* (New York: New Press, 1998). Information about globalization can also be found on the website of the World Economic Forum, www.weforum.org, and on the website of Global Exchange, www.globalexchange.org.

2. Naomi Klein, "A Speech about the Movement," e-mail communication, February 2001.

3. Kevin Danaher and Roger Burbach, eds., *Globalize This!* (Monroe, Maine: Common Courage, 2000). For more information on the anti-globalization movement, see the Global Exchange website, www.globalexchange.org.

4. I use both terms, anti-globalization movement and global justice movement, throughout this chapter to describe the same phenomenon. Increasingly, movement activists embrace the latter more than the former, but not universally.

5. I also use these and several other terms interchangeably, partly because many movement activists do, and partly because "developing," "Third World," and "Global South" are not completely accurate depictions of the geographic areas and conditions they purport to describe, which is also true of "developed," "First World," and "Global North."

6. William Greider, "Waking Up the Global Elite," *The Nation* 271, no. 9 (October 2, 2000): 17–18; "Trading with the Enemy," *The Nation* 272, no. 12 (March 26, 2001): 11–13; and the website of the World Economic Forum, www.weforum.org.

7. I have been a participant in and observer of the anti-globalization movement for nearly two decades in some capacity or another. I worked in the anti-apartheid movement and did solidarity work in Latin America during the 1980s and have participated in numerous protest actions in the United States more recently. While I have attempted to augment my experience with research and through interviews with movement activists, my account of this widely diverse, fragmented, and sometimes incoherent movement inevitably reflects my experience and interpretation, and therefore is open to disagreement.

8. Ute Pieper and Lance Taylor, "The Revival of the Liberal Creed: The IMF, the World Bank, and the Inequality in a Globalized Economy," working paper for Center for Economic Policy Analysis (June 1996); Hans-Peter Martin and Harald Schumann, *The Global Trap: Globalization and the Assault on Democracy and Prosperity* (New York: Zed, 1997).

9. John Williamson, "What Washington Means by Policy Reform," in *Latin American Adjustment*, ed. John Williamson (Washington, D.C.: Institute for International Economics, 1990), 7–25; Susan Strange, "Rethinking Structural Change in the International Political Economy: States, Firms and Diplomacy," in *Political*

Economy and the Changing Global Order, ed. Richard Stubbs and Geoffrey R. D. Underhill (New York: St. Martin's, 1994), 103–115; Mark Levinson, "The Cracking Washington Consensus," *Dissent* (Fall 2000): 11–14.

10. Joseph K. Roberts, "Multilateral Agreement on Investment," *Monthly Review* 50, no. 5 (1998): 26.

11. Mark C. Gordon, *Democracy's New Challenge: Globalization, Governance, and the Future of American Federalism* (New York: Demos, 2001), accessed February 9, 2002 www.demos-usa.org/Pubs/Global/.

12. Barry Bluestone and Bennett Harrison, *The Deindustrialization of America: Plant Closings, Community Abandonment, and the Dismantling of Basic Industries* (New York: Basic, 1982) and *The Great U-Turn: Corporate Restructuring and the Polarization of America* (New York: Basic, 1988).

13. Sassen, *Globalization and Its Discontents*; Castells, *End of the Millennium*.

14. Nancy Folbre and James Heintz, *The Ultimate Field Guide to the U.S. Economy* (New York: New Press, 2000); Richard B. Freeman, *The New Inequality: Creating Solutions for Poor America* (Boston: Beacon, 1999).

15. William K. Tabb, *The Amoral Elephant: Globalization and the Struggle for Social Justice in the Twenty-First Century* (New York: Monthly Review, 2001); Doug Henwood, personal communication to the author, March 12, 2001.

16. Sarah Anderson, ed., *Views from the South: The Effects of Globalization and The WTO on Third World Countries* (Oakland, Calif.: Food First, 2000).

17. Jeremy Brecher, Tim Costello, and Brendan Smith, *Globalization from Below: The Power of Solidarity* (Woods Hole, Mass.: South End, 2000); Sidney Tarrow, *Power in Movement: Social Movements, Collective Action, and Politics* (Cambridge: Cambridge University Press, 1994); Frances Piven and Richard Cloward, *The Breaking of the American Social Compact* (New York: Norton, 1997).

18. Kevin Danaher, ed., *Corporations Are Gonna Get Your Mama* (Monroe, Maine: Common Courage, 1996); Danaher and Burbach, eds., *Globalize This!*; Brecher, Costello, and Smith, *Globalization from Below*.

19. George McKay, ed., *DiY Culture: Party and Protest in Nineties Britain* (London: Verso, 1998); Stephen Duncombe, *Notes from Underground: Zines and the Politics of Alternative Culture* (New York: Verso, 1997).

20. Jackie Smith, "Globalizing Resistance: The Battle of Seattle and the Future of Social Movements," paper presented at the Workshop for Contentious Politics, Columbia University, 1999.

21. Tarrow, *Power in Movement*.

22. Jeffry A. Frieden, "Invested Interests: The Politics of National Economic Policies in a World of Global Finance," *International Organizations* 45, no. 4 (1991); David Moberg, "Power Grab: Big Business Wants to Tighten Its Hold with a New Global Trade Pact," *Progressive* 62, no. 3 (March 1998): 24.

23. Lorna Mason, "Breaking the Neo-Liberal Consensus: The Multilateral Agreement on Investment and its Links to Seattle Protests Against the World Trade Organization," paper presented at the American Sociological Association, Washington, D.C., 2000; Maude Barlow and Tony Clarke, *The Multilateral Agreement on Investment and the Threat to Canadian Sovereignty* (New York: Zed, 1997).

24. Freeman, *The New Inequality*; David Meyer, "Claiming Credit: The Social

48   *Ronald Hayduk*

Construction of Movement Success" (Irvine, Calif.: Center for the Study of Democracy, 2000).

25. People's Global Action, "What Is PGA?" accessed January 30, 2002 www.nadir.org/nadir/initiativ/agp/en.

26. People's Global Action, "What Is PGA?"

27. L. A. Kaufman, "Back Story," *Free Radical*, no. 10, accessed September 13, 2000, www.free-radical.org.

28. Doug Henwood, personal communication. See also Henwood's website for his journal *Left Business Observer*, www.panix.com/~dhenwood/LBO_home.html.

29. Will Hathaway and David S. Meyer, "Competition and Cooperation in Movement Coalitions: Lobbying for Peace in the 1980s," in *Coalitions and Political Movements: The Lessons of the Nuclear Freeze*, ed. Thomas R. Rochon and David S. Meyer (Boulder, Colo.: Lynne Rienner, 1997).

30. Tarrow, *Power in Movement*.

31. Brecher, Costello, and Smith, *Globalization from Below*; Danaher and Burbach, *Globalize This!*; Freeman, *The New Inequality*; Sassen, *Globalization and Its Discontents*; Martin and Schumann, *The Global Trap*.

32. Kevin Danaher, ed., *Democratizing the Global Economy: The Battle against the World Bank & the IMF* (Monroe, Maine: Common Courage, 2001); Danaher and Burbach, *Globalize This!*

33. Quoted on the Global Exchange website www.globalexchange.org.

34. George Rude, *Ideology and Popular Protest* (London: Lawrence and Wishart, 1980).

35. Brecher, Costello, and Smith, *Globalization from Below*, 7.

36. Global Exchange website; Danaher and Burbach, *Globalize This!*; Brecher, Costello, and Smith, *Globalization from Below*; Aspen Institute, *The Great Conversation* (Aspen, Colo.: Aspen Institute, 2000); John Madeley, *Big Business, Poor Peoples: The Impact of Transnational Corporations on the World's Poor* (New York: Zed, 1999).

37. Michael Massing, "From Protest to Program," *American Prospect* 12, no. 12 (July 2–16, 2001).

38. Simon Rodberg, "The CIO without the CIA," *American Prospect* 12, no. 12 (July 2–16, 2001).

39. Brecher, Costello, and Smith, *Globalization from Below*; Danaher and Burbach, *Globalize This!*; Amory Starr, *Naming the Enemy: Anti-Corporate Movements Confront Globalization* (New York: Zed, 2000).

40. Greider, "Waking Up the Global Elite" and "Trading with the Enemy"; Henwood, personal communication.

41. Danaher, *Democratizing the Global Economy*.

42. Anderson, *Views from the South*.

43. Quoted in Danaher and Burbach, *Globalize This!* www.globalexchange.org/wto/GlobalizeThisIntro.html.

44. Brooke Lehman, unpublished paper for the Institute for Social Ecology (Fall 1999); see also the website of the Direct Action Network (DAN), www.directactionnetwork.org.

45. Meyer, "Claiming Credit."

46. Levinson, "The Cracking Washington Consensus"; Massing, "From Protest to Program."

47. Greider, "Waking Up the Global Elite" and "Trading with the Enemy"; Henwood, personal communication.

48. Massing, "From Protest to Program."

49. The Internet address is www.unglobalcompact.org.

50. Massing, "From Protest to Program."

51. Klein, "A Speech about the Movement."

52. Brecher, Costello, and Smith, *Globalization from Below*. Similarly, "Alternatives for the Americas," a work in progress drafted by the Hemispheric Social Alliance, a coalition of labor, religious, environmental, and various activists from North and South America, codifies principles into an alternative to the FTAA as a tool for discussion and organizing; see Jeff Faux, "The Global Alternative," *American Prospect* 12, no. 12 (July 2–16, 2001).

53. Kirsten Moller, Medea Benjamin, and Kevin Danaher, "2000 in Review: Letter from the Global Exchange Founders," *Global Exchange Newsletter* (Winter 2001), accessed January 31, 2002, www.globalexchange.org/update/GXfounders Win2000NL.html.

54. Quoted in Brecher, Costello, and Smith, *Globalization from Below*.

55. Author interview with Kevin Danaher; information from two Global Exchange videos, *Globalization: Its Impact at Home and Abroad* and *Whose Globalization?*

56. Interview with Kevin Danaher; see also Global Exchange's website.

57. Massing, "From Protest to Program."

58. Danaher quoted in Massing, "From Protest to Program," 4.

59. Alexander Cockburn and Jeffrey St. Clair, *Five Days that Shook the World* (New York: Verso, 2001); Jim Davis, "This Is What Bureaucracy Looks Like: NGOs and Anti-Capitalism," in *The Battle of Seattle: Debating Corporate Globalization and the WTO*, ed. Eddy Yuen, Daniel Burton-Rose, and George Katsiaficas (New York: Soft Skull, forthcoming); Massing, "From Protest to Program." See also Cockburn's various "Beat the Devil" columns in the *Nation* for 2000.

60. Cockburn and St. Clair, *Five Days That Shook the World*; see also Davis, "What Bureaucracy Looks Like"; Massing, "From Protest to Program."

61. Cockburn and St. Clair, *Five Days that Shook the World*.

62. Frances Piven and Richard Cloward, *Poor People's Movements: Why They Succeed, How They Fail* (New York: Vintage, 1979).

63. Davis, "This Is What Bureaucracy Looks Like."

64. Danaher, *Democratizing the Global Economy*; see also Global Exchange's website.

65. Massing, "From Protest to Program."

66. Massing, "From Protest to Program."

67. William Greider, "Waking Up the Global Elite."

68. Davis, "This Is What Bureaucracy Looks Like"; Massing, "From Protest to Program."

69. Faux, "The Global Alternative."

70. Klein, "A Speech about the Movement"; Sheri Herndon, "No Logo: A Con-

versation with Naomi Klein," *Indymedia* (March 28, 2000); Brecher, Costello, and Smith, *Globalization from Below.*

71. Mancur Olson, *The Logic of Collective Action: Public Goods and the Theory of Groups* (New York: Schocken, 1968).

72. Other 2001 actions included protests in Barcelona against the meeting of the World Bank's annual conference on Economic Development in June; simultaneous protests in seventy-five cities against Citigroup in April; and the Zapatista mass mobilization and march to Mexico City in March, to name but a few. Information about the three actions named can be obtained respectively from Campanya BCN2001, accessed March 20, 2002 www.rosadefoc.org/ct/index.htm; Rainforest Action Network, "Citigroup: Not with My Money!" accessed March 20, 2002 www.ran.org/ran_campaigns/citigroup/; and Harry Cleaver et al., eds., *Chiapas 95*, accessed March 20, 2002, www.eco.utexas.edu/faculty/Cleaver/chiapas 95.html.

73. Victor Wallis, "A Radical Approach to Justice in 9/11," *Socialism and Democracy* 16, no. 1 (Winter–Spring 2002): 156–161.

74. President Bush's statements about the need to protect "our way of life" against "barbaric terrorists" and an "Axis of Evil" that the United States must guard against gave new life to a renewed militarism and the simmering cultural wars. These polarities are reflected in the outpouring of commentary that pits modernity—associated with globalization—against tradition as culturally backward, such as the updated versions of Samuel P. Huntington's *The Clash of Civilizations and the Remaking of World Order* (New York: Simon & Schuster, 1996) and Benjamin R. Barber's *Jihad vs. McWorld* (New York: Ballantine, 1996). See also Hester Eisenstein, "Globalization and the Events of September 11, 2001," *Socialism and Democracy* 16, no. 1 (Winter–Spring 2002): 133; and Edward Said, "The Clash of Ignorance," *The Nation* 273, no. 12 (October 22, 2001): 11–13.

75. Eisenstein, "Globalization," 131–136; Max Elbaum and Bob Wing, "Some Strategic Implications of September 11," *Socialism and Democracy* 16, no. 1 (Winter–Spring 2002): 161–164.

76. Leslie Kaufman, *Free Radical: A Chronicle of the New Unrest*, no. 19 (September 2001), accessed March 20, 2002, www.free-radical.org.

77. Quoted in Marc Cooper, "From Protest to Politics: A Report from Pôrto Alegre," *The Nation* 274, no. 9 (March 11, 2002): 11–15.

78. Cooper, "From Protest to Politics," 12.

79. Quoted in Cooper, "From Protest to Politics," 12. Other points of unity included: (1) redefining the movement from being anti- to pro-: "It's they who are anti. We are a movement for democracy. For equality. For the environment. For health. They are for a failed status quo." (Lori Wallach, quoted in Cooper, "From Protest to Politics," 12); (2) escalating the fight against the WTO; (3) blocking the FTAA; and (4) proposing a New World financial architecture.

80. *The Narco News Bulletin*, no. 9 (March 2001). See their website at www .narconews.com.

Part I

MOVEMENTS BASED ON MATERIAL NEEDS

3

Unions and American Workers: Whither the Labor Movement?

IMMANUEL NESS

At the dawn of the twenty-first century, the American labor movement is considerably weaker than at any time since the 1920s, and less effective in advancing the interests of workers than are equivalent movements in Western Europe and Canada. In virtually every category of economic security, American workers lag far behind those in other advanced industrial countries. On average, American workers continue to earn less and work harder than workers in countries with stronger labor movements.

A stock explanation for this discrepancy in social well-being is that American workers are more conservative and less militant than their counterparts in other countries. Historically, however, though American workers have had fewer political channels of expression, they are neither less militant nor less interested in improving their living standards through collective action. Scholars often attribute the inferior position of workers in America to the weakness of labor unions as against capitalist interests, citing in particular the historical absence of a major labor-based political party in the United States. Whereas in the early twentieth century effective labor-based parties emerged throughout Europe, no such party has taken the stage in the United States. While industrial democracies in Europe with strong labor parties have constructed elaborate social safety nets, the Democratic party has produced an American welfare system that is far less comprehensive and far less compassionate toward the working-class majority.[1] The recent political consensus around neoliberal economic policies has eroded even these limited social protections.

The lack of a labor party reduces American workers' reliance on the electoral arena and pushes labor toward confrontation at the point of production. Indeed, historically, American workers have tended to engage in militant workplace struggles to a significantly greater degree than their European counterparts.

What has always mattered for the working class, more than consciousness or ideology, is the ability of unions to provide tangible evidence that they can realistically advance the material interests of workers through organization and protest. Thus, contrary to the dominant interpretation of labor's political quiescence in the United States,[2] American workers do not exhibit what many academics conclude to be a "proletarian conservatism"; rather, as Howard Kimmeldorf argues, they have tended to express their radicalism through syndicalism, causing them to "eschew the political arena in favor of the workplace, to generally prefer the immediacy of direct action at the point of production to the uncertainty of legislative action in the halls of Congress."[3] As Kimmeldorf notes:

> Washing across the industrial landscape of early-twentieth-century America, syndicalism represented a fluid mix of organizational practices that combined the institutional brawn of pure and simple trade unionism with the mobilizing muscle of contemporary working-class insurgency to produce a kind of "syndicalism, pure and simple"—defined by its point-of-production focus, aggressive job control, and militant direct action.[4]

Rather than being regarded as a social movement, labor unions are more commonly viewed—and operated—as special interest organizations; instead of seeking to advance the interests of workers as a whole through political means, unions—much like corporate interests—typically lobby government officials to gain special treatment for industries employing their members.[5] This system of interest group intermediation increasingly fragments the working class into labor market categories and identity groups competing for government largesse, a phenomenon starkly evident in the recent support of the International Brotherhood of Teamsters for an energy bill that would increase oil production through drilling in the Arctic National Wildlife Preserve in Alaska.[6] Thus, two years after the much-ballyhooed teamster-turtle, labor-environmental alliance at the WTO protests in Seattle, parochial trade union interests seem to have won out, revealing the alliance as little more than media spectacle and wishful thinking on the part of leftists seeking to build a broader social movement. Not only do labor's blatantly audacious forms of interest group politics divide the labor movement, they also split labor from the environmental movement and other progressive forces.

THE AFL-CIO'S NEW VOICE
AND THE CALL TO ORGANIZE

The spiraling decline in organized labor's density in the workforce, from about 35 percent in the mid-1950s to about 13 percent in the mid-1990s, is indicative of labor's lost political clout under Lane Kirkland's leadership. At century's end, union density in the private sector hovered below 10 percent—threatening to call into question the future status of unionized workers in the public sector, where density was stalled at around 60 percent. This overall decline reflects labor's decreasing capacity to organize the majority of workers not already in unions—and therefore attests to its growing irrelevance in national political debates. Indeed, by the mid-1990s many unions had abandoned organizing efforts altogether, having realized that antiquated labor laws and the renewed willingness of employers to engage in union-busting tactics made successful organizing drives nearly impossible.[7]

On balance, organized labor's efforts to enforce federal laws protecting workers have proven increasingly futile. Labor law crafted in the 1930s and compromised in the following decades seems ever more incapable of addressing the needs of workers, the vast majority of whom no longer work in traditional manufacturing environments. The National Labor Relations Board, created amid the sweeping reforms of the 1930s, has become increasingly passive. Even during Democratic administrations, board decisions have rarely defended, in any robust way, the right of workers to organize into unions of their choice.[8] Under the Republican congresses of recent years—anti-union and dead set against new organizing—attempts at labor law reform were stymied. Now, with a new Republican administration in place, prospects are more dismal than ever.

Though the results from the first six years of John Sweeney's leadership of the AFL-CIO are mixed, the call to organize new members has unquestionably resonated among a small core of unions. The most active of these unions include the Service Employees International Union (SEIU); the Hotel Employees and Restaurant Employees (HERE); United Needletrades, Industrial, and Textile Employees (UNITE), a manufacturing union branching out into the service sector; and the Communication Workers of America (CWA). Still, the federation's proposal that national unions radically increase organizing expenditures from less than 5 percent of resources to 30 percent has, with the few exceptions noted, gone unheeded.

Indeed, the AFL-CIO has little power to control the activities of national unions. As a decentralized and fragmented institution operating in an anti-labor environment, it has far less ability to control the internal affairs of national unions than national unions have vis-à-vis their local affiliates.[9] Most national union charters contain clauses that permit them to seize control of maverick locals that fail to organize or that engage in unauthorized organizing across jurisdictional boundaries, thereby jeopardizing relations with other nationals.

No one can deny that the leadership's rhetoric and at least some of its actions have placed renewed emphasis on including organizing, a serious search for new targets and strategies, and on increasing the labor movement's political influence. Still, despite early signs of membership growth in the late 1990s, new organizing has declined over the past two years and appears to be stalled, as labor laws remain inimical to organizing and unions remain mired in outmoded practices.

After six years of reform and outwardly energetic AFL-CIO leadership under Sweeney and the New Voice team, enough time has passed to evaluate the program's successes and failures. Has the change in leadership brought about any significant change in the representational and organizing practices of national unions and their local affiliates? The mantra at the December 2001 AFL-CIO convention in Las Vegas, as intoned by John Sweeney, was "We're doing more of what we've done before"— reaffirmation of the progressive agenda of mobilizing and organizing workers, electing Democrats, opposing neoliberal globalization, and supporting regional and community alliances. However exemplary this agenda is compared to the conservatism and complacency of the Meany-Kirkland era, the AFL-CIO's continued reliance on the capricious Democratic party and the federation's inability to force national unions to take its agenda seriously expose the weakness of organized labor, fragmented and decentralized, in seeking to transform itself into an effective social movement.[10]

On the political front, since Sweeney's ascent in 1995 in the wake of a Republican congressional resurgence, it must be said that unions have had remarkable success in energizing supporters and mobilizing members to vote Democratic. Despite this, however, unions have had no voice promoting an agenda favorable to working people in the executive branch, and little voice in Congress, the latter attested to of late by the absence of any legislative proposal to increase government spending to bring the economy out of recession. Thus, although organized labor can take credit for mobilizing its ranks to vote Democratic, its organizing failures have kept those ranks too small and weak to play any determinative role in setting national policy.

ORGANIZING THE NEW
ECONOMY'S LABOR FORCE

What is different today from the Kirkland years is that the federation recognizes its weakness and fallibility and the important need to organize and mobilize. The federation leadership understands that organizing and growth are linked to mobilizing outsiders in new labor markets, including new-new economy workers, people of color, women, and immigrant workers. Unorganized workers in postindustrial labor markets will want to join unions where they are assured a voice in determining their fate on the job—particularly in an uncertain and frail economic environment. As organized labor seeks to organize new social segments, unions will have to change the perception—and too often reality—that its leadership is dominated by white men. Clearly New Voice has promoted greater leadership diversity in its Union Cities program, but change has been slow—and remains confined to the lower echelons of organized labor. The national unions remain dominated by white males no longer representative of the membership, and clearly not of the labor force as a whole.[11]

As unions seek to change, they will have to wrestle with the problem of maintaining standards in industries where new technology is being introduced and the labor force is shifting from white male to predominantly African American, new immigrant, and female. It remains uncertain how unions will balance the need to maintain and improve industry standards with the concern to organize new workers entering labor markets at significantly lower standards.

To make organized labor and its leadership more representative of the labor force as a whole will require greater union democracy, as unions become a social movement embracing both organized and unorganized workers. Such a transformation entails the following components: union democracy; instilling in the rank and file a sense of ownership; decentralized union governance through giving members control over union affairs; and a radical break with business unionism, in which a union's main function is delivering the goods for members.[12] The labor movement must advance a broader notion of unions as class institutions whose motto is that an injury to one is an injury to all.

A major obstacle to building such a movement is the hierarchical culture of unions, which tends to discourage membership participation in key decisions. This absence of participation makes it harder for unions to negotiate contracts for their members and erodes workers' sense of power vis-à-vis management.

The problem of recruiting new members will not be easy. Organizing strategies and structures of governance forged in the industrial union movement of the 1930s, when labor was concentrated in mass production industries, do not mesh well with the reality of the postindustrial workplace. Industrial restructuring has changed the nature and location of the labor force, significantly weakening organized labor. The emergence and growth of a postindustrial economy in the United States—a shift from manufacturing to services—from the 1970s to the present has eroded the membership of unions in the basic industries that dominated the post–World War II era. The consequent necessity of organizing workers in the new economy is a challenge that most unions are ill equipped to confront. Technological developments have brought about shifts in the fabrication

and delivery of goods and services, altering the structure of labor markets
dominated by employment in vertically integrated firms and thereby
accelerating the decline of union density and the growth of nonunion
firms. The emergence of a new labor force as a result of dramatic demographic changes in major urban centers—primarily the exodus of white
workers to the suburbs and the growth of African American, Latino, and
new immigrant populations—calls for creativity if the latter groups are to
be organized. With union density hemorrhaging, labor must explore
forms of unionization that go beyond conventional membership based on
majority status in workplaces. A new form of representation, characterized by Freeman and Rogers as "open source unionism," makes extensive
use of the Internet and regional and local labor councils to coordinate the
activities of workers in traditional unions and those who can be organized into nonmajority unions.[13] New forms of organizing activity
through workers' centers and associate membership are only now beginning in a few unions, including CWA and the United Auto Workers
(UAW), who recognize that the new economy has made old organizing
models obsolete. But much greater work will be necessary in many more
unions.[14]

LABOR AND GLOBALIZATION

For much of the past century, national labor movements relied on their
home countries to defend worker interests through regulating and enforcing labor-management relations and providing social welfare programs.
Unions could count on national labor laws to protect workers from
employer abuse and guarantee workers the right to join unions of their
choice. Although the labor movements of the past century varied from
country to country, through much of the developed world they could
count on standards regulating wages and hours. Moreover, although
workers almost never had an easy time joining unions, workplace democratic rights were significantly stronger twenty-five years ago than they
are today. The ascendancy of neoliberal capitalism on a global scale has
significantly eroded worker rights and the ability of unions organized on
a national basis to defend workers.

Globalization has significantly compromised labor standards and
workers' rights, both here and abroad, as unions increasingly face
unchecked capital flows across national boundaries and a loss of bargaining power with employers who remain in place. The twenty-first-century
brand of globalized, deregulated capitalism provides legal protections for
multinational corporations while threatening labor and environmental
standards. In this context, state power to protect noncorporate interests

is severely undercut. As trade and tariff restrictions that once protected workers on a national basis are broken down by the rise of global and regional trade blocs, unions are stripped of the ability to appeal to the state for protection and relief. Since workers' rights are not adequately incorporated into these global and regional agreements, labor in most cases finds itself without a seat at the table.

National labor leaders and activists are currently debating how best to maneuver in a hostile, corporate-dominated world economy. The pressing need is to develop strategies addressing the reality of globalized capitalism today far less loyal to national interests. How does labor curb the seemingly ineluctable growth of capital and labor mobility? There is no single or easy answer to this question.

Key issues remain unresolved. What voice might labor have within the World Trade Organization (WTO), the International Monetary Fund (IMF), and other transnational organizations? How can labor rights be protected within regional blocs such as the North American Free Trade Agreement (NAFTA) and the European Union? Insofar as it is wise or even possible to participate in the policy deliberations of these bodies, national and international labor organizations must find mechanisms that will advance the interests of workers amid a system of predatory capitalism in many ways reminiscent of the late nineteenth century. Beyond this, strategies must be found for building a broader international labor movement capable of defending the interests of workers both in northern advanced countries and in the southern undeveloped world. Indeed, labor must consider whether it may be appropriate to opt out of the current system and call for a new one that will protect workers, the disadvantaged, and the global environment. The recent turn by the Teamsters and others to more familiar forms of business and interest group unionism will make it enormously difficult to build the kind of global justice movement that transcends more parochial concerns.

Beyond the internecine struggles within labor, unions will have to address their abjectly weak position vis-à-vis international capital in the neoliberal order. The economic and political priorities of WTO-member governments are determined in large measure by multinational corporations and so reflect little interest in correcting violations of core labor standards. Since governments alone can make formal complaints to the WTO, labor unions, human rights organizations, and environmental groups can only encourage member states to engage in such actions; since the WTO sanctions only governments and not corporations for labor rights violations, employers face few penalties and no real financial consequences. What little attention is paid to such violations is directed primarily to low-wage countries; the result is that violations of labor rights in the United States and other developed nations continue unchecked.

It is difficult for unions in these countries to demand compliance with international labor standards when their governments have not ratified or do not enforce many of these conventions and are in breach of their provisions. Ewing and Sibley argue that the most pressing need is to advance the rights of workers and the poor throughout the world, and that labor standards must achieve this goal for workers in the countries of both North and South. To raise standards, unions must understand specifically how corporations regularly violate worker rights and freedoms. Moreover, social clauses must be added to international agreements to both protect jobs in rich countries and promote economic development in poorer ones.[15]

THE WAR AND THE LABOR MOVEMENT

While in early 2002 the United States seemed set on expanding a war against a nebulously defined enemy, the labor movement finds itself with no program for revitalizing the economy and defending jobs. Amid a war buildup and recession, U.S. corporations were downsizing at a greater rate than at any time since the early 1990s. Strikingly absent from the military agenda crafted by Washington was any sense of shared cost. Indeed, corporate America brazenly used the crisis as a pretext for exacting economic concessions from the federal government at a time when many Americans faced a decline in their standard of living. Restrictions on civil liberties, rationalized by the Bush administration as necessary to the "war on terrorism," also impeded the efforts of workers to improve their economic conditions through organizing and political action.

By early 2002, the only unanimity in the United States appeared to be the steadfast opposition, by the president and most in Congress, to an economic stimulus package that would tangibly assist the growing ranks of working people now suffering the aftermath of the events of September 11, which pushed an already reeling economy over the edge.

We heard only two policy responses from Washington, neither of which would benefit the majority of working-class Americans struggling to pay their bills and maintain their living standards. Republicans in the House demanded further tax cuts for business—an economic stimulus plan that included $70 billion in tax cuts and concessions for corporations.

Though Democrats opposed these tax breaks, they advanced no plan of their own to revive the economy to help working Americans. Senate Majority Leader Tom Daschle repeated the mantra of federal spending limits, fearing that a stimulus package directed at middle-income Americans might undo the fiscal discipline achieved by the Clinton administration, another policy trend that disproportionately benefited business and those in upper-income brackets. Yet, as the recession percolated through the economy, the Democratic leadership suggested nothing that would ameliorate the hardships American workers were enduring. By backing off from any plan that would help working America, they in effect ceded the political agenda to the Republicans. Indeed, the first pro-business measure was taken immediately after the September 11 attack, a $15 billion federal bailout of the airline industry just as it was laying off thousands of workers. The insurance and tourism industries are now lining up for their share of government largesse.

No equivalent federal bailout was on the agenda for the more than one million newly unemployed who lost jobs before and after September 11. No federal plan was envisioned to assist states under budgetary pressure to slash health, education, and social services that serve the poor, the elderly, and low-wage workers, who were hit first and hardest by the economic downturn. Proposals for a federal budgetary stimulus package that would improve and expand unemployment benefits, provide health care and social services as more people fell into poverty, fund public works projects to repair the national infrastructure and protect the nation from further attacks, and give tax rebates to low- and lower-middle-income people excluded from the Bush spring 2001 tax cut have gone unheeded. Unfortunately there was little hope that a stimulus package would gain support in Congress. As always, Republicans remain opposed to government-sponsored economic security for the working class. What is new, but not so surprising in the neoliberal era of capitalism, is that the economic resuscitation plan has not gained ground among the Democratic congressional leadership, who in the past could be counted on to support stimulus programs to help working people.

There is no precedent for this historical anomaly. During World War II, the U.S. government actively engaged in macroeconomic policy initiatives, spending money to "lift all boats," not just corporate America and the affluent. The idea of a nation at war translated into efforts to reduce economic inequality and in particular help those most at risk. In early 2002, as our nation's leaders mobilized for war and asked for sacrifice, no similar efforts were being made.

LABOR'S RESPONSE

What does the war against terrorism mean for the labor movement? Organized labor entered the post–September 11 era weaker than at any time in the past sixty years. This stands in marked contrast to the situation during World War II, the last major conflict supported by a vast majority of Americans. By the end of the war in 1945, just ten years after passage of the National Labor Relations Act, union density had reached 35 percent, a figure not matched since 1954. Union density was lower than in any period since the Great Depression and continues to drop precipitously, having fallen to 13.5 percent in 2002 (9.1 percent in the private sector). In early 2002, the recession was projected to be a disaster for organized labor as union jobs hemorrhaged throughout the economy—good for businesses seeking to cut costs, but catastrophic for maintaining American labor standards.

The September 11 events intensified a national recession that was already under way. The initial responses of the federal government favored corporations and the affluent and disproportionately burdened working people. Apart from jingoistic, at times maudlin, media hype, Washington showed little interest in ensuring a lasting consensus through sharing the costs of war. Instead, those who can best weather the storm were rewarded and those most vulnerable were left to face uncertainty and economic pain. In the absence of a labor movement that can build a national consensus around policies benefiting working people, the unspoken class divide in this country will widen further, even as elected officials and the media call for shared responsibility and sacrifice.

To be sure, under the Bush administration labor already faced a hostile political climate. September 11 added severe economic and organizational stresses to this, beyond the tragic loss of life. Hotel workers and public sector workers—two major areas of trade union strength in the last six years under Sweeney—have been particularly hard hit. Hotel and restaurant workers, who unionized in remarkable numbers throughout the 1990s, now confront massive layoffs and membership loss. Public sector workers—the backbone of union growth in the past generation—face the threat of looming state and local budget cuts. Declining state revenues threaten the jobs of these workers, who are now unfairly expected to bear the burden of hard times through concessions and givebacks, even though they did not benefit economically during the boom years of the 1990s.

But can labor flex its flaccid muscles in time of war? Can workers organize and strike without appearing unpatriotic? Will restrictions on civil liberties now threaten organizing activity and collective bargaining? Will immigrant organizing, a leading component of recent union growth, be repressed as xenophobic fears increase? What is clear is that workers today cannot avail themselves of legal protections that restrained employer abuse during World War II. Over the past twenty years, private sector workers have faced relentless retribution for organizing from employers intent on maintaining union-free workplaces. This pattern can be expected to continue and gather steam in a time of war.

To resist these trends, a unified labor movement must articulate a program that would help American workers, not just corporations. Such a program should include an increase and expansion of unemployment insurance benefits. Unemployment is projected to reach 6 percent by early 2002, a figure that in fact ignores more than 60 percent of the jobless. Extending the duration of unemployment insurance, increasing the amount of benefits, and expanding coverage to those currently excluded from benefits would stimulate the economy while assisting people who have lost jobs. In addition, the plan could include rebuilding the federally financed infrastructure—roads, railways (including the introduction of high-speed trains), the air transport network—as well as protecting the environment from biological and chemical hazards, extending improved health care to more Americans, and constructing new schools.

CONCLUSION

To build a stronger union movement, changes in labor law are needed that would reduce impediments to joining unions and so allow workers to improve their wages and working conditions. Such changes would mitigate the damage to workers in a wartime environment and thereby engender a greater sense of national solidarity. However, a changed labor law does not appear on the horizon, given the absence of a strong and militant labor movement willing to challenge and break the rules of an unfair body of law enacted over the past six decades to restrict the power of workers. Organized labor will be unable to revitalize itself unless it is willing to risk its sadly watered down power to embark on a sustained social protest movement, encompassing the broader working class now employed in the new economy. To build such a movement will require that far-sighted leaders within and without the labor movement challenge the existing system more fundamentally than is currently being done. Such a movement must deal with labor leaders who at times seem to fear their own members (and potential members) more than management. Though many have rhetorically embraced the more progressive AFL-CIO platform, few are willing to put it into practice by devoting adequate resources to organizing, fighting employers, and engaging in more direct forms of action, both at the workplace and in the political sphere. Absent such a movement, change may have to be initiated from outside the ranks of organized labor.

NOTES

1. See Michael Zweig, *The Working Class Majority: America's Best Kept Secret* (Ithaca, N.Y.: Cornell University Press, 2000).

64 Immanuel Ness

2. See Louis Hartz, *The Liberal Tradition in America: An Interpretation of American Political Thought Since the Revolution* (Boston: Harcourt, Brace, 1955).

3. Howard Kimmeldorf, *Battling for American Labor: Wobblies, Craft Workers, and the Making of the Union Movement* (Berkeley: University of California Press, 1999), 13.

4. Kimmeldorf, *Battling*, 15.

5. Alan Draper, *Conflict of Interests: Organized Labor and the Civil Rights Movement in the South, 1954–1968* (Ithaca, N.Y.: ILR Press, 1994).

6. Following the events of September 11, 2001, the Teamsters have pushed for a reduction of dependence on foreign energy, combining appeals for drilling with anti-Arab sentiment. According to Jerry Hood, Jimmy Hoffa's special assistant on energy policy, "We're importing literally, hundreds of thousands of barrels of oil a day from Iraq and Saddam Hussein in a region that is not overly supportive of our goals or the war on terrorism. . . . It makes sense that America take every step possible to reduce our energy dependence in an environmentally sensitive and productive way. ANWR is the way." International Brotherhood of Teamsters, "Hood Presses Senate Leaders for Energy Plan," Teamsters Online, November 2, 2001, accessed February 17, 2002, www.teamster.org/01newsb/hn%5F011102%5F1.htm.

7. See Stanley Aronowitz, *From the Ashes of the Old: America's Labor and America's Future* (Boston: Houghton Mifflin, 1998); Steven Fraser and Joshua B. Freeman, eds., *Audacious Democracy: Labor, Intellectuals, and the Social Reconstruction of America* (Boston: Houghton Mifflin, 1997).

8. See James A. Gross, *Broken Promise: The Subversion of U.S. Labor Relations Policy, 1947–1994* (Philadelphia: Temple University Press, 1995).

9. Lloyd Ulman, *The Rise of the National Trade Union: The Development and Significance of Its Structure, Governing Institutions, and Economic Policies* (Cambridge: Harvard University Press, 1955), 422.

10. Hal Leyshon "Little Debate at Convention: AFL-CIO Stays the Course," *Labor Notes*, no. 274 (January 2002): 1.

11. Immanuel Ness and Stuart Eimer, eds., *Central Labor Councils and the Revival of American Unionism: Organizing for Justice in Our Communities* (Armonk, N.Y.: M. E. Sharpe, 2001).

12. Stanley Aronowitz. "Labor on Trial: Assessing Sweeney's Record," *Working USA: The Journal of Labor and Society* 5, no. 2 (Fall 2001): 10–31.

13. Richard Freeman and Joel Rogers, "Open Source Unionism: Beyond Exclusive Collective Bargaining," *Working USA: The Journal of Labor and Society* 5, no. 4 (Spring 2002): 8–40.

14. The Communications Workers of America have devoted significant resources to organizing high technology workers at Microsoft through funding and organizational support for Washtech (Washington Technology Workers). The National Writers Union, a local of the United Auto Workers, also organizes along these unconventional lines.

15. Keith D. Ewing and Tom Sibley, *International Trade Union Rights for the New Millennium* (London: International Centre for Trade Union Rights/Institute for Employment Rights, 2000).

4

Mass-Membership Senior Interest Groups and the Politics of Aging

LAURA KATZ OLSON AND FRANK L. DAVIS

Since 1935, with the passage of the Social Security Act, the elderly have been the focus of federal policies, programs, and expenditures. Many of their needs have met a sympathetic public, often resulting in government benefits that other sectors of society have been unable to achieve. Representing 13 percent of the population today, older people receive a whopping 40 percent of the federal budget, an amount that has been steadily increasing over the past several decades.[1] In 1999, Social Security's Old Age and Survivors Insurance alone cost $338 billion or 19.9 percent of all federal outlays, followed by Medicare, which reached $190.5 billion or 11 percent of the total. The latter program has risen by about 10 percent annually since its inception, surpassing both the Consumer Price Index (CPI) and the federal budget overall.[2]

What factors have contributed to such unbridled growth in entitlement and "discretionary" spending for the elderly? One explanation has been the political power of older people and their senior groups. Dubbed the "Gray Lobby" in 1976 by Henry Pratt, it encompasses mass membership senior interest groups as well as professional and business organizations that serve the elderly.[3] It has been suggested that any opposition by political leaders to old-age programs is like "touching the third rail" or fighting an 800-pound gorilla.[4]

HISTORICAL CONSIDERATIONS: THE INTERPLAY BETWEEN POLICY AND MOBILIZATION

Social, economic, and technological changes during the nineteenth and early twentieth centuries created growing challenges and adverse conditions for the elderly, forcing large numbers into unemployment, dependency, and poverty. The percentage of older people requiring some form of public aid steadily increased from 23 percent in 1910 to 33 percent ten years later, reaching 40 percent in 1930.[5] At the same time, the number and percentage of older people were growing, from 2.7 percent of the population in 1860 and 4.1 percent in 1900, to 5.4 percent by 1930.

Prior to the twentieth century, there was no sense of age consciousness among the elderly, nor were they viewed as a separate group worthy of special assistance by society. Older people in need were subject to restrictive assistance and herded into poor houses along with other impoverished groups.[6] However, beginning in 1922, a number of pensioner groups emerged as part of a diffuse social insurance movement; the growing grievances and demands of the aged were channeled by populist leaders into a number of ad hoc organizations, all calling for public responsibility for elders through the provision of public pensions.[7]

One of the most important was the Townsend movement in the early 1930s, the largest mass social movement of the elderly up to that time, claiming about two million members at its peak, or 10 percent of the sixty-and-over population.[8] Its leader, Francis E. Townsend, called for $200 a month for every person over the age of 65; in return, elders had to spend the entire amount within the month and agree not to work. The movement "mushroomed into a mass crusade . . . achieving remarkable grassroots strength."[9] Participants, who belonged to a large network of clubs, engaged in rallies, petitions, political campaigns, marches, and other protest activities, and in Long Beach, California, succeeded in ousting a congressman who did not support their cause; they replaced him with their own candidate, seventy-two-year-old John S. McGroarty.[10]

Most analysts have concluded that these early age-based social movements had, at best, only a limited impact on the Social Security legislation per se. Because of worsening economic conditions among the elderly, the bankruptcy of many union pension and relief funds, the escalating pressures for redistributive pension schemes, and growing discontent overall, public leaders attempted to maintain stability and deflect demands for radical change. The Social Security Act represented a successful co-optation of popular forces seeking more sweeping plans and/or systemic changes in society.[11]

The movements' major success was achieved through their ability to place the needs of the aged on the political agenda and frame the debate in such a way as to render older people worthy of public support. In a nation imbued with individualism, self-reliance, and familism, pension advocacy groups were able to portray the elderly as victims of external forces, especially big business; therefore, unlike other sectors of the poor, older people were no longer entirely blamed for their dire economic situation. These groups also insisted that because older people had helped build America during their working years, they had a right to a pension.[12] The broader social welfare movement, however, was more effective in influencing Social Security; lacking widespread support for its agenda, by the 1920s it began emphasizing the elderly as a legitimate concern of government.[13]

Significantly, leaders of the pension movements were conspicuously absent from the Committee on Economic Security, which was formed by President Franklin Roosevelt to design the Social Security system. And the eventual program that emerged was not shaped by their demands; rather, it reflected the agendas of other interests.[14] In particular, instead of using general revenues to support the program, the committee relied on individual contributions through the regressive payroll tax, thereby emphasizing earned rights instead of government responsibility for the elderly.[15]

Indeed, the Social Security legislation, based on an insurance model, not only disappointed the old-age pension activists but also defused the aging movement itself, which remained mostly dormant until the 1960s. However, the program did render older people "an identifiable client group of government"[16] as well as foster bonds and some sense of cohesion among them, thus setting the stage for their future claims.[17]

THE EMERGENCE AND GROWTH
OF SENIOR GROUPS

As recently as the mid-1960s there were only a few formal old-age organizations. The National Retired Teachers Association (later to become the American Association of Retired Persons or AARP), the leading senior group today, was founded by Ethel Percy Andrus in 1947, primarily to provide low-cost insurance to teachers. The National Council of Senior Citizens (NCSC), created by the AFL-CIO and consisting of retired trade union members, was not launched until 1961, mainly to lobby for Medicare. Currently, it is the second largest advocacy group of the elderly. In addition, the National Association of Retired Federal Employees (NARFE) was established in 1921 to aid federal employees receiving benefits under the newly enacted Federal Employees Pension Act and to push for its expansion.

Also in the 1960s, numerous national programs for the elderly were initiated and expanded, including Medicare, the Older Americans Act, improvements in Social Security, Supplementary Security Income (SSI), and the Employee Retirement Income Security Act (ERISA). Indeed, the needs and problems of the elderly became the focus of significant federal legislation, laying the foundation for the dramatic rise in public expenditures over the next several decades.

However, there is some debate about what part the aging organizations themselves played in establishing policies and programs for the elderly during the 1960s and 1970s. Several leading scholars maintain that, similar to the enactment of Social Security, they were peripheral to the political process at the time.[18] According to Binstock, it was national government officials, professionals, organized labor, and business leaders who brought about age-based entitlements, rather than universal benefits, as in most other industrialized nations. The main influence of age-based organizations was on those aspects of the programs benefiting gerontologists and social service workers rather than elders themselves. "Indeed," Binstock argues further, "the rise of many old-age political organizations mostly followed, rather than preceded and influenced, the creation of government programs benefitting older people."[19] Moreover, senior groups were able to use their limited power to lobby successfully for Medicare and Medicaid only because the programs were so narrow and did not threaten doctors, hospitals, and other beneficiaries of the American health empire.[20]

Several observers assert that it was the aging programs themselves that were instrumental in encouraging the establishment and subsequent political significance of old-age organizations. Many of these groups were formed primarily to take advantage of the political and economic benefits accruing from the programs themselves. The vast array of new subsidies, for example, enhanced older people's awareness of their gains, fostering an interest in maintaining and expanding them.[21]

Beginning in the late 1970s, but especially during the 1980s and later, public benefits for the needy increasingly came under attack. President Ronald Reagan, for example, set out to dismantle the social welfare state, including Social Security, which, along with Medicare, was growing rapidly. Using projected future shortfalls as an excuse, he announced in 1981 that Social Security was going bankrupt and that benefits must be cut. He warned that the program was not only experiencing a financial "crisis" but also contributing to the overall economic woes of the nation itself: "The declaration of a Social Security crisis also was used to redefine old people as a 'burden' to American society, draining resources, 'busting the budget,' and robbing younger generations."[22]

In response, senior organizations on both ends of the political spectrum multiplied rapidly, while those already in existence became more politicized.[23] Many of the newer organizations, which engaged primarily in direct mail solicitations, signed up millions of members.

Several groups composed mostly of the young and middle-aged elaborated on President Reagan's message, most notably Americans for Generational Equity (AGE), established in 1984. With most of its money accruing from banks, insurance companies, defense contractors, and other corporate interests, its ultimate goal was to undermine support for the universal features of Social Security and push for its privatization.[24] Focusing on growing middle-class tax burdens and benefits for the elderly at the expense of the young, AGE spread its ideas through academic publications, think tanks, and the mass media, appealing to liberals and conservatives alike.[25] Its major success was in shifting the terms of the debate about Social Security from meeting the needs of the elderly more adequately to concerns about generational inequities and cost-containment.[26] Other conservative groups, including the National Alliance of Senior Citizens (NASC), espoused free market reforms, reduced government spending, even for old-age programs, and partial or full privatization of the Social Security system.

Between 1989 and 1992, three new organizations emerged, all with similar goals: Seniors Coalition, United Seniors Association (USA), and 60/Plus Association. Beginning as direct-mail fundraising groups, they engage primarily in lobbying, testifying, and research activities for conservative interests, aimed mostly at undermining support for social programs, including Social Security, Medicare, and Medicaid.

Liberal groups proliferated as well. For example, the National Committee to Preserve Social Security and Medicare (NCPSSM) was formed in 1982 to defend Social Security and later Medicare and Medicaid. Though by 1990 it had over five million members, a $30 million budget, and was the wealthiest political action committee (PAC) among the aging groups, its mass mailings were never taken as seriously by Congress as those of some of the other mass membership old-age organizations such as AARP or NCSC.[27]

Moreover, existing senior advocacy groups, which in the past had lobbied for new programs and the enhancement of existing ones, were now forced to protect what they had from major cuts and at best could promote only small, incremental changes. Many of them countered the growing anti-elderly rhetoric by promoting themes such as interdependence among generations, the universality of the aging process, ongoing needs among older people, and Social Security as an earned right and middle-class entitlement. Some also espoused a class-oriented theme, pitting corporate executives and the rich against the poor rather than generational conflict. Powell, Branco, and Williamson state,

> Whereas neo-conservatives had chosen to focus on generational differences, thereby diverting attention away from the widening resource gap between haves and have-nots in American society, senior rights advocates adamantly insisted that class-related differences remained central to any conception of fairness, and accused the Reagan and Bush administrations of further aggra-

vating class divisions by unjustly diverting the nation's financial programs helping the "needy" and into the already-overstuffed pockets of the "greedy."[28]

By the 1990s, there were over sixty national organizations acting on behalf of older people, nearly 75 percent founded between 1970 and 1990.[29] AARP, NCSC, the Gray Panthers, and NASC have been the most salient of the mass membership groups. However, in a recent study, Day found that Seniors Coalition and USA gained the most influence when the Republicans took over Congress in 1994.[30]

Regardless of political goals, nearly all of the mass membership senior organizations, with the exception of the Gray Panthers, were created, expanded, and sustained through material benefits. While the older ones, including AARP and NCSC, offered solidary incentives to some of their members through local affiliates, the others have relied almost entirely on computerized mass mailings for their recruitment or what Day calls "checkbook affiliations."[31] This allows them to lobby for their respective agendas with only limited time or effort required of their membership. The Gray Panthers, however, originating in the social movements of the 1960s, continues to emphasize local organizing, grassroots activities, demonstrations, vigils, and radical political, social, and economic change. For example, in response to Reagan's proposed cutbacks in Social Security, NCSC dispatched "seniorgrams" to its four thousand clubs, and AARP sent "legislative alerts" to its volunteer leaders and local affiliates. The Gray Panthers, on the other hand, held vigils at the White House and demonstrations throughout the country.[32]

The fact that most senior groups pursue issues of economic security and almost all of their members are motivated by material benefits demonstrates that they do not fit Ronald Inglehart's expectations of postmaterial society.[33] This is not surprising. Inglehart theorizes that those born after World War II, socialized during a period of unprecedented prosperity, are more concerned with self-expression and quality of life issues, but membership in senior groups tends to be dominated by older citizens. In fact, to qualify for membership in AARP, or receive benefits from NCSC, individuals must be at least fifty years old. While the formative experiences of some members, those in their early fifties and younger, would have taken place during Inglehart's postmaterialist era, the socialization of most would fall squarely in the industrial period of scarcity. Inglehart would expect these individuals to be focused on material concerns. Perhaps Inglehart's new ethos will be better reflected in senior groups' efforts as a larger share of their membership ranks are populated by postmaterialist generations. However, that influence is not yet apparent, nor does it appear likely given the evidence to date.

AMERICAN ASSOCIATION
OF RETIRED PERSONS

As suggested earlier, AARP originated as a service organization in 1947 to offer low-cost insurance to teachers; by 1958 all people sixty and over were eligible for membership, an age that was lowered to fifty in 1983. Remaining out of politics through the 1960s, AARP eventually ventured into the political arena, stepping up its activities in the 1980s.[34] At the same time, the group steadily expanded its benefits and services to include health aid discounts, mail order drugs, travel and investment services, tax assistance, magazines, newsletters, and the like.[35]

Though most of the senior groups, including NCSC, NASC, and NCP-SSM, use such material incentives to recruit members, AARP uses the widest array. A survey in 1982 by Paul Light revealed that most members joined AARP specifically for these benefits, including its publications.[36] Although the group has nearly four thousand local chapters, only about 3 percent of its members belong to these chapters, thus limiting its associational inducements. For the most part, AARP maintains itself by providing material incentives rather than political ones and receives nearly two-thirds of its resources from its related business activities and advertisements.[37]

Today AARP is not only the most sizable senior group but also the largest interest group in the United States. In fact, it dwarfs all of the other mass membership senior organizations.[38] With 34 million members, over $400 million in revenues, 1,700 employees, 250,000 trained volunteers, and a legislative staff of over 100 people, AARP has the reputation as the most powerful of the age-based groups as well.[39] According to Binstock, "whatever AARP chooses to do (or not do) tends to define the overall position of the old-age lobby."[40]

It has been estimated that nearly one-fifth of all registered voters belong to AARP,[41] and that nearly 70 percent of its members actually vote.[42] However, the group assiduously avoids any partisan politics; indeed, 40 percent of its members are Democrats, 40 percent Republicans, and 20 percent Independents.[43]

Some analysts contend that AARP's power accrues from the direct lobbying power of its politically astute leaders, backed by a massive membership. Though it does not have a PAC, or contribute any money to individual candidates, by 1996 AARP had twenty-nine registered lobbyists, ran a public policy research institute, and employed forty-four people on its policy staff alone.[44] Their analysts and lobbyists tend to be highly experienced, many coming from Congressional Aging Committee staff and federal agencies serving the elderly. The group itself views its political role mostly as educational, through policy analysis, legislative testimony, and information and outreach programs for its members.[45] More recently it began promoting voter registration through its BEAVOT ER.org website, registering more than 164,000 people for the 2000 election.[46]

Other observers, however, point to AARP's ability to activate enormous grassroots drives, such as flooding Congress with mail and phone calls, a tactic that may be even more effective than financial contributions through PACs. There is some evidence that AARP and other mass membership senior groups increasingly have been mobilizing such widespread grassroots support, especially through innovative communication technologies, and in the case of AARP, its local networks.[47]

AARP, however, tends to be relatively cautious in its tactics. In 1995, for example, despite the huge proposed reductions in Medicare and Medicaid, the organization did not attempt to mobilize mass protests, sit-ins, or even a letter-writing campaign; rather, it engaged in behind-the-scene lobbying to change the most objectionable aspects of the bill.[48] Only the Gray Panthers has regularly utilized radical political tactics to gain the attention of political leaders, the press, and the general public. The group frequently has organized mass demonstrations, grassroots campaigns, high-profile media events, vigils near the White House, and rallies at the Capitol. They also have taken to the street with picket signs, have issued manifestos, and engaged in various other forms of militant actions. With the exception of the Gray Panthers, however, "vigorous protest activity and other unconventional forms of participation . . . are not the hallmark of old-age political involvement."[49]

AARP and the Gray Panthers provide contrasting organizational rationales with starkly different policy implications. While the Gray Panthers can inspire only a relatively small membership with its politically oriented incentives, a large proportion of that membership, with its shared commitment to the group's political goals, can be mobilized to work on behalf of the Gray Panthers' policy agenda. In contrast, while AARP has spawned an enormous membership using material incentives, the diversity of its broad-based membership with its questionable commitment to political causes compromises AARP's ability to launch and sustain political campaigns, especially on issues that may receive less than near unanimous support among seniors. The result is that AARP's membership numbers may overstate its clout on a range of political issues, and policymakers seem acutely aware of this fact.[50]

The 1988 Medicare Catastrophic Coverage Act debacle was particularly sobering for AARP. The legislation, which included respite care and coverage for prescription drugs, was funded through higher premiums and surcharges on the wealthiest beneficiaries. Despite AARP's strong support, the act generated what some have labeled the second social movement among the elderly in U.S. history; large numbers of older people opposed it through mass demonstrations, protests, petition drives, and congressional letter-writing and telephone campaigns, resulting in its repeal eighteen months later. Moreover, nearly six thousand AARP members canceled their memberships.[51] In 1994, when AARP endorsed the Democrats' healthcare reform bill, it was rumored that additional members had resigned. Consequently, since that time the group is particularly careful to take "moderate, non-threatening stands."[52] However, because of its size and growing cleavages, such as working versus retired elderly, membership infighting may be inevitable.[53]

AARP finds it particularly difficult to give priority to policies and programs on behalf of disadvantaged older people or to promote social change. At best, it can do so only through limited advocacy efforts and policy analysis while focusing most of its attention on defending the status quo for its largely middle-class, white-collar membership.[54] For example, although AARP has shown concern about social spending for low-income elderly, particularly women, it emphasizes equity over adequacy issues when addressing the Social Security program.[55] The group does lobby for some benefits targeted to the disadvantaged but only when they are part of a package designed for its better-off constituency. AARP most likely will become even more cautious politically since its tax-exempt status as a nonprofit organization recently has come under attack by several U.S. senators. It appears that AARP has been and will continue to be guided through the "imperative of organizational survival."[56]

POWER AND AGING POLICY

Despite its size, economic resources, and reputation, there continues to be considerable disagreement over how much power AARP (along with other senior groups) has over social policy today. Many analysts argue that old-age organizations overall increasingly have gained political legitimacy and recognition as a political force since the 1970s, ultimately becoming powerful and effective advocates for the elderly throughout the 1980s and 1990s. Rhodebeck contends, for example, that they now have the potential to structure policy debate and public opinion.[57] Others point to the ability of advocates for the elderly to pressure Congress both through interest groups and within-system lobbies such as the Administration on Aging (AoA) and the National Institute on Aging (NIA).[58]

Several observers argue that while Reagan was successful in slashing benefits for the poor, because of intense lobbying efforts by senior groups, especially AARP, services for the elderly sustained the least cuts, and he was unable to reduce significantly the middle-class old-age entitle-ments.[59] In fact, overall spending for the aged continued to grow both absolutely and as a percentage of the national budget. Further, after a three-decade campaign, AARP was instrumental in the successful effort to end mandatory retirement in 1986.

Binstock, on the other hand, concludes that while public officials do pay attention to senior groups such as AARP, they do so for symbolic rea-sons; they can claim that they have the backing of a mass constituency of elders. He observes that their actual impact has been limited and confined primarily to minor policies while real power accrues to groups based on major economic interests.[60] Many powerful businesses and providers have a substantial vested interest in old-age policies and programs, a stake that has grown significantly over the years. Their special interest groups have formed formidable trade organizations, each focusing on specific benefits, unlike the broader-based senior organizations such as AARP.[61] The former include the American Association of Homes and Ser-vices for the Aging (AAHSA), American Federation of Home Health Agencies, the American Health Care Association, the Assisted Living Federation of America, National Association of Home Care, the National Association for the Support of Long-term Care (NASL), the American Medical Association, the American Hospital Association, and more.

Their major concerns have been and continue to be the effects of various policy alternatives on their individual enterprises, regardless of the impact on elders. For example, the for-profit nursing home industry has had the largest impact on Medicaid policies.[62] The program is the major source of funding for these institutions, accounting for well over half of their total revenues in the 1990s, up from 20 percent in 1960.[63] During 1999, the federal government alone spent $39 billion for such care.[64] Yet national studies continue to document the poor care for and mistreatment of nursing home residents, including abusive practices and neglect.[65]

It seems that mass-based senior groups provide broad support for funding and influence the general contours of programs, but have less clout in defining the intricacies of such programs. Business and profes-sional associations are thereby freer to focus their influence on the spe-cifics of where and how program funds are spent. Aging groups may, in part, serve to justify spending while these economic interests pursue the task of channeling resources to their own specific benefit.

When necessary, business enterprises mobilize elders to advance their commercial needs without the assistance of aging groups. For instance, in October 2000 Michael Stocker, the president of Capital Blue Cross, sent letters to the company's Medicare HMO enrollees urging them to lobby national political leaders for increased payments to their plan. In panic, more than 60 percent of the forty-three thousand HMO participants mailed postcards to Congress demanding the funding.[66]

Even so, recent cutbacks in aging programs have adversely affected members of these trade organizations, spurring an intense lobbying effort to restore and even increase funding to them. For instance, in order to combat fraud and produce savings in Medicare, the 1997 Balanced Budget Act (BBA) reduced payments to hospitals, nursing homes, and home healthcare agencies. This legislative act, along with congressional debates over Medicare reform, engendered mass mailings and other grassroots campaigns, intense lobbying, television commercials, and newspaper ads by a vast array of interests during 1999. Citizens for Better Medicare, which represents the pharmaceutical industry, spent nearly $30 million to oppose any benefits that would entail cost controls over drugs. The Alliance for Quality Nursing Home Care, made up of eleven nursing home operators, spent approximately $15 million to influence Congress. Along with the American Health Care Association, the nursing home trade group, it sought the restoration of cuts to old-age facilities. While the American Hospital Association focused on funding for its member organizations, the Coalition for Medicare Choices, consisting of Health Maintenance Organizations, lobbied for higher reimbursement rates for HMOs, and the Biotechnology Industry Organization (biotech firms) opposed pharmaceutical benefits that would limit drug research. These campaigns cost $10 million, $5 million, and $50,000, respectively. At the same time, AARP, NCPSSM, and other senior groups put their efforts into the preservation of Medicare overall, along with a demand for prescription drug coverage; NCPSSM spent approximately $1 million.[67] Congress caved in to industry demands: as one of its last actions in 1999, it increased fees to Medicare providers by $30 billion over five years. On the other hand, consumer interests were ignored. For example, Congress failed to enact a nursing home patient rights bill or measures protecting HMO beneficiaries.

Although there are many small, single constituency senior groups that focus on blacks, Latinos, Indians, women, lesbians, gays, and other disadvantaged elders, they lack broad-based support and power. As Gelfand and Barresi put it, "no national group or organization purporting to represent minorities is playing a key role in the debates over Social Security, retirement and pension coverage, health care reform, or the development of long-term care policies."[68] Though senior advocacy groups have formed loose coalitions among themselves (i.e., Save Our Security [SOS] and the Leadership Council on Aging Organizations) and with other social organizations (i.e., Generations United), Day found that they cannot speak with one voice as do the for-profit trade associations. Moreover, the various aging groups are now in niches and therefore are not building a broader issue agenda or united front. According to her, they have become less interested in coalition building since it is costly in terms of group autonomy and the ability to claim exclusive credit for group achievement.[69]

THE "ELECTORAL BLUFF"

The primary power of senior groups is in their "electoral bluff."[70] Politicians tend to view older people as a potential bloc vote and do not want to risk the possibility that such a large number of people could turn against them, an image that is promoted by the mass media.[71]

Clearly, the elderly vote both in large numbers and at considerably higher rates than do other age groups. In the 2000 presidential election, 22.5 million people aged sixty and over voted, representing 22 percent of all voters,[72] a percentage that will most likely increase even further as their relative number expands over the next several decades. Older people also are more likely to pay attention to politics, contact a political official, and participate in campaigning than other age groups, including sending money to PACs and candidates.[73] In one survey, over 50 percent of elders said that they had called or sent a letter to their congressional representative, one-third had contributed to a campaign, and 17 percent to a PAC.[74] MacManus holds that one of the reasons for the wide gap between young and old is that the elderly "are more heavily involved in groups that send out policy alerts to their membership along with more information on how to contact public officials."[75]

As a result, Democrats and Republicans alike tend to target older voters, especially those in the middle and upper class, more than other age groups. This was apparent in the 2000 presidential campaign rhetoric and platforms, with leaders of both parties prioritizing such issues as prescription drug benefits for the elderly; nine states with the greatest number of seniors have 243 electoral votes.[76] Peterson and Somit conclude that "over the next few decades . . . the political influence of the elderly will almost certainly grow quite substantially. But that growth . . . will probably be based on a misperception of their actual political behavior."[77] Though the image is one of cohesive old-age voting, they actually are diverse in their views and, for the most part, lack a sense of identity based on chronological age. Even in local referenda on property taxes—though many elders are house rich but with limited disposable income and do not have children in public schools any longer—age is not a significant factor in voting behavior.[78]

The evidence suggests that socioeconomic, race, ethnicity, and gender divisions rather than generational ones affect political preferences; the elderly appear to be as split on party, candidates, and issues as other age groups.[79] In the 2000 presidential election, while Bush held a 9 percent advantage among elderly men, Gore was favored by older women by 14 percent.[80] In fact, there are more differences within age groups than among them. Critically, studies show that individuals tend to hold both their ideology and party affiliation as they move through the life cycle.[81] In 1995, the 65 and over population was divided almost evenly among Democrats, Republicans, and Independents.[82]

Older people are divided on policy questions affecting the elderly as well, including Social Security, particularly since some rely on the program as their sole means of support while others have substantial assets and/or supplementary retirement income. Clearly, older voters have different stakes in the various aging programs and in their specific provisions.

Even AARP cannot mobilize cohesive support on most issues. Nor is there any evidence that it actually influences voting behavior; it is difficult for any of the senior groups to deliver the vote for particular issues or candidates. There are no indications that AARP could shift the votes of the elderly even minimally.[83] Significantly, although senior organizations had vigorously opposed Reagan's Social Security cutbacks, 60 percent of older voters supported him in 1984, 6 percent more than in 1980.[84]

Not only is the senior vote split, but there also are different policy preferences among their various advocacy organizations. The labor-based NCSC, for instance, supported the Social Security retirement test while other senior organizations were adamantly opposed to it.[85] The Medicare Catastrophic Care Act of 1988 is indicative of the cleavages among the elderly. Although AARP and NCSC lobbied vigorously for its implementation, as suggested earlier large numbers of middle- and upper-income older people, both individually and collectively with other senior groups, including NCPSSM, Seniors Coalition, and the Gray Panthers, successfully fought for its repeal.

THE 1990s AND BEYOND

The politics of aging since the 1990s has become distinct in that it is shaped by the new ideological agenda of the United States overall: in an era of government retrenchment, privatization, devolution, and residualism, it is assumed that any growth in programs for the aged has a negative impact on all other budgetary requirements. This has allowed the gradual chipping away of some old-age benefits, including taxation of Social Security pensions, an elimination of the extra personal tax exemption for people sixty-five and over, decreases in cost-of-living allowances, and increases in Medicare deductibles, copayments, and part B premiums, despite opposition from AARP and other senior advocates.[86]

Most important, cost-cutting efforts now focus on serious structural changes to old-age programs that could have significantly negative impacts on the elderly, particularly the most vulnerable among them.[87] Inequality among the sixty-five and over population tends to be even greater than that among younger people. Single older women as well as elderly blacks and Latinos disproportionately face adverse economic and social circumstances, with the majority living in poverty or near-poverty conditions. Yet these groups are experiencing and will continue to experience the most severe effects of cuts in public programs.

The costs of full or partial privatization of Social Security would fall disproportionately on older single women and minorities who rely on the program for most of their income and benefit from its redistributive features. Further, in the mid-1990s political leaders tried to balance the budget by seriously reducing Medicare and dismantling Medicaid. While senior groups were attempting to defend the integrity of these programs, doctors, nursing homes, HMOs, hospitals, and insurance companies were working out their own deals with Congress.[88] Discretionary programs for the elderly poor, including subsidized housing, the Older Americans Act (OAA), Supplementary Security Income (SSI), food stamps, nutrition programs, and Title V senior employment have been particularly threatened.[89]

CONCLUSION

It appears that programs for the aged in the twenty-first century will be molded by business and professional interests, and to a lesser extent mass membership senior groups, all of which tend to be concerned primarily with the impact of policies and funding on their own organizational imperatives. The most powerful mass-based old-age association, AARP, faces diversity and a lack of agreement on policy issues within its own ranks as well as sharp ideological differences between it and other senior organizations. As the baby boom generation ages, senior power will likely become even more divided, particularly given the growing economic inequalities in American society, especially along racial and gender lines.[90] Consequently, there will be even more limited activist politics on behalf of the most frail and needy than we have today. And the "electoral bluff" of senior groups such as AARP may increasingly become less threatening to national leaders.

NOTES

1. Robert H. Binstock, "Challenges to U.S. Policies on Aging in the New Millennium," *Hallym International Journal of Aging* 1 (1999): 3–13.

2. Thomas Schlesinger, "The Politics and Policy of Entitlements," paper presented at the meetings of the American Political Science Association, Washington, D.C., 2000.

3. Robert H. Binstock, "The Politics and Economics of Aging and Diversity," in *Diversity in Aging*, ed. Scott Bass, Elizabeth Kutza, and Fernando Torres-Gil (Glenview, Ill.: Scott, Foresman, 1990), 73–99.

4. Henry Pratt, "Do the Elderly Really Have Political Clout? Yes," in *Controversial Issues in Aging*, ed. Andrew E. Scharlach and Lenard W. Kaye (Needham Heights, Mass.: Allyn and Bacon, 1996), 81–87.

5. Christine Day, *What Do Older Americans Think?* (Princeton, N.J.: Princeton University Press, 1990).

6. Lawrence Powell, Kenneth Branco, and John Williamson, *The Senior Rights Movement: Framing the Policy Debate in America* (New York: Twayne, 1996).

7. Day, *What Do Older Americans Think?*

8. Day, *What Do Older Americans Think?*

9. Pratt, "Do the Elderly Really Have Political Clout? Yes."

10. Powell, Branco, and Williamson, *The Senior Rights Movement.*

11. Day, *What Do Older Americans Think?*

12. Powell, Branco, and Williamson, *The Senior Rights Movement.*

13. Day, *What Do Older Americans Think?*

14. Binstock, "Politics and Economics of Aging."

15. Jill Quadagno, "Generational Equity and the Politics of the Welfare State," *International Journal of Health Services* 20 (1990): 631–649.

16. Day, *What Do Older Americans Think?*

17. Powell, Branco, and Williamson, *The Senior Rights Movement.*

18. Day, *What Do Older Americans Think?*; Robert Hudson, *The Future of Age-Based Public Policy* (Baltimore: Johns Hopkins University Press, 1997); and Robert H. Binstock, "A New Era in the Politics of Aging: How Will the Old-Age Interest Groups Respond," *Generations* 19 (1995): 68–74.

19. Binstock, "New Era in the Politics of Aging."

20. Powell, Branco, and Williamson, *The Senior Rights Movement*; Barbara Ehrenreich and John Ehrenreich, *The American Health Empire: Power, Profits and Politics* (New York: Vintage, 1970).

21. Christine Day, "Old-Age Interest Groups in the 1990s: Coalition, Competition, and Strategy," in *New Directions in Old-Age Policies*, ed. Janie Steckenrider and Tonya Parrott (Albany: State University of New York Press, 1998), 131–150.

22. Powell, Branco, and Williamson, *The Senior Rights Movement.*

23. Jill Quadagno, *Aging and the Life Course* (New York: McGraw-Hill, 1999).

24. Quadagno, "Generational Equity."

25. Andrea Campbell and Julia Lynch, "Whose 'Gray Power'? Elderly Voters, Elderly Lobbies and Welfare Reform in Italy and the U.S.," unpublished manuscript, 2000.

26. Laurie Rhodebeck, "Competing Problems, Budget Constraints, and Claims for Intergenerational Equity," in *New Directions in Old-Age Policies*, ed. Steckenrider and Parrott, 151–181.

27. Day, *What Do Older Americans Think?*

28. Powell, Branco, and Williamson, *The Senior Rights Movement.*

29. Susan MacManus, *Young v Old: Generational Combat in the 21st Century* (Boulder, Colo.: Westview, 1996).

30. Day, "Old-Age Interest Groups in the 1990s."

31. Day, *What Do Older Americans Think?*

32. Powell, Branco, and Williamson, *The Senior Rights Movement.*

33. See chapter 1 of this book.

34. David Van Tassel and Jimmy Elaine Meyer, *U.S. Aging Policy Interest Groups: Institutional Profiles* (New York: Greenwood, 1992).

35. Day, *What Do Older Americans Think?*

36. Day, "Old-Age Interest Groups in the 1990s."

37. Robert H. Binstock, "The Old-Age Lobby in a New Political Era," in *The Future of Age-Based Public Policy*, ed. Hudson.

38. Campbell and Lynch, "Whose 'Gray Power'?"

39. Schlesinger, "Politics and Policy of Entitlements."

40. Binstock, "The Old-Age Lobby in a New Political Era."

41. Powell, Branco, and Williamson, *The Senior Rights Movement.*

42. American Association of Retired People, *AARP Bulletin* 41, no. 10 (2000).

43. Van Tassel and Meyer, *U.S. Aging Policy Interest Groups.*

44. Schlesinger, "Politics and Policy of Entitlements."

45. Campbell and Lynch, "Whose 'Gray Power'?"

46. American Association of Retired People, *AARP Bulletin* 41, no. 10 (2000).

47. Day, "Old-Age Interest Groups in the 1990s"; Schlesinger, "Politics and Policy of Entitlements."

48. Binstock, "The Old-Age Lobby in a New Political Era."

49. Robert Binstock and Christine Day, "Aging and Politics," in *Handbook of Aging and the Social Sciences*, ed. Robert Binstock and Linda George (San Diego: Academic Press, 1996), 362–387. Its members, too, tend to prefer traditional political activities as does the current elderly population overall. Despite their high level of political activities, only 3 percent of older people had ever participated in a public demonstration. However, MacManus points out that the middle-aged civil rights/Vietnam cohort is the most involved in political activism today, such as attending political meetings and forums, signing and circulating petitions, joining groups in support of causes, contributing to PACS and even boycotting, demonstrating, and engaging in civil disobedience. Susan MacManus and Kathryn Tenpas, "The Changing Political Activism Patterns of Older Americans: Do Not Throw Dirt Over Us Yet," in *New Directions in Old-Age Policies*, ed. Steckenrider and Parrott, 111–129; and MacManus, *Young v Old.*

50. Binstock, "The Old-Age Lobby in a New Political Era"; Day, "Old-Age Interest Groups in the 1990s," 131–150.

51. Campbell and Lynch, "Whose 'Gray Power'?" and Quadagno, *Aging and the Life Course.*

52. Binstock, "The Old-Age Lobby in a New Political Era."

53. MacManus, *Young v Old*.

54. Binstock, "Politics and Economics of Aging."

55. Day, *What Do Older Americans Think?*

56. Binstock, "A New Era in the Politics of Aging."; Binstock, "The Old-Age Lobby in a New Political Era."

57. Laurie Rhodebeck, "The Politics of Greed? Political Preferences among the Elderly," *Journal of Politics* 55 (1993): 342–364.

58. Powell, Branco, and Williamson, *The Senior Rights Movement*.

59. Schlesinger, "Politics and Policy of Entitlements"; Van Tassel and Meyer, *U.S. Aging Policy Interest Groups*.

60. Binstock, "Politics and Economics of Aging."

61. Day, *What Do Older Americans Think?*

62. J. Wiener and D. Stevenson, "State Policy on Long-Term Care for the Elderly," *Health Affairs* 17 (1998): 81–100.

63. R. A. Kane, R. L. Kane, and R. Ladd, *The Heart of Long-Term Care* (New York: Oxford University Press, 1998); J. Rhoades, *The Nursing Home Market: Supply and Demand for the Elderly* (New York: Garland, 1998).

64. U.S. General Accounting Office, *Nursing Homes: Additional Steps Needed to Strengthen Enforcement of Federal Quality Standards* (Washington: GPO, 1999).

65. U.S. Senate, Special Committee on Aging, "California Nursing Homes: Care Problems Persist Despite Federal and State Oversight," 105th Cong., 2nd sess., 1998.

66. Robert Pear, "Congress Near to Deal to Raise Fee Payments to HMOs," *New York Times*, October, 12, 2000, 3.

67. Josh Goldstein, "Nursing Homes, Hospitals, Unions and More Want to be Heard," *Philadelphia Inquirer*, August 30, 1999, A1, 8.

68. Donald Gelfand and Charles Barresi, eds., *Ethnic Dimensions of Aging* (New York: Springer, 1987).

69. Day, "Old-Age Interest Groups in the 1990s."

70. Robert H. Binstock, "Do the Elderly Really Have Political Clout? No," in *Controversial Issues in Aging*, ed. Scharlach and Kaye, 87–91.

71. Schlesinger, "Politics and Policy of Entitlements"; Campbell and Lynch, "Whose 'Gray Power'?"

72. American Association of Retired People, *AARP Bulletin* 41, no. 10 (2000).

73. Campbell and Lynch, "Whose 'Gray Power'?"; Susan MacManus, *Targeting Senior Voters: Campaign Outreach to Elders and Others with Special Needs* (Lanham, Md.; Rowman & Littlefield, 2000); Steven A. Peterson and Albert Somit, *The Political Behavior of Older Americans* (New York: Garland, 1994).

74. MacManus and Tenpas, "The Changing Political Activism Patterns."

75. MacManus, *Young v Old*.

76. MacManus, *Targeting Senior Voters*.

77. Peterson and Somit, *Political Behavior of Older Americans*.

78. Binstock, "Politics and Economics of Aging."

79. Day, *What Do Older Americans Think?*

80. American Association of Retired People, *AARP Bulletin* 41, no. 10 (2000).

81. Binstock and Day, "Aging and Politics."

82. MacManus and Tenpas, "The Changing Political Activism Patterns."

83. Robert H. Binstock, "Older Voters and the 1992 Presidential Election," *The Gerontologist* 32 (1992): 601–606; Binstock, "Do the Elderly Really Have Political Clout? No"; Robert H. Binstock, "The Politics of Enacting Long-Term Care Insurance," in *The Future of Long-Term Care: Social and Policy Issues,* ed. Robert Binstock, L. Cluff, and O. Von Mering (Baltimore: Johns Hopkins University Press, 1996), 215–238.

84. Binstock, "Do the Elderly Really Have Political Clout? No."

85. Under the retirement test, older workers receiving Social Security were taxed 50 cents for every dollar earned over a basic amount if they were below age sixty-five and 33 cents for every dollar earned above another exempt amount if they were between the ages of sixty-five and seventy. Workers aged seventy and older were exempt from the earning test. The retirement test was eliminated entirely in the late 1990s.

86. Binstock, "The Old-Age Lobby in a New Political Era."

87. Binstock, "The Old-Age Lobby in a New Political Era."

88. Fernando M. Torres-Gil, "Policy, Politics, Aging: Crossroads in the 1990s," in *New Directions in Old-Age Policies,* ed. Steckenrider and Parrott, 75–87.

89. Torres-Gil, "Policy, Politics, Aging: Crossroads in the 1990s."

90. MacManus, *Targeting Senior Voters.*

5

Radical and Pragmatic: United Students against Sweatshops

CHRISTINE KELLY AND JOEL LEFKOWITZ

Out of the haze of 1980s and 1990s identity-based social movement ideology and practice, a new class politics is emerging in response to new power repertoires associated with globalization.[1] Specifically, U.S. social movements appear to be increasingly interested in the economic aspects of globalization in an effort to curb environmental destruction, to halt labor and other human rights violations, and develop meaningful international institutions of social, ecological, and economic accountability. Though spurred on by the supranational mobility of global capital and its concomitant patterns of decentralized production, this shift in social movement thinking and action is largely a testament to the power of ideas and suggests that social movements are our best bet for resisting and reforming what appears to many a fait accompli.[2]

At the same time, this shift in social movement attention and action is equally inspired by the realization on the part of organized labor in the United States that politics as usual cannot halt the most pernicious effects of globalization. Organized labor has recognized (remembered?) that social movements can be their greatest allies in the struggle for economic justice. The AFL-CIO, since 1996, has helped open a dialog with social movement sectors and has raised the level of class-consciousness there. Though globalization has until now brought mostly bad news for the poor, women, and racial and ethnic minorities worldwide, it may also be responsible for prompting the rediscovery and updating of important alliances that are crucial to creating real change. Instead of conceding to the power of global giants, both organized labor and social movements are now taking stock of new points of leverage under globalization and shaping a politics that is both radical and pragmatic. Perhaps the most inspiring example of this is the work being done by U.S. students since 1997 to halt the superexploitation of garment workers in global sweatshops.

Students have creatively raised consciousness about campus connections with sweatshops and militantly pressed universities to change the working conditions, and wages, of the people who produce college apparel. United Students against Sweatshops (USAS), the major organizational vehicle for this work, has become one of the most noteworthy contemporary movements. Its insights and strategies are drawn from an understanding passed on from organized labor working in the garment industry. The defining lesson passed on to students is captured in the economics of college apparel: a baseball cap with a college logo sells for around $20 in a campus store. The university receives $1.50 for licensing the logo. The workers who made the caps get 8 cents. All told, the caps, T-shirts, and other college apparel represent a $2.5 billion a year industry. The wages for Kenia Rodriguez of the Dominican Republic, who works a fifty-six-hour week under unsanitary and hostile working conditions, are only $40 per week. Forty dollars a week in the Dominican Republic is only one-third of what an average family needs to live. The BJ & B factory, where Rodriguez works, is typical of sweatshops producing college apparel; in this case, the Korean-owned factory operating in the Dominican Republic's free trade zone produces goods for Champion and Starter, who sell heavily in the college market. At BJ & B, as elsewhere, workers like Rodriguez can be fired for objecting to working conditions or even talking about the benefits of a union.[3]

In this chapter we consider the U.S. student movement against sweatshops in the context of the literature on social movements and suggest that social movements can be both radical and pragmatic. We consider the opportunities for such a politics in the context of the "new power repertoires" of globalization and then consider the development and successes of USAS. We emphasize that USAS activism challenges the tendency, in both social movement practice and theory, of the past fifteen years to submerge class considerations. Class concerns and movement interest in developing institutional constraints on the social and environmental impact of global capital are back. We concentrate on two central features of the student anti-sweatshop movement: the ideological adoption of a class ethic[4] and the strategic use of student power. The goals, ideology, and tactics of the movement are radical; the movement's strategy, pragmatic.

By radical in goals and ideology we mean that the movement challenges the logic of capital. By radical in its tactics we refer to the willingness to violate rules and norms to press that challenge. Like students who demanded divestment of university stocks in companies with operations in apartheid South Africa, students against sweatshops challenge the idea that university investment and production decisions should be private enterprise. The companies involved in college-logo apparel see the people who do the work of sewing the decorative stitches, and other tasks, only in terms of a commodity, their labor power; and the companies search for the cheapest labor power possible just as they would for the cheapest textiles from which to make garments. For consumers, these workers are usually invisible. For the student activists considered here, the people who do the work are people. Karl Marx termed the way in which "a definite social relation between [people] . . . assumes the fantastic form of a relation between things" the "fetishism of Commodities," the alienation of people from other people and from the products of their labor.[5] Student opposition to sweatshops seeks to overcome commodity fetishism and alienation, to relate to the producers of the clothes they buy as people rather than as things. For this reason, the testimony of sweatshop workers, like Kenia Rodriguez, visiting this country, and the reports of students visiting workers and factories abroad, have proved to be extraordinarily important.

By pragmatic we mean that the students are interested in pursuing strategies in conjunction with labor that emphasize their bargaining power. USAS, we will show, has two crucial insights into their power as students: first, they understand their leverage over campus administrators, and second, by association, they understand how the university licensing of logos provides for additional and substantial leverage over the producers of college logo gear and their various subcontractors. That is, students expanded their power repertoire by adding institutional pressure through the commodity chain to traditional point of consumption and point of production strategies.

From the point of consumption back through the commodity chain to the point of production, the nodes of commercial activity provide opportunities for students to support workers and oppose exploitation. That U.S. students have creatively and persuasively seized this opportunity is significant in many respects.

STUDYING MOVEMENTS

Perhaps ironically, much of the academic literature of the 1970s, 1980s, and 1990s suggested that social movements of the era had moved beyond the politics of class and were disinterested in institutional/state-oriented strategies for the resolution of social antagonisms generally. The so-called new social movements were accounted for by reference to large-scale systemic shifts variously labeled postscarcity, postmodern, postindustrial, post-Fordist, or postmaterialist.[6] Though new social movement (NSM) theorists have largely been correct in noting movements' emphasis on issues relating to culture, identity, autonomy, and ecology, the suggestion by some that such postures confirm, as Alberto Melucci maintains, that advanced capitalist societies "no longer have an economic basis; [that] they produce by an increasing integration of economic, political and cultural structures"[7] has always seemed overdrawn. One common feature of NSM theories is the abandoning of rough distinctions that conceptually distinguish between ideology, institutions, and the accumulation process. Such distinctions, it follows, require a theory of social movements that can thematize the semiautonomous but multifariously related developments in each. Instead NSM theory largely submerged class concerns, both empirically and ideologically, and rerouted concerns for resistance to the cultural realm, which received conceptual primacy. Radical politics, it followed, became divorced from class politics.

At the same time, the largely European NSM theory was searching for ways to come to grips with the increasing integration of class politics in the post-Keynesian era. Concerns with the deradicalization and integration of unions in their collective bargaining mode led many social movement thinkers (and participants!) away from state- and class-based politics as arenas for radicalism. Equally frustrating for NSM analysts were the dominant social movement paradigms, particularly those in the United States, that emphasized decision-theoretic (rational choice) models for analysis. The approach that has dominated social movement studies in the United States since the 1970s is known as resource mobilization theory. Resource mobilization, as an approach to studying movements, emphasizes the institutional logic of social conflict and focuses on evaluating movements' ability to maximize calculated interests based on the availability of "resources," variously defined in the literature.[8] Taking a cue from the behavior of interest groups and the pluralist model of competition between groups, resource mobilization theory assumes that movement success is defined by successful bargaining in the context of current arrangements. But, as is suggested by the trajectory of unionism in the United States, successful bargaining often means jettisoning those features, ideological or practical, that break out of the confines of dominant institutions and ideology. Pragmatism, defined as instrumental bargaining, becomes divorced from an alternative vision of society and social relations.

The general tension played out among social movement scholars is one that has its parallel in movement behavior. Just as strategic or pragmatic thinking dominates one tendency, and radical or prefigurative thinking the other, movements over the past fifteen years evidence a similar split. It is our aim here to take a cue from the emerging patterns of social movement behavior and to suggest that radicalism and pragmatism are not mutually exclusive categories for social movements, or social movement analysis, today. Moreover, as illustrated below, it is a powerful combination that underscores the need for both social movement thinkers and participants to acknowledge that, political opportunities and resources notwithstanding, movements are bearers of ideas and interpreters of the world. The ideological orientation of the movement discussed here keeps its commitment to radical economic justice while keeping an eye on the new opportunities for leverage and bargaining presented under globalization.

SWEATSHOP PRODUCTION AND GLOBAL POWER REPERTOIRES

For more than a century the term sweatshop has been used to describe work, primarily by women and children, for very long hours and extremely low pay, under terrible conditions and constant harassment. Emphasizing work paced to the limits of endurance and arbitrary firings, Leon Stein terms sweatshops "a state of mind as well as a physical fact" that "demeans the spirit by denying to workers any part in determining the conditions of or the pay for their work."[9] The term sweatshop also has a more precise, technical meaning. As defined by the Illinois Bureau of Labor Statistics in 1892 "sweating consists of the farming out by competing manufacturers as to competing contractors, of the material for garments, which in turn is distributed among competing men and women to be made up."[10] These meanings of sweatshop are related because the fragmented, competitive conditions of work hinder efforts to establish unions and secure dignity, adequate wages, and decent working conditions.

Contemporary analysts conceptualize the system of subcontracting, now widely dispersed geographically, as global commodity chains, "sets of interorganizational networks clustered around one commodity or product, linking . . . sequential stages of input acquisition, manufacturing, distribution, marketing, and consumption."[11] These commodity chains, as Gary Gereffi suggests, can be controlled either by manufacturers or by retailers.[12] Each type of commodity chain offers distinctive possibilities for greater leverage not only by capital over workers, but also by workers and their allies.

In producer-driven commodity chains, primarily capital-intensive industries, subsidiaries and subcontractors realize economies of scale in making components.[13] Frances Fox Piven and Richard Cloward suggest that "The single sourcing of parts along extended production chains gives particular groups of workers extraordinary potential power," citing the example of "a strike at two General Motors plants producing brakes [that] shut down virtually the entire General Motors operation in the United States, Mexico, and Canada."[14]

The same prospects are not available in the buyer-driven commodity chains, concentrated in labor-intensive industries, in which subcontracted factories produce finished goods rather than parts. Gereffi observes, "these businesses . . . are not 'manufacturers' because they have no factories. Rather these companies are 'merchandisers that design and/or market but do not make, the branded products they sell." In buyer driven commodity chains, profits depend on "research, design, sales, marketing, and financial services."[15] For this discussion, the relevant design feature is the college logo. While the labor and material costs of affixing college logos to T-shirts, baseball caps, backpacks, and other products are minimal; the logos add significant value to the product but also provide new opportunities for workers and their allies.

Consumers in the United States do not want to buy sweatshop products. A survey commissioned by Marymount University's Center for Ethical Concerns found that "If buying a garment for $20,"about five out of six consumers are "willing to pay a dollar more if it were guaranteed to be made in a legitimate shop." If consumers are willing to pay an extra 5 percent for a "sweat-free" $15 college-logo T-shirt, and those 75 cents went directly to the worker, her wages would increase twenty-six-fold.[16] In another survey, three-fourths of respondents said that they would rather buy a $25 garment "certified as not made in a sweatshop" than an identical $20 garment that was not so certified.[17]

This widespread attitude indicates the potential for success of point of consumption strategies, such as boycotts. Randy Shaw notes that "an active grassroots campaign that enabled the public to differentiate [the boycott target, Jessica McClintock, Inc.] from other garment companies" and "exposure to the personal testimony of sweatshop workers" were necessary for the boycott to succeed. Shaw also reports on the campaign against Nike and the boycott of Guess clothing organized by a coalition of religious groups and student activists.[18]

Piven and Cloward describe such boycotts as "New worker-community-consumer alliances . . . reminiscent in some ways of the community mobilizations that often accompanied labor strikes before the prohibitions of Taft Hartley virtually eliminated them from labor's repertoire."[19]

A further expansion of the repertoire of point of consumption strategies may focus on retailers rather than targeting the products of single companies. While most consumers think manufacturers "should be most responsible for preventing sweatshops," from 1995 to 1999 the proportion of survey respondents who thought retailers alone or with manufacturers bore such responsibility increased from 17 to 30 percent, and two-thirds of respondents said they would "be more inclined to shop at stores working to prevent sweatshops."[20]

Students against sweatshops have gone off campus to demonstrate at local outlets of, for example, The Gap, and retailers such as Kohl's, criticized for its connection to the Chentex factory in Managua, Nicaragua, which tried to ensure low wages by firing union supporters.[21]

But, as Piven and Cloward observe, students have their greatest leverage when they "act out their defiance within the universities where they were physically located and could thus act collectively, and where they played a role on which an institution depended, so that their defiance mattered."[22] Students have used that leverage to press for university adoption of business "codes of conduct" that would protect workers rights internationally as well as establishment of independent monitoring to verify compliance with the codes.

This student tactic is not a boycott, although it resembles one in some ways. As in a boycott, USAS threatens to sanction sweatshop operators by withdrawing buyers, but the buyers are institutional rather than individual. This leverage is not exercised at the point of consumption, that is, it does not involve convincing students not to buy particular T-shirts in stores, but at earlier stages in the commodity chain, when contractors and subcontractors are licensed to use the university's logo. Indeed, consumers could keep buying identical products even if some contractors who produce the same item are sanctioned by the withdrawal of access to networks of distribution and licenses to use logos that allow premium prices to be charged. In this sense of institutional pressure on a strategic point in the commodity chain, the leverage that students exercise is similar to a corporate campaign.

The students intend to use that leverage in coordination with workers mobilized at the point of production at places like BJ & B in the Dominican Republic, Chentex in Nicaragua, and Kuk-Dong in Mexico to help advance the interests of workers. As Richard Applebaum and his colleagues point out, student demands for public disclosure and third-party verification of compliance make it "more likely that manufacturers can be compelled to improve conditions in their existing factories, rather than blame the factory and move production elsewhere," to "cut and run."[23] Eric Bracken of USAS explains, "We want to change the question from 'what should I buy?' to 'who should I support?' This is much more than a consumer movement; this is a solidarity movement."[24]

UNITED STUDENTS AGAINST SWEATSHOPS

The student anti-sweatshop movement, though fully independent, can be traced to efforts by the AFL-CIO beginning in the summer of 1996 to reach out to students and repair the rift between organized labor and youth activists dating back to the Vietnam War. Under the new Sweeney administration, in 1996 the AFL-CIO began recruiting student activists into "Union Summer," a program through which student interns are placed in practical labor organizing training in mostly low-wage service-sector jobs throughout the United States. With assistance from Ginny Coughlin of the United Needle and Industrial Textile Employees (UNITE), a handful of Union Summer graduates went back to their campuses in 1997 and initiated the first coordinated sweat-free campaigns. By the next summer, in a conference sponsored by UNITE, students formed USAS and formulated the three major organizing demands (now known as the Campus Codes of Conduct) of the movement: (1) public disclosure of factory sites; (2) independent monitoring of factory conditions; and (3) a guaranteed living wage for workers. By the spring of 2001, USAS had grown to include over 150 campus affiliates and, in addition to its success in publicly linking the college apparel industry to sweatshop labor, it can count significant victories in the areas of independent monitoring under the Workers Rights Consortium and in direct international solidarity alliances.

At the 2000 national organizing conference at the University of Oregon in Eugene, USAS set the following agenda for 2001: (1) continue work on the sweat free campus campaign nationally; (2) develop and support local living wage campaigns for U.S. workers, and (3) develop joint strategies with workers engaging in unionization efforts in global sweatshops producing college apparel. In each case USAS has made progress.

NO SWEAT ON CAMPUS

The anchor for the campus-based anti-sweatshop movement is a straightforward strategy designed to raise public awareness of the exploitation of garment workers in the global economy and mobilize pressure on sweatshop producers by targeting the college apparel industry. At center, student leverage is mounted against university administrations that derive royalty income from companies like Nike, Gear, Fruit of the Loom, Starter, and Champion in exchange for licensing the manufacture of campus and athletic apparel featuring school logos. Like students who demanded divestment of university stocks in companies with operations in apartheid South Africa in the 1970s and 1980s, USAS affiliates have employed multipronged tactics to pressure administrators into dropping (in this case) licensing agreements with sweatshop companies and to adopt the Campus Codes of Conduct.

Since its origins in 1997, the campus anti-sweatshop movement has sought to raise the issues with university administrators and fellow students by engaging in a variety of consciousness-raising actions: mock fashion shows, a "knit-in," an educational coloring book depicting sweatshop production, and, in the case of the University of Wisconsin at Madison, the infiltration of the homecoming parade where activists, dressed as Indonesian sweatshop workers, carried a giant Reebok shoe.[25] Having explained the necessity of change, students insisted on change through direct action, taking over administration buildings at several campuses. In most cases, this first wave of protests succeeded in forcing publicly embarrassed university administrations to endorse (in some cases only partially) the Campus Codes of Conduct. Though these pronouncements were largely symbolic and conciliatory, these early victories encouraged and propelled the movement forward. Subsequent interest within the Clinton administration in campaigning against sweatshop production increased the campus movement's visibility, but generated new obstacles to movement success by encouraging the formation of an industry-dominated monitoring system under the auspices of the Fair Labor Association (FLA). Convinced the FLA could not curb sweatshop abuses in the college apparel industry, USAS turned this obstacle into an opportunity, helping to create a potentially more effective monitoring system through the Workers' Rights Consortium (WRC).

Students took the initiative to develop an alternative system of independent monitoring, founding the WRC along with human rights and labor groups in April 2000. The WRC has a fifteen-member board comprised of five student representatives, five administrators from university members, and five members from its advisory board. Its advisory board is made up of seasoned supporters from the human rights community, women's rights organizations, labor organizations, alongside thirty members of Congress. According to the WRC, their mission is to verify and inspect "conditions in factories producing apparel for colleges and universities" by accurately reporting on company practices. The WRC will rely on the following three methods for accuracy: self-reporting from the industry, worker's complaints, and pro-active investigations.[26]

Unlike the FLA, the WRC does not certify factories as "sweat free" since they assume that any "global" monitoring under current circumstances is flawed and such certification can, as Applebaum and his associates point out, "lull consumers into passivity, under-cutting pressures for systemic change." Since one of the major threats to holding manufacturers responsible (and a threat to garment workers' income stability) is the "cut and run" strategy of global factory production, the student movement hopes to strengthen the WRC's monitoring efforts by banning this practice in the Campus Codes of Conduct. As a result of the pressure of student activists on college administrations, the WRC "reasons that universities, through their licensing contracts, have the power to force manufacturers to sit at the same table with workers and to make changes in a system that is itself the underlying problem."[27]

Kim Moody points out that this development, inspired as it is by a social movement/labor alliance, "represents an interesting nongovernmental grass-roots approach, using the power of the students, and allied organizations" and is not a "sanction against an entire people as is the case in enforcement through trade agreements."[28] Such specificity in pressure is one of the reasons USAS's strategy has been successful. These strategies, developed by social movements, are powerful tools in fighting global exploitation in our era. These actions underscore a growing awareness on the part of U.S. college students that U.S. social movement leverage is a powerful tool that must be reflected upon and crafted around the interests of those whose lives are most affected by the conditions in question. In that respect, USAS has shown enormous intellectual maturity since beyond the rhetorical, their actions show that the freedom of workers to organize is what is at stake here. USAS is continuing to prioritize its campus sweat-free campaign and since the fall of 2000 counts ten new campaigns on campuses nationally, among them the University of Nebraska, Northwestern University, Loyola, and the University of Illinois at Chicago.

LIVING WAGE CAMPAIGNS

This interest is also evident in the work by USAS on domestic living wage campaigns. Following their summer conference, the membership of USAS felt strongly that they needed to support living-wage/unionization efforts in the United States as well as abroad. During the academic year 2000–2001, USAS affiliates have been involved in some noteworthy living wage campaigns. A twenty-one-day sit-in at Harvard University drew attention to the living wage issue, as dozens of newspaper articles described the take-over of a university building and the regular rallies held outside by students with other supporters, including Senators Ted Kennedy and John Kerry (D-Mass.), former Secretary of Labor Robert Reich, and AFL-CIO president John Sweeney.

The sit-in ended with formation of a committee, which included participants in the sit-in, to explore the issue. In a preliminary report, the committee revealed that, adjusted for inflation, the median pay for custodial workers and security guards had declined since 1994, when it was above the living wage threshold, to about $1 below that level in 2001.[29] On the heels of the Harvard protest, a two-day sit-in at the University of Connecticut won an agreement to increase pay for janitors to "the prevailing wage set by the state Department of Labor."[30]

Across the country, protests at the University of California–San Diego, including one in which fifteen students were arrested, led the school to agree to hire as university employees janitors who worked for a nonunion contractor, significantly increasing their wages and benefits.[31] Student activists have pressed for living wages for university employees at some two dozen campuses, with successes at Wesleyan University and the University of Wisconsin.[32]

Off campus, students at the University of Kentucky have played an important role in supporting unionization efforts by sanitation workers in Lexington. Additionally, USAS affiliate Students for Social Equality at New York University was the central student organization fighting for a union for graduate student teachers there in the fall of 2000. This highly successful effort led to the establishment of the first-ever union for graduate student teachers officially recognized by a private university in the United States.

SOLIDARITY

USAS's more recent involvement in support of striking workers at the Kuk-Dong factory in Puebla, Mexico, underscores the power of coordinated pressure in support of point of production organizing in the global economy. In that case, striking workers locked out of a Korean-owned plant and subjected to police brutality have found important allies in USAS. The Kuk-Dong plant produces for both Nike and Reebok almost exclusively for the college apparel market. USAS has two part-time organizers in the region working with locked-out workers to develop joint strategies. USAS will, in response, employ student direct action on campus to pressure university administrators to force Nike and Reebok to take responsibility for striking workers. It is a model, USAS organizer Eric Bracken says, of what is to come for USAS.[33] Although Nike initially dismissed a WRC report critical of labor practices at the factory, independent monitors chosen by Nike came to the same conclusions.[34] The workers' actions and solidarity efforts led to pay increases, better working conditions, and union recognition at Kuk-Dong, now known as Mexmode.[35]

In the summer of 2001, USAS launched a second solidarity campaign, supporting striking workers at New Era, who had made baseball caps for hundreds of schools as well as for Major League Baseball. Students at Ohio State University drew attention to the issues in the strike by staging a baseball game in which "Players on the Workers' team wore scarlet and gray jerseys ([the] school colors) with grievances written on them such as

'Union Busting,' 'Needle Puncture Injuries,' 'Musculo-Skeletal Injuries,' 'Drastic Wage Cuts,' and 'Blood Contamination.'"[36]

In addition to the leverage students have found in new power repertoires using market-based leverage, workers and their allies seek state action at a variety of levels to redress the grievances of sweatshop workers. At the local level, at times inspired by student actions, more than thirty municipalities from New York to San Francisco have passed anti-sweatshop procurement bills governing the purchasing of millions of dollars in uniforms.[37] Similar efforts may develop at the national level as well. Representative Cynthia A. McKinney (D-Ga.), a member of the procurement subcommittee of the House Armed Services Committee, criticized Pentagon purchases from the Chentex factory, which has been the target of frequent criticism by the National Labor Committee as well as the U.S. Trade Representative.[38] Possibilities also exist for action by multilateral organizations. Unions have been critical of the lack of enforcement power of the International Labor Organization (ILO)—since it holds no voting rights in the World Trade Organization and favors adding a "social clause" to WTO standards.[39] Social movement allies are generally distrustful of the credibility and impact of such clauses. It is a point that requires continued dialogue and experimentation. Speaking on the eve of the Seattle WTO meeting, AFL-CIO president John Sweeney asserted that the union would work "against any trade accords that do not include workers' rights and environmental protections."[40]

CONCLUSION

All of this signals some new trends on the part of social movements as well as organized labor. *What is new in organized labor* is an understanding of the role that social movement allies (and young people in particular) can play in expanding the scope of conflict over global labor standards. Some important labor leaders have moved from conventional procedures toward a social movement awareness and dramatically changed culture of union activity. And, as organized labor in the U.S. confronts the task of organizing an increasingly diverse rank and file at home, in the context of globalized production, there are signs of a deepened respect for the political experience of ethnic, racial, and gender-based social movements. *What is new in U.S. social movements* is an interest in economic justice and a willingness to employ direct action tactics in coordination with local and international labor campaigns for worker empowerment.

These changes in labor and social movements provide fertile ground for a new era of left politics. But even fertile ground yields little without thoughtful cultivation. From the perspective of U.S. social movements, there remains plenty of leeway, and therefore debate, as to which combination of postures, strategies, and tactics are most beneficial to those whose interests sit at the center of the new sensibility: the super-exploited workers of the global economy. Among the varieties of strategies, postures, and tactics evident—from the direct action mobilizations associated with Seattle and Prague to more traditional labor and NGO efforts in support of "social clause" standards in bilateral or multilateral trade agreements—a powerful combination is evident in the student anti-sweatshop movement that deserves special attention. It is through the combining of radical and pragmatic strategies that USAS has had its success. Its radicalism stems from the ideological adoption of a class ethic in response to the social consequences of new patterns in the accumulation process and students' willingness to engage in direct action tactics molded to this central commitment. Its pragmatism stems from the strategic use of point of consumption pressure tied to regional labor campaigns engaging in point of production organizing drives. Both radicalism and pragmatism seem evident in the support for *independent* international agencies set up to monitor production sites and enforce codes. Whether the WRC will be able to actually operate along the lines envisioned remains to be seen, but this is precisely the kind of radical institution-building that marks serious change. USAS represents the kind of thoughtful and reflexive ideology and practice required to reap significant benefits in the fight against the new super-exploitation fostered under globalization. Their efforts should be vigorously supported and replicated when- and wherever possible.[41]

NOTES

1. This concept is borrowed from Frances Fox Piven and Richard Cloward in their article "Power Repertoires and Globalization," *Politics and Society* 28, no. 3 (September 2000): 413–431. There they borrow Charles Tilly's term "repertoires," which he uses to refer to the "inventory of available means" of collective action. Piven and Cloward refocus the term to "describe a historically specific constellation of power strategies" available to popular movements; see Charles Tilly, "Social Movements and National Politics," in *Statemaking and Social Movements*, ed. Charles Bright and Susan Harding (Ann Arbor: University of Michigan Press, 1984), 308. Like Piven and Cloward, we use the term to indicate the availability of strategies for power without implying that power is actually realized by movements. Realization, it will be argued here, though always a tentative possibility, heavily relies on movements' reflexive awareness of possibilities and the thoughtful adoption of multipronged strategies and tactics suited to those possibilities.

2. See Ulrich Beck, *Risk Society* (London: Sage, 1991), for an exemplary argument that emphasizes the role of contemporary social movements in holding capital and technology accountable to public interests.

3. "A UNITE Report on Campus Caps made by BJ & B in the Dominican Republic,"accessed March 30, 2001 www.uniteunion.org/sweatshops/schoolcap/schoolcap.html. Among others, BJ & B made caps for Cornell, Duke, Georgetown, Harvard, Notre Dame, University of Florida, University of Michigan, University of North Carolina, UCLA, and USC. See also Bob Herbert, "In America: Sweatshop U.," *New York Times,* April 12, 1998, 13.

4. See Stephen Bronner, *Socialism Unbound,* 2d ed. (Boulder, Colo.: Westview, 2001).

5. Karl Marx, *Capital,* vol. 1 (New York: International, 1947), and Karl Marx, *Economic and Philosophic Manuscripts* (Buffalo: Prometheus, 1988).

6. For a discussion of various theories of "new" social movements, see Christine Kelly, "New Social Movements and Modernity: Continuity or Rupture?" in *Tangled Up in Red, White and Blue: New Social Movements in America,* ed. Christine Kelly (Lanham, Md.: Rowman & Littlefield, 2001).

7. Alberto Melucci, "The Symbolic Challenge of Contemporary Movements," *Social Research* 52, no. 4 (1985): 789.

8. For an exemplary exposition of resource mobilization theory see John McCarthy and Mayer N. Zald, "Resource Mobilization and Social Movements: A Partial Theory," *American Journal of Sociology* 82 (1977). For newer work that seeks to address criticism of the sort raised here, see the collection *New Social Movements: From Ideology to Identity,* ed. Enrique Larana, Hank Johnston, and Joseph R. Gusfield (Philadelphia: Temple University Press, 1994).

9. Leon Stein, "Introduction," in *Out of the Sweatshop: The Struggle for Industrial Democracy,* ed. Leon Stein (New York: Quadrangle, 1977), xv.

10. Quoted in John R. Commons, "The Sweating System," in *Out of the Sweatshop,* ed. Stein, 45.

11. Gary Gereffi, Miguel Korzeniewicz, and Roberto P. Korzeniewicz, "Introduction: Global Commodity Chains," in *Commodity Chains and Global Capitalism,* ed. Gary Gereffi and Miguel Korzeniewicz (Westport, Conn.: Greenwood, 1994), 2.

12. Gary Gereffi, "The Organization of Buyer-Driven Global Commodity Chains: How U.S. Retailers Shape Overseas Production Networks," in *Commodity Chains and Global Capitalism,* ed. Gereffi and Korzeniewicz, 97–99.

13. Gereffi, "The Organization of Buyer-Driven Chains."

14. Piven and Cloward, "Power Repertoires."

15. Gereffi, "The Organization of Buyer-Driven Chains."

16. International Communications Research, *The Consumer and Sweatshops,* Question 3, accessed March 29, 2001 www.marymount.edu/news/garmentstudy.

17. Program on International Policy Attitudes, "Americans on Globalization: A Study of U.S. Public Attitudes," question 102, accessed March 30, 2001, www.pipa.org/OnlineReports/Globalization/appendixe_.html.

18. Randy Shaw, *Reclaiming America: Nike, Clean Air, and the New National Activism* (Berkeley: University of California Press, 1999), 112, 13–96, 113–121.

19. Piven and Cloward, "Power Repertoires."

20. International Communications Research, *Consumer and Sweatshops,* questions 2 and 5.

21. See, for example, Rachel Wright, "Student Protestors Target New Michigan

State U.–area Gap Store," *The State News,* September 11, 2000; Jen Fish, "10 U. Michigan Students Arrested at Labor Protest," *Michigan Daily,* October 3, 2000; Steven Greenhouse, "Critics Calling U.S. Supplier in Nicaragua a 'Sweatshop,'" *New York Times,* December 3, 2000, 9.

22. Frances Fox Piven and Richard A. Cloward, *Poor People's Movements: Why They Succeed, How They Fail* (New York: Vintage, 1979), 22.

23. Richard Applebaum, Edna Bonacich, Jill Ebenshade, and Katie Quan, "Fighting Sweatshops: Problems of Enforcing Global Labor Standards," paper presented at the annual meeting of the American Sociological Association, August 2000, 23, 13.

24. Interviews with Eric Bracken, September 1, 2000, and April 5, 2001.

25. Richard Applebaum and Peter Dreier, "The Campus Anti-Sweatshop Movement," *American Prospect* (September–October 1999): 72–78.

26. Worker Rights Consortium, "Executive Summary," accessed April 21, 2001, www.workersrights.org.

27. Applebaum et al., "Fighting Sweatshops."

28. Kim Moody, "Closing the Door on U.S. Imperialism and Capitalist Globalization," *New Politics,* no. 30 (Winter 2001): 103.

29. Patrick Healy and Joe Spurr, "Harvard Custodians Are Making Less, Study Finds," *Boston Globe,* October 23, 2001, B1.

30. Robert A. Frahm, "Students Win Agreement; End Sit-In," *Hartford Courant,* May 11, 2001, A3.

31. Tony Perry, "UC San Diego Agrees to Hire Contract Janitors," *Los Angeles Times,* June 15, 2001, 10.

32. Jane Manners, "Joe Hill Goes to Harvard," *The Nation* 273, no. 1 (July 2, 2001): 16–18.

33. Interviews.

34. "Independent Monitoring Agency Backs Unfair-Labor Practices Findings at Nike Factory in Mexico," *Chronicle of Higher Education* (March 30, 2001): 35.

35. Steven Jones, "Mexican Workers Set to Tour American College Campuses to Speak on Role of Union," *Daily Trojan,* [University of Southern California], November 15, 2001.

36. USAS, "Major League Solidarity," "reportback," accessed November 20, 2001, www.usasnet.org/campaigns/newera/mainpage.shtml.

37. UNITE Stop Sweatshops Campaign, "Cities Against Sweatshops,"accessed March 30, 2001, www.uniteunion.org/sweatshops/cities/cities.html; Michele M. Melendez, "Oberlin Considers Stand on Sweatshops," *Plain Dealer,* May 19, 1998.

38. Greenhouse, "Critics Calling U.S. Supplier In Nicaragua A 'Sweatshop.'"

39. Edward Alden and Frances Williams, "Forced Labour in Burma Tests ILO's Will to Uphold Global Standards: Union and Human Rights Activists Say Firm Rhetoric Is Not Matched by Action," *Financial Times,* March 27, 2001.

40. Steven Greenhouse, "Trade Pacts Must Safeguard Workers, Union Chief Says," *New York Times,* November 20, 1999. For an excellent discussion of the strengths and weaknesses of this strategy see the discussion in Applebaum et al., "Fighting Sweatshops"; for more direct criticism of the strategy of trade agreements see Moody, "Closing the Door," and Robin Hahnel, "Imperialism, Human Rights and Protectionism," *New Politics,* no. 30 (Winter 2001).

41. USAS may be contacted at 1015 18th Street, NW, Suite 200, Washington, D.C. 20036, or at www.usasnet.org.

Part II

MOVEMENTS BASED ON POSTMATERIALIST IDENTITIES

6

From Women's Survival to New Directions: WAND and Anti-Militarism

MELISSA HAUSSMAN

This discussion traces the founding and growth of Women's Action for New Directions (WAND). The organization was formed as part of a heightened national response to military and nuclear proliferation issues, beginning in the late 1970s, based on mobilizing efforts driven by Australian pediatrician Dr. Helen Caldicott, then in the United States. Formed as the Women's Party for Survival in 1980, the organization became (Women's) Action for Nuclear Disarmament in 1982, and changed to Women's Action for New Directions in 1990. Since 1980, WAND has both kept to its original anti-nuclear weapons stance and expanded to become a regionally and nationally based organization involved in national electoral politics and an alliance with women state legislators in many states.

This chapter focuses on the organization's changes from a grassroots party to a multifaceted social movement organization, in response to perceived issue shifts among the U.S. public and governmental elites. The central research question is how the group has created a niche for itself across decades of different political control and issue emphasis and has emerged in the 1990s as strong and vibrant, especially compared to many other anti-nuclear and women's movement groups that have folded. The chapter begins with a general coverage of relevant new social movement theory, including resource mobilization (RM), political process/political opportunity structure, and postmaterialist theories. The discussion continues by tracing three "waves" of the organization's history: the founding "wave" as the Women's Party for Survival in 1980–1981; the second

101

wave of growth, change, and institutionalization as Women's Action for
Nuclear Disarmament, an anti-nuclear women's group from 1982–1990;
and its third wave, from 1990 onward, as both an electoral and issue-
based organization, concerned not only with arms proliferation but also,
centrally, with national budget priorities and electing more women to
change them.

WAND appears to contain multiple theoretical origins. First, it displays
a postmaterialist stance on issues, emphasizing the potential public divi-
dends for reduced military spending, including social and environmental
protections. As will be discussed, there are relevant points from both RM
and political process theory to explain the organization's founding and
growth as well. As for feminist theory, WAND incorporates a cultural
feminist vision that women can potentially be united on certain issues,
including anti-war, anti-violence, and anti-weapons stances. It also works
within the liberal feminist vision that more women must be elected in
order to change public policy, especially in terms of redirecting budget
priorities away from military spending.

THEORIES OF NEW SOCIAL MOVEMENTS

One influential area of new social movement theory has explored the
degree to which economic and social change, in the advanced industrialized world, from industrial to postindustrial societies, has altered the priorities of organized groups therein. In the first half of the twentieth
century, most organizing was viewed as economically based, such as
unions, the American Farm Bureau, and the Chambers of Commerce.

Since the 1960s, scholars have hypothesized that changes in economic
production and social organization (the truncation of class structures
through the rise of the "new" public-sector class) and increased "hot but-
ton" issues, such as the Vietnam War and student uprisings, have led to
social movement formation. These new issues formed cleavages that
could not be contained in the traditional two-party system in the United
States. New theorizing stated that these issues, once thought of as the
basis for a party realignment, were the basis for organizing outside the
party system as social movements and social movement organizations.

Examples of social movements and their representative organizations
include the environmental movement, which also incorporated the older
Sierra Club and the Appalachian Mountain Club, and the women's movement, incorporating both "woodwork" feminists who had grown up with
"first wave" concerns earlier in the twentieth century and second-wave,
rights-based groups. Other examples are the civil rights movement,
which incorporated both the older National Association for the Advance-

ment of Colored People (NAACP) and the newer Southern Christian Leadership Council (SCLC), Student Nonviolent Coordinating Committee (SNCC), and ultimately the Black Panthers; and the labor movement, including both the older AFL-CIO and the newer Coalition of Labor Union Women (CLUW) and 9 to 5, among others. These groups also adapted organizationally to the new universe of campaign finance regulations beginning in the 1970s, forming political actions committees (PACs) to donate money to candidates.

Ronald Inglehart is an important theorist of value change in economically advanced societies, formulating the postmaterialist theory as a basis for newer social movement organizing.[1] Overall, the postmaterialist view holds that the power grid between state and society, mostly in industrialized democracies, has changed in the latter half of the twentieth century in important ways. These include the decline of class as the primary social structure and thus its centrality as a basis for action.[2] This is true in that on the one hand unions are weaker in political power than prior to the 1970s; but on the other hand, corporations have increased their political clout. It is curious that the official view of postmaterialists is that class is less relevant to social movement organizing since the 1970s. Another point is that the relationship between individual and collective life is viewed as more enmeshed, where "everyday life becomes a major arena of political action."[3] Third, since class is no longer viewed as the most salient overarching structure of social life and state politics, it follows that social movement identities take on the quality of life, rather than the quantity of material goods amassed, as a central value. Related to this is the view that new social movements are more interested in "autonomy and democratization" than in "economic gain or power."[4]

With specific reference to feminist theory and organizing, it is possible to trace continuities from the 1960s, as well as some newer elements. The most obvious basis of feminist movement continuity in the United States across the twentieth century is its grounding in liberal feminism, including the emphasis on equal rights for women and women's ability to participate in the public sphere. Begun in the first wave of feminist activism in the woman suffrage movement of the nineteenth and twentieth centuries, the rights-based feminist framework continued to be used by "woodwork feminist" bureaucrats working in Washington from the administration of President Franklin D. Roosevelt onward. The liberal rights discourse has also been found in the emergence of second-wave organizations, such as the National Organization for Women (NOW) in the 1960s, and into current usage.[5] While the rights-based feminist framework has by no means been the only one in the United States, it has been described as the dominant approach within U.S. feminism this century. Another continuing element in the liberal feminist approach is its disproportionate adherence among middle-class women who have advocated materially based goals such as access to the workplace, better working and retirement conditions and wages, and overall increased security, since women are usually "one relationship away from poverty."[6] Liberal feminist activists believe that women are available for mobilization against unfair laws, as in the areas of jobs, reproductive freedom, and working proactively to pass the Equal Rights Amendment.

Another part of the founding of the second wave of feminist theory and activism in the 1960s is cultural feminism, based on the belief that women share certain attitudes across class and race and that they can be tapped for mobilizing purposes. Indeed, cultural feminists, along with radical feminists, were the first to borrow the Marxist "consciousness-raising" technique in the early 1960s, when small groups met to help women discover the damage wrought upon them by the patriarchal system of social relations. Unlike liberal feminists who view the mobilizing potential for women based on external factors, such as the existence of unfair laws, cultural feminists, beginning in the 1960s, appeared more interested in educating women about the interactive effect of male-controlled politics and economics and, thus, heterosexist norms in social interaction. While WAND did not call itself a feminist organization in the early years, it did appear to invoke, perhaps unwittingly, an important cultural feminist notion that women differ inherently on some values from men, including being more supportive of peace initiatives.

Newer areas of activism include the hypothesized third wave of feminist activism since the 1990s, which does not view gender as necessarily the core dividing line in society in the way attributed to second-wave feminism. Third-wave feminists state that "gendered" ways of acting in society no longer exist to a great extent, and that women and men must work together to solve social problems.

In addition to Inglehart's "postmaterialist" framework, other new theories of social movement organization and success are included, for they specifically assess the strategic options and success of social movement organizations. The theories to be relied on more heavily are political process theory and resource mobilization theory. The first theory, political process or its close relative, concerning the "political opportunity structure," is a macrolevel explanation. Scholars in this framework examine concepts such as the receptivity of political institutions, based on political parties controlling them and other factors, to change. As denoted by Tarrow, the political opportunity structure, a combination of continuous political institutional arrangements and changing alignments, is defined as receptivity by the state to the movement and its demands, instability of political alignments, and movement access to supporting actors and groups.[7]

In terms of the second-wave U.S. women's movement, political process theorists are able to explain the divergent opportunity structures for women from the 1970s through the 1990s. Anne Costain suggests that the receptivity of the state to women's movement demands in the 1960s and 1970s was based on the weakness of the government, due to a crisis of legitimacy, with a "nearly equal balance of power between the movement and the government."[8] On the other hand, when that balance is tilted in favor of the government, the movement will be repressed by the state. This is similar to other theorists' understanding that the government may allow a social movement to have success for only so long, then shut off governmental access altogether.[9] One crucial factor weakening the government of the 1960s and opening it to women's movement demands, according to Costain, was the crumbling of the New Deal coalition and the democratic administration's recognition of women and African Americans as swing constituencies needed to retain power. Thus, women gained early legislative victories, despite not having the usual perquisites for lobbying success (such as large cash reserves and sophisticated D.C. attorneys).[10]

For this discussion, all three political opportunity factors—state access, political alignment instability, and access to support groups—are viewed as important in explaining the formation of the Women's party and its transformation into WAND. For example, both receptivity to the state and changing political alignments were felt from the movement under President Jimmy Carter in the 1970s to arms limitation and downsizing nuclear arsenals, to the social, fiscal, and military conservatism of the Ronald Reagan years beginning in 1980. At the same time that access to the state was nearly eradicated, the issue basis for the Women's party expanded. Berry has described the change in political alignments in 1980 as a "sea-change."[11] In this new environment, the Women's party could join a national nuclear freeze movement in progress and increase its profile.

Another social movement model of the 1970s was resource mobilization. This model emphasizes the need for a movement organization to build up resources of support and money. It looks upon an organization's success as strengthening its internal structure and counts on the acquisition of external resources. Resources can also be defined as the organization's having a "conscience constituency," those who support a social movement but probably would not directly benefit from its existence.[12] These movements are said to emerge through the efforts of movement or organizational "entrepreneurs," charismatic people who can draw in supporters and money. This model describes movements with a small membership, that "gather resources . . . from the elite and conscience constituents."[13] One described drawback to the RM model is that its focus is primarily on internal organization-building strategies and ignores the effects of the larger political structure.

The RM model in some ways fits WAND perfectly. The movement entrepreneur in this instance was Dr. Helen Caldicott, who traveled the United States warning against the effects of exposure to nuclear byproducts and leading the group Physicians for Social Responsibility. Caldicott, by most accounts a charismatic, intelligent, and energetic personality, would speak around the country, and people would be drawn to her and seek to participate. Her presence as a noted medical expert was clearly a resource possessed by the nascent Women's Party for Survival in the late 1970s, which aided early mobilization efforts.

Given the resource mobilization framework's insistence on the importance of organizational structure as relating to how resources are amassed and used, some RM theorists have helped flesh out the understanding of how structural changes may hinder or aid a movement organization. Zald and Garner discuss the relationship of organizational structure to goal transformation in an organization, such as how changing issue emphasis in the political and social spheres may mean that organizations are acted upon as much as they have agency to act, and that these changes can affect the social movement organization's strength. Zald and Garner note that "three interrelated aspects of the environment of (social movement organizations) can critically affect their growth and transformation," including changes in society, which may lead to an "ebb and flow of supporting sentiments for the organization"; society may change in the direction of the organization's goals, or conversely, "events may indicate that the organization's goals will not be attained," which can "sharply influence member and potential member sentiments." Finally, they write of "interorganizational competition" for issue space within a social movement sector, for these purposes construed as the peace/anti-militarism area. This may, in the long run, hurt an organization.[14] The ability to relate the strength of social concerns to the health of an organization is a helpful facet of RM theory, as articulated by Zald and Garner. It ties in with one of the most helpful aspects of political opportunity theory, which is how changing political alignments affect the political opportunity structure for an organization and movement, for example from the 1970s to the 1990s.

Zald and Garner have thoroughly covered the link between support for the movement's and organization's objectives and in turn the organization's mobilizing potential. First, they note that generalized support may exist for a movement's goals, but that there may be different levels of accord with specific organizations. "Organizational maintenance" occurs when an organization is able to keep pace with changes in the larger society and sentiment toward the movement as a whole. Two aspects may "mediate" the effect that larger social views have on the fate of the organization: the type of membership requirements for the organization and "the extent to which operative goals are oriented to member or individual behavior change," rather than toward general societal change. In the first instance, the theorists distinguish between inclusive organizations, requiring "minimum levels of initial commitment," and exclusive types, which require long "novitiate" periods for new members, and to "require the recruit be subject to organization discipline and orders." Similarly, the inclusive organization allows its members to belong to other organizations, requiring "little activity from its members." The exclusive organization requires greater member energy and time and may even "permeate all sections of the member's life, including activities with non-members." WAND more closely approximates the inclusive organization in not having an official membership and in allowing supporters to be as active or inactive as they choose. Another point made by Zald and Garner is that "competing values and attitudes are more readily mobilized in the inclusive organization."[15]

In many ways WAND as an inclusive organization has been more vulnerable to changing currents in society than an exclusive organization. RM organizational theory predicts that the inclusive organization will be more permeable to society's ebb and flow of sentiments on an issue than an exclusive one, given its low barriers to membership and thus to the outside world. Another point is that exclusive organizations, such as religious organizations, may be viewed as less threatening to society since their main goal is to change individuals. Inclusive organizations, by contrast, seek to change society, so it is likely that pressure will be more likely brought to bear upon them by the state. The potential combination of internal discord and societal or state disapproval can lead to a high degree of pressure felt by the organization, particularly by its leadership.[16]

Other helpful points from Zald and Garner's exposition of RM theory emerge, such as the importance of the donor base, especially to an inclusive organization. Each strategic shift in response to changing social viewpoints may alienate some donors. Similarly, Zald and Garner point out that a movement "succeeds when its objective is attained; [it is] becalmed when, after achieving some growth and stability, its goals are still relevant to society but its chances of success have become dim; [and] fails when the society has decisively rejected the goals of the organization and the organization as an instrument is discredited."[17] These two points are important because WAND found itself becalmed in the late 1980s and early 1990s, when the immediate threat of military buildup had faded, and it needed to assess strategic options and donor sources.

This RM approach, in combination with political process theory, shows the strong linkage between issue development in the state and larger society and the health and strength of the organization. RM theory also enables an examination of strategic choices related to organizational structure. The Zald/Garner piece is helpful in positing three stages through which a movement organization may travel: success, failure, and being "becalmed."

THE FIRST WAVE: FOUNDING AND EARLY HISTORY OF THE WOMEN'S PARTY FOR SURVIVAL

The Women's Party for Survival was founded in 1980 as a "small, volunteer-staffed organization, a political party, built upon Helen Caldicott's belief in mobilizing women's common anti-military views. It does not seem that the Women's party's founders expected to significantly challenge the U.S. two-party system. Instead, the party seems to have been created more to tap into the perceived commonality of women's views and to transmit the anti-arms race and anti-nuclear sentiments of half the population to policymakers. Partly through her work with Physicians for Social Responsibility (which she later directed), Caldicott undertook a U.S. lecture tour on the dangers of overreliance on nuclear power and nuclear weapons, especially in the United States. One theme often articulated was the destruction that a twenty megaton bomb could wreak. In the party's first newsletter, Caldicott's piece stated that while many bombs were smaller, "some of the Russian bombs are that big because they're less accurate." Similarly, "most towns and cities with populations of 25,000 people or more are probably targeted, which is most people in this country." She described the likely damage if a twenty-megaton bomb were dropped on Boston; it would likely create a "crater about a mile wide and 300 feet deep . . . everything in that volume would be turned to radioactive fallout . . . up to a radius of six miles from the center, every person would probably be vaporized."[18]

Organizational Issues

The Women's Party for Survival first met in New York City on March 13, 1980, and established its legal status with the Federal Election Commission (FEC) in June 1980.[19] Nationally, nodes of chapters seemed to spring up after one of Caldicott's lectures, in which women, especially, would approach her and ask what they could do. Her reply was to start a single-issue, anti-nuclear political party.[20] While Caldicott's work and her speeches provided the catalyst for the group's formation, Caldicott as an entrepreneur did not feel particular ownership of the organization and would move on to speaking engagements while a small, dedicated membership performed the local organizational work.

The majority of the organizational work in Massachusetts was done by local volunteers, at first mostly in Cambridge, then in Watertown. From the first, the Women's party was interested in electing pro-peace, antinuclear candidates to office, although initially Caldicott, "as an Australian, hadn't realized that it was almost impossible for a women's peace party to make any progress within our two-party system."[21] As a former board president has written, "as I saw it, the Council was strong in energy, creativity, and commitment; less strong in experience, recognition, and funds."[22]

An early tension within the party, which was formed seemingly on the cultural feminist belief of women as a group being more peace-loving than men, was whether other women's issues could be addressed and how overtly feminist the group could be. The answers to these two questions were essentially negative and showed emerging fault lines common to early second-wave groups.

On one hand, the Women's Party came out of a group, active in spring 1980 in Cambridge, named Wo-Men for Survival, which spoke to women's inherent talent for nurturing the earth. Similarly, although Caldicott "denies she is a feminist, she speaks to emotions our culture has labeled . . . as 'feminine'—the life-affirming side of us which must overcome the destructive side."[23]

However, Caldicott also evinced a distrust of the label "feminist." Early materials highlighted the fact that men staffed the office, and that while it was a women's movement organization, "we must also bring in men too—no hatred of men—men who care are allies."[24] Including men in actions was viewed as following the wishes of Caldicott, who advocated that "we must be smart politically."[25] Early meeting notes concerned whether Caldicott's strong statements represented the rank and file views of the organization. One memo stated, " 'many people have perceived the Women's Party as being sexist, anti-feminist and elitist . . .' several groups have been alienated by certain statements made by Helen C. and taken to represent W.P.S. policy."[26] Some groups with which the Women's party had to mend fences early on included the more established Women's Strike for Peace and MUSE.[27]

Other early questions of group identification concerned issues of racial and lesbian inclusion, similar to second-wave feminist questions in general, and of the extent to which to participate in various movement coalitions (ecology, women's, peace). On the former question, an early Women's party letter inviting people to a general meeting on January 24, 1981, at the Arlington Street Church (Boston), stated in part that "it is absolutely vital to build a genuinely multi-racial women's movement," noting that the military buildup impoverished and repressed "our sisters and brothers in the third world," and economically deprived "minority and poor communities" in the United States through social welfare cuts, and the "sharp and very dangerous rise of racism across the country."[28] In its written communication, the Women's party demonstrated a sensitivity and desire to link to minority communities that had not been found as much in women's movement organizations formed ten years earlier.

Yet another early issue of the second-wave women's movement was the nearly automatic identification of women's organizing with lesbianism by the mainstream media and how to counter this framing. A letter by the Women's party treasurer to "a sister in Vermont" in 1981 illustrated the tension between recognition of different groups. This tension was something that many second-wave groups have had to address. The treasurer's letter was in response to a member of a Vermont-based peace group who feared that overtly lesbian groups were not welcome to participate in the public activities of the Women's party. Her response was that the Vermont group's understanding was a "gross misunderstanding and distortion of the truth," and mentioned that one of the members of the Women's party administrative council "is a radical lesbian feminist and is quite candid about it." The letter also went on to affirm that the Women's party wished to "combine the traditional values [of supporting peace] with the insight gained through feminism."[29] While the Women's party was thought to appeal mainly to mothers, it also wished to represent "single" women, and in the 1980s, these communities were thought to be mutually exclusive.

Strategic Options

In its 1980 founding statement, the Women's party articulated its goals: (1) stopping the arms race, (2) having zero nuclear weapons, (3) banning nuclear power, (4) funding human needs, (5) healing the earth, and (6) giving women political power in decision making at all levels of the political process.[30]

The Women's party participated in Mothers' Day nuclear disarmament coalitions, but made clear that it would not participate in civil disobedience at these events.[31] The Mothers' Day actions, held on a holiday started during World War I, were predicated on women as mothers being more pacifistic. Decisions at these meetings used consensus, a structure common in second-wave women's organizations. In the 1980 Mothers' Day action, there was an anti-nuclear march, then the next day, May 12, members were urged to go "with their babies, children, husbands and friends" to meet either in the district or Washington offices of their U.S. representatives or senators as a follow-up. They were urged, in this "Congressional Presence for Survival," to emphasize the "dangers posed to all life on earth by nuclear weapons," and to "stress the many alternatives to war that are available to work out the problems of the distribution of the world's resources," and to "share our willingness to work on these issues with them."[32] Members were urged to bring homemade apple pies to their representatives to show that the Women's party was "as American as motherhood and apple pie," perhaps in remembrance of the labeling of the Women's Strike for Peace as communist in its appearance before the U.S. House Un-American Activities Committee in 1962.[33]

The 1980 event was the first group action for the Women's party.[34] In an April 1980 circular letter, Caldicott stated that Women for Survival, as it was then known, was working on a series of events that would take place in Washington on April 25–28, 1980, under the name of the Non-Nuclear World Weekend, and that Women for Survival would try to fill a bus to participate in the event. Among the other groups with which Women for Survival had been working on these events were the Coalition for a Non-Nuclear World, Mobilization for Survival, National Organization for Women, Feminist Women for Peace, Survival Summer, Women for a Non-Nuclear World, Women of the Boston Indian Council, and the Aquarian Age Congregation of the First Unitarian Church in Roxbury, Massachusetts. Other groups with whom Women for Survival declared an early affiliation were the Clamshell Alliance, the YMCA/YWCA, and the American Friends Service Committee.[35] Caldicott addressed some of the group's early concerns in the letter, stating, for example, that "an informal poll . . . reveals that the word 'party' causes some controversy" and that, therefore, at least for the time being, she planned that the group's work would be mainly educational, working with the "grassroots educational outreach" of Survival Summer across the country and trying to reach all women across political party status. There was, however, also a recognition that the November elections were upcoming, and the Women's party was ready for such participation through its filing with the Federal Elections Commission in June 1980.[36]

In 1981, the Women's party participated in a similar Mothers' Day antinuclear action in Washington. It included a march, a nuclear war enactment, lobbying training, and then lobbying of members of Congress on the next day. Other groups with which the party worked on this included Women's Strike for Peace, Women's Equity Action, NOW, and Friends of the Earth. One interest expressed was for the party to "emphasize outreach beyond the Northeast," to start becoming an actor on a national basis.[37] While it worked in coalition with groups to put on the march, the costs were "singly paid by the Women's Party for Survival." In addition, the party's first newsletter estimated that many more than a few thousand could have been convinced to attend the march, if they had had more than two months' planning time.[38]

Given its single-issue focus on ending the nuclear arms race, another important early effort of the Women's Party for Survival was the nationwide nuclear freeze movement. As one of the "more than 30 groups nationwide" working on the Nuclear Freeze Petition, the party stated that its hopes for the freeze were to (1) reduce the tensions between the United States and the USSR; (2) halt development of first-strike weapons (U.S. MX, Trident II, and cruise missiles, and "improved versions" of the Soviet SS-17, 18, and 19 missiles); (3) maintain nuclear parity between the United States and the USSR; (4) set the stage for real nuclear arms reductions; (5) minimize the spread of nuclear weapons to other countries; (6) strengthen the economy by freeing up the federal funds earmarked for nuclear weapons development; and (7) increase national and international security by putting a halt to the rapidly escalating arms race.[39] The Women's party at the time could be seen as a group with an interesting mix of cultural feminist assumptions, but with the ability to speak in the traditionally male domain about weapons systems, strike launches, and reaction times.

The Women's party was aware of the potential opposition of labor at the plants where nuclear arms were produced. The party's 1980 organizational packet told women planning to picket such plants to contact the labor force prior to the demonstration, emphasizing that the party's goal was "peaceful [plant] conversion, NOT factory shutdowns."[40]

While postmaterialist theory can help explain the U.S. and global shift of grassroots movements toward anti-nuclear organizing in a time of relative prosperity, especially in part of President Carter's term, this explanation is problematic for the part of Carter's term when stagflation was rampant, and for the first two years of the Reagan presidency, when global recession took place. The more specific nature of political process theory is helpful here in that one of the factors identified by Tarrow, that of changing political alignments (takeover of the presidency and Senate), seems to explain the "window of opportunity" capitalized upon by the Women's party in its formation and early activism. Another relevant factor of political process theory—state access for groups—was not forthcoming in the early 1980s, as President Reagan worked to "defund the left" and increase military spending. The only potential help could come from the Democratic House.

In terms of resource mobilization theory, the charismatic movement entrepreneur Caldicott was both an asset and a liability in the early days; her national speeches attracted a great deal of attention, especially due to her medical credentials, probably helped by her lack of identification with feminism. She was viewed by some party members as a liability due to her disavowal of some key women's movement goals (such as feminism).

The discussion about this entrepreneur raises another interesting question about the point made by RM theorists Zald and Garner about inclusive versus exclusive organizations. While it seems clear that the Women's party was formed in its early days as an inclusive organization, it also appears that the degree of inclusivity may have been a challenged point between Caldicott and party members; whereas she wanted to use the "pure" definition of anti-nuclear sentiments on the part of child-bearing women, others, more active in the general women's movement, wanted a larger scope of issue definition to include other feminist issues. When the Women's party moved into its second phase, Caldicott became a board member, shifted more of her attention to Physicians for Social Responsibility, and returned to Australia for a time in the mid-1980s.

THE SECOND WAVE: RECONFIGURATION AND INSTITUTIONALIZATION IN WAND, 1982–1990

In 1982 the Women's Party for Survival split into a two-part organization renamed Women's Action for Nuclear Disarmament (WAND), incorporating an education fund and a PAC.[41] By the mid-1980s, WAND had adopted a more overtly liberal feminist stance, based on increasing the visibility of electoral action in its strategic mix. Compared to the reluctance of some of the early leadership to use the term "feminist," it is currently perceived that "most WAND members would consider themselves feminists."[42]

Organizational Issues

Some of the issues related to the organizational structure were continuations of questions related to the Women's Party for Survival; others surfaced for the first time. The decision to change the name from the Women's party rested on diverse factors and occurred after a membership poll.

The name change precipitated much mail. Some women expressed concerns over whether the organization would drop the designation "women's," for as one activist wrote, that was the basis of her connection to the anti-nuclear movement. Similarly, one letter from the executive director to the membership in December 1981 stated that "confusion has arisen from our 'political party' stance . . . we have found that the hassles of the . . . reputations of third parties has held up some of our work."[43] Another issue contributing to the name change was that the Women's party had been receiving unwelcome attention from survivalist groups, which existed on the opposite spectrum from anti-nuclear organizing. Similarly, in a letter to the membership Executive Director Diane Aronson noted that "the need to remove 'Survival' from the national identification [is] necessary. We don't want to SURVIVE a nuclear attack . . . we want to help PREVENT nuclear war."[44] This statement pointed to a more confident, proactive stance on the part of the organization in the height of its growth.

Structurally, as the Women's party, the model had included the national office in Massachusetts (which ultimately moved to Arlington, its current location), the national board of directors, and chapters. The chapters were to adopt the national agenda, as voted upon by the board, and could also adopt their own additional items. However, if the additional items seemed inconsistent with national board policy, they had to be cleared through the board.[45] At that time, there were over seventy local chapters in the United States.[46]

It was believed that the organization could cover more ground and be more efficient by splitting itself into the nonprofit, tax-exempt educational fund, to educate members and the public about the nuclear arms race, and WAND/PAC. The latter half was created to enable WAND to lobby on specific bills and give money directly to candidates.[47] However, a possibly confusing aspect of the name was that the term PAC seems to have been used rather loosely in the early years to denote any sort of political activity. Later, this distinction was clarified by acknowledging the separation of political (lobbying) activity and the PAC function to give political donations. Both the education fund and the PAC had their own boards of directors. Caldicott was a member of both, and Sayre Sheldon was their president.[48]

Another change was to give more flexibility to the chapters. One way was to shift from the designation "chapter" to "affiliate," to reflect the "local group's autonomy while allowing you to stay connected to the national organization." Another change was that each local affiliate group could either name themselves WAND or simply "AND"—Action for Nuclear Disarmament.[49] In the first few years after the structural change, some groups kept the AND designation, including Brookline, Massachusetts, but by the mid-1980s most had added Women's to the name. The idea of increasing affiliate groups' autonomy was also attractive to the national office, which would therefore "be spared the time lost in dealing with financial, legal, and structural questions of what 'chapters' must do." This would leave the PAC with three types of members: (1) national board members, elected annually and empowered to vote on overall policy; (2) individual contributing members; and (3) affiliated members, including all preexisting "chapters" as of February 1, 1982, and the new affiliated groups formed since then. Dues were assessed at $25 annually for groups with fewer than fifty members, and $50 for groups with more than that.[50] These changes had been accomplished with the help of a consultant "with much experience in both disarmament issues and setting up organizations."[51]

Other evidence of institutionalization and differentiation within a movement organization seen to be growing included the decision in 1985 to establish a Washington, D.C., office for the Education Fund, and around that time, to hire a full-time lobbyist for the organization.

Structural designations were made within the national office in Massachusetts, which formed a suggested blueprint for affiliates. These included creation of a committee structure and clarification of the role and responsibilities of the executive director. Suggested committees included nuclear freeze issues, political action, media response, event publicity, outreach, chapter coordination, volunteer recruitment, and newsletter. Fundraising strategies continued along previous lines, such as direct mail solicitation, selling books and printed materials, and having fundraisers with celebrities.[52] For example, the actress Jane Alexander was on WAND's board for most of the 1980s. Membership dues were highest for WAND in the years of 1984–1986, at $134,000 +, $132,000 +, and $145,583, respectively.[53] On the other hand, the combined income of WAND and the Education Fund has been highest in the years 1985 ($1.18 million), 1986, 1999, and 2000. In 1986, the combined income was $898,840, and in the past two years, has hovered just above or below $850,000, within a $10,000 range.[54]

One important organizational conclusion in the mid-1980s concerned the results of direct-mail efforts. WAND's policy was to do direct mailing to hundreds of people to raise funds, and the national office held any names gained through responses for the first year. In the second year, the names of people who made a repeat donation and/or checked off on the WAND form that they were interested in local action would be sent on to the local affiliates. Similarly, at that point there would be a sharing of half the dues with the local affiliate. Overall, the executive director concluded, "the recruitment of first-time donors . . . is so minimal that it doesn't even begin to cover the costs. Most first-time direct-mail respondents are strictly donors, not activists."[55] WAND therefore realized that while some donors might be reached through direct-mail efforts, activists were usually a separate pool and would have to be mobilized either through large nationally focused efforts (such as the annual Mothers' Day marches on Washington) or through local presentations by speakers, or connection to a community issue by the local affiliate (such as a nuclear freeze effort).

WAND wished to expand its affiliate groups in the early 1980s, and looked to do this in certain states designated as having good potential. These included New England states, Ohio and Michigan, and California and Oregon.[56] It is more accurate to assess WAND's membership strength by numbers of chapters or dues paid, since contributors to the Education Fund are not counted as "members," and many send money to the PAC without formally joining.[57]

Another organizational issue that resurfaced was how WAND would work in coalition with other types of groups. The policy was that WAND "endorses events or campaigns that have national impact . . . requests for local support for endorsements are generally turned down" (for example, the national board would not endorse local nuclear freeze efforts, while local affiliates could). One exception was the local effort to save the Quincy, Massachusetts, shipyard in 1986.[58] If WAND were approached for a donation of staff time or money for another organization's event, it would have to be approved by the executive committee and perhaps the entire board.[59] WAND did want to be able to work in coalition with anti-nuclear, environmental, and feminist groups and, especially in its early years, was sensitive to negative assessments by others, wanting to work, as various memos indicated, on repairing relationships with Women's Strike for Peace, and reaching out to NOW.[60] This earned the organization the designation of being "one of the least ideologically rigid of the peace groups."[61]

While by most accounts WAND appeared to be a growing, thriving organization through the mid-1980s, by spring 1986 written reports came out of the national office stating that WAND was in financial crisis. Fundraising had only been successful in a series of small grants, and Caldicott had gone back to Australia.[62] While WAND/PAC's income had gone up from the previous year, the Education Fund's revenues had been halved. Some of WAND's leadership felt that the organization was in decline, as would be expected according to the RM theory of Zald and Garner. Beginning in early spring 1986, numerous letters went out from the national office to affiliate groups, groups without formal association with which WAND had previously worked, and individuals known to the group who could contribute extra money in the case of a crunch, and there were internal communications to the WAND board as well. Some saw the lessening of Caldicott's role as critical to the organization's fundraising plans, since funds traditionally poured into the office after one of Caldicott's speeches. WAND's board recognized that alternate sources of funds would have to be developed. The largest change regarding fundraising was "deciding that the days of angels 'coming to the rescue' via Helen's prodding is over," and that WAND could only build "on that which is guaranteed through its systematic fundraising efforts."[63]

It was noted that, after Caldicott's departure, "from our re-evaluation and changes, we are considering WAND as a new organization." This series of changes would mark the turning point from WAND's existence as a social movement organization centered around a charismatic personality and her issue agenda. The new WAND described itself as an organization that could arrive at a consensus on goals after polling its membership, but also a group that would now be more "streamlined" and focus on "work that will make a difference and involve more women's participation in ending the nuclear arms race."[64]

Some changes in fundraising strategies included encouraging affiliate groups to hold "house parties," and then to commit part of the receipts to the national office. One highly visible fundraiser was held on Mothers' Day of 1986, with Marlo Thomas, Alice Walker, and Candice Bergen.[65] Overall, the strategy was to strengthen the grassroots funding base, which involved the framing of WAND's mission, as "all of our program focus has fundraising components." This new emphasis was said to draw from the recognition that by the late 1980s, more women were working outside the home and less available for volunteer activities. Also, after an internal review, WAND decided that the peace movement in general had to become more "professionalized" in the form of fundraising. Specifically, they hoped that a more secure organization would work to politically empower women, so as to involve them "in the shaping of U.S. nuclear disarmament policies."[66] This shift involved some questions from affiliate members as to whether fundraising was now WAND's priority, instead of activism, but the leadership responded that it was not an "either/or" choice.

Other important steps at this time included hiring a consultant from Washington to address questions of "financial crisis, expansion and growth, and difficult transition of leadership."[67] Changes in organizational structure after this review included working with a staff accountant to keep the "bills payable" account current, hiring an operations manager, hiring a mostly new staff who felt able to work together toward the "common goal of moving forward," and the development of a new team structure between new Board President Beverly Droz and Executive Director Diane Aronson.

Some of the 1986–1987 changes came after painful events, or themselves involved difficult decisions about restructuring. However, their success was noted one year after the initial alarm about WAND's financial base was sounded. By January 1987, it was noted that WAND had paid off all its outstanding bills and had money in the bank. One communication from the executive director to the Caldicotts in Australia noted that "I've raised $36,000 this month."[68] From a self-described funding crisis in 1986, WAND certainly seemed to have turned the corner early in 1987.

Strategic Options

Having survived two internal reorganizations within four years, WAND emerged stronger and with a clearer vision of its goals. In the terms of the resource mobilization framework, WAND was able to emerge as an organization with the ability to set its goals independently following the departure of its founder. WAND had been in a period of growth in the early 1980s, a short period of decline in 1986–1987 where internal reorganization as suggested by Zald and Garner's theory was necessary, then from 1987 onward experienced a couple years of growth. As for the political opportunity structure, cracks were beginning to form within the Reagan administration, and a series of nuclear and military mishaps in 1986–1987 helped WAND in terms of its anti-nuclear goals but also to build bridges with mainstream political groups and to widen its grassroots base. These developments put WAND back into a solid growth mode for at least a couple of years.

Political events happening at this time included the Challenger disaster, the bombing of Libya, the nuclear power plant accident at Chernobyl, the loss of the Senate by Republicans in 1986, and the public revelation of U.S. aid to the Nicaragua Contras.[69] Mention of these events was frequent in WAND communications, either with reference to "the current crisis in the Administration," or the need to "make the connections between what's going on in our government and the tragedy of our current course in this insane arms race."[70]

One of the noticeable alterations in WAND's strategic emphasis by this time was that it began to participate directly in contacting members of Congress, working with them, contacting President Reagan, and generally taking visible action on the national political debate over militarism. Part of this may be attributed to the desire to be more visible for fundraising purposes, but another part seems due to WAND's having weathered crises and emerged stronger and more able to act. Thus, part of the national activism came at the invitation of visible national figures.

One noticeable change, beginning with WAND's new letterhead (which relegated Caldicott's name to a side column, rather than featuring it under the heading), in 1986 was the strengthening of the advisory board by adding nationally known political figures. Perhaps this came at the recommendation of WAND's D.C.-based consulting firm. By 1986, people such as Dagmar Celeste of Ohio, Representative Claudine Schneider (R-R.I.), Representative Patricia Schroeder (D-Colo.), and Senator John Kerry (D-Mass.) had been added to the advisory board. WAND's new mission appeared to be to continue to pay attention to its grassroots base while also building its national profile among Congress and the arms-control community.

One initiative of the spring of 1986 was the publication of WAND's study titled "Turnabout," the results of research on the disarmament movement for a year, which gave strategic recommendations for the "arms control and disarmament community."[71] The publication of this report gave the organization a credential of publishing a scholarly report that was independent of Caldicott's publications. It was widely distributed, including to "arms control and disarmament groups, members of Congress, key media contacts, to members of the funding community," and other interested individuals.[72] Another initiative following shortly thereafter was WAND's decision to hold its advisory board meeting in Washington, D.C., on March 24, 1987; arrangements were made for a breakfast hosted by Senator John Kerry, a congressional briefing following that, and an evening party for the WAND boards (directors and advisory) at Kerry's home.[73]

Other indications of WAND's increased stature in the national disarmament community took place. One was the invitation of Executive Director Diane Aronson to a workshop hosted by the D.C.-based Women for a Meaningful Summit, including a lunch meeting at the Greek Embassy, hosted by the wife of Greek prime minister Andreas Papandreou.[74] In the summer of 1986, Professor James McGregor Burns of Williams College and his wife, Joan, invited WAND representatives, as "leaders of the peace movement," to their home to ponder the best way for a united peace movement to exert "electoral success" in the next presidential election, including through primary voting, delegate selection, and platform writing. Part of the networking that preceded this invitation included writing to Pam Solo, Peace Fellow at the Bunting Institute and connected to WAND, and the preexisting connections between John K. Galbraith and James M. Burns, who considered themselves longtime electoral peace and détente activists. Another major question to be debated was the extent to which peace groups should work in coalition with other types of groups for electoral gains in 1988.[75]

Other national events in which WAND took either a leadership or an active role included the WAND-sponsored Diaper Campaign directed at President Reagan in May 1986, which had been aided in its development by Pam Solo. The diapers were to be sent by various organizations to the White House "between Mothers' and Fathers' Day 1986" to show the president that these organizations "asked him to question the meaning of protection in the nuclear age . . . [and] to be sent on to a day care center that has felt the full impact of your policy and budget priorities."[76] In addition to starting to emphasize the budgetary impacts of military spending, another suggestion that trickled up to the national office in Massachusetts from San Francisco and Los Angeles WAND affiliates was to link environmental protection to ending the arms race.[77]

A few other initiatives pointed to WAND's confidence about acting in many arenas. The first was a media campaign, including sending WAND representatives to talk radio programs. In particular, this was said to strengthen WAND's disarmament efforts in the area of its Boston head-

quarters.[78] Another project was its Constitutional Peace Initiative, originally developed by some Boston College faculty and graduate students,
to "reclaim the central values of the Constitution for the Peace Movement." This project was conducted by the WAND Education Fund, and
WAND's participation was to develop "an action component for the
nationwide campaign."[79] Finally, a very critical initiative undertaken with
an eye toward increasing WAND's and women's national presence was
the "200 Club: A Proposal for Electoral Empowerment." It planned to
have two hundred women in Congress by the year 2000, and involved "a
need identified by the WAND Education Fund both at the national level
and the local level."[80] In essence, the project involved identifying, training, and supporting women candidates and campaign staff. In some
ways, while it had a liberal feminist goal, the 200 Club also returned to
the cultural feminist roots of assuming that elected women would hold
different policy priorities from men.

WAND's successes in its second wave of development and institutionalization from 1982–1990 have been identified as participation in the cancellation of the MX missile, the nuclear freeze, détente, and the end of the
Cold War.[81]

The aspects of social movement theory most helpful to explaining the
second wave of WAND's organizational growth include the political
opportunity/political process model, especially the components of
changing alignments and access to the state. Also, aspects of the RM
model explaining the stages through which an organization may progress
were found to be helpful. In particular, the changing party control of the
U.S. government and reduced access of women's and left voices to the
state and its militaristic program were important mobilizing tools of
WAND in the early 1980s. When WAND began to go into a financial
slump in the mid-1980s, in part because of the departure of Caldicott for
Australia, it began to go into decline, as discussed by Zald and Garner.
However, political opportunity elements came to the rescue in 1986,
including the propitious publicizing of the diversion of taxpayer funds to
the Contras, Chernobyl, and the U.S. plane accident over Korea. By the
late 1980s, WAND was in a position of needing to further institutionalize
itself according to steps taken after the 1986 changes, including tying
itself to more "mainstream" national political action, and starting, by the
Bush presidency in 1988, to find itself "becalmed," in Zald and Garner's
terms, due to the reduction in state attention to military buildup after the
Reagan years. With the end of the Cold War during Bush's term, WAND
would have to publicize other issues. Similarly, it would need to continue
its growth as both a grassroots and nationally based organization,
empowered to make its own decisions in a new model without its former
charismatic leader.

WAND'S "THIRD WAVE," 1990–2001: BUDGETARY AND ELECTORAL EMPHASES

To continue building upon the organizational review undertaken in 1986, which had moved WAND in its positive new directions, WAND decided to change its name in 1990. It kept the acronym, but to emphasize changes in state priorities and in its own organizational priorities, its new name became Women's Action for New Directions.

Organizational Issues

Many organizational changes were undertaken to reflect the new organizational dynamic, responding to the new political opportunity structure of the 1990s. First, following the selection of a new president in 1986, the executive directorship changed hands in the late 1980s. Since 1993, WAND's executive director has been Susan Shaer, who leads the National Office in Arlington, Massachusetts. Shaer has prior experience in leading the Massachusetts League of Women Voters. WAND's current president is former Massachusetts state representative Barbara Hildt, known for her work on peace and environmental issues when she served in the state legislature.

Affiliate development per se became a smaller priority after the mid-1980s structural changes. Following the lessened focus on internal affiliates, other critical structural changes took place. One was the opening of the national field office in Atlanta, given that WAND recognized that "field development could not be done inside the Beltway."[82] The establishment of this office was viewed as a turning point. Since its founding, the national office of WAND has been in Massachusetts, emphasizing its grassroots base, and the D.C. office, as it is called, was begun in 1982. The addition of the field office in Atlanta in 1996 has rounded out the current WAND organizational structure.[83]

The project of identifying and developing contacts to work with WAND has been given largely to the Atlanta field office. In addition to the change in relationship with internal affiliate organizations, WAND's strategy for coalition building has become more formalized. There are currently WAND affiliates in fewer than ten states, compared to almost half the states in the early 1980s.[84] In large part, this reflects the decline of antinuclear issues as a key mobilizing impetus. Since the early 1990s, there has been a shift in the ways of counting members internally. The membership list was pared down to only those members who are active (either through participation or sending money). A new complication is that people who join WAND have to indicate that they are members of both the Education Fund and the PAC, even though the former receives far more direct contributions. However, in order for the PAC to solicit donations from people, they have to have indicated that they are members of the PAC.[85]

With respect to the new definition of affiliation, the clear new direction implied by the title is in developing officially designated "partners" in a wider range of sectors than those with which WAND built coalitions in the 1980s. As an Education Fund publication states, "WAND Partners are primarily non-profit women's, human needs, and peace organizations, but also include programs in universities, religious organizations, and policy/research groups." They may occur at all levels, from local to international. The basis for the partner network is that partners are "organizations committed to working with WAND to address federal budget priorities so that human and environmental needs are better served."[86] The job of WAND partners is to "share information with their members and constituents about the connection between federal spending priorities and their own vital work," and to mobilize their network and members to take action on legislation when needed. Also, as "leaders in their communities, WAND partners are a vital part of WAND's growing *Women Take Action!* network of activists, women state legislators, and women in Congress." As of 2000, there were said to be more than four hundred WAND partners in more than twenty-five states.[87]

There are different types of partner organizations or categories into which their partnership falls. The first category denotes partner organizations who have actually signed partner agreements with WAND, stating that they are committed to working with WAND by sharing information, materials, contacts, and participation to broaden education on "federal budget priorities so that human and environmental needs are better served." A second category denotes organizations that are currently involved with WAND, but have not yet signed the formal partner agreement. The third category is comprised of organizations that have indicated future interest in partnering with WAND. The partnership development process has become much more institutionalized since 1999. Currently, of the four hundred partners WAND has identified, more than half remain potential, uncommitted partners.[88] In order to keep its national network strong, WAND recognizes the continual need to reach out to and include these organizations. The WAND field office has identified twelve states in which it plans to concentrate its efforts as the most important and likely for partner development.[89] Another field office initiative has been to develop the STAND network, which is college and high school Students Taking Action for New Directions.

At least two other programs have been developed to reach out to current and future partners in critical states. WiLL, the Women Legislators' Lobby, was established in the early 1990s to identify women state legislators who fit WAND's profile of supporting peace and human needs initia-tives and voting for human service items in their state budgets. WAND provides support through mentioning these female candidates in its newsletters and sending people to volunteer on a daily or weekend basis for campaigns. By law, its federal PAC can monetarily support only fed-eral women candidates, which it has done; this activity will be assessed in the "Strategic Options" section below.

Another initiative of the mid-1990s has been to develop training work-shops, when, if asked, the WAND field or national office will send leaders to a potential or current partner requesting it. These trainings cover "understanding the federal budget process" and how to activate mem-bers of the press to change discretionary spending priorities from military spending to social service spending, including that for human rights, wel-fare programs, anti-violence programs regarding battered women, and education. As Executive Director Shaer has stated, "in the 1990s, we planned to become the 'go-to' organization on federal military spending and budgetary priorities."[90]

Strategic Options

In response both to the end of the Cold War and to President Clinton's election in 1992, WAND realized it needed to broaden its issue focus from anti-militarization and nuclear arms control. The ways in which it still emphasizes arms and nuclear issues are evident in some WAND Educa-tion Fund fact sheets of January 1999, which covered such matters as plans by the Department of Energy to develop mixed oxide fuel (MOX) from plutonium from dismantled nuclear weapons and uranium to use in commercial nuclear power plants (with no record on this fuel's stability); problems of moving the more than 40,000 metric tons of nuclear waste already produced through populated areas on its way to being "dumped"; the status of the United States as the number-one arms dealer in the world and its participation in the global arms trade; that in the 1990s, "more than 36,000 nuclear weapons remain in the global arsenal . . . [and] 5,000 of them are on 'hair-trigger alert,' ready to fire within min-utes; and that 10% of the US budget since 1940 has gone to the production of nuclear weapons."[91]

Other issues that WAND has added to its mix include the national budgetary process (especially important since the federal budget surplus identification) and the direction of about 40 percent of discretionary spending to Pentagon programs.[92] WAND focuses on across-the-board military reductions, rather than on a particular weapons system.[93] One identified program of WAND and WiLL has been the introduction of local Better Budget Resolutions at the state and city levels across the United

States. The plan is to pressure congressional members to redirect excessive Pentagon spending to the states to reinvest money in social service, infrastructure (including transportation), healthcare provision, hunger elimination, education and school repair, and environmental protection.[94] In addition, WAND educates its members and partners on the need for year-round vigilance on the budgetary process, including the work of congressional authorizing committees. Another issue WAND has identified as a critical focus is obtaining more money to prevent violence against women.

Like other second-wave feminist organizations that have persisted into this millennium, WAND has identified the need to elect more women to state legislatures and Congress in the belief that this will change legislative and budgetary priorities. Since the early 1990s WAND has helped elect thirty women to Congress, eighteen of whom came up through the WiLL ranks. In the 105th Congress women sponsored by the WAND PAC voted progressively 94 percent of the time, compared to 73 percent of the time for all women, and 49 percent for all men.[95] On average, WAND PAC contributions have increased by about $5,000 per election cycle.[96]

From 1990 to the present, WAND's successes have been identified as provisions for peacekeeping and environmental cleanup in the military budget; military base closings; cancellation of a contract for twenty B-2 bombers; the Chemical Weapons Convention; and the signing of the Non-Proliferation Treaty.[97] In addition, the election of WAND-sponsored women to Congress and WAND-aided women to state legislatures must be mentioned as clear successes.

CONCLUSION

This study shows the continued organizational and strategic adjustments of WAND since its founding in 1980, under Helen Caldicott's direction, as the Women's Party for Survival. WAND has made these adjustments in response to changes both in political opportunity structure and in resources, as noted by resource mobilization theory. Overall, this organization may be declared an unconditional success, having moved from the relatively narrow peacekeeping and anti-nuclear sector of the early 1980s to being a crucial player on the national stage, with national political figures on its board of directors, working to educate both its members and its partner organizations about the federal budget process and priorities, not normally considered an easy or feminist issue, and to elect women to state legislatures and to Congress. These changes have been reflected in WAND's institutionalization, and particularly in its creating itself in a new mold, led by greater autonomy of affiliates and greater planning between the board and the national office about organizational and strategic priorities since 1986.

During the 1990s, the organization further strengthened its funding bases and its programmatic outreach and developed new partners to work with in various movement sectors. For some, these changes came at a cost of seeming to abandon its grassroots tradition, but for others, it was only through these changes that WAND could maintain its viability. WAND has shown itself to be a plucky and adaptable organization, able to change its name, mission, and structure while retaining its core commitment to anti-militarism and anti–nuclear weapons. It, like NOW, is one of the few organizations to have been founded during the second wave and to be even stronger by 2000 than in previous years.

Social movement theories found to be most applicable in explaining WAND's trajectory included political process theory and resource mobilization theory, particularly in the Zald and Garner explanations. As previously identified, the most relevant elements of political process theory have been changing political alignments, especially in 1980, 1986, 1988, and 1992. Following from this, access to the state opened up in 1992. Relationships to allies became important in the beginning of the 1980s, when WAND was forming as Women's Action for Nuclear Disarmament, and in the 1990s, when it was growing as Women's Action for New Directions. Resource mobilization theory has been helpful in explaining WAND's trajectory in relationship to state preoccupations and availability of members concerned with WAND's core mission, from growth in the early 1980s, to a short decline in the mid-1980s, to becoming becalmed in the late 1980s, and to growth in the 1990s. It has also been helpful in describing WAND's change from an organization framed but not actually led in day-to-day operations by a charismatic, well-known figure to one that had to decide on and solidify its organizational structure and leadership roles after 1986. As a movement organization relating to postmaterialist concerns, WAND has persisted and kept those concerns in its mix, and in some ways has become even more attentive to them in its third wave by trying to redirect federal budget priorities to issues of environment and social welfare priorities. Under the presidency of George W. Bush since 2001, WAND returned to including anti-militarism and anti–nuclear buildup as higher priorities in its profile.

The new Bush presidency and its response to the September 11, 2001, terrorist bombing of the World Trade Center and the Pentagon have emphasized the continuing relevance of WAND's message and energized its mission of demilitarizing the policy debate around the world. One major initiative that WAND has identified in its response to the September 11 events is its Women Take Action for Real Security campaign. Based on the five principles of "restraint, responsibility, resources for real security, respect for others, and reduction of risks," WAND and WiLL formulated this new program at a September 2001 meeting in Washington, D.C. The campaign is described as an opportunity for people to "join with others across the country to fight for true national and global security in a time when our voices are urgently needed." It has four action areas: "engaging the media, raising our voices, holding high-level briefings, and providing expertise/guidance." These areas cover many components; under the media relations concept, for example, it includes encouraging letters to the editor, "using radio and television to get our message out widely," and running advertisements. WAND and WiLL's operationalization of "raising our voices" includes holding workshops to help women understand federal budget facts and to share that information with their communities; to "develop and deploy a WAND/WiLL/STAND Speakers' Bureau, using women trained by WAND to speak on federal budget priorities pre- and post-9/11"; to brief federal politicians and candidates about the "costs of homeland security to federal and state budgets"; and finally, "to provide discussion guides/talking points, and action guides for the public," on "costs of the war (on terrorism), nuclear concerns, and homeland security."[98] By 2002, WAND may be viewed as an organization whose structure has matured, given that it is willing and able to deploy a range of tactics in opposition to the president's strategy, many of which were not available to it ten or fifteen years ago. Examples include WAND's ability to calculate and publicize the costs of the war on terrorism and the expansion of its speakers' bureau on these issues.

Some of WAND's action items continue directly from commitments voiced in summer 2001 and earlier. For example, in July 2001 WAND and WiLL released a statement in opposition to House Resolution 195, which commended the U.S. military and defense contractors on a "successful in-flight ballistic missile defense interceptor test on July 14, 2001."[99] WAND continues its emphases on funding women candidates who oppose militarization and nuclear arms, as well as on educating the public about the fact that more than 50 percent of discretionary spending in the federal budget goes to defense spending. After the president's December 2001 statement of his intention to abrogate U.S. participation in the ABM (Anti-Ballistic Missile) Treaty, WAND issued "Talking Points on National Missile Defense." This document pointed out that the ABM treaty's provisions prevented the Bush administration from going ahead with its "national missile defense shield," the utility of which has yet to be proved. WAND also stated that 2002 National Intelligence Estimates, formulated in part by the CIA, showed that the United States was not very likely to be attacked by long-range missiles, but rather by chemical, nuclear, or biological attacks, and that building a missile shield would send exactly the opposite message of what was needed to states such as

North Korea, Iraq, Iran, and China. Regarding the latter state, the WAND points stated, "missile defense will justify the desire of Chinese nuclear planners to enhance their nuclear weapons program."[100]

In addition, WAND has participated in broadly based mass actions in April 2002, including the Women's Equality Summit and Congressional Action Day, sponsored by the sixty-plus National Council of Women's Organizations, of which WAND is a member, and partnership participation in the Alliance for Nuclear Accountability's "D.C. Days." It is clear that WAND's (and WiLL's) emphasis on the dangerous nature of continued arms buildup and militarily aggressive dialogue over the years, from a bipolar world in the late 1970s, to a post–Cold War one in the 1980s, and to a "war on terrorism" conducted in the new millennium, still serves the U.S. and global community well. It is both a testament to their work and an acknowledgment of the continued necessity of "military strength" to a president's reelection agenda that the fundamental issues discussed by WAND do not go away. Another example of the WAND program's continued success is that on February 27, 2002, "House Democrats told the Missile Defense Agency's Director that he should not assume they will support a proposed 7.8 billion-dollar budget in fiscal 2003. . . . Democrats questioned further investments in the program."[101] In 2002, it is evident that neither the need for continued vigilance on arms buildup nor WAND's or WiLL's projects against it will wither away. WAND has weathered the years of being "becalmed" and in danger of being viewed as concerned with irrelevant issues; it is now growing in numbers, courage, repertoire of actions, and visibility.

NOTES

1. Ronald Inglehart, "Values, Ideology, and Cognitive Mobilization in New Social Movements," in *Challenging the Political Order*, ed. Russell J. Dalton and Manfred Kuechler (New York: Oxford University Press, 1990), 43–66.
2. Steven M. Buechler, *Social Movements in Advanced Capitalism: The Political Economy and Cultural Construction of Social Activism* (New York: Oxford University Press, 2000), 47.
3. Hank Johnston, Enrique Larana, and Joseph R. Gusfield, "Identities, Grievances and New Social Movements," in *New Social Movements*, ed. Enrique Larana, Hank Johnston, and Joseph R. Gusfield (Philadelphia: Temple University Press, 1994), 3–35, cited in Buechler, *Social Movements in Advanced Capitalism*, 47.
4. Jürgen Habermas, *The Theory of Communicative Action: Lifeworld and System*, vol. 2 (Boston: Beacon, 1987), cited in Buechler, *Social Movements in Advanced Capitalism*, 47; Dieter Rucht, "Themes, Logics and Arenas of Social Movements: A Structural Approach," *International Social Movement Research* 1 (1988).
5. The term "woodwork feminist" is discussed by Jo Freeman in *The Politics*

of Women's Liberation: A Case Study of an Emerging Social Movement and Its Relation to the Policy Process (New York: Longman, 1975), 222, 234.

6. Buechler, *Social Movements in Advanced Capitalism*, 141.

7. Doug McAdam, *Political Process and the Development of Black Insurgency, 1930–1970* (Chicago: University of Chicago Press, 1982); Sidney Tarrow, *Power in Movement: Social Movements and Contentious Politics*, 2nd ed. (Cambridge: Cambridge University Press, 1998).

8. Anne Costain, *Inviting Women's Rebellion: A Political Process Interpretation of the Women's Movement* (Baltimore: Johns Hopkins University Press, 1992), xv, cites McAdam, *Political Process*, and Sidney Tarrow, *Struggling to Reform: Social Movements and Policy Change During Cycles of Protest* (Ithaca: Cornell University Center for International Studies, 1983).

9. Jeffrey Berry, *The New Liberalism: The Rising Power of Citizen Groups* (Washington, D.C.: Brookings, 1999), chapter 3.

10. Costain, *Inviting Women's Rebellion*, xv.

11. Berry, *New Liberalism*, chapter 3.

12. John McCarthy and Mayer N. Zald, "Resource Mobilization and Social Movements: a Partial Theory," in *Social Movements in an Organizational Society: Collected Essays*, ed. Mayer N. Zald and John McCarthy (New Brunswick, N.J.: Transaction, 1987), 16; Jeffrey M. Ayres, *Defying Conventional Wisdom: Political Movements and Popular Contention against North American Free Trade* (Toronto: University of Toronto Press, 1998), 11–17.

13. As discussed in Ayres, *Defying Conventional Wisdom*, 12.

14. Mayer N. Zald and Roberta Ash Garner, "Social Movement Organizations: Growth, Decay, and Change," in *Social Movements*, ed. Zald and McCarthy, 121–141.

15. Zald and Garner, "Social Movement Organizations," 126.

16. Zald and Garner, "Social Movement Organizations," 126–127.

17. Zald and Garner, "Social Movement Organizations," 128–129.

18. "A Talk by Dr. Helen Caldicott," *Women's Party for Survival Newsletter* 1, no. 1 (Summer 1981): 4.

19. Women's Party for Survival, "Mother's Day Coalition for Nuclear Disarmament, Report of Steering Committee Meeting, February 15, 1981," 1, from the files of Diane Aronson, former co-director, Women's Party for Survival, Arlington, Mass.

20. Telephone interview with Susan Shaer, Executive Director, WAND; Arlington, Mass., January 21, 2001.

21. Sayre Sheldon, "Organising a National Campaign: Women's Party for Survival, USA," in *Keeping the Peace*, ed. Lynne Jones (London: Women's Press, 1983), 31.

22. Sheldon, "Organising a National Campaign, 32.

23. Sheldon, "Organising a National Campaign, 31.

24. Women's Party for Survival, "Mother's Day Coalition," 1.

25. Quoted in Women's Party for Survival, "Mother's Day Coalition," 1.

26. "Report of Administrative Council Meeting, Thursday, May 14, 1981"; "Women's Party Meeting," May 15, 1981, Aronson files.

27. Women's Party for Survival, "Meeting with Washington People," May 15, 1981 (internal memo), Aronson files.

28. Katherine Pettus (president, Women's Party for Survival), invitation letter, January 1981, Aronson files.

29. Janice Trickett (treasurer, Women's Party for Survival), letter to "A Sister in Vermont," March 20, 1981, Aronson files.

30. "Women's Party for Survival Founding Statement," April 1980, Aronson files.

31. "Women's Party for Survival Founding Statement," 3.

32. Wo-Men for Survival, "Dear Friend" letter, April 28, 1980, Aronson files.

33. For a description of the Women's Strike for Peace appearance before HUAC, see Amy Swerdlow, "Ladies' Day at the Capitol: Women Strike for Peace versus HUAC," in *Unequal Sisters: A Multicultural Reader in U.S. Women's History*, ed. Vickie L. Ruiz and Ellen Carol DuBois (New York: Routledge, 1994), 479–496.

34. Helen Caldicott and Mareba Jos (coordinators, Women for Survival), letter, April, 1980, 1, Aronson files.

35. Caldicott and Jos letter, 1–2.

36. Caldicott and Jos letter, 1.

37. "Mother's Day Coalition for Nuclear Disarmament," 4.

38. *Women's Party for Survival Newsletter* 1, no. 1 (Summer 1981): 1.

39. *Women's Party for Survival Newsletter* 1, no. 1 (Summer 1981): 2.

40. Women's Party for Survival, Organizational Packet, September 1980, Section II, p. 3. Aronson files.

41. Women's Action for New Directions (WAND) website www.wand.org/abtwand/herstory.html.

42. Telephone interviews with Susan Shaer, January 21, 2001, and Bobbie Wrenn Banks, WAND field director, Atlanta, February 20, 2001.

43. Diane Aronson, "Dear Friends" letter, December 15, 1981, Aronson files.

44. Aronson, "Dear Friends," February 5, 1982, Aronson files; emphasis in the original.

45. Women's Party for Survival, Organizational Packet.

46. Sayre Sheldon, "Organizing a National Campaign," 37.

47. Sayre Sheldon (president, board of directors, WAND/PAC), "Dear Coordinator" letter, February 5, 1982, 1, Aronson files.

48. Sheldon, "Dear Coordinator" letter, 1.

49. Sheldon, "Dear Coordinator" letter, 1

50. Sheldon, "Dear Coordinator" letter, 2

51. Sheldon, "Organizing a National Campaign," 34.

52. Jim Frieden, "Memo" re: Women's Party for Survival Education Fund, August 24, 1981, Aronson files.

53. "Budget Comparison for 1983–2000," prepared by Barbara Miranda, Staff, National Office, Arlington, Mass., February 2001.

54. "Budget Comparison for 1983–2000."

55. Aronson, letter to Muncie, Indiana, WAND local affiliate president, March 11, 1986, Aronson files.

56. Shaer telephone interview.

57. E-mail exchange with Susan Shaer, February 16, 2001.

58. Aronson, letter to Quincy Shipyard Save the Jobs Coalition, March 18, 1986, Aronson files.

59. "Endorsement Procedure Followed by Executive Director," Aronson files.

60. Women's Party for Survival, "Meeting with Washington People."

61. "Women's Party Reaches Out," *Renewal* (August 24, 1981).

62. Aronson, letters to WAND members, October 10, 1986, Aronson files.

63. Aronson, letter to Mrs. Ann Sperry, January 30, 1987, Aronson files.

64. Aronson, letter to Mrs. Ann Sperry.

65. Aronson, letter to Ms. Cheryl Marshall, April 25, 1986, Aronson files.

66. Aronson, letter to Ms. Elizabeth McGuiness, January 20, 1987, Aronson files.

67. Aronson, letter to Susan Gross, Management Assistance Group, Washington, May 1, 1986, Aronson files.

68. Aronson, letters to Linda Rinearson, board member, January 20, 1987; and to Drs. Helen and Bill Caldicott, January 30, 1987, Aronson files.

69. Aronson, letters to Mr. Frederick Allen, May 1, 1986; and Ms. Esmee Brooks, December 22, 1986, Aronson files.

70. Aronson, letter to Allen, and to Mr. Stewart Mott, April 1, 1987, Aronson files.

71. Aronson, letters to Mrs. Joan B. Kroc, August 8, 1986, and Mr. Richard Boone, The Field Foundation, August 8, 1986, Aronson files.

72. Aronson, letter to Boone.

73. Aronson, letter to Board President Beverly Droz, October 5, 1986, Aronson files.

74. Aronson, letters to Ms. Karen Mulhauser, Women for a Meaningful Summit, Washington, and Mrs. Andreas Papandreou, Greek Embassy, June 6, 1986, Aronson files.

75. Professor James M. Burns, Williams College, letter to Diane Aronson, WAND Executive Director, July 18, 1986, Aronson files.

76. Aronson, letters to Ms. Pam Solo, May 13, 1986, and to President Reagan, May 16, 1986, Aronson files.

77. Aronson, letter to Ms. Sarah Cowan, San Francisco WAND affiliate, August 8, 1986, Aronson files.

78. Aronson, letters to Mr. John Garber and Ms. Roz Winsor, May 1 and 21, 1986, Aronson files.

79. Aronson, letter to Ms. Betsy Taylor, Ottinger Foundation, Oct. 22, 1986, Aronson files.

80. Aronson, letter to Ms. Marcie Musser, General Service Foundation, April 7, 1986, Aronson files.

81. Susan Shaer, e-mail communication, February 15, 2001.

82. Banks telephone interview.

83. Banks telephone interview; telephone interview with Laurel Westmoreland, Director of Partnerships and Youth, National Field Office, Atlanta, February 20, 2001.

84. Shaer telephone interview.

85. Shaer telephone interview.

86. "WAND Partner Network," WAND Education Fund, September 2000.

87. "WAND Partner Network."

88. "WAND Partner Network"; Banks telephone interview; Westmoreland telephone interview; telephone interview with Ms. Abby Hickox, Field Program Associate, WAND Field Office, Atlanta.

89. These states are Arkansas, California, Georgia, Massachusetts, Michigan, Minnesota, North Carolina, New York, Ohio, Oregon, South Carolina, and Tennessee; from Banks telephone interview.

90. Shaer telephone interview.

91. From WAND Education Fund Factsheets, including "Women Take Action: Get Rid of Nuclear Weapons," March 1999; "Women Take Action: Control U.S. Arms Trade," March 1999; "Women Take Action: Pandora's Box for the Next Millennium;" January 1999.

92. "Women Take Action: The American Pie Exercise," WAND Education Fund Worksheet, March 1999.

93. Shaer, e-mail communication, February 16, 2001.

94. Shaer, e-mail communication, February 16, 2001; "The American Pie Exercise."

95. Communication from WAND PAC, February 7, 2001.

96. Telephone interview with Kimberly Robson, WAND PAC Director, February 7, 2001.

97. Shaer, e-mail communication, February 16, 2001.

98. WAND, "Women Take Action for Real Security Campaign," September 2001, accessed February 28, 2002, www.wand.org/9–11/realsecurity.html.

99. WAND, "WAND Statement on National Missile Defense: July 2001," July 2001, accessed February 28, 2002, www.wand.org.

100. WAND, "Talking Points on National Missile Defense," Winter 2001–2002, accessed February 28, 2002, www.wand.org.

101. "Democrats Get Vocal about Missile Defense in House Hearing," *CQ Midday Update* (February 27, 2002).

7

The AIDS Coalition to Unleash Power: A Brief Reconsideration

BENJAMIN SHEPARD

Something extraordinary has taken place over the past decade. Yet much of it stemmed from a single source. For all of my life as an activist, one group has remained a fixture on the cultural landscape: the AIDS Coalition to Unleash Power (ACT UP). I first heard about ACT UP when I was in college. SILENCE = DEATH, the group's mantra, immediately spoke to me, informing me that I should let go of the shame I felt as a teenager about needing to get tested (translated as having had sex without condoms or with strangers). SILENCE = DEATH meant the shame my godfather felt about having queer sex and testing positive was no longer necessary. In the years before he died, his veterinarian wrote that my godfather had had lots of pets as a justification for getting so many prescription medications that he was taking for himself. They were drugs that AIDS treatment activists knew saved lives. Unfortunately, these life-saving medications had not yet been approved by the Food and Drug Administration (FDA) for human use. "Situation normal, all fucked up . . . ," unofficial ACT UP scribe David Feinberg[1] concluded of the whole mess.

As the years went on, the notion that sexual freedom was okay would become a more and more embattled idea. Many of my friends from the club days of the 1980s would encounter discrimination, positive test results, and social derision for their choices to live autonomous sexual identities. By the early 1990s, we went from ecstasy to ACT UP meetings together. One of the most important notions of ACT UP was that no one ever asked you what your identity was as long as you cared to get involved. I protested, shared stories, watched friends die, and became queer with ACT UP. There was never an official membership list but at its peak in the early 1990s, cities around the world maintained ACT UP chapters. Today, chapters in New York and Philadelphia continue to thrive, while countless affinity groups have spun off into differing organizations. This report considers just a few of these tributaries. While I will not look at the group's history in its entirety here, this collection of vignettes serves as a brief reconsideration of ACT UP's history and legacy on the activist landscape.

FROM RAGE TO SARTORIAL SPLENDOR

Fall 1993: we poured the ashes of friends we'd lost to the virus all over the steps in front of the California State House for my first action with ACT UP. I met everyone in the Safeway parking lot at 18th and Market Street for the bus ride from San Francisco to Sacramento. G'dali, one of the organizers from ACT UP/Golden Gate, gave a brief orientation. Wearing faded, beaten-up jeans with "Clean Needles Save Lives" and "Free AIDS Drugs" stickers, leather boots, and jacket, this fierce activist gently explained the best ways to hold our hands if we were arrested, among other tricks. Later, we recalled the names of all the friends we'd lost. I recalled my godfather, who'd died only three years earlier. Armed with a bundle of emotions ranging from rage to grief, placards, and whistles, we marched to the state house to protest Governor Pete Wilson's vetoes of healthcare spending. Drummers hit solemn measured beats. The Sisters of Perpetual Indulgence walked alongside a coffin carrying the ashes; a Gregorian chant droned through the air. The police beat a number of us with batons as we poured the ashes. One of my favorite memories of the day is the image of a man in a leopard-skin leotard, rhinestone drop earrings, and a lush moustache, carrying a sign proclaiming, LOOKS DON'T KILL, WILSON'S VETOES DO!

ACT UP brought that sensibility—a certain sartorial splendor—to every action it did, and in so doing transformed the way activism was conducted. "Who do you have to fuck in this town to get arrested?" David Feinberg[2] wondered during an office takeover when it seemed no one could get arrested at the FDA. I remember laughing out loud reading Feinberg's words. It was the same feeling as reading Woody Allen's *Without Feathers*, except Feinberg was writing about maintaining a sex life, living, and ultimately dying with the virus.

That was the beauty of ACT UP. The group offered an outlet for an otherwise horrendous situation. Sometimes it was through humor, style, and camp; sometimes it was through direct action. The group recognized the subversive effectiveness of a joke, as well as the sentiment that many were tired of spending their days mourning lost friends, possibilities, and sexual communities. "Don't mourn, organize," Industrial Workers of the World (IWW) organizer Joe Hill pleaded on the eve of his execution after a frame-up for murder; ACT UP concurred. Long-time member Bill Dobbs explained the approach: "People have long wondered how we were able to cross the *au courant* downtown life with uptown politics. It combined sex, politics, and brains in an electric way. It drew the boys out of the bars and into the streets."[3]

AIDS/SEX PANIC . . .

The boys needed to be drawn out of the bars. AIDS threatened to wipe out many of the gains of the gay liberation years of the 1970s. For liberationists "gay" was a revolutionary identity capable of dismantling institutions that pathologized sexuality. Their movement would free sexuality from the constraining cultural prerequisites of sex and gender.[4] The overarching motto OUR BODIES, OUR SELVES, which served as both a health slogan and a call for self-determination, mobilized a generation of women's and gay liberation activists.[5] AIDS and the right-wing attack it signified threatened this notion. Panic constituted much of the early response to the epidemic. Sex panics, such as those that accompanied the AIDS years, stem from the larger overarching idea of moral panics that accompany periods of structural changes. AIDS panics become a specific irrational response to the disease in and of itself but are part of sex panics. Sex panics are generally the product of cultural backlashes. "During a sex panic, a wide array of free-floating cultural fears are mapped onto specific populations who are then ostracized, victimized, and punished."[6] Historian Allan Bérubé defines a sex panic as "a moral crusade that leads to crackdowns on sexual outsiders."[7]

Cultural institutions draw parameters around deviance during a moral panic. Stanley Cohen describes the process:

[A] condition, episode, person or groups of persons emerge to become defined as a threat to societal values and interests; its nature is presented as a threat to societal fashion by the mass media; the moral barricades are manned by editors, bishops, politicians and other right-thinking people. . . . Sometimes the panic passes over and is forgotten, except in folk-lore and collective memory; at other times it has more serious and long-lasting repercussions and might produce such changes as those in legal and social policy or even in the way that society perceives itself.[8]

Sex panics organize anxieties around stigmatized groups, from witches to communists to queers. The AIDS panic targeted queers, Haitians, prostitutes, and leathermen. Morality crusades always require their targets.

BATHHOUSE CLOSURES

Long before today's new gay right (Gabriel Rotello, Michelangelo Signo-rile, Andrew Sullivan, and Larry Kramer),[9] Randy Shilts, another gay journalist, lamented about queer sexuality in the *San Francisco Examiner*, the most widely distributed paper in that city. In story after story, Shilts supported the case for the closure of the baths, which he patronized. In *And the Band Played On*, Shilts used age-old stereotypes to describe those on the margins of gay life. The tone of his writing suggested that certain subgroups were to blame for the AIDS epidemic. In a famous passage, Shilts described Ken Horne, a leatherman and an early casualty of the epidemic, along conventional moralistic lines:

> As the focus of sex shifted from passion to technique, Ken learned all the things one could do to wring pleasure from one's body. The sexual practices would become more esoteric; that was the only way to keep it from getting boring. The warehouse district alleys of both Manhattan and San Francisco had throughout the 1970s grown increasingly crowded with bars for the bur-geoning numbers of leathermen.[10]

What leathermen endured in the early years of the epidemic, as their bars were padlocked, serves as a microcosm for the anatomy of sex pan-ics. Even though evidence to link leather sex with higher rates of HIV was never demonstrated,[11] the AIDS panic came close to wiping out an entire subculture, the leather underground of San Francisco.[12]

The process was repeated as bathhouses were closed. Scientific dis-course masked prejudice only thinly. Medical sociologists Murray and Payne note: "Traditional moralism better explains the public health pol-icy initiatives taken and not taken regarding the incurable diseases AIDS than does existing scientific evidence."[13] Centers for Disease Control data found use of the baths had no statistically significant effects. The authors of a San Francisco Department of Public Health study on the baths looked at two groups, bath-goers and bar-goers, concentrating on two self-reported behaviors. McKusick and his colleagues found those in the bath-going sample were no more likely to have had receptive anal intercourse with new or secondary partners than the bar-going sample. Fifty-six per-cent of the bath-going sample reported no anal sex in comparison with 50 percent of the bar-going sample. In spite of these results, McKusick et al. consistently referred to bath-goers as sexual compulsives.[14] Merv Silver-man, the head of the San Francisco Department of Health, who initiated the bathhouse closures, confessed that he had never had data to confirm bath-going as an HIV risk factor.[15] Yet the baths, a significant institution for a group with few safe havens in a culture that outlaws their sexual activity, were closed in San Francisco and New York.[16]

In the following years, good gays divided from bad as leatherfolk became scapegoats. Thompson continues, "Leatherfolk are well aware, too, of their betrayal by gay leaders who distance themselves for the sake of mainstream approval. There's a political naiveté about sacrificing the civil rights of a few for the acceptance of the many."[17] Yet, this is exactly what happened. Eric Rofes recalled, "As a community, we told ourselves that if we were the best little boys in the world"[18] and publicly distanced ourselves from the bad gays, the AIDS nightmare would end swiftly. It was a foundation built on sand. Leatherfolk "know that a duplicitous myth of 'good' versus 'bad' gay people is good for no one."[19] Nonetheless, AIDS phobia was real. A long-term survivor recalled the initial cultural message of getting HIV: " 'So and so I know has got the Gay Cancer but he was a slut.' It was that kind of a reaction, 'He deserves it.' It just reinforced what we had been told."[20]

AIDS panic built on a series of panics, from the Great Kiddy Porn Panic of 1977 to the Meese Commission Report of 1986. Both played on age-old stereotypes and fears. The Kiddy Porn Panic took hold after a number of states passed gay civil rights ordinances in the mid-1970s. In response, Anita Bryant and John Briggs began their national campaign to "Save Our Children" from homosexuality.[21] The ordinance would have banned gay teachers from the schools. Briggs and Bryant skillfully played on the fear of homosexuality and its contagion to stir grassroots opposition to gay civil rights ordinances in Florida, Minnesota, Kansas, and Oregon.[22] Child seduction hysteria was a key ingredient in this initial backlash against sexual liberation. The Reagan-era Meese Commission Report on Pornography seized on the same cultural anxieties and phobias to call for the censorship of adult materials almost a decade later.

Child seduction scares create mass hysteria to generate support for "otherwise unacceptable" investigation and prosecutorial powers. The child seduction model follows a careful schema by which we organize and evaluate information. It assumes "sex monsters" pose such a terrible threat to women and children that we must give up our most basic rights to stop them. Anyone who rejects this assumption either naively or perversely denies that sexual abuse, harassment, or discrimination exists or is a "sexual monster" himself.[23] While the sex monster schema achieves its maximum political potency when used to invoke fears for the safety of children, it can also be applied to those who enjoy nonnormative sexual practices and cultures.

Child seduction hysteria linked queer sexuality and criminality in a way that split the movement. In an effort to gain respectability, many of the "good gays" and lesbians turned their backs on the ravages of the panic. Their silence opened the door for a generation of intrusions of those on the margins of the queer world. Pat Califia explained:

> The police do whatever we let them get away with. They don't bust the biggest gay-lib organization or the most popular bar in town. They close the hustlers' bars, the drag bars, and the leather bars. Right now they can get away with collecting the names of men who might be pedophiles, entrapping boy lovers, and putting them in prison. They can get away with intimidating and prosecuting lesbian and gay minors. Does anybody seriously think they will stop there unless we force them to? There are enough archaic sex laws on the books—laws relating to pornography, sodomy, public sex, and prostitution—to put many of us in prison if the police are allowed to use entrapment and surveillance.[24]

And surveillance continued after 1977. Over the next two decades, surveillance only got worse as queers continued to be arrested for having sex—even in their homes.[25]

SEX PANICS BEGAN AT THE MARGINS

Literature for ACT UP/Golden Gate featured Pastor Martin Niemoller's saying from 1945: "First they came for the Jews but I wasn't Jewish, etc. . . ." In the AIDS panic, first they came for the leathermen, the fetish communities, the Haitians, the prostitutes, the promiscuous gay men, and finally everyone else. Cultural biases let this happen.

In the initial phases of the health crisis, with little information or epidemiological data, people fell back on cultural biases to explain the little understood new affliction. "Early on, we believed it was something that would only hit leather men, then we thought it only hit men in San Francisco and New York, then it hit my lover. That's how we learned about the disease," one long-term survivor remarked.[26] Before the disease spread across the world, leathermen, a group on the periphery of the gay, lesbian, bisexual, and transgender (GLBT) world, were thought somehow to be the cause of the new disease. Rubin notes, "Stereotypes that leather sexualities (particularly SM and fisting) were inherently dangerous, unsafe, undesirable, or unhealthy have been easily assimilated into concerns over AIDS-related hazards. Thus leather sexualities have been prominent among the ideological scapegoats for AIDS fear, panic, and loathing."[27] Mark Thompson notes, "Moral revisionists propagated the belief that men into leather were in some way responsible for AIDS; the perceived excesses of radical sexuality, in this case were seen to equal death."[28]

ACTING UP AGAINST A SCRIPT OF DOMINATION

By 1985 a new radical politics emerged to challenge this script of domination. "No matter how you look at it, you're being pushed," Vito Russo screamed at a crowd of seven hundred as the bathhouse closures were taking hold in New York. "And I don't want you to jump out of the windows. I want you to push back." The night was November 14, 1985. New York governor Mario Cuomo had just signed legislation prohibiting "high risk" behaviors—oral and anal intercourse—in commercial establishments (i.e., baths, tea rooms, etc.). Vaginal intercourse was not included in the ban, and GLBT activists cried foul. Bathhouse closures played into a pernicious homophobic cultural script.

Bad news continued in 1986 with a Supreme Court decision that further legalized the state-based attack on homosexuals. The story of *Bowers v. Hardwick* began in 1982, when Michael Hardwick was arrested in his own home for having sex with another man. He appealed the case up to the Supreme Court, who upheld Georgia's sodomy law in 1986. In essence, the Supreme Court was ruling that the constitutional right to privacy does not extend to gay people. In his dissent, Justice Harry Blackmun argued that the issue facing the court involved a fundamental question of self-determination. "In a country as diverse as ours, there may be many 'right' ways of conducting relationships." Blackmun, the author of *Roe v. Wade*, suggested the right to choose a partner should be considered along the same lines as the right to sovereignty over one's body. Just as there is a constitutional right for women to "choose" whether or not to have an abortion, there should also be a right for people to choose with whom they would like to form intimate bonds. Blackmun concluded:

> In a variety of circumstances we have recognized that a necessary corollary of giving individuals freedom to choose how to conduct their lives is acceptance of the fact different individuals will make different choices. . . . The court claims that its decision today merely refuses to recognize a fundamental right to engage in homosexual sodomy; what the Court really has refused to recognize is the fundamental interest all individuals have in controlling the nature of their intimate associations with others.[29]

The decision offered a glimpse of what Eve Sedgwick[30] would describe as a lack of benign sexual variance. Civil rights laws extend protections to people on the basis of race, class, and gender but fail to address choice of partners. *Bowers v. Hardwick* reaffirmed the usual criminal status assigned to queer identity. Its aftermath sparked a new wave of pro-sex, queer activism.

Vito Russo[31] and countless others like him became involved in an activism dedicated to speaking up after the decision. "Revolutions begin when people who are defined as problems achieve the power to redefine the problem," explains sociologist John McKnight.[32] Russo's anger embodied the beginning of a revolution in activism. ACT UP was formed under the rubric SILENCE = DEATH to condemn the placators. Crimp and Rolson wrote, "Silence = Death declares that silence about the oppression and annihilation of gay people, *then and now*, must be broken as a matter of our survival."[33]

Artist David Wojnarowicz articulated ACT UP's pro-sex argument in stating "I will not stop exploring the possibilities of my own body!"[34] Wojnarowicz's screams, before his death, refuted a culture that assumed gays should just give up on sex. The mantra SEXUALITY = LIFE became a kernel of AIDS activism. Faced with *Bowers v. Hardwick*, the bathhouse closures, and AIDS phobia, ACT UP sought to reverse a cultural narrative that defined AIDS within a moralizing lens. Legal and medical discourses advanced this script by utilizing science to label people with AIDS in terms of deviance and stigma.[35] Storylines were drafted in black and white contrasting terms: clean or dirty, hetero or homo, natural or immoral, pure or impure. Themes of morality and retribution, death, and cancer dominated a story cast with injection drug users, sex-crazed fags, whores, victims, disease carriers, and crack babies. This normalizing script privileged heteronormative cultural practices while utilizing the full administrative technology of the state to punish anything that deviated. ACT UP aimed to turn the storyline on its head.[36]

ACTING UP AGAINST THE PROFESSIONALIZATION OF REFORM

The first wave of AIDS activism was marked by the creation of institutions for service delivery. It was followed by a second angrier wave in the late 1980s that gave birth to ACT UP, the Names Project, World AIDS Day, and grassroots political and semipolitical actions. ACT UP led this second wave.

Cleve Jones, Eric Rofes, Stephen Genden, old-time gay liberationists and first-time activists converged for the National Gay, Lesbian, and Bisexual March on Washington, D.C., in June 1987. Sixty-four were arrested for stopping traffic in front of the Capitol as the Names Quilt, a collection of individual memorial quilts for those who had died of the virus, was first unfolded. ACT UP was but three months old. For a brief moment, gay and queer worlds, radicals and incrementalists, united against governmental indifference to the epidemic.[37] From that day forward, the schism between those who considered AIDS a day job and those fighting for their lives only grew.

For the next three or four years, ACT UP merged its anger with the legacy of gay liberation, snatching the gay movement out of the hands of an assimilationist civil rights lobby.[38] The group's 1989 Stonewall 20 rally clearly marked the link between AIDS and queer activism. AIDS topped the GLBT civil rights agenda. Carrying a banner reading: THE TRADITION, LESBIANS AND GAY MEN FIGHTING BACK!!! marchers chanted: Arrest us, just try it. Remember, Stonewall was a riot.

A definitive battle line of the second wave of AIDS activism involved the institutionalization of the epidemic. To receive funding dollars, organizations needed to look respectable. New York's Gay Men's Health Crisis (GMHC), the first AIDS organization on the east coast, provides a case in point. Originally formed to fight for people with HIV/AIDS, as funding increased the organization's grassroots character was overshadowed by public policy "advocacy" and service delivery. By the end of the decade, GMHC had become an arm of local and state governments seeking to enhance their legitimacy among the economically powerful gay community in Manhattan.[39]

By the early 1990s, GMHC had become caught up in contradictions of the welfare state dating back to Johnson's Great Society. War on Poverty programs encouraged community participation in handling local problems. Successful groups were funded. In turn, many used the money to lobby for more. By the early 1970s, a backlash emerged. Future grants were given with stipulations regulating speech and lobbying.[40] The result limited the message of cash-strapped groups, such as GMHC, who accepted federal monies.

The rapid growth of GMHC fell into a pattern Daniel Patrick Moynihan describes as the Professionalization of Reform (PoR). Moynihan identifies four components of this process:

Profound economic growth.
The exponential growth of knowledge within the social sciences.
The professionalization of the middle class.
The rise of foundations.[41]

Although a new class of professional reformers was employed, there is little evidence that these professional groups were able to achieve their stated goals of reducing poverty or ending the AIDS crisis.[42] With increased funding, GMHC shifted from critique to coexistence. Numbers of community participants dwindled as they were replaced by professional staff members. In the process, a community organization was supplanted by a social service agency. GMHC had undergone a mission slip.[43]

Funding has the effect on an organization of separating the management from its membership base. The base loses influence on the leadership as staff are hired and policy decisions are made based on criteria outside the needs of the membership.[44] The result is that those lobbying for community programs are not sufferers but professionals, confident they know what community members need.[45] Yet all too often groups such as GMHC, undergoing institutionalization, ignore their membership base.[46] The evolution of GMHC, as an organization, embodies a phenomenon that would divide the loyalties of gay community groups for the next decade.

ACT UP, FIGHT BACK!

"Do you want to start a new organization devoted solely to political action?" GMHC founder Larry Kramer screamed in front of a crowd at the Gay Community Center the night of March 10, 1987. Kramer, GMHC's founder, had grown increasingly frustrated with GMHC's reticence to use direct action or use its influence to aggressively fight for new AIDS drugs.[47] A generation earlier labor organizer Saul Alinsky had bid good riddance to a similar grassroots group for leaving his methods behind.[48] "Not only is pressure necessary to compel the establishment to make its initial concession, but the pressure must be maintained to make the establishment deliver. The second factor seemed to be lost on [The Woodlawn Organization]."[49] ACT UP was born in Alinsky's spirit. While GMHC represented mainstream interests and courted grant monies, ACT UP members racked up arrests. To the extent that AIDS activism had been defined by service provision, ACT UP redefined the crisis in terms of sexual politics.[50]

Not long after the Sacramento demonstration, I interviewed G'Dali Braverman about his life as an activist. He had been there at the very beginning, volunteering for GMHC in 1982 before joining ACT UP New York in 1988. The ethos of ACT UP clearly unfolds within his narrative. Braverman, who had known and worked with Feinberg before he died, reflected on his first days with the new group:

> I think the root of AIDS activism necessitated our looking at issues around basic gay homophobia to begin to identify why the world wasn't facing up to AIDS. . . . I had received a couple of flyers in the mail about ACT-UP. I breezed through them and, basically, tossed them. When ACT-UP passed where we stood on the sidewalk, at Gay Pride in 1988, a year after its forma-

tion, I took one look and said, "I am going to go to the next meeting of that organization." There was a sense of power, a sense of action. It didn't appear to be about pity or shame or sadness or guilt. It seemed to be about anger and action. I think that as the individual that I am and as a Jew those were things that I could identify with.

My first meeting was right after Gay Pride. It was on the first floor and it was packed. People flooded out the doors. People were in the hallways. There was no ventilation. But there was the sense that this was the place to be, all the energy, all the focus around HIV was happening in that room. And I just listened. It was probably young gay men mostly, 23–35, physically fit, an exceptionally large number of attractive people, energetic, articulate people. Probably 30 to 40 percent of the organization was composed of Jews. Jews have always been at the center of leftist movements which has always ended up fucking them over in the end. An agenda was put together. The meeting went on for three and half hours and people stayed. All ages, 16–60, the whole gamut. Men, women, boys, girls, parents, but mostly gay men and you didn't know who was HIV positive or not.

Even from that early time there were only a few of us who identified as positive. I was one of those people. I found out in early '87. I don't remember it definitely. By that time I had accepted the fact that chances were that everybody I knew was going to die and that I was going to die and it was just a question of time. It just seemed the logical conclusion. In retrospect it *was*.

Actions were proposed every week at that point. I can remember feeling a buzz in those earlier demonstrations. I'd be leaving my office or my apartment and walking or being on a subway and having this sense of the unknown in my gut this feeling that I was putting myself at risk and this response circulating through my blood of "You have to! You must. This is just something that you are going to do" and hearing myself think, "What's going to happen? Is there going to be brutality? Are people going to be fighting? Is there going to be a confrontation? What is my response going to be? Am I going to be able to stick to our non-violent guidelines? Am I not going to feel a need to reciprocate aggression on a physical level?" As a new person you go through this constant inner checks and balances because you are so filled with a fury. We helped perpetuate that anger in the discussions that we had around the actions so that you are a bottle of emotions with a great sense of purpose. When you were at the demonstration you sustained yourself on an adrenaline rush because you were chanting the whole time whether it was a half an hour or an hour and a half. Physically maintaining that energy level does incredible things to you. You walk away from the demonstration feeling elated, really elated and purposeful.

ACT-UP was working on a multitude of issues. There were probably a good 20 committees existing, treatment issues, housing, local issues, city issues, a media committee, etc. There were people working on those issues that were meeting several times a week outside of the regular Monday meeting.[51]

By the mid-1990s, the group could boast a list of accomplishments including forcing expedited FDA approval for new medications, pressuring Burroughs Wellcome to reduce the price for AZT, highlighting the need for healthcare reform, and pressuring the National Institutes of Health to increase spending on research, among others.

One of the group's more difficult tasks involved implementing the use of harm-reduction principles to HIV prevention. When New York health commissioner Woodrow Myers took the moralistic position that drug users need to face the consequences of their behavior, ACT UP New York organized an illicit needle exchange program in New York City's Lower East Side. Ten ACT UP members were arrested for distributing clean needles. They later challenged the case in court, successfully arguing that needle exchange was "a medical necessity" to stem the spread of HIV.[52] From a pragmatic approach to drug use to unapologetic queer identity, ACT UP taught America it had better face its demons and get over its biases.

Over the next decade, ACT UP would evolve with the ever-elusive nature of the virus, staying together longer than anyone could have expected. Leadership changed, activists died, and Monday night meetings continued. With each level of carnage, the task of halting the epidemic's progress became more daunting. AIDS was fully entwined within the mosaic of poverty. Within this context, the group struggled to maintain focus.[53] To deal with AIDS involved addressing endemic social problems of race, income inequality, and discrimination faced by the truly disadvantaged in America.[54]

In the 1960s, social theorist Herbert Marcuse outlined an idea called pure refusal, a position that stipulates that participation within a problematic system is tantamount to complicity. ACT UP would follow this mantra. Few social movements are able to remain entirely outside a policy framework of the provision of services, and ACT UP's adherence to this idea took its toll, yet the group persevered.[55] Along the way, some found a path to the policy table while others continued to scream from the street.

In, 1994, longtime gay liberationist Hank Wilson reflected:

> I want to be around. I want to fight it. I think when I look at my ACT-UP group, we've got these cycles too in our group. Sometimes you need to ride it through but sometimes it's important for people to keep together. I think sometimes we spent too much time fighting with people we disagree with and never coalesce with people.[56]

Under the surface, a number of burdens wore on the movement, most notably grief. Longtime ACT UP New York member Bill Dobbs observed:

> Consider the larger landscape. Nothing is happening on AIDS. Activist pressure has subsided. The best media coverage is in the obituaries. AIDS is just

one more given in an ugly world. More deaths and more memorials. Continued anti-gay and anti-sex attacks by all levels of government.

When I go to ACT UP meetings these days I keep feeling the ghosts in that room. Marty Robinson, Vito Russo, Bob Rafsky and many more. I hope to get the paper and read that Jesse Helms, Newt Gingrich, Phil Gramm, Ralph Reed and their ilk are no more. And I hope that a now-dead David Wojnarowicz will fly through walls to find Signorile and Rotello and the other collaborators. David will wake them up with that soft deep voice of his and say, "Your time's up."[57]

Cleve Jones elaborates:

You know, it's kind of hard to describe what it's like to lose everybody you know but that's what happened. The people who joined the struggle in ACT-UP, many died, many of them got burned out, or have chosen to stay home to take care of themselves or others. Others have gotten jobs in the industry. As for what's happening now, what we are seeing is the accumulated toll of 15 years of death. People like to talk about what's happened with ACT-UP but the single most fundamental thing with ACT-UP is that they have died.[58]

AIDS ACTIVISM AS QUEER POLITICS?

For a while, queerness and ACT UP walked hand-in-hand. By the early 1990s, this hegemony was slowly falling apart. Queers were linking the AIDS struggle with deeply embedded problems of outsider status in America. ACT UP was as much about the difficulties faced by intravenous drug users, welfare moms, and illegal immigrants as it was about homophobia. "Housing is an AIDS issue! Housing equals health!!!" a cross section of queer activists, PWAs, and social workers chanted in front of New York City Hall in 1998. Queerness, by association and identification with "outsider" status, was transforming and expanding a political arena. Once involved in the fight to end the AIDS crisis, queer identity was never quite the same. This is not to imply that queer no longer encompassed certain sexual acts; it did. But as Crimp posits, "it also entails a *representation* between those practices and other circumstances that make very different people vulnerable both to HIV infection and to the stigma" of outsider status.[59] Actions served to combine both acceptance of the gay-AIDS connection and active resistance to the link at the same time.[60] The interrelation between gay and AIDS identities proved increasingly vexing.[61] By confronting HIV and sexual stigma, activists from a wide range of movements became a little queerer.

Queer community organizing emerged from the AIDS wreckage, bending cultural identities, gender roles, and expectations. Some envisioned a

new politics, which rejected interest group representation, defining itself
against "the normal rather than the heterosexual."[62] Others considered
queerness as an essential separatist identity. As notions of queer entered
contemporary political discourse, battle lines were drawn as groups
sought to interpret and put their often elusive goals into operation. Queer
theory's anti-homophobic critique and its cultural riddles played out in
dramatic ways within the new AIDS/queer politics.

By the early 1990s a vast array of organizations dedicated themselves
to this new politics. Queer Nation grew out of ACT UP New York, posing
profound questions about social categories using graphic arts, kiss-ins,
and political theater.[63] "From the first time I joined ACT UP, there has
been tension over what is and is not AIDS related activism," reflected
New York activist Ann Northrop. While combat against AIDS and homophobia had been dubiously interlinked as the chief targets, questions
about what could be AIDS activism persisted. Northrop recalled:
"Repeatedly in ACT UP meetings someone would bring up some particular incident that seemed to be only lesbian and gay related. Someone
would inevitably stand up and say, 'What does this have to do with
AIDS?'"[64]

By the early 1990s, queer identity was emerging with more and more
cultural recognition. As visibility increased, so did the attacks. ACT UP
did not have the energy to take on both fronts of the AIDS battle—
homophobia and the pandemic itself.[65] Ten years into the seemingly
unending epidemic, the need to outline an agenda for a homophobic critique outside the parameters of AIDS activism became an emotional
necessity.

The group sought to apply ACT UP's grassroots tactics to transform
public sexual discourse. Public space needed to be safe not only from discrimination but for demonstration, spectacle, and joy.[66] Queer Nation utilized once ordinary space for rituals capable of transforming a culture,[67]
queering hostile public space with fun and merriment. The group built
on ACT UP's successful work of occupying unfriendly geography, challenging what had been assumed was heterosexual space. One project
involved planting a billboard with the slogan, FAGS AND DYKES BASH BACK
on top of Badlands, a gay bar off Christopher Street, facing the West Side
Highway. The sign stopped traffic.[68] Within such actions, Queer Nation
broadcast the all-encompassing problem of compulsory heterosexuality
dominating public space.[69]

From Jesse Helms's "no promo homo" campaigns to *Bowers v. Hardwick*, queer bodies were marginalized while Anglo Saxon, seronegative,
heterosexual bodies maintained privilege. Queer Nation sought to scram-
ble this convoluted message of citizenship by openly denying closeting
assimilation as they built on the legacies of the black power and feminist

movements. If queers did not take care of themselves, few else would. As such, Queer Nation called for gays to appreciate a mutuality of queer power. In so doing, they conceived of a GLBT nationality as a fixed ethnic model.[70]

The slogan WE'RE HERE. WE'RE QUEER. GET USED TO IT firmly placed notions of Queer Nationality within a public sphere. Actions included "Queer Nights Out" in the park after a sniper shot several gay men in Central Park's Ramble, and "Kiss-Ins" meant to queer those spaces where violence loomed. Combinations of excitement and pressure, merriment and menace, eros and anxiety always accompany the presence of the other. Through "Kiss-Ins," official spaces such as an administrative plaza or a bland mall became the location for the juices of unofficial fun: pleasure, longing, jealousy, and even reaction—formations capable of producing public scandal or social transformation.[71]

WOMEN, HIV, AND THE LESBIAN AVENGERS

Women endured perhaps the most painful brunt of the AIDS pandemic. A full decade ensued as women suffered from a full range of HIV-related opportunistic infections not recognized by the Centers for Disease Control. As such, many women did not qualify to receive appropriate benefits, despite suffering from any number of OB/GYN related opportunistic infections.[72]

Through ACT UP and Queer Nation, lesbians led fights along with gay men against the inherent sexism, racism, and homophobia endemic to the health crisis. The 1970s questions, however, never went away. Coexistence between lesbians and gay men was not without its problems, particularly as female contributors were taken for granted. Like much of the rest of the culture, ACT UP and Queer Nation chapters were never devoid of racism, patriarchy, or sexism. Conflicts over gender, class, and race tore at the fabric of a number of ACT UP and Queer Nation chapters. And much of the time, lesbians and gay men seemed to be just as estranged along the lines of gender as heterosexuals.[73]

In response to this picture, the Lesbian Avengers cropped up after the 1992 New York Gay Pride Parade. Founder Sara Schulman recalled their beginnings:

We were in ACT UP and we realized that younger women were not getting it together and learning the skills that we had. And we thought we'd just start this small group in New York to teach them basic skills. And the people who started the Avengers were just hardcore political people, you know, people that had been in the Cuban Revolution, Irish Republicans, a woman who had been in CORE and me and people who really knew what they were doing. And we came up with this idea and it just went boom! It just became so large so fast and then it just fell apart.

The best thing was the march on Washington that we did without a permit. Forty thousand dykes. We started the Dyke March. That was the best thing that we ever did. No permit. That was so great because the official march on Washington that year was so lame. 1993 it must have been. That was great. We ran a few ballot measure campaigns in other states that were really wonderful.[74]

One of the ballot propositions drew particular attention. November 9, 1994, Californians passed Proposition 187, a ballot measure banning immigrants from use of basic social services including education. The same night gays gained seats on the San Francisco Board of Supervisors. Instead of celebrating a narrow victory, the Lesbian Avengers marched during the Night of Rage, the next day participating in the student walkouts against Proposition 187. Members of the group ate fire in protest to the state and national swerve to the right, embodied in the three strikes law, anti-homeless ordinances, and the defeat of national healthcare. Such thinking suggested a new queer universalizing politics, opposed to narrowly defined minoritizing lenses of interest group participation.[75] Despite its complexities, throughout the 1990s branches of queer community distinguished themselves by linking the struggle for sexual social justice with broader cultural questions.[76]

SEX AND SOCIAL JUSTICE

ACT UP emerged from a series of movements, community groups, and cultural battlefronts. The group's members played key roles within the feminist sex wars, debates over outing, and the introduction of queer theory into political discourse. And countless groups and movements were born from ACT UP. Former ACT UP New York member author Sara Schulman recalled, "All those groups: Church Ladies for Choice came out of ACT UP; Queer Nation came out of ACT UP; Lesbian Avengers came out of ACT UP; everything came out of it; you know, Housing Works, they all came out of ACT UP."[77]

Yet, by the mid-1990s, times were changing. The legacy of ACT UP's pro-sex position was challenged as a number of former ACT UP members, including Gabriel Rotello, Larry Kramer, and Michelangelo Signorile, argued against the central tenets of the Gay Liberation movement that ACT UP had helped nurture. Long-term ACT UP New York member Bill Dobbs explained:

In 1995, 26 years after we pushed the police back at Stonewall, gay men now spark raids on queer gathering places. Freedom means the ability to make choices, whether wise or stupid. Plenty can and should be done to improve AIDS prevention, but get the sexcops—those with and without badges—out of our lives. Who are these creeps who tell me with whom I can have sex or whom I can love?[78]

What ensued was a five-year sex war between social justice–minded queers and the new gay assimilationists.[79] Eric Rofes outlined what was at stake: "Among the most effective ways of oppressing a people is the colonization of their bodies, the stigmatizing of their desires, and the repression of their erotic energies."[80] Former leaders of ACT UP formed the AIDS Prevention Action League and SexPanic! to challenge the new gay right. The result was a dynamic conversation and debate about the meaning of queer sexuality and AIDS's impact on it.

In 1997, ACT UP celebrated its ten-year anniversary with another trip down to Wall Street as a new generation of activists was coming of age with the group. By that time, ACT UP spin-off groups were evolving into still further offshoots as SexPanic! members moved on to organize countless ad hoc rallies within the rubric of a new formation, the Fed Up Queers (FUQ). In fall of 1998 FUQ organized a small political march that would turn out to be the largest queer riot since Stonewall. New Yorkers remember it as the Matthew Shepard political funeral. Some eighty of us would be arrested within the evening.

FROM ACT UP TO THE WTO

Throughout the 1990s, conversations about ACT UP involved postmortems. What ever happened to ACT UP? people would ask. Over the years, ACT UP members died, high-risk groups have changed, three presidents have retired, yet Monday night meetings have gone on as the group continued to set the tone for AIDS and cultural activism. As the years wore on, ACT UP recognized that what had happened to queer communities would happen to people all over the world. Cleve Jones, the founder of the Names Project AIDS quilt, reflected, "That's part of it. That terrible feeling of screaming as loud as you can scream and no one can hear you."[81] Yet ACT UP built on these years.

Of course, for twelve years before Seattle, ACT UP and AIDS activism were becoming an international movement. After returning from South Africa and observing long lines of people waiting for treatments they were not going to get, Cleve Jones, the founder of the AIDS quilt, recalled a strange déjà vu: "It felt like 1981 at San Francisco General Hospital all over again,"[82] ACT UP made battling drug companies a cornerstone of its work. By the late 1990s, queer/AIDS activists were taking these lessons and applying them to the inequalities of access to AIDS drugs across the world. ACT UP and its offshoots played an important role in the history and the battle for AIDS drugs and global justice. In the months before the Seattle protests, the group pushed for one of their greatest wins.

BATTLING GLOBAL APARTHEID

Long-term ACT UP member Ann Northrop explained, "I got into the streets with ACT UP because I was taken with the tactics—direct action. We don't have the corporate power or the media. Our tool is our public humiliation."[83] In the months before the Seattle WTO meeting, ACT UP used these tools to make Al Gore's life miserable. The problem was in South Africa, where an estimated 25 percent of the population has HIV. In accordance with WTO rules, the South African government under Nelson Mandela had passed a law stating that the country could bypass global intellectual property laws. During the planning of a demonstration in opposition to the African Growth and Opportunities Act, members of ACT UP obtained a copy of what ACT UP founder Eric Sawyer called the "smoking gun memo." As he explained, the February 5, 1999, memo from a State Department staff member intended to convince a New Jersey representative that the Clinton/Gore administration was doing everything in its power to support the interest of several large international pharmaceutical companies in the representative's state in their battle to prevent the South African government from producing their own generic versions of AIDS and cancer medications. The memo listed courses of action, including 301 Trade Watch List inclusions and threats to withhold trading rights and foreign aid from South Africa if the country did not stop pursuing the production of inexpensive drugs. The vice president threatened to sanction South Africa for manufacturing generic versions of expensive patented life-saving drugs. The U.S. Trade Department bragged that Gore had held firm against poor countries standing up to world trade laws. Sawyer was outraged at this information and at the fact that Vice President Al Gore had taken an active role in issuing some of these threats at various meetings.[84]

In response, ACT UP members drove to Nashville for Gore's announcement of his plans to run for president, picketing his speech and placing signs in between Gore and the cameras proclaiming, GORE'S GREED KILLS! By the time the weekend was over, ACT UP had disrupted appearances in New Hampshire and New York, garnering significant news coverage and throwing Gore into a frenzy. Within the week, Gore's rhetoric on drugs had changed and he backed down. In a testament to the efficacy of a smart, well-targeted campaign, by the end of the year the group had forced a sitting vice president to reverse the U.S. trade policy.[85]

Jimmy McNulty worked with ACT UP on that campaign. He recalled some of the direct action involved: "The target was Charlene Barshefsky, the U.S. Trade Representative (USTR), reporting directly to Al Gore, who was that day off to Seattle for the first of the WTO talks. So this was timed and targeted carefully and was the method that would, among other things, raise critical awareness and get some attention that led to the embarrassment, which led people to make public statements which bring the issue up out of their own mouth. Two weeks, three weeks later Al Gore acknowledged, 'the activists were right.'"[86] A number of activists from ACT UP/New York, ACT UP/Philadelphia, New York's Fed Up Queers, and Health GAP Coalition used a decoy to clear the entrance to Barshefsky's office, where they locked themselves down and asked for a meeting with the trade representative. All this occurred within a federal building, on federal property close to the White House.

McNulty explained, "As everybody knows, the whole fucking world is a con game. You walk in with confidence, and we walked up the stairs. You can practically walk through armed guards. Then we walked right into the metal detector. I can't even remember because it was so intense, but I'm sure it went 'beep, beep, beep, beep, beep.'"[87] The activists were on the second landing before anyone on the ground floor noticed to point out they could not go there. Calmly they explained, "This is an office takeover. No one is going to be hurt. This is nonviolent. We have someone we want to talk to, Charlene Barshefsky." Once inside the activists locked themselves inside Barshefsky's office where they remained for an hour before being arrested and taken away. But that one hour was enough to force a change in federal trade policy. The November 27, 1999, *Time* magazine on the upcoming "Battle in Seattle" specifically mentioned the USTR office takeover. The following spring the Clinton/Gore administration softened its stance on defending AIDS drug patents.

There is a famous poster that hangs in South Africa now. With an image of Nelson Mandela's face, it reads, "Survived Apartheid, Killed by Drug Company Greed." By 2001, Nelson Mandela and South Africa were sued by thirty-nine drug companies for trying to produce their own AIDS drugs at cost.[88] Given how many people are affected by the virus, South Africa's democracy is threatened by lack of access to AIDS drugs. ACT UP's argument is that Africa needs the sovereignty to make its own decisions about what is best for its people. Community sovereignty versus corporate greed. It's a civil war being fought on a thousand fronts across the world.

FROM ACT UP TO CHIAPAS

"ACT UP was the embodiment of queer theory," recalled Ricardo Dominguez, a veteran of ACT UP Tallahassee who borrowed on his experience with ACT UP to create a theory of electronic civil disobedience used by hactivists around the world. The point was that a theory existed within an action, a question, a principle. ACTION = LIFE. Dominguez explains:

> One of the things that really occurred out of these massive actions was that ACT UP really brought to the foreground that is the politics of the question as opposed to the politics of the answer. ACT UP was really calling for a single question to be answered: "Is there a cure?" It wasn't that we were saying that we were going to overthrow the state, that we were going to overtake the world or that we had answers. But we were asking the single question that was very difficult, one for the therapeutic state to answer, another for pharmaceuticals to answer, and, of course, one for the regulatory bureaucracy to answer. Why wasn't there a cure? What was going on? What was the hold-up?

The politics of the question became a central tenet of the successful international Zapatista rebellion, in which Dominguez played a role. He continued:

> But you saw it again in 1994, this kind of rise up of the ACT UP tradition of the politics of the question. What the Zapatistas soon learned out of net war was to begin to ask a question: "What does democracy mean for indigenous communities in Mexico? What is it? Is there a democracy for Mexico?" This began to break all sorts of barriers and questions, constitutional questions.[89]

FROM 9/11 TO GLOBAL APARTHEID

In the days since the World Trade Center disaster, the questions ACT UP has asked all along have only become more and more resonant. In the days after 9/11 and before the next round of World Trade Organization talks in Doha, Qatar, global attention turned to root questions about global poverty. Even the often unsympathetic *New York Times* has followed ACT UP's position, editorializing, "for millions of AIDS sufferers, patents that keep drug prices high are a major reason that AIDS treatment is out of reach. Anthrax has killed a handful of Americans so far. AIDS has killed 22 million worldwide. Americans today can surely understand the need to give poor countries every possible weapon to fight back."[90]

Three weeks after 9/11, Archbishop Desmond Tutu called HIV/AIDS South Africa's "new apartheid" and criticized his country for dithering while people died of the disease.[91] In many ways, the global justice movement has inherited the mantle of the anti-apartheid movement: An injury to one is an injury to call. ACT UP has said it all along. "8000 people die every day. Demand AIDS DRUGS FOR ALL."

A PROLIFERATION OF STORIES

In 1988 Vito Russo argued, "After we kick the shit out of this disease, I intend to be able to kick the shit out of this system, so that this never happens again."[92] In other words, fighting the AIDS pandemic meant fighting institutional racism, sexism, the class system, as well as homophobia. Over the next fifteen years, "kicking the shit out of the system" would grow to mean fighting undemocratic international trade laws, the prison industrial complex, poverty, unresponsive government, budget cuts, a disaster in healthcare, and countless mechanisms of a bureaucracy that puts profits ahead of people.

To a certain extent, ACT UP helped open up countless culture tales—from Housing Works' anti-racist AIDS discourses to the Church Ladies' implicit point that AIDS/QUEER activism equals sexual liberation and translates into reproductive rights, to the Zapatistas' use of ACT UP's politics of the question to force the world to reconsider, "What does democracy mean for indigenous communities in Mexico?" ACT UP left few stones unturned while helping us see how science nor theology nor the state was outside the influence of cultural bias or interpretation. No one has a monopoly on the truth.

ACT UP taught us to recognize that AIDS was more than a disease, it functioned as discourse.[93] Recognizing this, ACT UP opened up the storylines for countless movements and ways of being in the world, reminding us of routes outside of imposed ideological structures and expectations about gender and culture, creating spaces for personal and social transformation,[94] all the while placing sex and social justice at the center of the new global justice movements. Without justice there can be no pleasure.[95] ACT UP helped teach us that without pleasure, there can be no justice.

NOTES

1. David B. Feinberg, *Queer and Loathing: Rants and Raves of a Raging AIDS Clone* (New York: Viking, 1994).
2. Feinberg, *Queer and Loathing.*
3. Quoted in Chris Bull, "Still Angry after All These Years," *The Advocate,* August 17, 1999, 19–20.

4. See Dennis Altman, *Homosexual Oppression and Liberation* (Sidney: Angus Robertson, 1972) and Annamarie Jagose, *Queer Theory: An Introduction* (New York: New York University Press, 1996).

5. See Nancy Stoller, "From Feminism to Polymorphous Activism: Lesbians in AIDS Organizations" in *In Changing Times: Gay Men and Lesbians Encounter HIV/AIDS*, ed. Martin P. Levine, Peter M. Nardi, and John H. Gagnon (Chicago: University of Chicago Press, 1997), 172–173.

6. See Eric Rofes, *Dry Bones Breathe: Gay Men Creating Post-AIDS Identities and Cultures* (Binghamton, N.Y.: Harrington Park, 1998).

7. Bérubé quoted in "Sex-Lib Activists Confront 'SexPanic,'" *Gaywave*, December 2, 1997.

8. Stanley Cohen, *Folk Devils and Moral Panics: The Creation of the The Mods and Rockers* (London: Martin Robinson, 1972).

9. Conservative gay writers Michelangelo Signorile, Larry Kramer, Andrew Sullivan, and Gabriel Rotello have been called "the Gang of Four" of gay journalism. In a series of books and articles published in the mid- and late 1990s, they narrated gay life from an apologist perspective, describing AIDS as punishment for queer sexuality, asking good gays to divorce themselves from their liberationist queer history. The most famous of these books include: Michelangelo Signorile, *Life Outside: The Signorile Report on Gay Men: Sex, Drugs, Muscles, and the Passages of Life* (New York: HarperCollins, 1997); Andrew Sullivan, *Virtually Normal: An Argument about Homosexuality* (New York: Vantage, 1996); Gabriel Rotello, *Sexual Ecology: AIDS and the Destiny of Gay Men* (New York: Dutton, 1997); and Larry Kramer, "Sex and Sensibility," *The Advocate*, May 27, 1997, 59. While Larry Kramer helped start ACT UP, in his later years he continued to maintain a sex negative approach toward gay sexuality and publicly attacked queer activists for fighting to maintain queer spaces (see Larry Kramer, "Gay Culture, Redefined," *New York Times*, December 12, 1997). In sum, their storyline of gay life favors gay marriage, the pro-life movement, military service, tax cuts, law and order policies such as hate crimes laws, and minority interest special rights. It restricts gays to a strait-jacketed monologue. For a critique see Michael Warner, "We're Queer, Remember?" *The Advocate*, September 17, 1997, 7.

10. Randy Shilts, *And the Band Played On: Politics, People, and the AIDS Epidemic* (New York: St. Martin's, 1987), 46.

11. Allan M. Brandt, *No Magic Bullet: A Social History of Venereal Disease in the United States since 1880* (Oxford: Oxford University Press, 1985).

12. See Gayle Rubin, "Elegy for the Valley of the Kings: AIDS and the Leather Community in San Francisco," in *In Changing Times*, ed. Levine, Nardi, and Gagnon, and "The Catacombs: A Temple of the Butthole," in *Leatherfolk: Radical Sex, People, Politics, and Practice*, ed. Mark Thompson (Boston: Alyson, 1991).

13. Stephen O. Murray and Kenneth W. Paine, "Medical Policy Without Scientific Evidence: The Promiscuity Paradigm of AIDS," *California Sociologist* 11 (Winter–Summer 1988): 13–14.

14. Lwon McKusick, William Hortsman, and Arthur Caragni, "Reactions to the AIDS Epidemic in Four Groups of San Francisco Gay Men" (San Francisco: Department of Public Health, 1984).

15. Mervyn Silverman, "Addressing Public Health Concerns of the City of San Francisco," in *AIDS and Patient Management*, ed. Michael D. Witt (Owings Mills, Md.: National Health Publications, 1986), 34.

16. See Allan Bérubé, "The History of the Gay Bathhouses," in *Policing Public Sex: Queer Politics and the Future of AIDS Activism*, ed. Dangerous Bedfellows (Boston: South End, 1996); "A Century of Sex Panics," in *SexPanic!* (New York: Sheep Meets Sheep Collective, 1997).

17. Thompson, *Leatherfolk*, xii.

18. See Eric Rofes, *Reviving the Tribe: Regenerating Gay Man's Sexuality and Culture in the Ongoing Epidemic* (Binghamton, N.Y.: Harrington Park, 1996), 3.

19. Thompson, *Leatherfolk*, xii.

20. Benjamin Shepard, *White Nights and Ascending Shadows: An Oral History of the San Francisco AIDS Epidemic* (London: Cassell, 1997), 68.

21. Pat Califia, *Public Sex: The Culture of Radical Sex* (San Francisco: Cleis, 1994), 41.

22. Randy Shilts, *The Mayor of Castro Street: The Life and Times of Harvey Milk* (New York: St. Martin's, 1982), 156–157.

23. Philip Jenkins, *Moral Panic: Changing Concepts of the Child Molester in Modern America* (New Haven, Conn.: Yale University Press, 1998).

24. See Califia, *Public Sex*, 59.

25. See "Entrapment: Are Outdoor Cruisers Sex Offenders? Outdoor Cruise Spots Nationwide Find Increased Police Entrapments Arrests Up In New York, San Diego, Atlanta, Salt Lake City," compiled by *Badpuppy Gay Today*, August 27, 1997.

26. Shepard, *White Nights*, 58.

27. Rubin, "Elegy for the Valley of the Kings," 109.

28. Thompson, *Leatherfolk*, xii.

29. Harry Blackmun, quoted in "Blackmun's Opinions Reflect His Evolution Over the 24 Court Years," *New York Times*, March 5, 1999.

30. Eve Kosofsky Sedgwick, *Epistemology of the Closet* (Los Angeles: University of California Press, 1990), 22–27.

31. See Vito Russo, "Why We Fight," www.actupny.org/documents/whfight .html; and Eric Marcus, *Making History: The Struggle for Gay and Lesbian Equal Rights, 1945–1990: An Oral History* (New York: HarperCollins,1992), part 5, "The Film Historian Vito Russo."

32. John McKnight, *The Careless Society: Community and Its Counterfeits* (New York: Basic, 1995), 16.

33. Douglas Crimp and Adam Rolson, *AIDS Demo Graphics* (Seattle: Bay, 1990), 14.

34. An East Village artist who died of AIDS in 1992. This quote is from a video installation at "Fever: The Art of David Wojnarowicz" at New York's New Museum in 1999.

35. Paula Treichler, "AIDS, Homophobia, and Biomedical Discourse: An Epidemic of Signification," in *AIDS: Cultural Analysis/Cultural Activism*, ed. Douglas Crimp (Boston: MIT Press, 1988).

36. Joshua Gamson, "Silence, Death, and the Invisible Enemy: AIDS Activism

and Social Movement 'Newness,'" in *Ethnography Unbound: Power and Resistance in the Modern Metropolis*, ed. Michael Burawoy, et al. (Berkeley: University of California Press, 1991), 43–49.

37. Jane Rosett, "Dressed for Arrest: The Day the Suits Seized the Street," *Poz Magazine* (May 1997).

38. Crimp and Rolston, *AIDS Demo Graphics*.

39. Stanley Aronowitz, *The Death and Rebirth of American Radicalism* (New York: Routledge, 1996), 134.

40. Daniel P. Moynihan, *Maximum Feasible Misunderstanding: Community Action in the War on Poverty* (New York: Free Press, 1971).

41. Moynihan, *Maximum Feasible Misunderstanding*, 24.

42. Althea K. Nagai, Robert Lerner, and Stanley Rothman, *Giving for Social Change: Foundations, Public Policy, and the American Political Agenda* (Westport, Conn.: Praeger, 1994), 29.

43. See John Meyers and Brian Rowan, "Institutionalized Organizations: Formal Structure as Myth and Ceremony," *American Journal of Sociology* 83, no. 2 (1977): 240–263.

44. J. McCarthy and M. N. Zald, *The Trend of Social Movements in America: Professionalization and Resource Mobilization* (Morristown, N.J.: General Learning, 1973), 18.

45. Moynihan, *Maximum Feasible Misunderstanding*, 24.

46. McCarthy and Zald, *Trend of Social Movements*, 17.

47. Crimp and Rolston, *AIDS Demo Graphics*, 26.

48. Alinsky had assisted The Woodlawn Organization (TWO), a Chicago community group which had successfully fought the University of Chicago's encroachment into the surrounding neighborhood. Like GMHC and countless other community groups, TWO had taken on 501C3 status as a nonprofit organization once it achieved a certain level of success through direct action; 501C3 status regulated the group's future advocacy work. For two excellent summaries of the difficulties of the group and the backlash it received once it strayed from its mission, see: J. H. Fish, *Black Power/White Control: The Struggle of the The Woodlawn Organization in Chicago* (Princeton: Princeton University Press, 1973), and Manuel Castells, *The City and the Grass Roots: A Cross Cultural Theory of Urban Social Movements* (Berkeley: University of California Press, 1983).

49. Saul Alinsky, *Rules for Radicals* (New York: Vintage, 1971), 142.

50. Aronowitz, *Death and Rebirth*, 141.

51. Shepard, *White Nights*.

52. Edith Springer, "Effective AIDS Prevention with Active Drug Users: The Harm Reduction Approach" in *Counseling Chemically Dependent People with HIV Illness*, ed. Michael Shernoff (Binghamton, N.Y.: Harrington Park, 1991), 149.

53. See Steven Epstein, *Impure Science: AIDS, Activism, and the Politics of Knowledge* (Berkeley: University of California Press, 1996), 290, 294; Robin Hardy, "Die Harder: AIDS Activism is Abandoning Gay Men," *Village Voice* (July 1991): 33–34; Donna Minkowitz, "ACT UP at a Crossroads," *Village Voice* (June 1990): 19–20; Chris Nealon, "ACT UP Splits Up," *Gay Community News* (March 18–24, 1991): 1, 6; Rachel Pepper, "Schism Slices ACT UP in Two," *Outweek* (October 10, 1990):

12–14; Dan Levy, "Queer Nation in S.F. Suspends Activities," *San Francisco Chronicle*, December 27, 1991.

54. Nancy E. Alder and W. Thomas Boyce, "Socioeconomic Inequalities in Health: No Easy Solution," *Journal of the American Medical Association* 269, no. 24 (June 23–30, 1993); Hugh Heclo, "The Social Question," in *Poverty, Inequality and the Future of Social Policy: Western States and the New World Order*, ed. Katherine McFate, Roger Lawson, and William Julius Wilson (New York: Russell Sage Foundation, 1995); Richard D. Moore and David Stanton, "Racial Differences in the Use of Drug Therapy for HIV Disease in an Urban Community," *New England Journal of Medicine* 330, no. 11 (March 17, 1994); William Julius Wilson, *The Truly Disadvantaged: The Inner City, the Underclass, and Public Policy* (Chicago: University of Chicago Press, 1987); Stanley L. Witkin, "Chronicity and Invisibility," *Social Work* 43, no. 4 (July 1998): 293–295.

55. Aronowitz, *Death and Rebirth*, 138–139.

56. Shepard, *White Nights*.

57. Interview in 1996 with Bill Dobbs of *Fruit Magazine*, mosaic.echonyc.com/~meehan/DOBBS/Dobbs.html; found under the auspices of a Web page titled, "Surmising a Future."

58. Shepard, *White Nights*.

59. Douglas Crimp, "Right On, Girlfriend!" in *Fear of a Queer Planet: Queer Politics and Social Theory*, ed. Michael Warner (Minneapolis: University of Minnesota Press, 1993), 37.

60. Gamson, "Silence, Death, and the Invisible Enemy," 43.

61. Eric Rofes, "Gay Groups vs. AIDS Groups: Averting Civil War in the 1990's," *Out/Look* 2, no. 4 (Spring 1990): 8–17.

62. Michael Warner, "Introduction" to *Fear of a Queer Planet*, ed. Warner, xxvi.

63. Alexander S. Chee, "A Queer Nationism," *Out/Look* (Winter 1991): 15–19; Allan Bérubé and Jeffrey Escoffier, "Queer/Nation," *Out/Look* (Winter 1991): 13–15.

64. Marcus, *Making History*, 487–488.

65. Crimp, "Right On, Girlfriend!" 316.

66. Lauren Berlant and Elizabeth Freeman, "Queer Nationality," in *Fear of a Queer Planet*, ed. Warner, 198.

67. Victor Turner, *The Ritual Process: Structure and Anti-Structure* (Chicago: Aldine, 1969).

68. Marcus, *Making History*, 488–489.

69. Berlant and Freeman, "Queer Nationality," 198–201, 205, 207, 208.

70. Lisa Duggan, "Making It Perfectly Queer," in *Sex Wars: Sexual Dissent and Political Culture*, ed. Lisa Duggan and Nan D. Hunter (New York: Routledge, 1995).

71. Berlant and Freeman, "Queer Nationality," 205, 207, 208; Turner, *Ritual Process*.

72. See Benjamin Shepard, "Maria," *Antioch Review* 53 (Spring 1995): 156–168.

73. Arlene Stein, "The Decentering of Lesbian Feminism" in *Social Perspectives in Lesbian and Gay Studies: A Reader*, ed. Peter Nardi and Beth Schneider (New York: Routledge, 1998), 561.

74. Sara Schulman, interview with the author, August 3, 2000.

75. See San Francisco Lesbian Avengers, "1994 Actions," www.lesbian.org/sfavengers/old/1994SFAvenge.html, and Sedgwick, *Epistemology of the Closet.*

76. Stein, "Decentering," 561.

77. Sara Schulman, interview with the author, August 3, 2000.

78. "Interview with Bill Dobbs," *Fruit Magazine* (1996), mosaic.echonyc.com/~meehan/DOBBS/Dobbs.html.

79. See Benjamin Shepard, "Queer and Gay Assimilationists: The Suits vs. the Sluts," *Monthly Review* (May 2001); and "Culture Jamming a SexPanic!" in *From ACT UP to the WTO: Urban Protest and Community Building in the Era of Globalization,* ed. Benjamin Shepard and Ron Hayduk (New York: Verso, 2002).

80. Rofes, *Dry Bones.*

81. Shepard, *White Nights,* 261.

82. Cleve Jones, book tour lecture, spring of 2000.

83. Ann Northrop spoke at a session titled "Strategy Problems for Social Movements" at the CUNY conference Independent Politics in a Global World, October 7, 2000.

84. Eric Sawyer, "An ACT UP Founder 'Acts Up' for Africa's Access to AIDS," in *From ACT UP to the WTO,* ed. Shepard and Hayduk.

85. Ann Northrop, conference talk.

86. Jimmy McNulty, interview with the author, August 14, 2000.

87. Jimmy McNulty, interview with the author, August 14, 2000.

88. Henri E. Cauvin, "Access to AIDS Drugs at Issue in South African Trial This Week," *New York Times,* March 5, 2001.

89. Ricardo Dominguez, "Mayan Technologies and the Use of Electronic Civil Disobedience," in *From ACT UP to the WTO,* ed. Shepard and Hayduk.

90. "The Urgency of Cheaper Drugs," *New York Times,* October 31, 2001.

91. "Tutu on AIDS: 'New Apartheid,'" Reuters, October 7, 2001.

92. Vito Russo, "Why We Fight."

93. Treichler, "AIDS, Homophobia, and Biomedical Discourse."

94. David M. Halperin, *Saint Foucault: Towards a Gay Hagiography* (New York: Oxford University Press, 1995), 102.

95. Carter Heyward, *Touching Our Strength: The Erotic as Power and the Love of God* (New York: Harper & Row, 1989).

8

The Disability Movement: Ubiquitous but Unknown

DAVID PFEIFFER

The disability movement is quite diverse. It includes all types of physical and mental disabilities. In addition disability cuts across divisions of gender, class, sexual orientation, race, ethnicity, nationality, and culture. In part because of this complexity it is very difficult to do empirical research on the disability movement. It is difficult also because there is no generally accepted aggregate data about disability, people with disabilities, and the disability movement itself. The parameters of the population are not known. And there is no central archive that contains unpublished documents of the movement to consult. It is difficult, but not impossible, to do empirical research on the disability movement.

The writing of this chapter was possible because the author, who is a wheelchair user, participated in many of the victories and defeats of the disability movement over the past fifty years. Consequently, it is written partly from the viewpoint of participant observation. It also relies upon conversations with other leaders and members of the disability movement, the reading of primary documents, and research on the topic.

CHARACTERISTICS

There is a twofold emphasis within the disability movement. One part emphasizes rights and the other part services.[1] The rights advocates emphasize civil rights, which guarantee people with disabilities equal protection and due process—in other words, being treated like other citizens and in a fair manner. Buttressed with these rights, they argue, the services can be obtained. The services advocates emphasize the various services (such as in-home services), without which many people with disabilities could not demonstrate and lobby for their rights. Today, however, the two divisions are largely melded together within the disability movement.

A comment must be made about the services for which people with disabilities advocate. They are not "special needs." They are such things as access to various parts of society where people without certain characteristics (such as using a wheelchair or being blind) easily go. For example, many male high school students are provided services in terms of coaches, football and baseball fields, basketball courts, locker rooms, uniforms, and other assistance in order to train to become rich as professional athletes. Granted that high school athletic teams have other functions as well, so do things for which the disability movement fights. Curb cuts are convenient not just for wheelchair users, but also for people pushing baby strollers, bicycle riders, in-line skaters, or anyone who is pushing a heavy object on wheels, such as a furniture mover.

Other services include public transportation systems, which everyone can use. People with disabilities pay taxes and are entitled to use services paid for by taxes. In Kansas the Wichita Metropolitan Transit Authority labeled some bus routes inaccessible, implying that people needing some type of "accessible" bus were denied access to those areas.[2] More to the point, if a bus that was equipped with a lift was on one of those routes, the driver would not allow access to a person requiring the lift because it was designated an inaccessible route.

Another example is health services. Instead of providing health services to members who had disabilities, Kaiser Permanente of California used inaccessible medical equipment. One member had pressure sores that his doctor had not examined for over a year because the examination table was not accessible. Another member had not had a gynecological exam for fifteen years for the same reason. A third member was not weighed for fifteen years because there was no wheelchair accessible scale in his doctor's office.[3]

To their credit, once a suit was filed Kaiser Permanente agreed to install accessible medical equipment, remove other barriers, and begin training programs to educate the medical staff. But the question remains, why did Kaiser Permanente wait until a law suit was filed to act? Under Section 504 (which will be discussed later) the requirement had existed for at least twenty-five years and under the Americans with Disabilities Act (ADA) (also discussed later) for ten years.

There are disagreements as to how many people are disabled in the United States as well as worldwide. There are numbers, but these numbers are not reliable. One reason is that there is no commonly accepted definition of a disability.[4] Another reason is the way in which numbers are determined. In the decennial census the U.S. Census Bureau asks screening questions that exclude many people who identify as a person with a disability. The screening questions embody a limited definition of disability. Census data today give a figure of about 20 percent of the population as disabled, and it is widely accepted because the Census Bureau is a federal agency.[5] Other research gives quite a different result.

For example, one study found that in the U.S. population aged eighteen to sixty-four, 44 percent can be identified as people with disabilities.[6] Another study found that 46 percent of the U.S. population have one or more chronic conditions that are described in terms implying a disability.[7] As a compromise many researchers use the figure of 30 percent because of the number of people who refuse to identify as disabled, who may not know that they have a particular condition, or who do not realize that they fit one of the definitions of disability.

Although the disability movement is similar to other social movements, it is also distinct from them. About half of the members of the disability movement are people who are poor, unemployed, unmarried, and not homeowners. Typically they did not receive a good education and lack adequate access to health care and transportation.[8] Many of them are imprisoned in nursing homes, community residences, or institutions.[9] And they truly are imprisoned! In these places, even though they are quite capable individuals, they are not allowed to leave on their own or at all, are told when to wake up, when to bathe, when to eat meals they cannot choose, and when to go to bed. They cannot make the simple decisions that nondisabled people make every day, even though most of the people with disabilities are perfectly capable of making these decisions.

If they do not live in an institution, members of this segment of the disabled population are segregated in public housing or poverty ghettos. If they are in need of in-home care funded by Medicaid (42 USC 1396d), they are afraid to leave their homes because they would lose this assistance due to a federal regulation that assumes that anyone needing in-home services must be incapable of traveling outside. Recently there was a loosening of these restrictions, now allowing the person to travel for medical care and once a week to attend religious services. Yes, they truly are imprisoned.

People with disabilities are often disenfranchised. They are prevented by barriers such as steps into the polling place, which wheelchair users cannot climb; voting machines with written instructions and printed ballots, which blind people cannot read; and instructions that even nondisabled persons cannot understand; or they are denied the chance to register because the public official does not think they can make a decision on their own. In Philadelphia only 46 of the 1,681 voting places are wheelchair accessible. Nationwide there are over twenty thousand voting places not physically accessible.[10]

If a person is disabled from birth or before the age of adulthood, they are usually poorly educated in segregated special education classrooms. Most people with disabilities think that special education in public schools is a farce. There are notable exceptions, but special education teachers are usually overworked and confronted with situations for which they are not trained. In many states a high school diploma from special education classes carries with it none of the prerogatives (such as admission to community colleges) that a regular high school diploma does.

People who are disabled are vulnerable to being euthanized by professionals and relatives who cannot imagine that they have an acceptable quality of life or who just want to be rid of them.[11] When checking into a hospital for any type of care, people with disabilities are pressured to sign DNR (Do Not Resuscitate) orders to be placed in their charts.

Many persons believe that it is "socially irresponsible" to give birth to an infant when it is known that the infant has a serious genetic disorder. Dorothy Wertz found that in the United States a quarter of the geneticists, over half of the primary care physicians, and almost half of their patients concurred.[12] The same view is embodied in the argument against human cloning because cloning can produce babies with a defect.[13] To a person now living who was born with a genetic disorder ("serious" is a term variously defined), this position is tantamount to saying that his or her life is not worth living and should have been terminated before birth.

ATTITUDES

No one seems to like people with disabilities. People in every culture and nationality have pejorative views of people with disabilities.[14] Studies have shown that various groups tend to shun those with disabilities.[15] Disability is seen as a personal tragedy, a disgrace to the family, and/or a punishment from God. People with disabilities are to be pitied and they are regarded as a burden to society, to the family, and to themselves. With such attitudes toward people with disabilities it is difficult to see how a disability movement could even exist, but it does.

In part these attitudes are due to the fact that people with disabilities are diagnosed. They are viewed as having a deficit named in that diagnosis.[16] Unlike members of other social movements they are not allowed to self-identify. In fact, many refuse to self-identify (even if they could in a formal sense) and if possible they pass as nondisabled. At the same time many do identify as a person with a disability for ideological reasons.

People with disabilities are also feared and they are seen as deviant and abnormal.[17]

Ron Amundson does an excellent job of establishing that "normal" and "abnormal" are value judgments about how physical and mental activities should be performed.[18] In fact, disability is a very normal part of everyone's life because each and every person will become disabled at some point in his or her life. And a number of studies describe how prejudice against people with disabilities is ingrained in U.S. history and society.[19] It is within this environment of ignorance and bigotry that the disability movement exists.

ORIGINS

It can be argued that the disability movement started in the 1920s with the actions of some disabled adults and the concerns of parents of disabled children. Earlier dates could also be chosen based on different events.[20] There is a chronology of the disability movement beginning in 1817 and going up to 1996 at www.sfsu.edu/~hrdpu/chron.htm. It begins with the founding of the first school for children with disabilities in the western hemisphere, the American School for the Deaf in Hartford, Connecticut.

In the 1920s, however, there were individuals who became blind as adults, many of whom were World War I veterans. The only option for some of them was to be sent to a state institution for the blind. The ones who stayed with their families and the ones in institutions had but one occupation: making brooms and caning chairs. Not being willing to do that for the rest of their lives, a group of them banded together and in 1921 founded the American Foundation for the Blind. Using education and awareness strategies it accomplished important goals concerning the civil rights of persons with disabilities (not just blind persons) and needed services. It continues to be quite active today.

In addition to these and other actions by disabled adults, the parents of children with disabilities of all types were distressed by the fact that the public school systems excluded their children.[21] They joined together locally, then statewide, and finally (in the late 1940s) nationally to bring about change so that their children, like other children, could receive a free public education to prepare them for life. Out of these two beginnings came the disability movement.

During the 1930s, 1940s, and 1950s various single disability groups appeared and grew to a national presence. The American Foundation for the Blind was mentioned earlier. In 1940 blind people who disliked the idea of sighted people playing a major role in that organization created the American Federation of the Blind, which emphasized self-advocacy.

More recently, in 1961, blind people who opposed some of the ideological
and operational issues of the American Federation of the Blind founded
the American Council of the Blind.

Returning World War II veterans with spinal cord injuries organized
the Paralyzed Veterans of America in 1947. Composed of veterans who
are using wheelchairs (mainly) because of service-connected disabilities,
it is very successful in operating different types of activities including a
strong advocacy program.

The National Association of the Deaf had been organized in 1880. It
was composed of people who use American Sign Language and identify
as a linguistic minority. More recently the Self Help for the Hard of Hearing (SHHH) arose. Other groups such as United Cerebral Palsy (UCP)
and the Easter Seals Society were formed. A group of parents formed the
National Association for Retarded Children. The political development of
the disability movement is reflected in their changes of name from the
National Association of Retarded Children to the National Association for
Retarded Citizens as the children aged and finally to simply the Arc.
These groups and others were quite active.

The bad boy of the disability groups is the Muscular Dystrophy Association. It runs the annual Labor Day Marathon, which is widely criticized
in the disability movement for its use of Jerry Lewis as a spokesperson.
The problem with Lewis is that he stresses how pitiful people (especially
children) with disabilities are. He was quoted recently as saying that if
people in wheelchairs do not want pity, then they should stay home. The
reaction by members of the disability movement caused Lewis and the
Muscular Dystrophy Association to offer an apology. Other groups—
such as UCP and Easter Seals—which also ran telethons at one time,
either discontinued them or radically changed their nature to avoid making people with disabilities appear pitiful.

Are these organizations part of the disability movement? In some
sense, yes. The American Federation of the Blind, the American Council
of the Blind, the National Association of the Deaf, and the Paralyzed Veterans of America all play a role in the disability movement. But generally
the other organizations are viewed by activists in the disability movement
as marginal at best. Many people are appreciative for help received, but
they see these organizations as raising funds to maintain themselves and
keeping this money from going to people who actually need it.

There are many organizations that are clearly part of the disability
movement but are largely autonomous. In many urban areas there are
groups with the name Disabled in Action (DIA). They and state coalitions
for people with disabilities, like the Massachusetts Coalition of Citizens
with Disabilities, carry out advocacy on the state and local levels. In addi-

tion many local centers on independent living provide services and carry out advocacy.

Out of the disability movement came the field of disability studies.[22] It first appeared as a section of the Western Social Science Association. Although the section continues today, many members of the section founded their own organization in 1986 and took the name Society for Disability Studies (SDS), an organization of academics, advocates, agency people, artists, and others (its Web page is located at www.uic.edu/orgs/ sds/). Although distinctly separate from any other organization in the movement, it clearly remains within the movement.

SDS has its own journal, *Disability Studies Quarterly*, of which I am the editor. It is now an entirely electronic journal, which can be viewed at www.cds.hawaii.edu/dsq. In each issue the mission statement of the society is stated. The current one reads:

> The Society for Disability Studies (SDS) is an international non-profit organization that promotes the exploration of disability through research, artistic production, and teaching. Disability studies encourages perspectives that place disability in social, cultural, and political contexts. Through our work we seek to augment understanding of disability in all cultures and historical periods, to promote greater awareness of the experiences of disabled people, and to contribute to social change.

Through scholarly writing, only some of which is published in *Disability Studies Quarterly*, and through its annual meeting, members of the society contribute to the understanding of disability, the awareness of disability issues, and the need for social change.

In addition to *Disability Studies Quarterly* two popular magazines present news and information and serve as a place to discuss disability issues. Struggling against major odds, *The Ragged Edge* (www.ragged edgemagazine.com) and *The Mouth* (www.mouthmag.org) are grassroots publications for the disability movement.

The disability movement is related to other movements in the United States. Most of the older leaders of the disability movement were trained in organizing and advocacy in the civil rights movement. Some were participants in activities of the American Friends Service Committee. In addition they gained experience in the anti-Vietnam War movement, the women's rights movement, and in Democratic party politics. There is a solid liberal legacy among the older leaders. At the same time they recognize that the constituency of the disability movement cuts across both the Democratic and the Republican parties, much to the dismay of some people on the left.[23] And many of the younger leaders share the alienation from politics that is found in the United States today.

SIGNIFICANT EVENTS

With the advent of the 1970s things began to happen. In 1970 the Urban Mass Transportation Act of 1964[24] was amended to require that systems receiving funds under the act (virtually all public transit systems in the United States) be accessible to persons who are disabled or elderly.

In 1971 the Mental Patients' Liberation Front was founded in Boston, reminding the disability movement that physical disabilities were not the only ones that existed. This lesson has still not been learned by parts of the disability movement.

During the next year, in 1972, the Berkeley Center for Independent Living in California and two years later, in 1974, the Boston Center for Independent Living appeared. From these two centers grew a number of other local independent living centers offering advocacy and services.[25]

In 1973 the Rehabilitation Act[26] was passed by Congress. Although mainly concerned with rehabilitation of persons with disabilities, it contained Section 504, which was the first civil rights statute for people with disabilities. The promulgation of the federal regulations to implement it, however, was several years away.

The Education for All Handicapped Children Act (well known as Public Law 94–142) was passed in 1975. Its present version is known as the Individuals with Disabilities Education Act (IDEA).[27] It requires that a free, appropriate, public education (FAPE) be provided to all children with disabilities in the least restricted environment.

The Developmental Disabilities Assistance and Bill of Rights Act of 1975[28] created state developmental disabilities councils, which provide a governmental focus (in the councils) for the planning of services and advocacy for people with developmental disabilities. It also provided funding for the councils.

In the spring of 1977 two events galvanized the disability movement. The regulations for Section 504 of the Rehabilitation Act of 1973 still had not been promulgated four years after its enactment.[29] Demonstrations were held in April 1977 at all ten U.S. Department of Health, Education, and Welfare (HEW) regional offices and in Washington, D.C., by people with disabilities who brought their frustration to the notice of the media. In Berkeley the demonstrators occupied the regional office of the HEW (the lead agency in writing the regulations) and in Washington, D.C., demonstrators occupied the office of HEW's secretary. They refused to leave. After some tense weeks, the secretary announced that he would sign the regulations and did so on April 28, 1977. This event was a significant victory for the disability movement.

One of the reasons for the capitulation of the secretary was the scheduled meeting in May 1977 of the White House Conference on Handicapped Individuals. More than three thousand people (delegates, alternates, and their supporters, most of them being people with disabilities) were on their way to Washington. If the regulations had not been signed when they arrived, they would have forcefully occupied numerous government buildings.

The White House Conference not only aided in having the Rehabilitation Act regulations signed, but was also a notable event in the history of the disability movement. For a week in Washington leaders of the movement from around the nation met, discussed, argued, and socialized. The networking that happened as a result of the White House Conference was remarkable.

Policy victories that can be traced back to the White House Conference are numerous. Some of them are:

- The Voting Accessibility for the Elderly and Handicapped Act in 1984,[30] which requires that polling places in federal elections be accessible for citizens with disabilities or those who are elderly.
- The Air Carrier Access Act of 1986, which prohibits discrimination by airlines on the basis of a disability.[31]
- The Fair Housing Amendments of 1988, which added people with disabilities as protected individuals in the field of housing. Landlords cannot refuse to rent a unit because the person has a disability. Common areas of buildings must be accessible and adaptations must be made as needed.
- And what has been called the most important piece of civil rights legislation since the Civil Rights Act of 1964: the Americans with Disabilities Act (ADA).[32] On July 26, 1990, then President George H. W. Bush signed it into law in a public ceremony on the lawn of the White House.

The ADA prohibits disability-based discrimination in public and private employment by employers with fifteen or more employees. Disability discrimination in the delivery of services, programs, and activities by state and local governments is prohibited. And it requires that public accommodations be accessible (in the very broad sense) to people with disabilities. These statutes and their policy framework are discussed in Silverstein.[33] Appendix 2 of that article gives an extensive list of federal laws related to persons with disabilities.

While these statutes and similar ones on the state level are very important policy victories achieved by the disability movement, note that they all concern basic civil rights and access to society, which nondisabled persons routinely enjoy. Granted that other individuals' rights are violated and that other groups are also hated and feared, people with disabilities

David Pfeiffer

have received as harsh a treatment from other people as any group. Today they are imprisoned without due process. They are sterilized without their knowledge on the assumption that they could never care for a child. If they have a child, it is not unusual for the child to be taken from them by the state. They are put to death in the name of mercy. They are pitied and loathed. They are forced into poverty by unemployment. They are unable to go freely on the streets and byways of society.

This treatment of people with disabilities is hard to reconcile with the English Common Law, which is the philosophical basis for the U.S. political and legal system. The Common Law is set forth by Blackstone in his *Commentaries* where he wrote that:

> personal liberty consists in a power of locomotion, of changing situations, or removing one's person to whatever place one's own inclination may direct, without imprisonment or restraint, unless by due course of law.[34]

Perhaps it is too romantic to cite philosophical foundations and expect society to live up to them. Being trained in public choice under the late William Riker, I could produce a hard-bitten economic model that supports the position taken by the disability movement. But no matter what justification is offered for better treatment of people with disabilities, there is no doubt that the disability movement has won some significant victories and will continue to do so.

THE MOVEMENT TODAY

People with disabilities today are still fighting for their basic rights and for survival.[35] There is no single organization that represents the movement. Instead there are a number of grassroots organizations, state groups, and some national associations that are tied together over the Internet. There are a number of e-mail discussion groups that discuss strategies, exchange views, and mobilize locally, on the state level, and on the national level when necessary. And there are a number of academic programs in the United States and elsewhere that are creating disability studies programs to educate both the disabled and the non-disabled and to change public policy.[36]

However, there are two organizations today that come close to being the tangible disability movement: ADAPT and Not Dead Yet. These two organizations deserve some closer examination.

American Disabled for Accessible Public Transportation (ADAPT) was founded at the Atlantis Independent Living Center in Denver in 1983. Using demonstrations, sit-ins, lobbying, and public relations strategies it had largely, not completely, won its fight for accessible transportation by 1990.

ADAPT then began to focus on getting people with disabilities who were imprisoned in nursing homes out and living in the community. The initials now stand for American Disabled for Attendant Programs Today, although it still works for accessible transportation. There are chapters of ADAPT in at least forty-five cities. While the Denver chapter is the focus for organizing and information, there is no nationwide organization. It does have its own Web site (www.adapt.org) and is well known in the disability movement.

Although ADAPT earned its reputation through demonstrations—such as the crawl-in on the steps of the Capitol in Washington, D.C., during which ADAPT members slid out of their wheelchairs and crawled up the steps, and sit-ins in the office of any public official who did not follow mandated nondiscriminatory policy or simply refused to take action—it is now using lawsuits to achieve its goals, in addition to its previous tactics.

In March 2001 ADAPT participated in a suit against the District of Columbia Housing Authority for failing to make 5 percent of its public housing units accessible as required by federal regulations. Local chapters all across the country also use sit-ins, demonstrations, and law suits to ensure access for people with disabilities. ADAPT is truly central to the disability movement.[37]

The other group, Not Dead Yet (NDY), also was formed around a specific issue and remains focused on that issue. The issue is euthanasia and the possibility that a person will be put to death against his or her will.[38] Not Dead Yet was founded by Diane Coleman, who is disabled, a lawyer, and was radicalized by the case of Elizabeth Bouvia.[39]

In 1983 Bouvia asked the courts to allow a hospital to help her die through starvation while providing pain killers. Bouvia, a licensed social worker, was disabled, had just had a miscarriage, was going through a divorce, and was not able to find a job because of her disability. She was receiving legal representation from the ACLU. Coleman, a member of ACLU, attempted to convince the local ACLU chapter to cease their representation of Bouvia. The ACLU board refused to do so because they thought it was the appropriate thing to do since Bouvia was a person with a disability. Coleman was outraged.

Over the next dozen years Coleman joined ADAPT and was trained in advocacy and protest. She eventually moved to Chicago in 1996. She and Carol Gill, presently the national executive of the Society for Disability Studies and a faculty member at the University of Illinois at Chicago, wrote testimony to be delivered in Washington, D.C., giving the disability movement's opposition to assisted suicide.

Stopping at the policy summit organized by the National Council on

Disability in Dallas in April 1996, Coleman talked with ADAPT leader Bob Kafka. He said that he had a name for her just organized group. Drawing on the movie *Monty Python and the Holy Grail*, he said it should be named Not Dead Yet. Coleman liked the idea and started recruiting members.

The first demonstration by Not Dead Yet, in June 1996, was at the home of Dr. Jack Kevorkian, who was "assisting" people with disabilities to commit suicide. During the same week another protest was held at the University of Michigan at a bioethics conference. During these conferences assisted suicide was put forth as a merciful and reasonable way for people with disabilities to end their "useless" lives. Abortion and euthanasia were presented as ways to keep any more of those "useless" people with disabilities from being born.

Stephen Drake, then a graduate student at Syracuse University and who is disabled, heard about the Michigan demonstration and joined the movement. Today Coleman is the executive director of an independent living center in Chicago and president of Not Dead Yet. Drake, as research analyst, does the organizing, research, and writing for Not Dead Yet. As Coleman said:

> There's never a dull moment as far as something happening about this issue—be it the latest family member killing their disabled relative, the latest "angel of mercy" in a nursing home or hospital, the latest referendum being introduced, the latest conference that again left us out.[40]

And their position is quite clear. Diversity is a fact of life and any law that protects some people and considers others as having a life not worth living is discriminatory. Diversity is valuable. People with disabilities already have dignity and do not need to die in order to have it.

Not Dead Yet has its own Web site (www.notdeadyet.org). It carries out activities to publicize its cause and to protest proposed social policies. It participated in defeating bills legalizing assisted suicide in California, New Hampshire, and Maine. In September 2000 it carried out a protest at the International Euthanasia Conference in Boston. In June 2001 there was a protest at the U.S. District Court in Detroit against Kevorkian's request to be released from prison pending the outcome of his appeal of his conviction for murder. Kevorkian is described as a serial killer who preyed upon the despair of people with disabilities.

Like ADAPT, Not Dead Yet is a central part of the disability movement, which works today to assist people with disabilities to survive through education, awareness, and policy advocacy. They are two of the most active organizations in the disability movement. According to Barnartt and Scotch, during the 1980s and 1990s ADAPT was involved in 219 out of 401, or 55 percent, of the protests staged by disability organizations. The closest other organization was the Independent Living Centers (actually a confederation of centers in various locations across the country) with 22 protests or 6 percent. NDY and the now defunct American Coalition of Citizens with Disabilities (ACCD) were involved in 14 protests or 4 percent each.[41]

THEORETICAL QUESTIONS

In his instructions to chapter authors, John C. Berg, editor of this volume, posed several theoretical questions. The responses in terms of the disability movement are dealt with below. But before turning to Berg's specific questions, there is one problem to discuss about theory.

This chapter is written with a firm foundation in rational choice theory, not the version most public choice analysts use. The differences lie in the way that utility is operationalized. Most rational choice (or public choice) theorists operationalize utility as dollars or some currency. I have (and some other public choice theorists) operationalized utility in several different ways. Whatever a person says has utility for him or her (in the public choice sense) is accepted.

From Berg's viewpoint the difficulty in dealing with social movements from the rational, public choice perspective is twofold: the free rider problem (free riders who contribute nothing but will share in the social, common good), and that the costs to the individual who does work to attain the social good always exceed the return. Operationalizing utility in different ways that are relevant to the participant resolves these problems.

Riker and Ordeshook presented a clear resolution of these two challenges. Using the rational calculus they argued that $R = PB - C + D$, where R is the return for carrying out an act, B is the direct benefits realized from the act that is modified by P, which is the probability of obtaining those benefits by carrying out the act, C is the cost of carrying out the act, and D is the nondirect benefits from carrying out the act.[42]

Riker and Ordeshook were concerned with voting and D represented a sense of civic duty and other things. Regretfully they later dropped their use of the term D.[43] However, as Berg points out in chapter 1 of this volume, the D term (he does not use that expression) consists of benefits from participating in the movement because they enjoy the activities, feel a civic duty to do something, or a similar benefit that free riders do not receive and that is always greater than C (the costs) for persons who are not free riders.

In other words, people are maximizers of expected utility who participate in a movement if the return is greater than the costs. Some persons with disabilities, being poor, rejected, segregated, and despised, often do not receive any clear benefit from the movement and are not active. Other persons with disabilities do perceive a return greater than zero and are active. In this way the disability movement is not different from other social movements. The disability movement does differ in the type of benefits and the costs that individuals bear.

In his early draft of the introduction Berg wrote, the "problem is how to account for such nonmaterial incentives without reducing the theory to circularity." The answer is easy. The incentives clearly are not all nonmaterial. I, as well as many others, have made a career out of being a policy analyst focusing on disability issues and being an advocate. Further, many nonmaterial benefits are of great value. Utility functions of diverse people are different, and it is fallacious to operationalize utility as money, as economists do. It is clear that Berg differs from my views of theory, the rational calculus, and how to operationalize utility.

Turning to Berg's theoretical questions, each of them is discussed in order. The first question concerns the debate about Ronald Inglehart's theory that postmaterialist needs are displacing material needs as the basis of the political left. Inglehart says that as industrialized countries achieved peace and prosperity, concerns with material equality disappeared and a "postmaterialist" perspective appeared.[44] In his words:

> Throughout most of history, the threat of severe economic deprivation or even starvation has been a crucial concern for most people. But the historically unprecedented degree of economic security experienced by the postwar [World War II] generation in most industrial societies was leading to a gradual shift from "Materialist" values (emphasizing economic and physical security above all) toward "Postmaterialism" priorities (emphasizing self-expression and the quality of life).[45]

Berg raises the question if this actually happened.

What has been presented so far in this chapter clearly supports the position that for the disability movement economic and physical security are still major concerns. Of course people with disabilities are interested in self-expression and quality of life, but first they must survive. And they continually find nondisabled people congratulating them on self-expression either in a childish way (they are courageous and how unusual for a cripple to be able to paint a picture or write a poem) or in a hostile reaction (that handicapped person never accepted his handicap). The quality of life of a person with a disability is generally denigrated and used as the basis for assisted suicide.

The key data for Inglehart come from the 1990 World Values surveys.[46] The values that it asks about are white, male, Western, ablist ones. Inglehart played a major part in gathering this data and he shows a prejudicial view of people with disabilities through acceptance of these questions and their answers as satisfactory data. This prejudiced view keeps him from recognizing that the disability movement is not postmaterialist. The anti-disability bias of the survey is shown by the wording of three sets of questions.

The first set of questions asks about agreement with these statements: "When jobs are scarce, men have more right to a job than women." "When jobs are scarce, people should be forced to retire early." "When jobs are scarce, employers should give priority to [name nationality where survey is being done] people over immigrants." "It is unfair to give work to handicapped people when able-bodied people can't find jobs."[47] Why does the wording change to the phrase "it is unfair" in the last question? The first three questions have the key terms "more right," "should be forced," and "priority." In the fourth question "unfair" is used. This switch in wording violates the rules of good question construction because it prejudices the answer. Of course Inglehart and others cannot see this unfairness because of their prejudice.

The second set of questions asks, "Do you approve or disapprove of abortion under the following circumstances?" "Where the mother's health is at risk by the pregnancy." "Where it is likely that the child would be born physically handicapped." "Where the woman is not married." "Where a married couple do not want to have any more children."[48] Having a child born with a disability is equated with negative things such as health dangers, violation of sexual standards, and population control. However, being born with or later acquiring a disability is neither good nor bad. It happens to everyone. Inglehart and others do not see this double standard.

The third set of questions presents a series of moral actions and asks, "Please tell me for each of the following statements whether you think it can always be justified, never be justified, or something in between." The statements cover such things as tax cheating, buying stolen merchandise, lying, suicide, and murder. Part way through the list is "Euthanasia, terminating the life of the incurably sick." Aside from the fact that many people are "incurably sick," but will live quite comfortably and contribute to society for twenty, forty, or sixty more years, it avoids the issue of active and passive euthanasia.[49] Again Inglehart and others see nothing wrong in how they ask this question.

Inglehart may or may not be aware of many of the issues that the disability movement raises. He says that postmaterialist parties (like the Greens) include these issues in their concerns: "they are relatively favorable to women's rights, disabled groups, gay and lesbian emancipation, ethnic minorities, and a number of other causes."[50]

On the next page Inglehart writes that the Green party in Germany actively supported a number of postmodern, postmaterialist causes including "rights for the physically disabled." This support can be found in the Green parties in other countries also.

In the United Kingdom a disability advocate, Simone Aspis, who is also disabled and is the disability spokesperson for the Green party, was a candidate for Parliament for the Greens in the June 2001 election and received twice the number of votes their candidate got in the previous election. Clearly the Green party in the United Kingdom has some awareness.

Bob Brown details the Australian Green party's support of disability issues. He is the Green's senator from Tasmania and shows a considerable knowledge about and insight into disability issues.[51] Another Green party shows awareness of the issues of the disability movement.

There is evidence that the Green parties in Germany, United Kingdom, and Australia support disability issues with varying insight into what that means. How about the United States? A partial comparative content analysis of the 2000 presidential election party platforms for the Greens, the Democrats, and the Republicans was carried out focusing on traditional liberal issues. Acknowledging that platforms are notoriously bland and can be very misleading, the results are interesting. They are presented in table 8.1.

It is interesting that the two issues most frequently mentioned were the same for all three parties. The Greens ranked the environment first (not surprising) and children's issues second. Both the Democrats and the Republicans ranked children's issues first and the environment second. Disability issues were fifth for the Greens and sixth for both the Democrats and the Republicans.

The Greens gave class and ethnic/racial issues more mentions than disability issues. The Democrats gave women's, racial-ethnic, and elderly issues more mentions than disability issues. The Republicans gave women's, elderly, and class issues more mentions than disability issues. It is also interesting that the Greens gave disability issues more mentions, fourteen, in fewer pages of their platform, fifty-four, than did the Democrats, twelve in fifty-seven pages, and the Republicans, ten in seventy-four pages.

A Spearman's Rho was run comparing the three parties. The correlation between the Greens and the Democrats was 0.71 ($p = 0.03$). The correlation between the Greens and the Republicans was 0.67 ($p = 0.05$). The Greens are more like the Democrats than like the Republicans, but not by much. The correlation between the Democrats and the Republicans was 0.87 ($p = 0.003$), which means that they were more similar to each other than either one was similar to the Greens.

All of this evidence shows that the Greens paid more attention (based

TABLE 8.1
**Partial Content Analysis of the 2000 Presidential Election Platforms
for the Greens, the Democrats, and the Republicans**

Mentions by Issue	Greens	Democrats	Republicans
Environment	62	27	43
Women's issues	12	20	24
Racial and ethnic issues	19	16	6
Native American issues	10	2	4
Children's issues	42	96	62
Class issues	19	9	11
Gay, lesbian, transgendered, bisexual issues	6	4	0
Elderly issues	10	13	13
Disability issues	14	12	10
Civil rights	6	0	0
ADA	1	1	0
Number of platform pages	54	57	74

Source: Calculated by the author from the Green Party Platform 2000 as ratified at the Green Party National Convention, June 2000, www.gp.org/platform/gpp2000.txt (accessed July 11, 2001); the 2000 Democratic National Platform: Prosperity, Progress, and Peace, www.dems2000.com/AboutTheConvention/03_partyplat.html (accessed July 11, 2001); and the Republican Party Platform adopted in July 2000 by the delegates to the 2000 Republican National Convention in Philadelphia, Pennsylvania, www.ucsub.colorado.edu/~curepub/platform.html (accessed July 11, 2001).

on mentions) to disability issues in their platform than did either the Democrats or the Republicans. It could be argued that the Greens paid a lot more or paid a little more than the other two parties.

A peculiarity did arise. The Greens used the terms disabled, mentally ill, and blind along with the term government benefits six times. Neither the Democrats nor the Republicans ever mentioned a disability term along with government benefits. This statistic could be interpreted to mean that the Greens think about disability issues more in terms of a welfare state frame of mind than either the Democrats or the Republicans. If correct, then it is not one which the civil rights part of the disability movement would like. The services part of the disability movement might like it, however.

To answer Berg's first question then, other movements may have switched to concern for self-realization and quality of life, but the disability movement is still focusing on economic and physical security.

The next question concerns the distinction between movements and interest groups and whether this distinction is blurring. Berg (in his introduction) writes: "Movement organizations are likely to be short-lived, low in resources, and driven by a demand for justice; interest groups [are] more permanent, with budgets and staffs, and concerned with the material interests of their members." (Berg cites other writers also.)

Under this distinction the disability movement is clearly a movement. Groups like ADAPT and Not Dead Yet are movement organizations. They are relatively short-lived, have almost no resources, and are very much driven by a demand for justice.

Groups like UCP, The Arc, the Easter Seals Society, and the Muscular Dystrophy Association are interest groups. They are more permanent, have budgets, and have staffs. Whether their concern is with the material interests of their members depends on the definition of the term "member." Most members of these organizations pay dues and volunteer their time for various reasons including concern for family members and civic duty. The funds raised are divided between the organization's staff and persons in need who usually are not dues paying members. It is for this reason that these groups are considered to be on the margins of the disability movement.

The answer to Berg's question is that his distinction between movements and interest groups is viable, but in the disability movement there are few if any interest groups. The groups that are clearly interest groups are marginal. In the disability movement, at least, the distinction between the two is not blurring.

Berg's third question concerns the range of tactics available to movements and the relation of the choice of such tactics to the characteristics of groups and issues. The range of tactics available to the disability movement are those used by protest movements in the 1950s, 1960s, and 1970s. That is, they carry out demonstrations and sit-ins and file lawsuits with free legal representation. The legal representation comes from nonprofit foundations that raise money specifically for this purpose and/or (in a few cases) law firms performing pro bono.

So my answer to the third question is that the tactics used by the disability movement are those employed by protest movements in earlier decades with the added sophistication of the Internet. Apparently issues of economic and physical security require protests.

Question four concerns how left movements are affected by the growing weight of money in politics. The disability movement does not have money so it relies on organizing people in various locations and carrying out demonstrations, sit-ins, and occasional lawsuits when pro bono representation is available. It would be hoped that in a democratic political system these tactics would be sufficient. In some cases they are effective, but in many other cases (such as influencing members of Congress who receive considerable amounts of campaign funds) they fail.

My answer to this fourth question is that the disability movement is definitely at a disadvantage because money is becoming more influential in politics. The way to overcome this "handicap" is blocked by members of other movements who will not allow people with disabilities to become employed or to work in high paying occupations.

Berg's final question concerns prediction of issues that will become more important in the future. These issues, listed below, are very important now and will become more important in the future because the disability movement has so much to overcome. It is society itself that oppresses people with disabilities and it is society that must change. This change will be revolutionary if it does not come in an evolutionary way— and soon.

The U.S. Supreme Court has attacked the Americans with Disabilities Act (and to a lesser extent Section 504). Some persons will object to the term "attacked," but in the face of considerable evidence of pervasive discrimination by the states against people with disabilities and in the face of an extensive set of hearings by Congress during the passage of the ADA, the Court in *Alabama v. Garrett*[52] weakened the ADA. With a basis neither in logic nor in law it relieved states of the threat of a suit for damages as a result of employment discrimination.

If the Court continues to weaken the ADA and other civil rights statutes protecting (in a flimsy way) people with disabilities from disability discrimination, there will be blood in the streets.[53] This threat to the civil rights of people with disabilities is little recognized because it is so pervasive. The assumption behind the threat is that these violations of the rights of people with disabilities are not based on myths, fears, stereotypes, and bigotry, but are necessary because the people concerned are disabled.

A second issue is the implementation of the Olmstead decision, which (to give the devil his due) was a good ruling by the U.S. Supreme Court. Before *Olmstead v. L.C.*,[54] states frequently just locked up people with disabilities in institutions as the easiest way to provide services. In *Olmstead* the Court ruled that it was a violation of the ADA and the civil rights of people with disabilities to deny them their right to live in the community where the same services could be obtained. However, states are slow to implement this decision. It will become more and more important in the future.

A third issue, and one that underlies the slowness of change of policies, is the widespread acceptance of the medical model to deal with disability policy and people with disabilities. The medical model assumes that disability is a personal deficit only the professionals can "cure." Since disabilities are permanent, people with disabilities are kept in the "sick" role, in which they have no rights. They must obey the "doctor's orders."[55] Failure to do so gets the person with a disability labeled noncooperative and can result in the cessation of services and even death. Furthermore, people with disabilities are kept in nursing homes because the medical model assumes that that is the only place for them. The medical model underlies the payments of many millions of dollars a year to nursing homes. The nursing home industry, well supplied with money, is hard to defeat.

The fourth issue, which will become worse in the future, is the widespread adoption by states of laws that allow mental health professionals to enter the homes of people with disabilities and to force them to take medications. They also can monitor and control the personal lives of people with disabilities without any showing that there is some danger to themselves or to others.

The fifth issue is euthanasia and assisted suicide. The discussion of the issue in the United States (and worldwide) is based on the tacit assumption that people with disabilities are better off dead, that they cannot possibly have a satisfactory quality of life. Not Dead Yet is a forceful opposition to this movement, but the popular discussion of cloning human beings has injected a fresh principle that "defective," that is, disabled, infants are better off never born.

These are some of the important issues facing the members of the disability movement in addition to questions of economic and physical security. If these issues continue to unfold in the way they are today, then the future for people with disabilities is dark.

CONCLUSION

In the introduction to this volume John Berg wrote:

> The movements discussed in this book are united, first of all, by the sense that they have a common enemy. They are less united about how that enemy should be defined—"capitalism," "the corporations," "imperialism," or "the power structure," for example—but they have more or less the same social forces in mind, whatever the term.

Berg is wrong in his assumption that the disability movement sees certain elements of society as a common enemy.

The disability movement is different from the other movements discussed in this book. The people in the disability movement see all of society as the enemy. To use Berg's examples, capitalists and workers, corporations and the public, the imperialists and the dispossessed, and persons in and out of the power structure all tend to loathe people with disabilities and want them out of the way. Because of the way people with disabilities are treated, the disability movement has no interest in joining some new, broad movement.

Why is this pervasive dislike and oppression of people with disabilities not perceived by people in the other movements? Simply because it is so pervasive. The workers, the public, the dispossessed, and the powerless are not seen as being such because of a deficit in them, while people with disabilities are seen to have a deficit (named by their so-called disability), which makes their unjust, prejudiced treatment seem to be natural. Building codes ensured the lack of ramps and curb cuts while requiring two exits and certain types of building materials in the name of a fire code. Educational policy required the offering of foreign languages while not recognizing Braille and American Sign Language as languages. Because people with disabilities are seen to be abnormal, their civil rights can be routinely violated.

The disability movement will continue to fight this oppression using the tools available to it. Unless changes happen in society, there will be no disability movement nor people with disabilities. Their "useless" lives will be terminated.

NOTES

1. Doris Zames Fleischer and Frieda Zames, *The Disability Rights Movement: From Charity to Confrontation* (Philadelphia: Temple University Press, 2001), chapter 12; Steve Brown, *Freedom of Movement* (Houston: ILRU, 2000); David Pfeiffer, "Divisions in the Disability Community," *Disability Studies Quarterly* 8, no. 2 (Spring 1988): 1–3; Gerben DeJong, "Defining and Implementing the Independent Living Concept," in *Independent Living for Physically Disabled People*, ed. Nancy M. Crewe, Irving Kenneth Zola, and Associates (San Francisco: Jossey-Bass, 1983), chapter 1.

2. *Incitement* (Winter/Spring, 2001): 11. *Incitement* is the newsletter of American Disabled for Attendant Programs Today (ADAPT).

3. *Incitement* (Winter/Spring 2001): 10.

4. Robert Silverstein, "Emerging Disability Policy Framework: A Guidepost for Analyzing Public Policy," *Iowa Law Review* 85, no. 5 (2000): 1715–1718.

5. U.S. Census Bureau, "Americans with Disabilities: 1997," accessed July 20, 2002 www.census.gov/hhes/www/disable/sipp/disab97/asc97.html. Data are from the 1996 panel of the Survey of Income and Program Participation.

6. Barbara M. Altman, "Definitions of Disability and Their Operationalization and Measurement in Survey Data: An Update," *Research in Social Science and Disability* 2 (2001): 77–100.

7. Catherine Hoffman, Dorothy Rice, and Hai-Yen Sung, "Persons with Chronic Conditions: Their Prevalence and Costs," *Journal of the American Medical Association* 276, no. 18 (1996): 1473–1479.

8. National Organization on Disability, *2000 N.O.D./Harris Survey of Americans with Disabilities* (New York: Harris Interactive, 2000), 12–17.

9. Myron G. Eisenberg, Cynthia Griggins, and Richard J. Duval, eds., *Disabled People as Second-Class Citizens* (New York: Springer, 1982); Sonny Kleinfield, *The Hidden Minority*, (Boston: Little, Brown, 1979).

10. "Philadelphia Lawsuit Puts Focus on Voting Booth Accessibility," *wemedia* (June/July 2001): 15.

11. Henry R. Glick and Amy Hutchinson, "The Rising Agenda of Physician-Assisted Suicide: Explaining the Growth and Content of Morality Policy," *Policy Studies Journal* 27, no. 4 (1999): 750–765; David Pfeiffer, "Eugenics and Disability Discrimination," *Disability & Society* 9 (1994): 481–499; Peter Singer, "On Being Silenced in Germany, *New York Review of Books*, August 5, 1991, 36–42; Peter Singer, *Practical Ethics*, 2d ed. (New York: Cambridge University Press, 1995); Jack Kevorkian, *Prescription: Medicide—The Goodness of Planned Death* (Amherst, N.Y.: Prometheus, 1991); Garland E. Allen, "The Eugenics Record Office at Cold Spring Harbor, 1910–1940: An Essay in Institutional History," *Osiris*, 2d Series, 2 (1986): 225–264; Helga Kuhse and Peter Singer, *Should the Baby Live? The Problem of Handicapped Infants* (Oxford: Oxford University Press, 1985).

12. Dorothy C. Wertz, "Eugenics Is Alive and Well: A Survey of Genetic Professionals Around the World," *Science in Context* 11, no. 3–4 (1998): 100–109.

13. John Travis, "Dolly Was Lucky: Scientists Warn that Cloning Is Too Dangerous for People," *Science News* 160, no. 16 (October 20, 2001): 250–252.

14. K. Heyer, "Between Equality and Difference: The Politics of Disability in Japan," *Japanstudien* 11 (2000): 105–133; K. Heyer, "From Special Needs to Equal Rights: Japanese Disability Law," *Asian-Pacific Law & Policy Journal* 1 (2000), accessed October 17, 2001, www.hawaii.edu/aplpj/pdfs/7-kh.pdf; M. Miles, "Disability on a Different Model: Glimpses of an Asian Heritage," *Disability & Society* 15 (2000): 603–618; J. Paterson and M. Jamieson, "The Attitudes of Community Based Rehabilitation Workers Towards People with Disabilities in South India," *International Journal of Rehabilitation Research* 22 (1999): 85–92; Colin Barnes, "Theories of Disability and the Origin of Oppression of Disabled People in Western Society," in *Disability and Society: Emerging Issues and Insights*, ed. L. Barton (Essex: Addison Wesley Longman, 1996); M. T. Westbrook and V. Legge, "Health Practitioners' Perceptions of Family Attitudes Toward Children with Disabilities: A Comparison of Six Communities in a Multicultural Society," *Rehabilitation Psychology* 38 (1993): 177–185; R. E. Hardy, J. G. Cull, and M. E. Campbell, "Perception of Selected Disabilities in the United States and Portugal: A Cross-Cultural Comparison," *Journal of Human Behavior & Learning* 4 (1987): 1–12.

15. M. Turmusani, "The Economic Needs of Disabled People in Jordan: From the Personal to the Political Perspective," *Disability Studies Quarterly* 19 (1999): 40–54; L. Habib, *Gender and Disability: Women's Experience in the Middle East* (London: Oxfam, 1998); A. Rose, "'Who Causes the Blind to See': Disability and Quality of Religious Life," *Disability & Society* 12 (1997): 395–405; B. Ingstad and S. Whyte, *Disability and Culture* (Berkeley: University of California Press, 1995); M. Miles, "Disability in an Eastern Religious Context: Historical Perspectives," *Disability & Society* 10 (1995): 49–68; N. L. Mary, "Reactions of Black, Hispanic, and

White Mothers to Having a Child with Handicaps," *Mental Retardation* (1990) 28: 1–5; M. Mardiros, "Conception of Childhood Disability among Mexican-American Parents," *Medical Anthropology* 12 (1989): 55–68; R. P. Strauss, "Genetic Counseling in the Cross Cultural Context: The Case of Highly Observant Judaism," *Patient Education & Counseling* 11 (1988): 43–52; P. Abberely, "The Concept of Oppression and the Development of a Social Theory of Disability," *Disability & Society* 2 (1987): 19–55.

16. David Pfeiffer, "The ICIDH and the Need for Its Revision," *Disability & Society* 13 (1998): 503–523.

17. Uta Gerhardt, *Ideas About Illness: An Intellectual and Political History of Medical Sociology* (New York: New York University Press, 1989); Erving Goffman, *Stigma: Notes on the Management of Spoiled Identity* (Englewood Cliffs, N.J.: Prentice-Hall, 1963).

18. Ron Amundson, "Against Normal Function," *Studies in History and Philosophy of Biological and Biomedical Sciences* 31, no. 1 (2000): 33–53.

19. Douglas C. Baynton, "Disability and the Justification of Inequality in American History," in *The New Disability History: American Perspectives*, ed. Paul K. Longmore and Lauri Umansky (New York: New York University Press, 2001), 33–57; Paul K. Longmore and Lauri Umansky, "Introduction: Disability History: From the Margins to the Mainstream," in Longmore and Umansky, *The New Disability History*, 1–32; Fleischer and Zames, *The Disability Rights Movement*.

20. C. W. Bledsoe, "Dr. Samuel Gridley Howe and the Family Tree of Residential Schools," *Journal of Visual Impairment and Blindness*, 87, no. 6 (1993): 174–176; Paul K. Longmore and David Goldberger, "The League of the Physically Handicapped and the Great Depression: A Case Study in the New Disability History," *Journal of American History*, 87, no. 3 (2000): 888–922.

21. Fleischer and Zames, *The Disability Rights Movement*, chapters 1 and 2; J. B. Fine, "Catalysts for Change: Parents of the Handicapped, 1930–1960," Ph.D. dissertation, Loyola University of Chicago, 1989.

22. David Pfeiffer, "The Disability Paradigm," in *Disability Policy: Issues and Implications for the New Millennium—A Report on the 21st Mary E. Switzer Memorial Seminar, Held September 1999*, ed. L. Robert McConnell and Carl E. Hansen (Alexandria, Va.: National Rehabilitation Association, 2000), 81–82 [reprinted in *Journal of Disability Policy Studies* 11, no. 2 (Fall 2000): 98–99]; Susan Brown, ed., *An Independent Living Approach to Disability Policy Studies* (Oakland, Calif.: World Institute on Disability, 1993); David Pfeiffer and Alexa Novak-Krajewski, "The Emergence of Disability Studies," *AHSSPPE Bulletin* 1 (1983): 116–122.

23. Ravi Malhotra, "The Politics of the Disability Rights Movements," *New Politics* 8, no. 3 (New Series) (2001): 65–75.

24. 49 USC 1612.

25. Fleischer and Zames, *The Disability Rights Movement*, chapter 3.

26. 29 USC 790.

27. 20 USC 1400; see Fleischer and Zames, *The Disability Rights Movement*, chapter 11; Richard Bryant Treanor, *We Overcame: The Story of Civil Rights for Disabled People* (Falls Church, Va.: Regal Direct, 1993).

28. 42 USC 6001.

29. Fleischer and Zames, *The Disability Rights Movement*, chapter 4; Richard Scotch, *From Good Will to Civil Rights: Transforming Federal Disability Policy*, 2d ed. (Philadelphia: Temple University Press, 2001), chapter 5; Treanor, *We Overcame*, chapters 3 and 4.

30. PL 98–435.

31. PL 99–435; see Treanor, *We Overcame*, chapter 8.

32. 42 USC 12100; see Fleischer and Zames, *The Disability Rights Movement*, chapter 6; National Council on Disability, *Equality of Opportunity: The Making of the Americans with Disabilities Act* (Washington, D.C.: Author, 1997); Treanor, *We Overcame*, chapters 6 and 7.

33. Silverstein, "Emerging Disability Policy Framework."

34. Quoted in Robert L. Burgdorf, *The Legal Rights of Handicapped Persons* (Baltimore: Paul H. Brookes, 1980), 442.

35. David Pfeiffer, "Overview of the Disability Movement: History, Legislative Record, and Political Implications," *Policy Studies Journal* 21 (1993): 724–734.

36. Devva Kasnitz, Sharon Bonney, Raffi Aftandelian, and David Pfeiffer, "Programs and Courses in Disability Studies at Universities and Colleges in Canada, Australia, the United States, the United Kingdom, and Norway," *Disability Studies Quarterly* 20, no. 2 (2000): 155–184.

37. *Incitement* (Winter/Spring 2001): 5, 12–19.

38. Fleischer and Zames, *The Disability Rights Movement*, chapter 8.

39. Laura Hershey, "Dedicated Couple Leading the Not Dead Yet Movement," accessed October 17, 2001, www.cando.com.

40. Quoted in Hershey, "Dedicated Couple."

41. Sharon N. Barnartt, and Richard Scotch, *Disability Protests: Contentious Politics, 1970–1999* (Washington, D.C.: Gallaudet University Press, 2001).

42. William H. Riker and Peter C. Ordeshook, "A Theory of the Calculus of Voting," *American Political Science Review* 63 (1968): 25–43.

43. William H. Riker and Peter C. Ordeshook, *An Introduction to Positive Political Theory* (Englewood Cliffs, N.J.: Prentice-Hall, 1973), 62–65.

44. Ronald Inglehart, *Culture Shift in Advanced Industrial Society* (Princeton, N.J.: Princeton University Press, 1990), 5367; Inglehart, *Modernization and Postmodernization: Cultural, Economic, and Political Change in 43 Societies* (Princeton, N.J.: Princeton University Press, 1997), 4.

45. Inglehart, *Modernization and Postmodernization*, page 4.

46. Inglehart, *Modernization and Postmodernization*, Appendix 5.

47. Inglehart, *Modernization and Postmodernization*, 402. The questions quoted are V128,V129, V130, and V131 of the World Values survey.

48. Inglehart, *Modernization and Postmodernization*, 412, World Values survey items V237-V240.

49. Inglehart, *Modernization and Postmodernization*, 420–421, World Values survey item V312.

50. Inglehart, *Modernization and Postmodernization*, 244.

51. Bob Brown, "The Greens on Disability Issues," *Access: The National Issues Journal for People with a Disability* 3, no. 3 (June–July, 2001): 3–6.

52. U.S. Supreme Court, *Alabama v. Garrett*, 99–1240, February 2001.

53. David Pfeiffer, "'We Won't Go Back': The ADA on the Grass Roots Level," *Disability & Society* 11, no. 2 (1996): 271–284.

54. U.S. Supreme Court, *Olmstead v. L. C.*, 527 US 581, 1999.

55. Talcott Parsons, "Illness and the Role of the Physician: A Sociological Perspective," *American Journal of Orthopsychiatry* 2 (1957): 146–150; "The Sick Role and the Role of the Physician Reconsidered," *Health and Society* 53 (1975): 257–278.

Part III

ALTRUISTIC MOVEMENTS

9

Growing Green: Can It Happen Here?

JAMES R. SIMMONS AND SOLON J. SIMMONS

Among the new social movements that have emerged over the past forty years in the advanced industrial countries, the Green movement is one of the most promising. In nearly every Western nation the Greens social movement has undertaken perhaps the first sustained and substantial challenge to the hierarchical model of modern institutions with an alternative vision of direct democracy, social justice, rotating leadership, and a merger of the personal and the political.[1] In much of Europe, Green parties are a complex confluence of social movements that have come to realize that winning state power is the only way to influence decision making. They are also a repository for all those who are disaffected or apolitical and feel they have nowhere else to go. Placing them on the conventional ideological continuum is difficult. While their antagonism to big corporations, the military, and traditional morality places them close to the left, they are also part of a naturalistic and communitarian tendency that is hostile to rapid industrial or agricultural development and some forms of technological change.

The Green parties have become a regular feature of European elections. In countries like France and Germany they are often partners with the Social Democrats, hold ministerial positions, and have won concessions on policies like nuclear power, mass transit, and eco-taxes. The United States, however, remains "exceptional" in that it has stood alone as the only major Western industrial country without a significant Green political formation. Even though there have been attempts to create a U.S. Green party at least as early as the formation of the Citizens party in 1979, most of these efforts by U.S. Greens have been off the radar screen of the nation's mass media and therefore have gone largely unnoticed by the general public. Nevertheless, a Green movement did develop here by fits and starts in the mid-1980s. Its many heterogeneous affiliates had been unobtrusively active at the state and local levels in various parts of the country until the 2000 presidential election finally placed the party into the public eye.

In the United States the environmental movement has been very large and active, but because of the confining features of the two-party system, it has been restricted to pressure group activity or protest. From the outset during the Progressive era, this movement has been torn by a debate over priorities, strategies, tactics, management, and organizational forms. Although the common denominator has always been the environment, the multiple and competing organizations of this heterogeneous movement are made up of a complex amalgam of pragmatic reformers, conservatives, radicals, professionals, and volunteers. The U.S. Greens constitute a value-oriented environmentalism that wants to change the way society operates. While it distrusts efforts to work through conventional political processes and organizations, it also contends that neither protest nor pressure will ensure sustainable systemic transformation.

In this chapter we want to examine and attempt to answer the question that asks if a broadly conceived environmentalism can be organized around a political party that can succeed in electoral politics. Thus, after a brief overview of the U.S. Greens, we will review the party's electoral performance (particularly in the 2000 presidential contest) and attempt to determine if the party can develop the kind of social base that would make it a significant threat to the conventional parties. Next our analysis will look at not just the potential popular support for this insurgent movement but also a number of other features of the U.S. political system that might limit or bolster the party's chances. Finally, we will ask how different social movements might work together and what role the Greens might be able play in a near future political realignment.

GREEN POLITICS

The Green party is almost the quintessential exemplar of the organizational tendencies and essential subcultural and identity features that have come to define the new social movements.[2] Since its inception in 1984 at a meeting of activists in St. Paul, Minnesota, the Green movement has remained more of a loose network of like-minded individuals than an organized political party.[3] Both in Europe and in the United States the Greens can best be described as an electoral expression of the New Left. It is just one of many social movements that can trace its origin to the 1960s reaction to post-war–boom America by college students and disgruntled professionals. Like these other new movements, the Green movement can be distinguished from more traditional groups by the way in which it offers an oppositional version of progress in a consumption-obsessed society.[4]

While external observers have tended to see the Greens as a single-issue party because of the close association with ecological ideals, the Green movement is not just another environmental interest group. Although Greens are deeply concerned with the environment, they view their own ecological principles as the fundamental basis for the transformation of life on the planet.[5] They envision their movement-party as simply a specific response to the fundamental crises that members see facing the nation as well as the specific agent or vehicle that will help move the country toward a "sustainable" future.[6] Not all environmentalists identify with the Greens and, more important, Green activists have been drawn from a wide variety of disparate political currents of which environmentalism is only one part.

As with the more conventional public interest groups, ecological principles rather than the advancement of member interests act as the glue that provides the movement's common reference point. There are no special benefits or advantages accruing from membership. Activists hope that unaffiliated individuals and members of environmental, women's, peace, and other countercultural formations can all come together in a progressive coalition under the banner of the Greens' core values. Although the movement has seemed on the verge of implosion since its founding, there has been a consensus over the statement of "Ten Key Values" formulated at the original gathering These essential principles embrace diversity, social justice, grassroots democracy, feminism, community, decentralization, ecological wisdom, nonviolence, personal and global responsibility, and a future focus. They envision a postmaterialist society in which technology is judged by its use, and the quality of life is given priority over economic growth.

Unlike most conventional leftist parties, the Greens do not identify capitalism as their primary opponent. Activists view both unregulated markets and bureaucratic collectivism as their targets. The party does not advance socialism or even social or industrial democracy as a panacea for social ills. Activists are suspicious of all statist solutions and hierarchical forms. Instead, while it is critical of corporate power and runaway multinational firms, the Green platform calls for an ambiguous "community-based economics" that encourages employee ownership and workplace democracy. Activists want to establish some form of reconfigured work structure that redistributes income, promotes the informal household and community economy, encourages volunteer work, develops appropriate technology, and restricts the size and power of corporations.

A central characteristic of the Green camp has been its considerable diversity and the divisions within its ranks. Activists have become notorious for their opposition to hierarchy and their internal disputes over both tactics and principle. The Greens have not one but two institutional expressions that have only recently begun to discuss merger seriously, and then without success. While the two competing networks have many similarities, the Greens/Green Party USA (G/GPUSA) has attempted to become a national dues-paying membership party tied to grassroots movements that emphasize direct action and nonelectoral activities, the Association of State Green Parties (ASGP) is made up of dissidents from a federation of locality-based affiliates that are geared to party-building and elections.[7] Little should be made of this division since much of the conflict reflects left sectarianism and personality clashes more than it does severe differences over strategy or program.

Thus, rather than sprouting up from out of the fringes of one of the major parties in response to a divisive issue, the Greens claim to be a "party of a different kind." Like their European counterparts, U.S. Greens like to say that they are neither left nor right. Their potential as a new party may stem from the fact that their program does not fall neatly along the classic dimension bisecting the two major parties. The Green program focuses on quality of life or self-expressive values rather than on basic economic needs. They do not call for an expansion of the welfare state but for a decentralized polity. Although Greens have made some overtures to blue-collar workers, trade unionists, minorities, and the poor, their primary following tends to be concentrated in such "new class" occupations as teaching, social and human service work, small business, professionals, and students.

Rooted in an all-encompassing worldview rather than fleeting issues or a charismatic individual personality, the Green movement has managed to persist since its founding almost two decades ago, despite internal quarrels, limited resources, low visibility, and meager electoral success. Since its first foray into electoral politics back in 1986, the party has concentrated on races in contests for offices like city council or county board where its candidates stood some chance of success. Nevertheless, Green candidates have entered unwinnable races for posts like governor or Congress for strategic purposes such as ballot access or issue promotion. There has been a slow but steady increase in the number of government offices contested by the Greens. The 2000 national election was the Green party's most ambitious effort yet with, in addition to the Nader campaign, 283 other Greens seeking office, including four candidates for governor, fifty for the House of Representatives, and thirteen for the U.S. Senate.[8]

Despite disappointing showings in the two most recent presidential contests, the Greens now claim to hold ninety-one local government offices in twenty states. Consequently, this movement party has forged ahead in 2001 fielding 281 candidates in twenty-five states for sixty-six types of state and local office with a record sixty victories for these efforts. It has also stepped up its direct action on behalf of various social causes. It maintains large regular chapters in New York and California along with affiliates in thirty-one other states. Despite extensive criticism from embittered Democratic loyalists and spokesmen from other groups that their efforts cost Al Gore the presidency, the Greens seem undeterred. They are now organizing for the 2002 mid-term congressional elections and planning for the long haul.[9] In fact, many state parties are prepared to compete for more elective offices even if this hurts liberal Democratic candidates, as their last national campaign was accused of doing.

ELECTION 2000

In its early days, the political landscape surrounding the 2000 presidential election seemed to present minor-party candidates with windows of opportunity. In recent years U.S. politics has opened up a substantial degree of political space to independents and minor parties. The past three decades has seen a growing number of such candidates rise to contest the slates offered by the major parties.[10] Although the meaning of these outsider entrants is controversial, many analysts attribute this phenomenon to the rise of the independent voter and partisan dealignment. A combination of the growth of candidate-centered campaigns, social fragmentation, partisan disarray, political scandal, and declining voter turnout all seemed to point toward an impending eclipse of the old party system and the demand for something else.[11] As the election approached, surveys indicated that over half of the public saw little essential difference between the two major parties as well as a majority favoring the emergence of a third party.[12]

From the outset these circumstances would seem to have favored both political pundit Pat Buchanan and consumer advocate Ralph Nader, who already enjoyed substantial name recognition prior to their respective nominations by the Reform and Green parties. Despite the relative celebrity status of the two candidates, most of the media attention in the early days of the campaign focused on Buchanan. Most pundits thought that his nationalist, isolationist, socioreligious, and cultural themes were more likely to attract alienated voters.[13] Nader, on the other hand, was largely ignored early on until the weight of his persistent 4 to 8 percent standing in public opinion polls and a computerized Web-based campaign by the Greens forced greater media attention. The closeness of the election's final days combined with the tactical positioning by Bush and Gore put Nader even more in the spotlight, albeit for the wrong reasons from the stand-point of his supporters and admirers.

Buchanan proved not to be a factor in the election. After a divisive split at the Reform party's convention, Buchanan sank in the polls and his campaign became almost invisible despite a favorable Federal Elections Committee ruling that provided him with the $12.6 million in federal funding earned by Ross Perot's showing in 1996. While Buchanan emphasized traditional themes like abortion that have resonance across much of the center-right, he increasingly identified himself with a populist "paleo-conservatism" by asserting that the nation was now governed by a pluto-cratic elite that had turned its back on "Middle America" by colluding with multinational capital. Globalization with its corporate flight and waves of immigrants, he claimed, was undermining an America that he identified with white ethnic communities. This message had less reso-nance for him than it had had in 1992 because his forecast of socioeco-nomic decline had been undercut by eight years of sustained growth, declining crime rates, and falling unemployment levels.[14] He was also now running as a minor-party candidate in a general election and subject to the usual "lesser-evil" argument.

While a strong economy, greater financial security, and the higher lev-els of satisfaction of the late 1990s may have undermined Buchanan, the final Nader result is more difficult to interpret. It can be explained, at least in part, by his opponents' efforts in the waning days of the campaign to conjure up the specter of a conservative triumph. The Democratic party, labor unions, and environmental and pro-choice groups funded commer-cials and sponsored celebrity spokespeople in key states attacking Nader as a stalking horse for Bush and an unwitting antagonist who would undercut all that he had long fought to achieve. The Republicans gave credence to these charges by running their own spots in key states, using statements by Nader critical of the Democratic party and its candidate, expressly created for the purpose of undermining Gore.[15] The wasted vote and narcissistic "spoiler" themes proved effective, causing some of Na-der's constituency to melt away by election day.

In the end, Nader gained nearly three million votes or just under 3 per-cent of those who went to the polls. This figure was less than the 5 percent needed to qualify for federal matching funds and less than half of Nader's peak position in the polls. Exit poll results showed that Nader voters were very similar demographically to those who ordinarily vote for third par-ties. That is, they tended to be young, male, independent, unmarried, low-income, and first-time voters.[16] Nearly one-third of them claimed they would not have voted in a two-way race. On the other hand, spatial analysis by county indicated that Nader's support extended beyond his predictable strength in college towns, "new lifestyle" cities like Santa

Monica, Burlington, or Seattle, and enclaves in liberal suburbs. The Green candidate also did well in largely rural counties of the northeastern states and Pacific northwest as well as pockets in similar regions of the upper midwest and central western states. Overall, Alaska proved to be Nader's best state.

In the aftermath of the election, the Greens were unrepentant. Nader had not achieved his goals, but the former Green party candidate was upbeat. The veteran citizen crusader had his party-building hat on and was looking forward to a bright Green future.[17] Activists seemed less concerned with the final vote count than they were with the grassroots activities and membership growth the campaign had produced. Instead of disappointment, most Greens were stimulated by the result and anxious to move ahead with efforts to expand their activist network. A national university Campus Greens has been formed, and adherents have attempted to merge the two rival Green associations by forming the Green Party of the United States. Despite his age, Nader seemed amenable to taking his volunteers and list of seventy-five thousand donors and forming them into an identifiable entity for a presidential challenge in 2004. Even if he does not, the Greens are optimistic about their prospects. Their leaders insist local races matter more than the national contest and that issues will ultimately count for more than famous personalities.

NEW POLITICAL ALIGNMENT?

Among the enduring paradoxes of election 2000 is the meaning of the Green vote. Most pundits have written off the Naderites as disgruntled liberals who would have made part of a comfortable 52 percent Democratic majority if that party had offered a more attractive choice to lead the ticket. Other analysts saw a deeper meaning in these results and have used terms like *dealignment, overload, fragmentation,* or *crisis* to explain the unexpected turbulence in recent elections. According to this second line of reasoning, increased third-party voting, weakening partisanship, declining turnout, ticket-splitting, and government gridlock are all part of a general weakening of the two major parties organized along the traditional fault lines. How else can we explain during an extended period of peace and prosperity the weakness of conventional candidates or the willingness of so many to protest and organize themselves outside of established groups and political institutions?

One popular variant on this latter theme is a theory that suggests that all advanced industrial societies are going through a postindustrial "cultural shift" that will ultimately realign their politics. Ronald Inglehart, the most prominent spokesmen for this position, has argued that the growing support for Green parties is simply one sign of the fact that a "silent change" in basic values is altering the political climate in Western nations in ways that undercut the traditional parties.[18] Affluence and the security provided by the welfare state, Inglehart asserts, have shifted the political axis away from class-based issues and economic productivity to more expressive values and self-actualization for the generations born since World War II. Therefore, the old parties aligned along the "materialist" dimension will find themselves increasingly confronted by new movements and parties on both the right and left contesting a "new politics" cleavage that pits "postmaterialist" demands for greater self-gratification and personal expression against efforts to secure order and restore traditional norms.[19]

If this latter perspective is correct, the Nader vote should reflect a substantial base in postmaterial values. Although exit polls have been useful in giving a gross picture of Nader support along various dimensions, more crucial to an understanding of his support are the relative contributions of these features. In order to test the validity of the postindustrial thesis and other assertions about the Naderites we have turned to the election-timed surveys conducted by the University of Michigan. The National Election Study (NES) is a particularly useful data source for this exercise, given the range and quality of its variables. Among their most important variables, for our purposes, was a measure for postmaterialism. In previous waves of the NES, Inglehart's preferred priority ranking question was offered. This was not true in the 2000 survey. However, NES did ask several questions that allowed us to develop our own measure. We selected the appropriate available scaled items (environment vs. jobs, religiosity vs. secularism, immigration perspectives, reactions to crime, lifestyle, and childrearing) to create a "tally of extremes" (see table 9.A1). This approach generated a variable that matches other estimates of the purported material/postmaterial divide in U.S. society.

The strategy we have pursued consists, first, of separating those who actually voted for Nader from those who listed him as their second choice but voted for someone else; and second, of an analysis of the postmaterialist values and the various other characteristics of these voters that differentiate them from the rest of the electorate. For both sets of Nader supporters we have examined various bivariate cross-tabulations, logistic regression models that statistically control for the individual influence of variables, and multinomial logistic regression models that introduce statistical control while allowing for separate influences on several categories of the outcome variable (Gore, Bush, Nader, etc.). While none of these specific approaches can uniquely describe Nader's support base, each acts as another window on the phenomenon. Taken together, certain patterns of support become obvious. As table 9.1 suggests, when voting prefer-

TABLE 9.1
Social Values and Vote Choice

	Gore	Bush	Nader	Buchanan	Other	Total
Materialist	29.1	68.4	1.5	0.5	0.5	17.8
Mod-M	44.0	53.7	1.2	0.5	0.5	36.5
Mixed	57.3	41.7	1.0	—	—	18.7
Mod-PM	64.5	29.5	4.4	—	1.4	19.7
Postmaterialist	73.4	8.9	16.5	—	1.3	7.2

Source: Calculated by the authors from data in Nancy Burns, Donald Kinder, Steven Rosenstone, Virginia Sapiro, and the National Election Studies. *National Election Studies (NES), 2000.* Pre-/Post-Election Study (dataset) (Ann Arbor: University of Michigan, Center for Political Studies [producer and distributor], 2001).

ences and basic values are aligned in this way, candidate choice tends to fall into predictable places on the resulting continuum. Gore's support increases as we move away from the materialist end of the continuum while Nader's support is overwhelmingly from strong postmaterialists.

Perhaps our most dramatic finding about the Green support is the partial validation for some aspects of the postmaterialist thesis. Table 9.2 demonstrates the relationships we found from our postmaterialist scale. These results indicate that the more consistently respondents held postmaterialist values, the more likely they were to vote for Nader. Postmaterialists were eleven times more likely to vote for Nader than materialists. Among those we classified as either moderate or strong postmaterialists support for Nader also dramatically increases. Notwithstanding this strong base of support, a serious problem for any Green candidate is the fact that the actual number of postmaterialists is a small segment of the entire population. By our accounting, fewer than 30 percent of the respondents fall into this classification and, of this select group, roughly just under one in three gave Nader any support. Taken together, less than 10 percent of the electorate can be said to hold values fully consistent with the Green program. Worse yet, from this standpoint, is the apparent materialist social values basis for a prospective "New Right" candidacy.

Another aspect of the postmaterialist thesis seems weaker. Central to the claim of a progressive culture shift is the projection of intergenerational change generated by an increasingly secure condition of growth and abundance. If the older generation, with values shaped by war and depression, is giving way to the children of the "baby boom," we should expect especially strong Green values and voting patterns among the young. However, table 9.3 suggests that these younger cohorts (whose parents were themselves the products of an affluent society) are not very different from their elders. Although fully 33 percent of those under

TABLE 9.2
Level of Nader Support

	None Recorded	Second Choice	Nader Voter	Total Population
Materialist	94.4	4.1	1.5	17.8
Mod-M	89.1	9.7	1.2	36.5
Mixed	87.9	11.2	1.0	18.7
Mod-PM	76.0	19.4	4.6	19.7
Postmaterialist	54.4	20.1	16.5	7.2
Total	84.7	12.3	3.0	100.0

Source: Calculated by the authors from data in Nancy Burns, Donald Kinder, Steven Rosenstone, Virginia Sapiro, and the National Election Studies. *National Election Studies (NES),* 2000. Pre-/Post-Election Study (dataset) (Ann Arbor: University of Michigan, Center for Political Studies [producer and distributor], 2001).

thirty-five can be classified as postmaterialists, their support for Nader was only slightly stronger than that of the older generation. It should be noted, however, that these younger postmaterialists were more likely to vote for Nader. And, among those over sixty, only 18 percent can be classified as postmaterialist, and among these, just one in fifty cast a Nader vote. The generational values shift indicated by these data suggests social change that is much more modest than the veritable transformation anticipated by either Inglehart or many of the Greens.

Along with this elementary, cross-tabular investigation, we examined the possibility that this seeming association between postmaterialist values and Nader support might be a spurious result driven by its associa-

TABLE 9.3
Young Nader Support (age < 35)

	None Recorded	Second Choice	Nader Voter	Total Population
Materialist	100.0	0.0	0.0	12.0
Mod-M	89.8	7.1	3.1	35.8
Mixed	90.0	10.0	0.0	18.2
Mod-PM	81.7	13.3	5.0	21.9
Postmaterialist	51.5	21.2	27.3	12.0
Total	84.7	12.3	3.0	100.0

Source: Calculated by the authors from data in Nancy Burns, Donald Kinder, Steven Rosenstone, Virginia Sapiro, and the National Election Studies. *National Election Studies (NES),* 2000. Pre-/Post-Election Study (dataset) (Ann Arbor: University of Michigan, Center for Political Studies, [producer and distributor], 2001).

tion with other variables. That is to say, the apparent postmaterialistic
Nader base might be explained away by demographic, economic, political, or attitudinal factors that have nothing to do with these values per se.
This, however, does not seem to be the case (see table 9.4). Both our logistic regression and multinomial techniques indicate the same unique
determinants. In nearly all specifications with robust vector of opinion
and participation controls, this dimension seems to lie at the root of

TABLE 9.4
Logistic Regression of Vote for Nader on Selected Independent Variables

	B	Std. Error	Wald	df	Sig.	Exp(B)
Male	0.65	0.73	0.79	1.00	0.37	1.91
Black	2.32	1.49	2.41	1.00	0.12	10.15
Hispanic	5.55	1.58	12.37	1.00	0.00	256.38
Age	−0.04	0.03	2.07	1.00	0.15	0.96
Education	0.11	0.20	0.29	1.00	0.59	1.11
Married	0.76	0.89	0.73	1.00	0.39	2.14
Urbanicity	−0.01	0.16	0.01	1.00	0.94	0.99
Family Income (thousands)	0.01	0.01	0.40	1.00	0.53	1.01
Ideology (squared)	−0.05	0.04	1.56	1.00	0.21	0.95
Postmaterialism	1.04	0.40	6.77	1.00	0.01	2.84
Lean to Democrats or Republicans	3.07	1.20	6.50	1.00	0.01	21.48
Independent	4.54	1.45	9.79	1.00	0.00	93.28
Favor Strong Third Parties	3.12	1.45	4.67	1.00	0.03	22.76
Favor No Party Labels	3.45	1.47	5.47	1.00	0.02	31.36
Sociotropic	0.59	0.38	2.39	1.00	0.12	1.80
Doesn't Matter Which Party Manages Economy	2.10	0.78	7.33	1.00	0.01	8.18
Favor Tax Cut	0.05	0.20	0.06	1.00	0.80	1.05
Use Surplus for Social Security	−0.89	0.29	9.23	1.00	0.00	0.41
Favor Government Health Plan	0.50	0.21	5.66	1.00	0.02	1.65
Favor Campaign Finance Reform	0.10	0.21	0.25	1.00	0.62	1.11
Against Affirmative Action	0.27	0.20	1.91	1.00	0.17	1.31
Sexist	5.16	1.44	12.92	1.00	0.00	174.15
Volunteered in Community	−1.96	0.86	5.15	1.00	0.02	0.14
Contacted Government Official	1.33	0.75	3.13	1.00	0.08	3.76
Attended Community Meeting	1.56	0.92	2.91	1.00	0.09	4.77
Involved in a Protest	−0.95	1.06	0.80	1.00	0.37	0.39
Intercept	−18.06	4.98	13.17	1.00	0.00	

Source: Calculated by the authors from data in Nancy Burns, Donald Kinder, Steven
Rosenstone, Virginia Sapiro, and the National Election Studies. *National Election Studies
(NES)*, 2000. Pre-/Post-Election Study (dataset) (Ann Arbor: University of Michigan, Center
for Political Studies [producer and distributor], 2001).

Nader support either in the form of an actual vote or a second-choice preference. The most sophisticated of these analyses shows that, net of all other factors, a strong postmaterialist is over fifty-five times as likely to support Nader as to have offered him no support (see table 9.A2). This elementary result seems only to get stronger in tighter cross sections.

The association between the Nader vote and postmaterialist values is less than surprising. Given the details of his biography, the content of his public pronouncements, and the platform of his party, we might expect this type of voter to drift haltingly toward the Greens over time. Also unsurprising was the fact that strong partisans of the two major parties were less likely to support him than self-described independents and leaners or those rejecting party labels and favoring a third option. The successful economic performance of the Clinton administration years did not move Naderites because they did not think it mattered which party managed the economy. Voters who thought it would make a difference if either Gore or Bush became president were fully eighteen times less likely to vote for Nader. Nor were strong Naderites economically distinctive in other ways except in their greater support for equality and in their tendency to identify with the working class. Nader voters were also predictably somewhat younger, slightly left of center, and more liberal on such issues as gays in the military

Other findings were unexpected. For example, among Nader voters one may count African Americans, rugged individualists, gender traditionalists, citizens uninvolved with their communities, and even extreme materialists. Perhaps the most surprising finding was Nader's appeal in the Hispanic population. In model after model, the fact that Hispanics were more likely to vote for Nader stands firm. He captured 8.5 percent of the Hispanic respondents and, in controlled models, he was the overwhelming choice. Why such a disparate conglomeration of voters turned to Nader may well become important in future efforts by the Greens to develop working coalitions. What we are to make of this heterogeneous following is not entirely clear. At the very least, this strange assortment of adherents suggests that Nader may have appealed to many voters for reasons other than his progressive record or Green values. It also suggests that the image of an elite, white, and well-educated Green voter is somewhat of a stereotype. Through all of this the threads of an independent politics and a postmaterialist disposition are what appear to hold the Nader support together in what seems to be a lonely crowd.

STRATEGIC POTENTIAL

Despite their electoral work over the past sixteen years, the Greens still face all the obstacles of the U.S. political process that have led minor parties of the past to the graveyard.[20] They face institutional barriers including lack of ballot access, inadequate media exposure, legal hurdles, and difficulties with campaign finance.[21] Nader, for example, was on the presidential ballot in just thirty-two states and the District of Columbia, and received no votes at all in four states that did not allow write-ins. The Greens never raised enough money for a substantial electronic media outreach campaign. They did run a notorious ad parodying a "Mastercard" commercial, but this briefly gained the public's attention only because of the offended corporation's lawsuit. The free time they did get was mostly negative since it focused almost exclusively on the finances and personal qualities of their candidate or the comparative impact of a Green vote on the major-party contenders and the probable policy consequences of a Republican victory. Even journals of left opinion gave candidate Nader a mixed reception.

Many of these obstacles might be overcome by an effective grassroots effort. However, there is still the more fundamental question about the size of the party's social base. When the first effort to found a Green party was under way in the early 1980s, it was said that the Citizens party had everything but a constituency.[22] Unlike Barry Commoner's efforts in 1980, Nader's presidential candidacy was met with a much more promising response than the meager 3 percent of the popular vote that he ultimately received. Early polls showed Nader at more than twice his final vote total, and fully one-sixth of the electorate listed Nader as either their first or second choice. This support is very much in line with the performance typical of the European Greens since, despite their greater success and higher visibility, these parties normally manage a vote in the 6 to 8 percent range in parliamentary elections and have been able to exceed 10 percent of a national vote only in Luxembourg.

In European elections under proportional rules, 5 to 9 percent of the vote allows the Greens to have representation in government. The winner-take-all plurality and district system in the United States severely limits this possibility. Although U.S. federalism and nonpartisan local elections will allow the Greens some prospects at the regional level denied to most of their European counterparts, they are severely handicapped in the more visible national contests. And, unless the unlikely happens and U.S. Greens are successful in getting the nation's multiple governments to enact forms of "preference" voting (instant runoff, Borda count, proportional representation, fusion), the party's prospects will be limited in much of the country to such elective positions as city council, mayor, county assembly, school board, or state legislator.[23] Elections for offices such as governor, senator, and the presidency will continue to entail purely symbolic or strategic entry.

Greater success would require the Greens to expand their base. Even if Nader had won over all the postmaterialist voters, he would still have garnered just over one-quarter of the electorate by our measure. Although Inglehart's projections for a realignment based on continuing value change suggest optimism, U.S. Greens cannot be certain that their political base will grow. Despite its affluence, the United States provides less of the security that is the fertile social environment in which the "new politics" is supposed to thrive. Income inequality has risen since the early 1970s, wages have stagnated, wealth is more concentrated, there is a much less generous welfare state, and the government safety net has become more porous.[24] Therefore, the Green movement cannot expect to simply ride a postmaterialist tide. It will have to reframe emerging issues and move mass opinion, not just respond to it.

A logical move by the party would be to attempt a "Blue-Green" alliance. Although efforts to work with organized labor have been suggested and even attempted by some Green chapters, there is as yet no sign that pressures of globalization on the economy can move workers or their unions away from their moorings with the Democratic party. The poor and disaffected are another potential source of support since they are most alienated from the system and most dissatisfied with the major parties. However, they do not vote in large numbers nor do they protest in normal times. Not only are the poor difficult to organize under the best of circumstances but their socially conservative values are at odds with the Green program.[25] In any case, neither blue-collar workers nor the nation's poor are likely to be easily drawn to a party that emphasizes "quality of life" issues and promises them little in the way of immediate or tangible relief.

The environmental interest groups are another potential source of support. While national associations like the Sierra Club, National Resources Defense Council, and Audubon Society were hostile to Nader's presidential bid, their memberships and revenues had been stagnant or declining during the disappointing Clinton years. The environmental community has struggled to remain pragmatic "players" in national policy while at the same time maintaining the zeal of their most committed members.[26] This Washington, D.C.–centered emphasis on lobbying has led to charges of "corporate" environmentalism and generated intramural disputes over goals and tactics. Still, even with such signs of dissatisfaction, it seems unlikely that the Greens can win over an environmental lobby that blames them for making possible the anti-environment agenda of the Bush administration. They might, however, win over large numbers of militant dissidents with their emphasis on direct action, local coalitions, and grassroots issues.

There are other elements that might make up a larger Green coalition. Racial minority groups may be socially conservative, but they might be attracted by the party's strong human rights and equality planks. Hispanics seem to be the best match. Their demographic ascendancy and relative political passivity make them a sleeping giant.[27] And, unlike African Americans, they have a weak attachment to the Democratic party. Furthermore, the data we uncovered indicate that they gave surprising support for Nader. Even a "Green-Camouflage" coalition with hunters, fishers, farmers, and recreationists or organizations such as Ducks Unlimited seems plausible. This unlikely linkage might be possible given Nader's solid vote in several rural counties and the anti-government rugged individualist support we found in surveys. European Center parties often possess this latter character and follow along with a Green program.

Crises of the kind predicted by the Greens might offer an opportunity for growth. Experience shows that popular mobilization is easiest to achieve in the compelling context of a national emergency with strong leadership from a political party. A severe economic downturn might spur a favorable realignment if it were attributed to corporate malefactors. But it might be possible in more normal times for a vigorous grassroots movement to stimulate change if eco-catastrophes like pollution, energy shortages, and global warming point the way. These problems would have to be framed in ways that go beyond criticism and emphasize Green alternatives. The ability of the major parties to co-opt these issues would be somewhat limited given the fact that they are captive "duopsonies" closely tied to the financial interests that invest in their expensive campaign efforts.[28] However, our analysis has shown that such crises might favor a right-wing populism over a progressive alternative, given the large number of Americans holding materialist beliefs.

The terrorist attacks on the Pentagon and World Trade Center towers on September 11 could have either a galvanizing impact or depressing effect on Green mobilization, depending on events. On the one hand, the party's opposition to the Bush administration's violent response to this tragedy could isolate the movement from the public in an emerging climate of patriotic fervor. Campus protests and civil disobedience by Green affiliates might even spawn various forms of government repression. On the other hand, a long drawn-out and expensive military campaign against terrorism with an unsatisfactory outcome like the Vietnam War or war against drugs could generate a sizable humanitarian movement in which the Greens could play a leading role. Burning issues like peace, globalization, poverty, and recession just might provide the glue that would make the Greens more than simply a minor electoral vehicle and more of the kind of organizational umbrella through which disparate social movements could achieve unity and learn to work together.

Finally, the Green party may be limited by its own internal contradictions. Even if the Greens had been able to merge, there would have been no guarantee that the resulting formation would not dissolve into myriad factions, hostile groups, and dissenting individuals. Like all of the new social movements, the ideology that unites everyone favors individual self-expression over reflexivity, identity over social solidarity, and arbitrariness over binding norms.[29] It is not clear whether Green activists are willing to sufficiently submerge their own individualistic personalities for the sort of organized effort required for effectively mobilizing people. Internalized democratic mechanisms are important in ensuring a generalized feeling of ownership over group decisions, but they also allow for an extended deliberative process in which a few contentious egoists can slow or even prevent action. Opportunities for insurgency can be lost if the decentralized Green framework and a subculture that distrusts authority prevents effective coordination.[30]

CONCLUSION: A GREEN FUTURE?

American history is littered with fledgling movements and alternative parties that failed in their efforts to succeed on the scale envisioned by today's Greens. Nevertheless, considering the peculiar way in which issues divide the public and the volatility of the electorate, it is by no means certain that the Green party has no future. Given the patterns we analyzed, it should be clear that the paltry vote Nader garnered in the 2000 presidential election was much less than the party's potential following. While the Green vote may not be the clear harbinger of a major realignment, it should be obvious that many salient national issues have only a marginal relationship with the programmatic stances of the two major parties. A marked social base does seem to exist for the party. In fact, the ideological space we found along the postmodern axis could, under fortuitous circumstances, create opportunities for both a left-leaning ecology party and a new-right reactionary party.

The vagaries we find in popular opinion, however, are no guarantee of the onset of the form of thoroughgoing transformation envisaged by the Greens. For the party to become a significant change agent, it will have to demonstrate greater organizational capacity, networking ability, electoral reach, and educational effort than the Greens have to date. Most important is the predicament, from a strategic perspective, of how a "new-age" radical movement can win over the working-class, minority, and environmentally conscious citizens now aligned with the Democrats. Declining loyalties, cross-cutting social pressures, and emergent political cleavages may provide the party with windows of opportunity. But the moralism, spontaneity, and subjectivism of the movement may have to give way to a more mundane emphasis on immediate benefits, material demands, and practical solutions if the Greens are to grow.

On balance, it is hardly implausible to imagine future circumstances under which the contemporary climate of political disengagement, partisan erosion, and vaguely defined discontent is replaced by a contentious period of realignment during which the Greens emerge as a significant third party. The party does have a constituency base, it maintains a cadre of committed ideologues, and its focus on local activism seems well suited to the U.S. political process with its federal government structure. In the end, however, the actual prospects for this or any other comparable new movement party may depend upon circumstances over which the Greens have little or no control. Successful campaigns at the local and regional levels will prove to be empty victories unless the Greens can win enough of the higher-level public offices to allow them to transform the national policy agenda. They can stage events and protest, but without sufficient financial resources or adequate media exposure they will not be able to prevent distortions of their program and message. Therefore, even the onset of economic crises and multiple eco-catastrophes might not automatically improve the party's chances.

Declining public confidence in traditional authority and all hierarchical institutions has undermined support for political leaders throughout the industrial world. New social movements, like the various national Green parties, tend to thrive in an environment of generalized affluence that permits increasing space for the open expression of individual autonomy and dissent. Nevertheless, despite its great wealth, the United States may well be the one advanced country that offers the least hospitable setting for a Green party. The nation's greater market volatility, culture of privatism, socioreligiosity, restrictive electoral apparatus, truncated welfare system, and high and growing levels of material inequality make for a societal framework that is much less suited than elsewhere for the emergence of a postindustrial politics. Given all of these circumstances, it is unclear if a viable Green political movement can truly prosper here or if we will remain "exceptional" as the only advanced industrial democracy with neither a large Social Democratic or Labor party nor anything resembling a significant Green presence.

APPENDIX

Variables Used in the Analysis

Among the most important variables in the study is the measure of postmaterialism. There has been much discussion about how to think about postmaterial values and what kinds of measures are most appropriate to tap them. In previous waves of the National Election Studies, Inglehart's preferred priority type measure was offered. This was not true in the 2000 pre- or postelection surveys. However, attitudes of respondents that would suggest that they hold such values are included in the surveys in several items. We have selected scales on the following areas of opinion as the basis of our scale: Approaches to reducing crime, religious observance, environment vs. jobs, immigration, moral traditionalism, and approaches to childrearing. For each of the areas a five- or seven-point scale was constructed from the available items. In line with Inglehart's criticism of scale-type measures and in light of our concerns regarding the nonlinear nature of such measures, we elected to create a "tally of extremes" type measure. For this, we assigned respondents a positive score if they fell in the extreme upper range of a measure and a negative score if they fell in the extreme lower range of a measure. We then tallied the positive and negative scores, generating a variable that ranged from −6 to +6. Based on within-group similarities we then reclassified these values into five classes ranging from extreme materialist to extreme postmaterialist. This approach generated a variable that matches other estimates of the material/postmaterial divide in American society. For the multinomial logistic regression we selected the extreme values of this scale as dummy variables. Only respondents who fell in the extreme of all five variables would be classified as either a strong postmaterialist or materialist.

In order to assess the role of a hypothetical value shift such as that described by Inglehart, we have explored both marginal descriptions of the vote choice relative to the list of variables in table 9.A1 while also testing their joint associations in logistic regressions (see table 9.A2). All variables were taken from the standard items of the 2000 NES. They either conform directly to these variables or were adapted from them. The variable numbers to the right correspond to the NES release variable numbers.

TABLE 9.A1
Variables Used in the Analysis

Variable	Release Variable Number	Level of Measurement
Male	v001029	Binary
Black	v001006a	Binary
Hispanic	v001006a	Binary
Age	v000907	Continuous
Education	v000910	Continuous
Married	v000909	Binary
Urbanicity	v001016–v0001018	8-point scale
Family income (thousands)	v000993, v000996	Continuous
Ideology (squared)	v001368	Squared 7-point scale
Postmaterialist	v001530–v001533, v001586–v001589, v000874–v000875, v001482–v001484, v000508–v000509	Binary, 5-point scale
Working-class consciousness	v000998–v001004	Binary
Lean to Democrats or Republicans	v000519, v001409	Binary
Independent	v000519, v001409	Binary
Favor strong third parties	v001650	Binary
Favor no party labels	v001650	Binary
Rugged individualist	v000617–v000618	Binary
Favor tax cut	v000688–v000689	5-point scale
Use surplus for social security	v000691–v000692	5-point scale
Favor government health plan	v000608a–v000612	7-point scale
Favor campaign finance reform	v001490	7-point scale
Racist	v001575, v001579, v001583	Binary
Against affirmative action	v000671a, v000671b, v000672, v000673	5-point scale
Sexist	v000756a,b, v000758	Binary
Homophobic	v000724	Binary
Pocketbook	v000398	5-point scale
Sociotropic	v000488a,b, v000489, v000490	5-point scale
Future pocketbook	v000496a,b, v000497, v000498	5-point scale
Future sociotropic	v000403–v000405	5-point scale
Doesn't matter which party manages economy	v000505	Binary
Volunteered in community	v001491	Binary
Contacted government official	v001492	Binary
Attended community meeting	v001493	Binary
Involved in a protest	v001506	Binary

Source: Nancy Burns, Donald Kinder, Steven Rosenstone, Virginia Sapiro, and the National Election Studies. *National Election Studies (NES)*, 2000. Pre-/Post-Election Study (dataset) (Ann Arbor: University of Michigan, Center for Political Studies [producer and distributor], 2001).

TABLE 9.A2
Multinomial Logistic Regression of Nader Support
on Selected Independent Variables

	B	Std. Error	Wald	df	Sig.	Exp(B)
Nader Voter						
Intercept	−19.09	6.76	7.98	1.00	0.00	
Male	2.13	1.16	3.39	1.00	0.07	8.45
Black	3.78	2.04	3.44	1.00	0.06	43.78
Hispanic	7.64	2.16	12.48	1.00	0.00	2079.64
Age	−0.09	0.04	4.02	1.00	0.05	0.92
Education	0.17	0.31	0.28	1.00	0.59	1.18
Married	1.13	1.34	0.72	1.00	0.40	3.09
Urbanicity	−0.04	0.24	0.02	1.00	0.88	0.96
Family income (thousands)	0.01	0.01	0.31	1.00	0.58	1.01
Ideology (squared)	−0.11	0.06	3.11	1.00	0.08	0.90
Strong postmaterialist	4.01	1.29	9.64	1.00	0.00	55.08
Strong materialist	1.52	1.68	0.81	1.00	0.37	4.55
Working-class consciousness	1.51	1.06	2.03	1.00	0.15	4.53
Lean to Democrats or Republicans	3.83	1.55	6.14	1.00	0.01	46.13
Independent	5.16	1.69	9.29	1.00	0.00	173.53
Favor strong third parties	4.66	2.41	3.75	1.00	0.05	105.92
Favor no party labels	5.21	2.30	5.14	1.00	0.02	182.74
Rugged individualist	1.45	1.19	1.47	1.00	0.22	4.25
Favor tax cut	0.31	0.28	1.20	1.00	0.27	1.36
Use surplus for social security	−1.04	0.47	4.91	1.00	0.03	0.35
Favor government health plan	0.63	0.29	4.70	1.00	0.03	1.88
Favor campaign finance reform	0.28	0.32	0.74	1.00	0.39	1.32
Racist	0.46	1.54	0.09	1.00	0.77	1.58
Against affirmative action	0.54	0.35	2.43	1.00	0.12	1.72
Sexist	5.70	1.93	8.73	1.00	0.00	298.35
Homophobic	−0.62	0.47	1.74	1.00	0.19	0.54
Pocketbook	0.28	0.61	0.21	1.00	0.65	1.32
Sociotropic	0.48	0.50	0.94	1.00	0.33	1.62
Future pocketbook	−0.39	0.62	0.40	1.00	0.53	0.68
Future sociotropic	−0.27	0.59	0.21	1.00	0.64	0.76
Doesn't matter which party manages economy	2.92	1.22	5.71	1.00	0.02	18.53
Volunteered in community	−2.99	1.27	5.51	1.00	0.02	0.05
Contacted government official	2.18	1.01	4.69	1.00	0.03	8.87
Attended community meeting	1.96	1.24	2.48	1.00	0.12	7.08
Involved in a protest	−2.28	1.90	1.45	1.00	0.23	0.10
Second Choice						
Intercept	−3.61	1.72	4.39	1.00	0.04	
Male	0.44	0.27	2.63	1.00	0.10	1.55
Black	−0.03	0.51	0.00	1.00	0.95	0.97

TABLE 9.A2 (Continued)

	B	Std. Error	Wald	df	Sig.	Exp(B)
Hispanic	−0.94	1.18	0.63	1.00	0.43	0.39
Age	0.01	0.01	2.59	1.00	0.11	1.02
Education	0.08	0.07	1.28	1.00	0.26	1.08
Married	−0.61	0.31	3.92	1.00	0.05	0.55
Urbanicity	0.14	0.06	4.74	1.00	0.03	1.15
Family income (thousands)	0.00	0.00	0.27	1.00	0.60	1.00
Ideology (squared)	−0.02	0.01	1.78	1.00	0.18	0.98
Strong postmaterialist	1.38	0.41	11.14	1.00	0.00	3.98
Strong materialist	−1.23	0.61	4.09	1.00	0.04	0.29
Working-class consciousness	0.08	0.28	0.08	1.00	0.78	1.08
Lean to democrats or republicans	0.11	0.28	0.17	1.00	0.68	1.12
Independent	0.21	0.54	0.15	1.00	0.70	1.24
Favor strong third parties	1.12	0.32	12.27	1.00	0.00	3.05
Favor no party labels	0.87	0.37	5.52	1.00	0.02	2.39
Rugged individualist	−0.19	0.30	0.41	1.00	0.52	0.83
Favor tax cut	0.08	0.08	0.89	1.00	0.35	1.08
Use surplus for social security	−0.09	0.10	0.92	1.00	0.34	0.91
Favor government health plan	0.05	0.07	0.57	1.00	0.45	1.05
Favor campaign finance reform	0.07	0.08	0.68	1.00	0.41	1.07
Racist	−0.61	0.47	1.68	1.00	0.20	0.54
Against affirmative action	0.03	0.08	0.15	1.00	0.70	1.03
Sexist	−1.25	0.98	1.64	1.00	0.20	0.29
Homophobic	0.07	0.10	0.42	1.00	1.07	1.07
Pocketbook	0.22	0.15	2.05	1.00	0.15	1.24
Sociotropic	−0.20	0.13	2.31	1.00	0.13	0.82
Future pocketbook	−0.37	0.17	4.51	1.00	0.03	0.69
Future sociotropic	−0.09	0.19	0.25	1.00	0.62	0.91
Doesn't matter which party manages economy	0.22	0.26	0.70	1.00	0.40	1.24
Volunteered in community	0.02	0.32	0.01	1.00	0.94	1.02
Contacted government official	0.04	0.32	0.02	1.00	0.90	1.04
Attended community meeting	0.04	0.32	0.01	1.00	0.91	1.04
Involved in a protest	0.82	0.51	2.61	1.00	0.11	2.26

Source: Nancy Burns, Donald Kinder, Steven Rosenstone, Virginia Sapiro, and the National Election Studies. *National Election Studies (NES),* 2000. Pre-/Post-Election Study (dataset) (Ann Arbor: University of Michigan, Center for Political Studies [producer and distributor], 2001).

NOTES

1. Carl Boggs, *Social Movements and Political Power: Emerging Forms of Radicalism in the West* (Philadelphia: Temple University Press, 1986).

2. Enrique Larana, Hank Johnston, and Joseph Gusfield, eds., *New Social Movements: From Ideology to Identity* (Philadelphia: Temple University Press, 1994).

3. David Reynolds, *Democracy Unbound: Progressive Challenges to the Two Party System* (Boston: South End, 1997).

4. Alain Touraine, *The Self-Production of Society*, trans. Derek Coltman (Chicago: University of Chicago Press, 1977).

5. Greg Jan, "The Green Party: Global Politics at the Grassroots," in *Multiparty Politics in America*, ed. Paul S. Herrnson and John C. Green (Lanham, Md.: Rowman & Littlefield, 1997).

6. John Rensenbrink, *Against All Odds: The Green Transformation of American Politics* (Raymond, Maine: Leopold, 1999).

7. Since this was written, the ASGP has transformed itself into the Green Party of the United States (GPUS).

8. Association of State Green Parties (ASGP), "Green Party Election Results: Summary 2000 and Summary 2001," accessed December 23, 2001 www.greens.org/elections.

9. Jon Margolis, "Nader Unrepentant," *Mother Jones* (July–August 2001).

10. John C. Berg, "Beyond a Third Party: The Other Minor Parties in the 1996 Elections," in *The State of the Parties: The Changing Role of Contemporary American Parties*, 3d ed., ed. John C. Green and Daniel Shea (Lanham, Md.: Rowman & Littlefield, 1999), 212–228.

11. Walter Dean Burnham, "Whole Lotta Shakin' Goin' On," *The Nation*, April 17, 2000.

12. Pew Research Center, "Retro-Politics," release, November 11, 1999.

13. Kevin Philips, "The Wrecking Crew," *Milwaukee Journal Sentinel*, July 9, 2000.

14. Edward Ashbee, "The Also-Rans," *Political Quarterly* 72, no. 2 (April–June 2001).

15. William Crotty, ed., *America's Choice 2000* (Boulder, Colo.: Westview, 2001).

16. Voter News Service, "Exit Poll Results," November 12, 2000.

17. Lenora Todaro, "Ralph Nader Lashes Back," *Village Voice*, December 20, 2000.

18. Ronald Inglehart, "Value Change in Industrial Societies," *American Political Science Review* 81, no. 4 (December 1987): 1289–1319; Inglehart, *Culture Shift in Advanced Industrial Society* (Princeton, N.J.: Princeton University Press, 1990).

19. Ronald Inglehart, *Modernization and Postmodernization: Cultural, Economic, and Political Change in 43 Societies* (Princeton, N.J.: Princeton University Press, 1997).

20. Steven J. Rosenstone, Roy L. Behr, and Edward H. Lazarus, *Third Parties in America: Citizen Response to Major Party Failure*, 2d ed. (Princeton, N.J.: Princeton University Press, 1996).

21. Diana Dwyre and Robin Kolodny, "Barriers to Minor Party Success and Prospects for Change," in *Multiparty Politics in America*, ed. Herrnson and Green.

22. Marty Jezer, "Citizens' Party: Can It Live Up to Its Name?" *The Progressive* 46, no. 10 (October 1982).

23. Douglas J. Amy, *Real Choices/New Voices: The Case for Proportional Representation Elections in the United States* (New York: Columbia University Press, 1993).

24. Benjamin I. Page and James R. Simmons, *What Government Can Do: Dealing with Poverty and Inequality* (Chicago: University of Chicago Press, 2000).

25. Pew Research Center, "Independents Still on the Fence," release, September 14, 2000; "The Two Strains of Swing Voters," release, March 15, 2000.

26. Christopher J. Bosso, "Seizing Back the Day," in *Environmental Policy in the 1990s: Reform or Reaction?* 3d ed., ed. Norman J. Vig and Michael E. Kraft (Washington, D.C.: CQ, 1997).

27. Kevin P. Phillips, *Post-Conservative America: People, Politics, and Ideology in a Time of Crisis* (New York: Vintage, 1983).

28. Thomas Ferguson, *Golden Rule: The Investment Theory of Party Competition and the Logic of Money-Driven Political Systems* (Chicago: University of Chicago Press, 1995); James R. Simmons, "The Economic Theory of Democracy Revisited and Revised," *New Political Science* 23 (Fall 1992): 29–49.

29. Christine A. Kelly, *Tangled Up in Red, White, & Blue: New Social Movements in America* (Lanham, Md.: Rowman & Littlefield, 2001).

30. Sidney Tarrow, *Power in Movement: Social Movements and Contentious Politics*, 2d ed. (New York: Cambridge University Press, 1998).

10

Human Rights Watch: American Liberal Values in the Global Arena

CLAUDE E. WELCH, Jr.

Human Rights Watch is dedicated to protecting the human rights of people around the world. We stand with victims and activists to bring offenders to justice, to prevent discrimination, to uphold political freedom and to protect people from inhumane conduct in wartime. We investigate and expose human rights violations and hold abusers accountable. We challenge governments and those holding power to end abusive practices and respect international human rights law. We enlist the public and the international community to support the cause of human rights for all.

—Mission Statement, HRW

The emergence of human rights as a factor in interstate relations and, more important, in the domestic politics of states, is one of the most significant post–World War II political developments.[1] How individual governments treat their citizens and resident aliens no longer is claimed as a matter of exclusive domestic sovereignty. In a steady and accelerating process, what classic, post-Westphalia theory had left to states alone has become an item of legitimate international concern. This evolution was encouraged (and continues to be encouraged) by concepts long associated with U.S. liberal political thought: the rule of law, sovereignty vested in the people, ultimate responsibility of governments to their citizens, and constitution-style documents setting forth basic principles.

This chapter examines the most significant international human rights nongovernmental organization (NGO) based in the United States. Human Rights Watch (HRW) has, in the relatively brief period since 1978, become a—and quite likely *the*—paragon of effective advocacy on behalf of millions of victims of abuses. HRW concentrates on abuses by governments against their own citizens that are contrary to international human principles and to values enshrined in national constitutions. It weds incisive, detailed research on a variety of human rights issues with continued monitoring of (largely) civil and political rights in more than seventy countries. HRW is a large, complex organization. With five regional divisions (Africa,[2] the Americas, Asia, Europe and Central Asia, and the Middle East and North Africa), three thematic divisions (arms, children's rights, and women's rights), and a variety of special issues (including academic freedom, corporations and human rights, drugs and human rights, labor rights, prisons, refugees, international justice, and the International Criminal Court, or ICC), HRW is rivaled only by Amnesty International (AI) in terms of breadth and depth of coverage. HRW's staff of approximately 180 persons is divided among several offices: two-thirds are housed in its headquarters in the Empire State Building; a significant number are posted in Washington (most notably the Americas division); and smaller numbers serve in regional offices in Brussels, London, and Los Angeles (an office is being planned for Bangkok).

To understand HRW as an exemplar of U.S. liberal political thought and action, it should be viewed first in the domestic context of civil rights organizations such as the National Association for the Advancement of Colored People (NAACP) and the American Civil Liberties Union (ACLU), and second in the international human rights context following World War II, and most particularly in the mid-1970s, when U.S. internal conditions and global shifts encouraged new approaches.

The NAACP, founded in 1909, built a strong record of litigation through its associated Legal Defense and Educational Fund on behalf of civil and political rights for U.S. blacks and, by extension, for other groups denied equal opportunity. The ACLU, established in 1920, fought long and persuasively on behalf of constitutional principles through court cases—though often (like the NAACP) under strong attack. The emphasis of both organizations on civil rights meant the broader term "human rights" was not widely used in the United States until well into the last quarter of the twentieth century.

On the international level, several steps occurred. The establishment of the United Nations resulted in the rapid declaration of a set of human rights principles; the Cold War accentuated contrasting Western and communist approaches to human rights; the post-Vietnam and post-Watergate syndromes underscored the importance in the United States of a "moral" as contrasted with a "realist" view of foreign policy; détente, and particularly the Helsinki Accords, offered new opportunities for networks of human rights activists to cooperate across borders; and the United Nations drafted a series of treaties through which governments pledged to promote and protect human rights. The 1978 establishment of

Helsinki Watch, the initial constituent of HRW, is discussed in more detail below.

HRW also provides an object lesson in the growing political significance of NGOs. NGOs form the heart, or perhaps better the brains and nervous system, of civil society. Their growth in numbers has been extraordinary. According to the Union of International Associations, five times as many human rights groups existed in 1993 when contrasted with 1953; overall they constituted about a quarter of international nongovernmental social change groups.[3] Human rights NGOs constitute a distinctive genre of organization. They stand for "principled ideas." Unlike interest groups, they do not advocate the economic advancement or protection of a narrowly defined sector of society (unless, of course, it is being discriminated against), nor do they claim to advance the interests of a single group.[4] Unlike political parties, they do not seek to exercise power directly. To change the metaphor used at the start of this paragraph, the tree of international human rights has its roots in the UN Charter, its trunk in the Universal Declaration of Human Rights and the major treaties discussed below, its branches in networks of activists, and its life-giving, energy-producing leaves in NGOs.

EMERGENCE OF HUMAN RIGHTS AS AN INTERNATIONAL ISSUE

U.S. liberal political thought has long shown a strong, moralistic international character. It looks favorably on multilateral institutions. Cooperation among governments for common good will achieve more satisfactory results in the long run than "power politics" based on narrow conceptions of national interest, economic advantage, or coercive strength. Idealism through the voluntary association of the many is considered preferable to realism based on calculations of trading patterns, military threats and alliances, or cultural affinities. However, U.S. resistance for many years to ratifying human rights treaties is linked to "U.S. exceptionalism," the belief that the United States has successfully achieved higher levels of human rights performance than other countries, and that ratification of such treaties would be irrelevant and possibly inimical. These concerns interact with security and economic interests, resulting in U.S. opposition to the ICC or establishment of binding human rights policies within international financial and trade institutions. The result is a mixed record, in which early U.S. leadership has passed to other governments. It has been the task of HRW, in conjunction with other NGOs, to remind the U.S. government of its historic role and current needs in an interdependent world.

The UN Charter sets forth the principle of "promoting universal respect for, and observance of, human rights and fundamental freedoms for all without distinction as to race, sex, language or religion" as a basic objective. This clause and parts of the Charter reflected intense lobbying by a wide variety of U.S. citizen groups at the 1945 San Francisco conference.[5] Soon after the United Nations' establishment, its Economic and Social Council (Ecosoc) created the Commission on Human Rights, chaired by Eleanor Roosevelt. The document the Commission prepared, the Universal Declaration of Human Rights (UDHR), provided the essential foundation for the elaborate UN machinery developed since 1948.

The UDHR was drafted by a small, distinguished group whose five major participants had been well trained in Western legal concepts.[6] The document bore the mark of U.S. constitutional thought, many of its articles about civil and political rights echoing the Bill of Rights. Nondiscrimination was its central value: All persons should be treated equally. The UDHR also set forth economic, social, and cultural rights, while guaranteeing to members of minorities the right to live with others in a community and to maintain their language and other aspects of solidarity.

The day on which the UDHR was adopted—December 10, 1948—is now celebrated internationally as Human Rights Day. The strong margin by which the UN General Assembly voted in favor of the UDHR—forty-eight votes in favor, none against, two absent, and eight abstentions—testified to the drafters' sensitivities and the document's qualities.[7] In the enthusiastic words of a recent analyst, the UDHR "would rank in historic significance with the Magna Carta, the French Declaration of the Rights of Man and the American Declaration of Independence."[8]

As its name suggests, the UDHR expresses aspirations rather than sets rigid legal requirements. It represented, in the words of its preamble, "a common standard of achievement." Several years were to pass, however, before the UDHR would be complemented by companion treaties establishing specific obligations for governments.[9] In chronological order, here are the major human rights "conventions," which provide the basis for HRW's activities, the ICCPR being particularly significant:

- The International Convention on the Elimination of All Forms of Racial Discrimination (CERD, 1965)
- The International Covenant on Economic, Social and Cultural Rights (ICESCR, 1966)
- The International Covenant on Civil and Political Rights (ICCPR, 1966)
- The Convention on the Elimination of All Forms of Discrimination against Women (CEDAW, 1979)

- The Convention against Torture and Other Forms of Cruel, Inhuman, or Degrading Treatment or Punishment (CAT, 1984)
- The Convention on the Rights of the Child (CRC, 1989).[10]

Each of these agreements obligates the ratifying governments (the "States Parties," in international legal jargon) to bring their laws into conformity with the international standards embodied in it and take other necessary action steps progressively, and to submit a periodic report on the progress made in implementation. The reports go to committees (ranging from ten members [the Committee Against Torture] to twenty-three members [the Committee on the Elimination of Discrimination Against Women]) of elected independent experts, for discussion with official representatives. These groups, often referred to as Treaty Bodies, prepare "concluding observations" based on the reports and discussion about each country; they also issue occasional General Statements, which are authoritative interpretations of the particular treaty, and may require governments to submit special supplementary information in addition to the periodic reports.

The reporting obligation placed on states has opened perhaps the most important area of activity for human rights NGOs: documentation of abuses. One of the world's leading experts deems the process of information gathering, evaluation, and dissemination one of the two "absolutely indispensable functions" of human rights NGOs.[11] HRW has established a high standard of performance in this respect. Its reports have become must reading for all persons and groups concerned with implementation of human rights. Monitoring how governments meet their constitutional and international requirements lies at the heart of such activism. HRW has learned how to shame states by well-documented, incisive, and accurate reports, followed up by careful advocacy and media pressure. In Korey's words, "Publicity—pitiless, potent and persistent—has been the continuing and ultimate aim of the organization's numerous projects. And, at this specialty, HRW has developed an expertise unrivaled in the human rights business."[12] As we shall now see, this emphasis dates from its earliest years.

BRIEF HISTORY OF HUMAN RIGHTS WATCH

The founding personalities and the temporal context provide important clues to the successes HRW has enjoyed in its nearly quarter century of existence. From 1978, when Helsinki Watch was created by Robert Bernstein, up to the present, HRW has been characterized by high professional standards, attention to emerging issues, increasing prominence in international media as a source of valuable information, and growth in income that has permitted extensive expansion of staff. Leadership has been remarkably stable, with Bernstein as chair of the board for thirty years, with first Executive Director Aryeh Neier serving for fifteen years, and with the Associate Executive Director Ken Roth moving into the top position following Neier's resignation in 1993.

HRW has focused most of its advocacy efforts on the U.S. government, media, and public opinion. Although its staff members come from a wide variety of national backgrounds, the organization's dominant ethos is American in style—an aspect with positive and negative consequences, as I shall note in the conclusion. Although started and run for many years with a nearly exclusive focus on civil and political rights,[13] HRW has moved cautiously toward recognizing the indivisible nature of human rights.[14] Its history and development are fascinating to explore, starting with its initiation as Helsinki Watch.

Helsinki Watch grew from a little-noted provision of the 1975 Helsinki Accords, officially titled the Final Act of the Conference on Security and Cooperation in Europe.[15] This epochal conference balanced interests of East and West in a masterful fashion not fully appreciated in the United States at that time. The accepted principles were placed into three "baskets," the third mentioning "Respect for Human Rights and Fundamental Freedoms, Including the Freedom of Thought, Conscience, Religion or Belief." Whether this was operative political principle or pious platitude would soon be tested.

As Eastern European governments ratified the accords, local activists began to press for their full implementation. Groups sprang up under the leadership of eminent individuals, such as playwright Vaclav Havel (who established Charter 77 in Czechoslovakia) and 1975 Nobel Peace Prize winner Andrei Sakharov (who had formed the Moscow Human Rights Committee in 1970), demanding the "respect for human rights" politicians had promised. Their struggles attracted the attention of some Americans, including Bernstein (the highly influential president, chair, and CEO of Random House, and also chairman of the Association of American Publishers) and McGeorge Bundy (president of the Ford Foundation). Bundy, who had broad experience in foreign affairs (he had moved from his Deanship at Harvard to Washington in 1961, serving as Kennedy's chief adviser on foreign policy), had both an acute sense of international politics and millions of dollars at the Ford Foundation's disposal.[16] Bernstein had earlier formed the Fund for Free Expression, through which the Ford Foundation underwrote the establishment of Helsinki Watch in 1978. The first executive director of Helsinki Watch, Aryeh Neier, moved from his position as executive director of the ACLU to bring the fledgling organization into existence, bringing with him many ACLU values and strategies.

Both the international and domestic political contexts facilitated new human rights efforts at that juncture. Let me briefly note important facets of both contexts, starting with the global setting.

- As already noted, the Conference on Security and Cooperation in Europe had recognized basic human rights principles that governments had pledged to uphold; they could be publicly embarrassed by NGOs for failure to meet them.
- Radio was undermining the old regimes of eastern and central Europe. The Voice of America, Radio Free Europe, and the BBC carried powerful human rights messages, despite Soviet efforts to jam their programs. Contacts among NGOs, east and west, were becoming increasingly common, thanks to direct dial telephones, fax machines, and eased international travel. Increasingly, they could establish and maintain transnational advocacy networks.
- A global treaty basis for human rights was taking shape. The principles of the UDHR were increasingly complemented by major agreements setting precise legal obligations for states. For example, by 1966 negotiations had been completed, texts adopted, and the process of ratification started for CERD and the two International Covenants (ICESCR and ICCPR); all three had come into force by 1976.
- Awarding of the 1977 Nobel Peace Prize to Amnesty International gave an important cachet to human rights NGOs. The prize recognized Amnesty's leadership on behalf of Prisoners of Conscience, who had been imprisoned for their advocacy of nonviolent political change and its support for an end to human rights abuses such as torture. Without question, the honor AI received encouraged formation of other human rights NGOs.

Within the United States, profound shifts in the domestic political climate had also created a more hospitable atmosphere for human rights by the mid-1970s:

- Popular disillusionment with "politics as usual" as manifested in Vietnam and Watergate meant the U.S. government, encouraged strongly by NGOs advocating "principled interests," could pursue different, more moral or idealistic purposes.
- Congressional initiatives late in the Nixon presidency resulted in legislation denying U.S. economic assistance or military aid to countries marked by persistent patterns of gross violations of human rights, unless special presidential certification was given. Congress also

mandated that the Department of State prepare an annual report on the human rights practices of all U.S.-aid–receiving countries, the basis for what has since become an increasingly sophisticated, detailed compendium.

- Jimmy Carter's successful 1976 presidential campaign, in which human rights figured prominently, and the early years of his presidency, in which he and Secretary of State Cyrus Vance tried to implement this option, provided further political credence for human rights as central to American foreign policy.
- Underlying all of these steps was the broad U.S. interest in human rights through moral, citizen involvement, as had been manifested in NGOs' pressure at the 1945 San Francisco conference and which forms a crucial part of the liberal point of view.

In short, the international and national political climates in 1978 were auspicious for creating and linking human rights NGOs. And, with vigorous leadership and increasing resources, Helsinki Watch widened its areas of concern. It took a giant step toward a broader international role with the establishment of other regional groups. Americas Watch followed in 1981, Asia Watch in 1985, Africa Watch in 1987, and Middle East and North Africa Watch in 1989. The various nonregional divisions (arms, women, children) and the special interests mentioned earlier were initiated at varying times and as resources permitted.

The establishment of Americas Watch represented in crucial respects a reaction to changes in national politics, away from what were portrayed by conservatives as the "failed" policies of Carter. The election of Ronald Reagan in 1980 initiated a sharp rightist reorientation of U.S. foreign policy. Reagan appointees made a facile distinction between authoritarian and totalitarian governments: the former could be effective partners in the paramount global struggle against communism, despite their often horrendous records of human rights abuses.[17] The new Republican president deliberately insulted human rights activists by nominating Ernest Lefever, an avowed opponent of human rights activists, as Assistant Secretary of State for Human Rights. (Congress rejected the nomination, a result of strong mobilization by NGOs.) Strong Reagan administration support for "Freedom Fighters" or for military regimes in Central America escalated violence there, with the White House blaming the violence on opponents of the region's U.S.-supported groups or governments. Reports to the contrary from Americas Watch, though sharply and harshly questioned by the Reagan administration, proved ultimately to be far more accurate than the rosy official portrayals emanating from the State Department or the White House. The mobilization of shame through the provision of detailed, accurate information had started.

It was not the Reagan administration that received the strongest criticisms from human rights NGOs, however, but rather other governments. There were villains aplenty. Americas Watch, Asia Watch, and the others could choose among multiple possible targets. One of their toughest issues was deciding how to allocate resources, balancing other governments' susceptibility to external influence (Could pressure from the U.S. government and public opinion sway a rights-abusing regime to change its policies?), heinousness of abuses (Was the worst abuser of human rights necessarily the best target if NGOs or other governments could exercise little external or internal leverage over its policies?), and ability to maintain pressure over time (Given that many human rights issues arose not only as a result of deliberate national policies but also from long-standing practices embedded in national cultures, could change be expected in a brief period?). These dilemmas remain.

Let us fast forward our analysis of HRW—which still did not formally have this identity—to the early 1990s. All regions of the world were covered by "Watch" groups. However, serious problems had surfaced. "The extraordinary growth of the organization in the course of a mere decade from simply a European- (Helsinki)-focused operation to one that embraced global human rights issues exposed grave inadequacies and liabilities that plunged it into a serious crisis," Korey observes.[18] Regional divisions had proliferated and expanded, with resultant confusion. The strong-willed style of Neier ("authoritarian leadership" was a term frequently employed) accentuated internal friction. Thanks to a grant from the Ford Foundation, a management study was completed in late 1993, and a difficult decision was made to subsume the semiseparate groups into the broader HRW context. What had been largely autonomous fiefdoms, some with high degrees of name recognition and renown, were now to cooperate more closely and adopt a common name. It is to the credit of Ken Roth, who succeeded Neier as executive director, that the process has gone relatively smoothly.

HUMAN RIGHTS WATCH AND AMERICAN LIBERALISM

HRW and most other major Western-based human rights NGOs share a common faith in the efficacy of study and exposure. They focus upon accountability and the mobilization of shame. Accountability means that external human rights groups may hold a government responsible for its actions, irrespective of the former's claims that it is shielded by domestic sovereignty.[19] International NGOs, in other words, criticize actions taken by individual governments. Effective mobilization of shame means that, if a government is concerned about its international image, it will not necessarily respond to external critiques by denial of them, but by concrete steps for rectification. Obviously, mobilization of shame fails when a state simply brushes off pressures from human rights NGOs, or when the human rights issue arises from deeply embedded cultural practices well beyond rapid transformation by political fiat. HRW, like most other human rights NGOs, finds it more satisfying and effective to concentrate on acute but solvable issues under some degree of government control, rather than on chronic and likely unsolvable problems rooted in social mores or economic circumstance. For example, while rampant discrimination based on caste constitutes a fundamental abuse of human rights, HRW can more fruitfully concentrate on caste-based violence that may be abetted (or certainly not halted) by the government of India.[20]

Liberal organizations generally share a strong faith in the impact of informed public opinion. They "are organized to promote causes, principled ideas, and norms, and they often involve individuals advocating policy changes that cannot be easily linked to a rationalist understanding of their 'interests.'"[21] NGOs such as HRW or AI invest significant resources in research, publication, and advocacy. By mobilizing members and supporters, they believe change can be wrought by persuading states to change existing policies and adopt more rights-protective ones. However, this belief—that shame can be effectively mobilized through the publication of carefully researched reports and follow-up advocacy—cannot be readily or directly confirmed. HRW has invested mightily in investigation and publication, with 556 reports totaling 30,433 pages published from 1986 to 1995.[22]

Recognizing that information does not speak for itself, HRW places far greater stress on advocacy.[23] All its studies are accompanied by detailed, specific policy recommendations.[24] Analyses should lead to action, not to filing. But who is HRW's most significant audience? Without question, it remains the U.S. government. HRW pursues a policy Keck and Sikkink describe as "leverage."[25] It seeks access to decision-makers; and, as a U.S.-based organization in the media capital of the world but with a sophisticated Washington office, it lobbies the world's most powerful government. Favorable mention of HRW reports by members of Congress, the Executive branch, or the leading media counts as success. Public pressure by the United States to influence the human rights policies of other countries along lines suggested by HRW is a significant triumph for the organization.

Although the overwhelming majority of its research and advocacy centers on approximately seventy target governments, HRW does not overlook the domestic front. It makes common cause with other organizations—most notably the ACLU—in preparing reports and calling for change.[26]

Clearly, it is far more efficient to use resources to lobby leading policy-makers directly than to affect their behavior indirectly through public opinion. A significant contrast exists in this respect between HRW and other organizations discussed in this book. Contrasts also are manifest between HRW and its giant partner in the human rights world, Amnesty International. AI works hard to engage its million members in campaigns, whether to free individual prisoners of conscience or to pressure major governments to change their policies. Keeping this enormous base of people active, interested, and (perhaps above all) regular in their dues and donations involves a great deal of effort.

Neither AI nor HRW accepts allocations from governments, lest its independence be threatened. For reasons of efficiency, HRW strongly prefers to raise a few large gifts rather than many small ones.[27] A small number of major foundations have been generous in their support,[28] most notably the Ford Foundation. Ford has granted an estimated $200 million in support to international human rights groups over a twenty-five-year span.[29] However, it is also fair to say that the overwhelming majority of U.S. foundations have never made a significant grant for explicit human rights work.[30]

CONCLUSION

In the introduction to this book, the editor posed a series of questions about left and liberal movements in U.S. politics. HRW, it should be clear at this point, draws its resources overwhelmingly from the United States, spends much of its effort trying to influence the U.S. media and especially the U.S. government, yet finds all but a small fraction of the abuses it seeks to have corrected in other countries. HRW acts domestically and globally in order to have its primary impact outside the United States.

The issue of postmaterialist versus material needs has never arisen for HRW, nor indeed for other human rights NGOs, in the fashion for movements examined in other chapters. HRW operates on the basis of principled values, emphasizing legal and political remedies based on ideas drawn in substantial measure from the liberal U.S. political tradition. As an earlier reference to the NAACP and ACLU suggested, HRW's techniques of analysis, exposure, and advocacy within the framework of the rule of law were tested by many decades of application within the United States before being utilized in the global arena.

A sharp critic has labeled HRW (along with AI and several other human rights NGOs) "conventional doctrinalists because they are

marked by a heavy and almost exclusive reliance on positive law in treaties and other sources of international law." Supporters for such organizations, Mutua continues, "come from the private, nongovernmental, and
civil society segments of the industrial democracies: prominent lawyers,
academics at leading universities, the business and entertainment elite,
and other professionals. In the United States, these circles are drawn from
the liberal establishment; the overwhelming majority vote for and support the Democratic Party and its politics."[31] He argues that they do not
pay sufficient attention to economic, social, and cultural rights, and that
their rhetoric about the "indivisibility" of human rights is not matched
by commensurate action. For HRW, this comment is historically fair, but
increasingly less accurate. The organization recognizes the interconnec-
tion of what are often called two "generations" of rights. As of January
1997, HRW departed from its historical pattern of privileging civil and
political rights, first, where protection of an economic, social, or cultural
right is "necessary to remedy a substantial violation" of a civil or political
right, and second, where the violation of the former is a "direct product
of state action, whether by commission or omission."[32] More substantial
steps have followed. Asia Division has been most active in expanding
HRW's ambit of concern, particularly through studies of bonded child
labor and caste-based violence against Dalits ("Untouchables").

The introduction to this book also asked whether the distinction
between movements and interest groups is eroding. For human rights
NGOs such as HRW, this question has not arisen. They concentrate on
principled norms, not on material interests.

Human rights organizations enjoy and utilize a range of tactics,
detailed in the preceding pages. Their tactics derive from their basic characteristics, notably their dedication to the rule of law. Two recent books
set forth short lists of NGOs' preferred modes of action. Keck and Sikkink
examine information, symbolic, linkage, and accountability.[33] Welch
stresses "three Ds and three Es": documentation, democratization, development, education, enforcement, and empowerment.[34]

All human rights organizations "march on their pocketbooks." Obviously, they can function only with regular (and preferably growing!) contributions. Most sedulously eschew funding from governments, which
are their usual target of criticism and/or pressure. HRW relies heavily on
foundation grants and donations.[35] Its endowment fund is relatively new,
the Ford Foundation having given $5 million to it in mid-1999.[36]

In terms of emerging issues, the chief arenas for HRW and similar
NGOs lie in economic issues, treating them increasingly as rights as international norms emerge. But this will require attention to targets in addition to governments. IFIs—international financial institutions—and
TNCs—transnational corporations—are obvious ones. But can (say) the

International Monetary Fund (IMF), the World Trade Organization (WTO), or Nike be held to standards similar to those applied to governments? Will the "mobilization of shame" prove effective against entities that are economic rather than political in nature? Human rights groups have advocated consumer boycotts (witness the campaign against Nestlé because of its aggressive marketing of breast milk substitutes), but their "success" has been mixed, at best. Corporate bottom lines or public images may need to be seriously threatened before change occurs. Much-touted codes of conduct have turned out to be as much public relations exercises as serious changes in policy.[37] The glass is at least half full to those seeing the campaigns as establishing a new moral threshold for companies' policies, but mostly empty to those stressing concrete results. And, while the World Bank has (with great flourish) established human rights checklists for projects it considers, application of this policy has been spotty, while the IMF and WTO have proven far more reluctant to broaden their economic mandates. Among international organizations, far and away the most effective has been the ILO (International Labor Organization), thanks to a series of 180-plus agreements with precise standards and careful review of performance by professional staff.[38]

International treaty standards can be both broadened and deepened. HRW played a primary role in two major recent campaigns that involved scores, indeed hundreds, of other NGOs. The International Campaign to Ban Landmines[39] built a coalition of human rights groups with like-minded governments to propose, draft, and adopt a treaty banning an entire weapons system—no mean accomplishment, in theory. Implementation of the landmines convention is far more problematic, however, given opposition by several permanent members of the UN Security Council. Continued U.S. resistance to the establishment of the ICC deeply disappointed leaders of HRW. Despite U.S. rhetoric about the rule of law globally, the need to ferret out, try, and punish violators of crimes against humanity and war crimes, and the establishment of international criminal tribunals for the former Yugoslavia, Rwanda, and Sierra Leone, the Clinton administration tried, unsuccessfully, to write numerous restrictions into the draft treaty and rules of operation. Nonetheless, the ICC is edging ahead, a sign of the serious erosion of the leadership role the United States once played with respect to international human rights.

And, as final and exceptionally complex frontiers of action, HRW and other human rights NGOs must deal with abuses that are structural in nature or based in family relations or civil law and closely linked to culture. An example of the latter is domestic violence; an example of the former is life-threatening economic deprivation resulting from the workings of world markets. No easy target for advocacy, and particularly for solution, exists in such cases.

Is HRW an "American" or an "international" institution? Clearly, it combines elements of both. Its major target of pressure remains the U.S. government; its headquarters are situated in New York City; large numbers of Americans serve on the staff; and its dominant values derive from U.S. civil and political rights. On the other hand, as its mission statement indicates, HRW examines human rights abuses irrespective of where they occur (contingent, of course, on resources and perceived importance). Its offices outside the United States bear witness to its international aspirations: it is far easier, more efficient, and politically sensitive to lobby the European Union from Brussels and the members of the Association of Southeast Asian Nations (ASEAN) from Bangkok than to do either from New York and Washington. But I concur with Korey's assessment: "Even with the thrust toward internationalization, HRW still [is] rooted in the American scene and utilize[s] its connections with the American power structure to affect other governments on human rights issues."[40]

Ultimately, HRW and its sister NGOs are restricted in their impact because they advocate rather than implement policies. They influence governments and public opinion, rather than direct them. Frustration and shortfalls are inevitable. But, when one compares the context of human rights now with that of 1948, when the Universal Declaration was adopted, the contrasts are striking. An armature of international standards exists, based on the UDHR's "common standard of achievement." The number of governments espousing democracy and responsibility to their citizens has leaped, with the disappearance of colonialism and the collapse of communism. Dense networks of human rights NGOs exist, their transnational advocacy exchanging best practices and coordinating campaigns. The contributions of HRW to such development, in its history of less than a quarter century, have been significant.

NOTES

Several HRW staff members were interviewed at varying dates including Ken Roth, Reed Brody, Mike McClintock, Janet Fleischmann, Peter Takirumbudde, Julia Hall, Alison Des Forges, Smita Narula, Dorothy Thomas, and Widney Brown.

    1. I am not claiming that only after 1945 did the Westphalian model come under attack. Moral claims on behalf of the rights of persons not citizens of the states making the claims led to intervention—for example, in the nineteenth century to end the slave trade internationally (especially associated with Great Britain), to protect religious minorities from persecution (as in French "protection" of Maronite Christians in Lebanon against the Ottoman Empire), or to abolish specific social practices (foot-binding in China). Unfortunately, many of these efforts became justifications for colonialism.

2. For clarity and self-disclosure, I have served as a member of the Africa Division's advisory committee since its inception in the late 1980s—a far from onerous responsibility involving one or two meetings per year, to provide input to highly professional staff members about the priorities they have established and the mandates within which they work.

3. In absolute terms, the number climbed from 23 to 168. Margaret E. Keck and Kathryn Sikkink, *Activists Beyond Borders: Advocacy Networks in International Politics* (Ithaca, N.Y.: Cornell University Press, 1998), 10–11.

4. Critics of the liberal paradigm embodied in much of the international human rights machinery do not agree with this statement, to be certain. They assert that human rights NGOs' claims of neutrality or service to humanity as a whole in fact mask the interests and especially the values of a restricted, privileged group, namely largely white, educated, bourgeois, and northern males. Several lines of attack can be mentioned, none of which can be discussed here because of space and time limitations. One argument is that civil and political rights are unduly privileged, giving short shrift to economic, social, and cultural rights; this critique has come from many quarters, most markedly during the Cold War from Communists and from Third World spokespersons who stressed the argument that economic development should precede enhanced civil and political rights since, in their view, human rights was a "luxury" associated with wealth rather than power. A second line of attack, identified often as the "Asian values" argument, criticizes the liberal emphasis on the rights rather than the duties of individuals, and advocates greater recognition of the importance of groups. A similar emphasis on the rights of groups comes from indigenous peoples and their spokespersons, who assert that individualism has eroded communal solidarity and contributed to "ethnocide." A third area of questioning arises from the lack of attention (perhaps because of the lack of a clear target or means of remediation?) to structural violations of human rights; trends in world market prices, for example, are seen as causing massive problems, although the remedy is by no means clear. Criticized as well is the attention given to "public" as contrasted with "private" law: while assault is a clear violation of law and of human rights, domestic violence has been culturally rationalized as "discipline" and only recently given attention in national laws. Women's groups have taken a leading role in reducing the public-private distinction. Interestingly, while the values and modalities of international human rights clearly fit within the liberal paradigm, so too do most of the criticisms made of it!

5. William Korey, *NGOs and the Universal Declaration of Human Rights: "A Curious Grapevine"* (New York: St. Martin's, 1998), 31–41; Felice D. Gaer, "Reality Check: Human Rights NGOs Confront Governments at the UN," in *NGOs, the UN, and Global Governance*, ed. Thomas G. Weiss and Leon Gordenker (Boulder, Colo.: Lynne Rienner, 1996), 52. Among the groups called to San Francisco were several traditionally associated with liberal causes in the United States: the NAACP, the American Jewish Committee, the American Federation of Labor, the League of Women Voters, and the American Bar Association; however, the National Association of Manufacturers and the Chamber of Commerce also participated, a sign of the breadth of the U.S. NGO and interest group community.

In the words of one well-informed specialist, the lobbying of these important U.S. nongovernmental groups "planted several firm human rights seeds in the UN that, in time, would bear considerable fruit. The secret of their strategy was to persuade the U.S. government of the value of human rights in the Charter, relying on its leadership to affect decisively the perspective of others. . . . It was a strategy that would be pursued at various intervals later on in UN history. And it was, to a large extent, the key to human rights advancement. Only rarely would a major breakthrough in human rights occur at the UN without the determination and power exercised by Washington." Korey, *NGOs and the Universal Declaration of Human Rights*, 39.

6. Johannes Morsink, *The Universal Declaration of Human Rights: Origins, Drafting, and Intent* (Philadelphia: University of Pennsylvania Press, 1999).

7. The majority of abstaining states came from the communist bloc; South Africa abstained because of the mention of equality among races, and Saudi Arabia because of the mention of equality between the sexes.

8. Korey, *NGOs and the Universal Declaration of Human Rights*, 43.

9. Drafting of what became the two International Covenants had been largely completed by late 1951, but Cold War squabbles and major disputes in the United States over the relative roles of treaties and the Constitution delayed final consideration. The swelling of the General Assembly by newly independent Asian and African states introduced new priorities, notably self-determination, national control over natural resources, anti-colonialism, and opposition to apartheid. Only in 1966 did the General Assembly unanimously adopt the two International Covenants—and it took a full decade before both received sufficient ratifications to enter into force. Meanwhile, the Universal Declaration itself became increasingly prominent, leading in 1962 to (in the words of the UN Office of Legal Affairs) the "strong expectation that Members of the international community will abide by it." Quoted in Korey, *NGOs and the Universal Declaration of Human Rights*, 49.

10. There are, of course, numerous other treaties that embody human rights norms and standards: the 1926 Slavery Convention (the League of Nations' Slavery, Servitude, Forced Labour and Similar Institutions and Practices Convention) and the 1956 Supplementary Convention (the Supplementary Convention on the Abolition of Slavery, the Slave Trade and Institutions and Practices Similar to Slavery); agreements adopted by regional organizations (the [European] Charter of Human Rights and Fundamental Freedoms, the [Inter-]American Convention on Human Rights, and the African Charter on Human and Peoples' Rights); the four Geneva Conventions of 1949 and the Supplementary Protocols of 1977, which form the core of so-called humanitarian law; and several conventions adopted by the ILO (International Labor Organization). That is not all. The International Criminal Court, when established, will provide a venue for trials of persons accused of crimes against humanity; human rights courts have already been established by the Council of Europe and the Organization of American States, and one has been proposed by the Organization of African Unity. For general remarks on reporting as a strategy for promoting and protecting human rights, see Claude E. Welch, Jr., *Protecting Human Rights in Africa: Roles and Strategies of Non-Governmental Organizations* (Philadelphia: University of Pennsylvania Press, 1995), 140–169.

11. Laurie Wiseberg, "Defending Human Rights Defenders: The Importance of Freedom of Association for Human Rights NGOs" (Montreal: International Centre for Human Rights and Democratic Development, 1993), 4.

12. Korey, *NGOs and the Universal Declaration of Human Rights*, 339–340.

13. The bulldog commitment of Aryeh Neier to civil and political rights seems to be the chief reason. Makau Mutua cites Neier's remarks to a 1993 symposium at Harvard Law School: "When it comes to the question of what are called economic rights, I'm on the side of the spectrum which feels that the attempt to describe economic concerns as rights is misguided. I think that when one expresses this opinion, it is often thought that one is denigrating the significance of economic misery and inequities. I would like not to be accused of that. I regard economic equity and economic misery as matters of enormous significance. I just don't think that it's useful to define them in terms of rights." Quoted in Makau Mutua, "Human Rights International NGOs: A Critical Evaluation," in Welch, *NGOs and Human Rights*, 162, n 22. Also see Korey, *NGOs and the Universal Declaration of Human Rights*, 344.

14. The strongest statement along these lines came from the 1993 World Conference on Human Rights. The Vienna Declaration and Programme of Action stressed the universal, indivisible, interrelated, and interdependent nature of human rights. Although attention was to be given to cultural contexts, limitation of human rights based on the principles and values of a ratifying state was rejected.

15. Korey, *NGOs and the Universal Declaration of Human Rights*, 229–240; Claude E. Welch, Jr., "Amnesty International and Human Rights Watch: A Comparison," in Welch, *NGOs and Human Rights*, 94–95.

16. The Ford Foundation had been heavily influenced by Cold War politics in its early decades; it also chose to steer most of the resources directed overseas through governments rather than NGOs. Major changes in the Foundation's policies can be traced to the impact of Latin American military dictatorships, sketched recently by one of the major participants; see William D. Carmichael, "The Role of the Ford Foundation," in Welch, *NGOs and Human Rights*, 249–251. Keck and Sikkink quote one observer, who noted that Carmichael "cared passionately about human rights" and "fanned the HR flame" in the foundation. Keck and Sikkink, *Activists Beyond Borders*, 99.

17. The Reagan administration's "point person" was Jeanne Kirkpatrick, specialist on Argentina and U.S. representative to the United Nations. She argued that combating the Soviet Union would be enhanced by cooperation with self-proclaimed anti-communist right-wing governments, many of them in Central or South America. The United States thereby turned a blind eye toward massive human rights violations in countries such as Argentina, El Salvador, or Guatemala. For an understanding of Argentina much at odds with Kirkpatrick, see Iain Guest, *Behind the Disappearances: Argentina's Dirty War against Human Rights and the United Nations* (Philadelphia: University of Pennsylvania Press, 1990).

18. Korey, *NGOs and the Universal Declaration of Human Rights*, 347.

19. Keck and Sikkink consider accountability one of the four major "tactics" utilized by transnational advocacy networks. Other tactics include information, symbolic, and linkage policies. Keck and Sikkink, *Activists Beyond Borders*, 18–25.

20. Human Rights Watch, *Broken People: Caste Violence against India's "Untouchables"* (New York: HRW, 1999).

21. Keck and Sikkink, *Activists Beyond Borders*, 8–9.

22. Korey, *NGOs and the Universal Declaration of Human Rights*, 365.

23. Author's interview with Ken Roth, December 14, 1998; compare with Korey, *NGOs and the Universal Declaration of Human Rights*, 366.

24. A very well-informed analyst of human rights contrasts the approaches of AI and HRW to human rights reports and advocacy in the following words: "Most policy makers and members of the political elite *know* the facts already; what they want to know is what they should *do* about them. AI, because it addresses many governments, addresses none in particular, and as a result AI's reports are rather light on political analysis and recommended options for policy makers. HRW is more cunning than AI in this regard, but mainly because it addresses much of its reporting specifically to the U.S. government." Morton E. Winston, "Assessing the Effectiveness of International Human Rights NGOs: Amnesty International," in Welch, *NGOs and Human Rights*, 37.

25. Keck and Sikkink, *Activists Beyond Borders*.

26. Noteworthy examples include prison conditions and discriminatory aspects of the imposition of the death penalty.

27. Welch, "Amnesty International and Human Rights Watch," 104.

28. Jay S. Osviovitch, "Feeding the Watchdogs: Philanthropic Support for Human Rights NGOs," *Buffalo Human Rights Law Review* 4 (1998): 341–363.

29. Carmichael, "The Role of the Ford Foundation," 252.

30. In fact, American foundations tend to shy away from issues that can be viewed as political, as international human rights certainly are—involving as they do direct criticism of governments and lobbying for political action. For an interesting albeit dated perspective, see Waldemar A. Nielsen, *The Big Foundations* (New York: Columbia University Press, 1972).

31. Mutua, "Human Rights International NGOs," 151.

32. "Human Rights Watch's Proposed Interim Policy on Economic, Social and Cultural Rights," cited in Mutua, "Human Rights International NGOs," 155.

33. Keck and Sikkink, *Activists Beyond Borders*, 18–25.

34. Welch, *Protecting Human Rights in Africa*, 50–74.

35. Details in Welch, "Amnesty International and Human Rights Watch," 95–97, 104.

36. Carmichael, "Role of the Ford Foundation," 254.

37. See chapter 5.

38. Virginia Leary, "Lessons from the Experience of the International Labour Organisation," in *The United Nations and Human Rights: A Critical Evaluation*, ed. Philip Alston (Oxford: Clarendon Press, 1992), 580–619.

39. Korey, *NGOs and the Universal Declaration of Human Rights*, 363–364, 433–434.

40. Korey, *NGOs and the Universal Declaration of Human Rights*, 361.

11

The Peace Movement:
Voices in the Wilderness

MEREDITH REID SARKEES

Attempts to promote peace and to encourage the government to eliminate or reduce military adventures have been a consistent element of United States political history. The peace movement has endeavored (with occasional success) to play a role in shaping U.S. foreign policy. Peace movement activities have changed over time, and their specific foci have been very much determined by the political issues of the day. The overarching goal of this chapter is to examine a couple of issues in which the peace movement has been interested and the tactics it has employed to express its positions.

At the beginning of the twenty-first century, one of the more significant American uses of force, both political and military, is the U.S. sanctions policy against Iraq, which has endured since the 1991 Gulf War. One of the peace movement organizations that have been working to promote a change in U.S. policy toward Iraq is Voices in the Wilderness. This chapter discusses Voices in the Wilderness within the broad context of the peace movement and as an example of the tactics by which nongovernmental organizations can have an impact on U.S. policy formation.

DEFINITIONAL ISSUES

What exactly is peace? *Webster's* dictionary initially defines peace as "freedom from war or stopping war."[1] Yet generally for both members of the peace movement and scholars who study it, peace has a much broader meaning. For instance, in her examination of the role of the Women's

International League for Peace and Freedom (WILPF), Katherine Meerse noted that "League members believed that peace was not simply the absence of war. True peace could be constructed only on a solid foundation of freedom, justice, and equality for all."[2] Bruce Kent traced a similarly broad definition of peace to religious origins:

> If Pope Paul VI in his 1967 encyclical *Populorum Progressio* was correct ("Peace is the fruit of anxious daily care to see that everyone lives in the justice that God intends") then all those working for justice are working for peace. Amnesty International, the World Development Movement, the United Nations Association, the Red Cross, and a host of other individuals and groups made up the wider peace movement.[3]

In this broad context, the peace movement can be conceived of as people who seek to promote justice by opposing governmental uses of violence. Consequently, the peace movement seeks to challenge foreign policy decisions that pursue goals and utilize tactics that are inconsistent with peace and justice. Despite the seemingly laudatory connections between peace and justice, Kent also indicated that peace did not always have such a positive connotation: "The term peace movement frequently appeared in the press in the 1980s as 'peace movement.' The quotation marks indicating a warning. 'Peace' was not then an ideologically clean word."[4] In contrast to such pejorative views, changes in the international system since the 1990s have contributed to a corresponding evolution of the peace movement. Not only has the number of peace movement organizations increased, but the peace movement is now being seen in a more global context, acknowledging the international interplay among peace organizations. As Michael True has noted, there has been a "steady increase in resistance movements against direct and structural violence around the world since the 1980s, dramatizing the interconnectedness of regions, nations, people, and the natural environment."[5] This shift has led some scholars to substitute the term "movement for global nonviolence" for the "peace movement" in order to highlight the new convergence of initiatives for peace and campaigns for social justice around the globe.[6] The "global nonviolence" emphasis goes beyond our desire to focus on attempts to change public and specifically foreign policy. Thus the term "peace movement" in its broad context will be retained here to highlight endeavors to change government policies, while still being cognizant of the ways in which the peace movement has changed over time.

HISTORY

The focus on peace or peaceful resolutions to conflicts has been a constant theme (though frequently ignored) in American politics. During the revolutionary period, there were those who sought a peaceful resolution to the conflict with Britain, such as John Dickinson, who persuaded Congress to pass the Olive Branch Petition urging George III to restore peace.[7] Subsequently, the core of President George Washington's foreign policy was isolationism, or the desire to eschew foreign entanglements in order to avoid being dragged into war. Yet the peace movement as an organized interest in America really began at the beginning of the nineteenth century as an outgrowth of utopian movements and religious convictions, particularly among the members of the historic peace churches, such as the Quakers, Mennonites, and Church of the Brethren.[8] Peace societies' work for world peace was often correlated with advocacy of other reforms such as abolition of slavery and women's rights. Internationally, the Napoleonic wars and the War of 1812 in America precipitated the creation of nonsectarian peace societies, especially in New York and Massachusetts in 1815.[9] These groups varied in ideological perspective from the fairly conservative position of the American Peace Society (founded in 1828), which accepted "defensive" war, to the more radical pacifism of the New England Non-Resistance Society (founded in 1837 by William Lloyd Garrison). Yet during this period, they generally agreed on seeing journalism as a form of activism, and a primary focus was on utilizing the power of the press through their own publications to change public opinion.[10]

The Civil War divided the peace movement over the aims and purposes of the peace movement relative to war and slavery. For example, the American Peace Society supported the Civil War, while the Copperheads or Peace Democrats campaigned against the war, yet they opposed emancipation of the slaves.[11] Though the popularity of the peace movement declined during this period, it reemerged afterward, frequently in a more organizational form that combined peace activities with other social goals. For instance, the Women's Christian Temperance Union (WCTU) created a Department of Peace and Arbitration in 1887. The outlawry of war was to be the third of the great trio of abolitions (along with the eradication of slavery and liquor), which they viewed as their historical legacy.[12] The left, as such, had little to do with these movements until the period of U.S. imperial expansion of the 1890s. Anti-imperialism became the specific focus of groups not usually associated with the peace movement. For instance, intellectuals formed the Anti-Imperialism League in 1898 and carried out a campaign to educate the American public about the horrors of the Philippine war and the evils of imperialism.

This activism was heightened by the approach of World War I. Now, however, the Socialist party and the educated pacifist constituency led the anti-war movement. The People's Council of America for Peace and Democracy was formed in 1917 as a coalition of labor-farmer, left, and pacifist forces. "Among other groups, the Women's Peace Party (later the U.S. branch of the Women's International League for Peace and Freedom [WILPF]), the Fellowship of Reconciliation, and the National Civil Liberties Bureau (later the American Civil Liberties Union [ACLU]) all had active socialists in their leaderships and ranks."[13] However, U.S. entry into World War I led to a decline in peace activities. The socialists were divided by the war and ultimately were crushed by defections and government suppression. Yet, "[t]hey had by 1919 nevertheless conducted the most important radical antiwar movement until the 1960s."[14]

In terms of the sheer quantity of participants and organizations, the American peace movement reached a height during the interwar years.[15] The primary focus was on the construction of peacekeeping mechanisms including disarmament pacts. The Committee on the Cause and Cure of War (CCCW), founded by Carrie Chapman Catt, became the largest women's peace organization of the 1920s, with a focus on developing legal institutions to prevent war.[16] Two other women's peace groups of the period were more "radical." The WILPF articulated the connection of economic and racial oppression with colonialism and war, while the Women's Peace Union consisted of suffragists and absolute pacifists.[17] During the 1920s, the peace movement was able to play a role in shaping American policy, especially by building grassroots public support for the Kellogg-Briand pact.[18]

The popularity of the peace movement declined during World War II, yet it was revived in the immediate post-war era (1946 through 1949). However, the post-war period involved different issues and correspondingly different organizations. Nuclear proliferation became the primary concern, and pacifists were the vanguard of the anti-nuclear mobilizations (1957 through 1963). The Albert Einstein–Bertrand Russell appeal of July 1955 united prominent scientists worldwide to call for measures of peace and nuclear survival. Peace research began among social scientists, with pacifist Kenneth Boulding as its leading figure.[19] A "peace delegation" was even developed in Congress, which contributed to the ratification of the 1963 Test Ban Treaty. Otherwise the movement was relatively unsuccessful in restraining the nuclear buildup.

Meanwhile the peace movement became linked to the civil rights movement, and opposition to the Vietnam War attracted more leftist groups to the peace movement. "The sudden swelling of the peace movement and radicalization of its participants, especially visible on campuses, created, more than any other influence, the largest U.S. radical movement since the 1930s. . . . Peace indeed tended to be equated with social transformation."[20] The antiwar momentum spread among other vocal elements of the population, including press commentators, corporate executives, the clergy, and prominent personalities, whose attitudes appeared in the media coverage.[21] The growing anti-war sentiment among disparate vocal elements of the population contributed to the peace movement having an impact on ending the Vietnam War. (The details of this will be discussed below.)

Yet after the Vietnam War began to wind down, many of the peace movement groups fragmented and all but disappeared. The nuclear freeze remained the primary issue for the peace movement in the 1980s, though it had limited success. There also was a shift to a focus on Latin America, with groups such as Human Rights Watch documenting atrocities, and Amnesty International lobbying on behalf of political prisoners. In the United States there was growing opposition to the School of the Americas at Fort Benning, Georgia. Groups like School of the Americas (SOA) Watch have sponsored demonstrations each November and have initiated lobbying efforts with members of Congress. This effort has had some limited success in that the public scrutiny caused sufficient embarrassment in Congress that the government changed the name of the school to Western Hemisphere Institute for Security Cooperation. So far, however, the peace movement has been unable to force its closure.[22]

Despite the demise of many peace movement organizations during the 1980s, the Grassroots Peace Directory indicated the existence in 1988 of 7,700 peace groups (yet 7,200 had annual budgets of less than $30,000).[23] However, it is estimated that 35 percent of the peace movements active in 1988 had ceased operations by 1992.[24] Many of the core peace constituencies and key organizations, such as the historic peace churches and world federalists, have remained, while the newer groups and those with more specific interests tended to vanish. Conversely, organizations that undertook state and local insider political action were less likely to disband.[25]

TACTICS

If the goal of the peace movement has been to influence government policy on issues of peace and social justice, how has it proposed to accomplish this? In the United States, the foreign policy decision-making apparatus is significantly different from that in the domestic politics sphere. It is more hierarchically structured, with the central roles being played by the president and the senior foreign policy advisors and a less prominent role played by Congress. The foreign policymaking structure is frequently pictured as a series of concentric circles, with the president in the middle, or as a pyramid-type structure, with the president at top, as represented by figure 11.1.

The actual policymakers are in the top three categories. Those in the

FIGURE 11.1
U.S. Foreign Policy-Making Structure

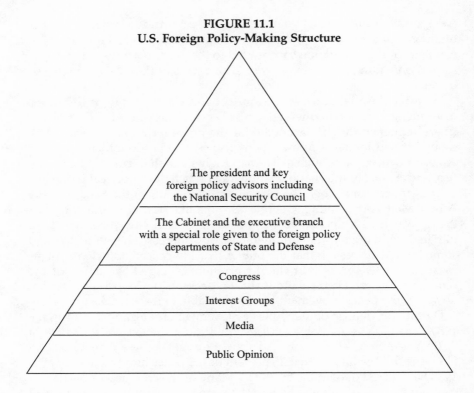

The president and key
foreign policy advisors including
the National Security Council

The Cabinet and the executive branch
with a special role given to the foreign policy
departments of State and Defense

Congress

Interest Groups

Media

Public Opinion

bottom three have no direct role in policymaking, and thus can generally have a significant impact only by trying to influence those in the top three levels. "Interest groups" could be subdivided into five basic types: economic groups, identity groups, political issue groups, state and local governments, and foreign governments.[26] From this structural perspective, the peace movement would fall under the category of political issues groups. However, of the interest groups, the category that has frequently been seen as the most influential is the "economic groups," especially, for foreign policy, the military-industrial complex.[27] Yet, as globalization has increased both the number of interest groups and the intertwining of economic and other issues, the influence of other types of interest groups will undoubtedly increase as well. Consequently, the government will be under increased pressure to incorporate the interests and positions of interest groups and activists into decision-making processes.

Interest groups in general have three basic options for influencing policy: influencing the executive branch, influencing Congress, and influencing public opinion.[28] To influence the executive branch, interest groups can convey information to executive agencies, become involved in presidential elections, or attempt to have an impact on executive appointments. Interest groups can also lobby Congress or become involved in congressional elections. Finally, interest groups can try to get the help of the media and public opinion to amplify their message. Similarly, public opinion can be seen as having influence in five general ways: (1) by setting parameters for policy options; (2) by restraining or pulling the president toward the center; (3) by having an impact on Congress, through public opinion polls and by communication of policy preferences to members of Congress; (4) directly, by setting a range of diplomatic solutions that would be possible (politically acceptable) at home; and (5) by affecting the outcome of elections.[29]

However, there are some ways in which the peace movement differs from other interest groups. As mentioned above, the foreign policy structure itself limits opportunities for influence; domestic policy groups have more options. For instance, the civil rights movement could use the courts to obtain policy changes, but the peace movement has few opportunities to use the judicial branch. Electoral influence to obtain policy changes is also more limited, since elections are more often decided upon domestic rather than foreign policy issues. The peace movement's utilization of public opinion is also more constrained because in general the foreign policy elite do not see the public as being informed about international issues, and thus public opinion is frequently ignored.[30] The peace movement has no natural ally in the bureaucracy; in fact, it confronts powerful adversaries, particularly in the Department of Defense and Congress, in its attempts to contain military spending.[31]

The peace movement is also different from other interest groups on broader theoretical issues. Johan Galtung has argued that the peace movement faces a particular dilemma because it poses a fundamental challenge to the state's use of force. The basic argument of the peace movement is that the state abuses military power.

> The essential task of the peace movement in a historical perspective is to challenge monopoly control over coercion in general, and military power in particular, by the government in the modern state. . . . The peace movement stands not only for a challenge to government monopoly, but also for a general reduction of the instruments of violence, all the way to the abolition of war as a social institution.[32]

The dilemma is that the peace movement lacks the fundamental tools to make such a change, since there is no recognized right for citizens to refuse military service or to withhold taxes from a government that wages war.[33]

The influence tactics available are also being changed by the globalization of the peace movement. In their discussion of peace movement organizations, Edwards and Marullo identified thirty-eight separate influence activities or tactics targeting individuals, national governments, and intergovernmental institutions. These tactics were then combined into seven distinct technical play lists that could be performed by peace organizations. Three of the seven can be considered to be conventional *insider* tactics: (1) national insider legislative activity; (2) state or local insider legislative activities; and (3) party electoral activities. The other four were considered *outsider* activities: (4) monitoring congressional voting records and peace-related legislation; (5) grassroots electoral activities like voter registration drives, public meetings, and getting people to the polls; (6) actions, including participation in a rally or demonstration or letter-writing campaign; (7) nonviolent direct action, including boycotts, civil disobedience, war tax resistance, nonviolent training, and draft counseling.[34] Discouragingly, their findings indicated that only those who are willing to accept the rules and legitimacy of the status quo, who utilize insider tactics, are allowed access to insiders and perhaps even to survive.[35] Jackie Smith categorized the tactics available to transnational social movement organizations (TSMOs) in a similar fashion (see table 11.1).

TABLE 11.1
Examples of TSMO Tactics, 1983–1993 (listed by the *target* of the activity)

Individuals	*National Governments*	*Intergovernmental Institutions*
Education	Letter-writing campaign	Draft international conventions
Citizen exchanges	Fact-finding missions	Document violations of international law
Work camps	Protest demonstrations	Early warning activities
Speakers bureau	Direct actions	Promote "international" days
Legal aid	Lobby national policymakers	Advise IGO officials
Alternative marketing	Petitions	Lobby delegates
Networking	Observer missions	Monitor transnational corporations
Nonviolence training	Advise national governments	Monitor international agencies
Technical training	Draft national legislation	Political socialization
Media campaigns		

Source: Jackie Smith, "Characteristics of the Modern Transnational Social Movement Sector," in *Transnational Social Movements and Global Politics*, ed. Jackie Smith, Charles Chatfield, and Ron Pagnucco (Syracuse, N.Y.: Syracuse University Press, 1997), 44.
Note: Categories are illustrative, not necessarily mutually exclusive.

In the course of history the peace movement has used a number of tactics in pursuit of its goals. For instance, nineteenth-century peace advocates emphasized the significance of writing as a form of activism and focused upon the power of the press to change public opinion to oppose war. Attempts to mold public opinion were also characteristic of the pre–World War I peace movement, though more emphasis was given to public demonstrations and speeches. Attempts to influence Congress through the election of sympathetic legislators were also made during this period. The interwar period saw a focus on education and cultural exchanges and the promotion of legal mechanisms to stop war (which ultimately proved ineffective). Opposition to the Vietnam War was characterized by attempts to change public opinion by spreading information and having demonstrations. The key elements were the role of the media in changing public opinion and the ability to create a strong coalition of groups, which then utilized a variety of tactics.

Mary Anna Colwell examined 1980–1990s peace movement activities in terms of the tactics they utilized to influence public policy. She wanted to answer four basic questions: whether the peace movement was serious about influencing policy, whether it was organized effectively to do so, and whether the tactics were expressive (aimed at making the actors feel better), or instrumental (aimed at changing policy). The data were derived from a 1988 survey of organizations working for peace and a 1992 follow-up survey. The overarching finding of her research suggests that most peace movement organizations are concerned about foreign policy, claim to want to change policy, yet generally had few specifics of how to do this.[36] Very few engaged in trying to work for the election of congressional representatives opposed to war policies. They did not work for legislation that would provide for access by citizen groups into the foreign policy process. Few seemed highly involved in lobbying Congress. The justification for these decisions was unclear.[37]

The only groups that Colwell found to be successful were some of the expert foreign policy organizations such as the Council on Foreign Relations and Carnegie Endowment. Such groups have become recognized participants in the policy process under certain circumstances: when issues are particularly salient to the group; or when there is a split within the policymaking elite; or when an issue is marginal to the primary foreign policy agenda.[38] These elite groups are deeply involved in foreign policy issues but are not normally linked to the peace movement. On occasion, these elite foreign policy organizations share the policy goals of the peace movement, which increases their chances that these goals will be adopted.

Utilizing data from the same survey, Marullo and Chute compared the specifically pacifist organizations to nonpacifist peace organizations.

One-third of the peace movement organizations could be classified as pacifist.[39] The study found that the pacifist groups were more united, more radical, and had broader goals than general peace movement organizations. They also differed in the tactics they used, being more likely to engage in direct action, more likely to undertake civil disobedience and participate in boycotts, and more likely to sponsor resistance training. Both pacifist and nonpacifist groups utilized educational activities and were equally likely to take part in demonstrations. Overall, the pacifist groups "often serve as the vanguard of the movement. . . . It has been the pacifist groups that have articulated the most visionary or comprehensive goals for the movement."[40] Since the pacifist groups are more likely to believe that policy changes result from the process of changing individuals rather than elites, they are less likely than nonpacifist groups to work within the political system. The authors conclude by arguing that for real change to take place, the activities of both wings of the peace movement are necessary.[41] This is true partially because the alternatives posed by the more radical pacifist groups make the reforms of the nonpacifist groups seem more acceptable. Such findings would also seem to suggest that if the pacifist portions of the peace movement wish to be more successful, they will need to expend more energy working to modify the political structure itself to make the process of foreign policymaking more open to alternative perspectives.

IMPACT

Though the peace movement has been active in a number of policy realms, the question remains as to whether it has been successful in influencing public policy. Ultimately the reasons for governmental policy choices are rarely clear. Consequently, as the historical account and the discussion of tactics have revealed, it is hard to assess the impact of peace movements on government policy. Overall, however, one can conclude that its successes in actually changing public policy have been relatively limited. Rarely has it ever been able to prevent the use of military force, yet it has been more successful in goals with a more limited scope, such as inhibiting U.S. entry into World War I and promoting disarmament measures. Here we would like to discuss three of the instances in which the peace movement has had an impact since the end of World War II. In these instances the peace movement has emerged as an avenue for popular influence.[42] "It is clear, however, that both policymakers and activists act as if protest does matter."[43]

Vietnam

Probably the most often-cited instance of the power of the peace movement was its activities to end the war in Vietnam. The peace movement is seen as having played a significant role, primarily through activities to influence public opinion. Though public opinion certainly did change, from supporting the war to wanting peace agreements, it is difficult to disentangle the degree to which the peace movement helped in causing public opinion to shift. Initially, the anti-war movement utilized more "insider" tactics related to providing information. "We tend to forget that this phase of the anti-war movement began as an attempt to educate the government and the nation."[44] This very much reflected the acceptance of the pluralist model of policymaking with its belief in the role of citizens in a democracy. "People believed that the government would respond to them because they believed in American democracy and rectitude."[45] However, those in Washington were trying to conduct the war without hindrance, and when the government did respond with disinformation and new waves of repression, tactics shifted more to "outsider" tactics of protest demonstrations and direct action.[46] Yet the focus on providing information remained. Bruce Franklin gives the peace movement credit particularly for encouraging the public to change its view of the North Vietnamese. "Countless Americans came to see the people of Vietnam fighting against U.S. forces as anything but an enemy to be feared and hated. Tens of millions sympathized with their suffering, many came to identify with their 2,000-year struggle for independence, and some even found them an inspiration for their own lives."[47] The shift in focus to demonstrations and direct action was assisted by the increasing cooperation of the disparate anti-war organizations. This broad coalition not only increased the visibility of their activities, but also expanded the types of tactics utilized, including attempts to have an impact on government decision makers and upon the electoral process. Although college anti-war activism did hamper those in policy positions, the most decisive opposition to the war came ultimately not from the campuses but from within the cities and the army itself.[48] Yet, the anti-war movement did influence the course of the war since its more "radical" positions made the more gradual options for ending the war more acceptable.[49]

Despite the peace movement's successful role in encouraging the end of the Vietnam War, the mediocre status of the peace movement today is revealed in the extent to which current organizations and individuals want to distance themselves from its activities, and people who were in the movement now feel embarrassed or ashamed of their participation.[50]

Nuclear Freeze

The nuclear freeze campaign was the largest segment of the peace movement in the early 1980s. Scholars have argued that the peace movement's attempts to limit nuclear weapons during this period were successful in influencing both the legislative process and the media.[51] The "freeze movement" generally meant CND (Campaign for Nuclear Disarmament) and its various specialist sections, including Pax Christi, the National Peace Council, the World Disarmament Campaign, and the Society of Friends. Overall, the freeze movement has been characterized as one of the "mainstream" elements within the peace movement since its goals were more reformist than radical in nature. The movement had several foci, but initially it tried to educate the public about the dangers of nuclear weapons and nuclear proliferation by creating something like an open public debate on defense and security. One of the groups that became most energized by the issue was women, and there was a "rapid growth of an informed, determined and courageous feminist constituency. For instance, the persistence of the Greenham women caught the imagination of the world."[52] The freeze movement also had an impact on the media, and its activities helped to put nuclear issues on the media agenda.[53] Furthermore, elements of the entertainment industry provided support to the movement. *"The Day After*, a made-for-television movie about a nuclear war actually occurring, was both indicative of and a further contributor to a widespread fear that the buildup was going too far and that things might be careening out of control."[54]

The freeze movement also wanted to have an impact on governmental policy, in terms of establishing arms control plans and winning defense spending cuts. In this vein, it acted in ways that are typical of nonpacifist peace movement organizations, in that it utilized more elements of an "insider" electoral lobbying strategy.[55] At the time, the Reagan administration was much more skeptical of arms control than its predecessors. It had proposed developing a nuclear war–fighting capacity, dubbed NUTS (for Nuclear Utilization Targeting Strategy), and had promoted the deployment of SDI (the Strategic Defense Initiative), dubbed Star Wars. Initially the administration dismissed the information provided by the freeze movement. However, as the freeze movement began to gain in popularity and receive wide support from religious communities, its strategy included more "outsider" tactics. A freeze rally in New York City attracted a crowd estimated at 700,000 to 1,000,000, which made it the largest U.S. demonstration of any kind up to that point.[56] Large demonstrations also were held in Western Europe, protesting the Pershing and cruise missile deployments. Though it was unsuccessful in stopping the increased missile deployments, it contributed to slowing the Reagan buildup. In this vein, the nuclear freeze movement has been credited with setting policy parameters that pulled the Reagan administration back from the political right and more to the political center.[57] The public discussions precipitated by the freeze activities were also able to emphasize the judgment that security was not only to be found in a numerical nuclear balance,[58] an argument that contributed to the signing of the Intermediate Nuclear Forces (INF) Treaty in 1987. An indicator of the success of the freeze movement in this vein is that many of the arguments put forward by peace movement activists in the 1980s are reappearing in more respectable, or insider, organizations in the 1990s.

On the other hand, there were also negative aspects to the peace movement's preoccupation with the nuclear freeze issue during this period. For instance, it has been argued that many critical issues of the time were ignored both by the peace movement and by the public, including health hazards, environmental dangers, economic collapse, and the social divisions between rich and poor, black and white.[59] Reagan administration policies vis-à-vis the contras were also not fully discussed. The experiences of the freeze movement thus highlight both the benefits of utilizing insider tactics and its pitfalls. As a critic has concluded, "The merging of SANE [the successor to the Committee for a Sane Nuclear Policy of the 1950s and 1960s] and Freeze, in 1986, also exemplified the victory of professionalism over grassroots enthusiasm within Left-connected anti-war work—at least for the time being."[60]

The Gulf War

The peace movement has had a discouraging record regarding the Middle East. In general, this is true both because the movement has been divided over the issue of Palestine and because many other peace activists have failed to address the Palestinian case at all. Indeed, some prominent peace activists and their organizations have supported political candidates who take anti-peace positions: for instance, a number of former peace activists who subsequently held political office even supported Israel's 1982 invasion of Lebanon.[61] Thus, "Without the support of mainstream peace groups, groups working for peace in the Middle East have remained on the fringes of popular consciousness."[62]

The peace movement was revitalized, however, by the possibility of U.S. intervention into the Gulf crisis, and the movement's subsequent activities had certain elements of success. Initially the peace movement was able to engender support for their opposition to U.S. intervention across a broad spectrum of individuals and groups. Despite President George H. W. Bush's claim that there was no anti-war movement opposing the Gulf War, hundreds of thousands of people were mobilized in opposition. There were several interesting attributes of the peace movement at this stage. To a great extent, the intellectuals did not lead the movement and were in fact generally behind, rather than ahead of, public opinion. Another interesting aspect of the anti-war movement was its popular appeal in the west and the midwest of the United States, areas that are not usually known as strongholds of dissident politics. The strongest anti-war sentiment was among the elderly, and a smaller proportion of the movement was made up of students. Yet the movement began to develop several strengths. Politically, in terms of coalition formation, it became intergenerational, uniting new activists on campuses with those who had fought for peace and social justice for decades. The peace movement also gained support (immediately prior to the war) from key segments of organized labor, the majority of the larger Christian denominations, and women.[63] Congress was also initially hesitant about U.S. war involvement.[64] Consequently, this united peace movement forced the Bush administration to go to extraordinary lengths to legitimize the war effort, such as asking for formal congressional and UN backing and emphasizing principles of self-determination and enforcement of UN resolutions as justifications for the war. Yet, the anti-war movement, while widespread, was shallow. Most Americans became increasingly resigned to the fact that the U.S. government would prosecute the war as it saw fit regardless of public opinion. Once the war began, public opinion shifted to support of President Bush.

Ultimately, the Gulf War not only exposed the movement's weakness, but also resulted in its increasing marginalization. Part of the peace movement's difficulties stemmed from a fundamental split between those who condemned Iraq and those who did not.

For example, in 1991 during the peace movement's mobilization against the U.S. military buildup in the Persian Gulf, two "warring" coalitions formed to oppose U.S. intervention. The smaller coalition refused to condemn Iraq's invasion of Kuwait, while the larger, more mainstream, coalition did so in its platform. This culminated in rival national-level demonstrations on successive weekends in Washington D.C. These intra-movement conflicts were played out publicly in the national press and exacerbated public disaffection with opposition to the Gulf War.[65]

The peace movement's position was also weakened by a highly effective propaganda barrage by the Bush administration, the censorship of the press at the war front, falsification of reports to exaggerate military successes, the underestimation of civilian casualties, the low number of American casualties, the short duration of the war, and the nature of the Iraqi regime. The media played largely a "cheerleader role," with opponents of the war, including Middle Eastern experts, largely ignored. "Prowar sentiment was stage-managed from the highest level and was no match for an underfunded grassroots movement."[66] The relatively low number of American casualties and the brevity of the ground war, in contrast to the dire predictions of the peace movement, helped undermine the movement's credibility. As a result, after the war the anti-war movement was in disarray, and once again the Middle East was on the back burner of the peace movement's agenda.

> Though the traditional pacifist groups, such as the Fellowship of Reconciliation and the American Friends Service Committee, have continued to address the situation in Iraq—particularly the devastating humanitarian crises resulting from the war and the ongoing sanctions—such efforts have failed to create much popular support. . . . Similarly, periodic bombing raids by the U.S. Air Force in Iraq since the war has met with little organized opposition."[67]

There were some positive outcomes from the peace movement's efforts in this case. The anti-war sentiment expressed forced President Bush to go to great lengths to justify and legitimize the war, seeking both congressional and UN approval. Consequently, in the future it may be hard to legitimize further military interventions without such a clear mandate. "In effect, while the peace movement was unable to stop the Gulf War, it may have effectively prevented future wars. . . . As a result, there are many reasons to believe that anti-war sentiment is seen by those in positions of political power as a force with which to be reckoned."[68]

These three cases reveal some tactical lessons for the peace movement. The most striking lesson is the importance of coalitions. With thousands of relatively narrow peace organizations in existence, their impact will be limited unless they unite. As the Vietnam case demonstrated, the cooperation of anti-war groups from disparate orientations not only provided numerical support for demonstrations, but it also provided a broad array of tactics, ranging from more "radical" direct actions to insider lobbying. With the support of the media, the success of the movement was its encouragement of the government to end the war. Yet its ultimate failure was in not seeking a more fundamental change in the policymaking process, which might have ensured greater access for future peace movement concerns and activities. This lack of access was initially problematic for the freeze movement. Though the movement was partially successful in trying to utilize coalition formation, the narrowness of its focus limited its appeal. The primacy that the freeze movement gave to insider tactics served it well on some levels, yet also restricted its options and proposals. The opposition to the Gulf War similarly had its success during the initial period when anti-war sentiment existed within a wide variety of groups and institutions. Yet the breadth of the incipient coalition was hurt by internal disagreements, which also contributed to massive defections from the movement when it was confronted with sustained opposition from the government. Thus, these cases would seem to indicate that if peace movements are going to be successful, they need to involve as many organizations as possible, including the media; cooperate and coordinate their efforts; utilize a broad array of tactics, both insider and outsider; and include efforts for institutional policymaking reform.

Current Trends

The post–Cold War era is showing contradictory trends within the broad peace movement. On the positive side, a core of the peace movement's organizations has survived; the American Friends Service Committee, the Fellowship of Reconciliation, Pax Christi, War Resisters' League, and the Women's International League for Peace and Freedom continue to maintain organizations. Recently there has also been another period of revitalization of the American peace movement, with an expansion of peace and justice concerns and issues, such as human rights, the environment, women's rights, peace, and economic development on the national and global levels. In addition, the process of globalization has fueled the growth of both national and transnational social movement organizations. Such cross-national organizations in many instances have sprung from, or are linked to, domestic peace movement organizations. For instance, Pax Christi (a group open to anyone interested in nonviolence) has seen not only its U.S. membership grow to twelve thousand, with five hundred local chapters, but also the development of a Pax Christi International, with branches in twenty-two countries on four continents.[69] Data drawn from the Yearbook of International Organizations show rapid growth in such transnational social movement organizations. Between 1973 and 1993, the number of TSMOs grew from fewer than two hundred to more than six hundred. Of these, the number of groups focused specifically on peace issues was eight in 1973, six in 1983, and nine in 1993.[70] Many of these organizations are becoming internationally accepted "for bilateral and multilateral consultation, arbitration, mediation, second-track diplomacy, peacekeeping, and even disarmament."[71] These organizations can provide resources and greater access to intergovernmental organizations to the local peace movement organizations. As Ronald Deibert concludes, "For Liberals, this type of political activism has become a beacon of hope in the quest to create a mode of political participation linking individuals at the local level to issues of global concern."[72] Specifically, Deibert argues that this growth of citizen networks has been fueled by the Internet, which enables organization members to communicate easily among themselves and to share information with activists around the world.[73] In so doing, it binds individual activists and groups into a more cohesive force. The Internet also serves as a means of putting pressure on politicians and policymakers.

> Such a technological capacity may be responsible for the creation of a new type of "armchair activism" where people could get involved in campaigns . . . without even leaving their home or office, thus reducing the physical commitment and/or risks made by participating in traditional demonstrations.[74]

In contrast to these positive trends, the peace movement also faces a number of specific challenges. Most generally, it seems to lack a coherent identity or presence, leading Nat Hentoff to ask, "Where is the peace movement?" He sees small groups such as the War Resisters League, the Fellowship of Reconciliation, Catholic Worker, and Pax Christi as doing what they can. But the networks of people around the country that had nurtured those groups during the Vietnam War have fragmented. " 'We feel lost,' a previous resister told me."[75]

In a similar vein, Oegema and Klandermans ask why sympathizers do not actively participate in the peace movement. They argue that although the proportion of a movement's sympathizers in society is relatively stable over time, the motivation of people to participate has declined. Motivation to participate can be seen as a function of the existence and magnitude of the grievances and the existence and appeal of a movement addressing these grievances.[76] Consequently, the lack of participation must reflect a low concern with the grievances and/or the lack of appeal of groups addressing these issues.

Another reason for the difficulties currently facing the peace movement is the complexity of many issues the movement confronts. This can lead to disagreements over goals and/or tactics, thus there is no one clear "peace position." For instance, opposing views over the Gulf War splintered the peace effort, fueled public disenchantment with the movement, and increased the suspicion with which the peace movement is seen within policymaking circles. The decline in the peace movement's fortunes has also been fueled by the growing public disgust at or alienation from political issues in general. Thus, despite the growth of peace issues and peace movement organizations, the resulting situation of the public's and policymakers' distrust is one in which the peace movement will find it even more difficult to have an impact.

Though the peace movement organizations in the United States today are attempting to address a wide variety of issues, one of the more problematic ones is U.S. policy toward Iraq. This policy has a number of different components, including economic sanctions, military missions, and attempts to topple the Iraqi regime. Much of this policy was adopted in the wake of the Gulf War, when the peace movement's influence was at a low ebb. Now, however, peace movement organizations are increasingly beginning to espouse opposition to U.S. actions and are attempting to promote a change in U.S. policy. One such organization is Voices in the Wilderness. A case study of Voices in the Wilderness is included here as an example of the issues confronting the contemporary movement and as a means of addressing the tactics by which peace movement organizations can have influence on U.S. policy.

VOICES IN THE WILDERNESS AND
U.S. POLICY TOWARD IRAQ

Since 1991, the American role in Iraq has remained relatively invisible to the public. The United States continues to apply trade sanctions on Iraq, enforces the no-fly zones in northern and southern Iraq, funds Iraqi opposition groups, and periodically bombs Iraqi targets, all without serious opposition. There has, however, been the development of a portion of the peace movement that is trying to mobilize public concern over the effects of U.S. policies.

Voices in the Wilderness is an organization dedicated to working toward the changing of U.S. policy toward Iraq, specifically to the lifting of the sanctions and the ending of the bombing campaigns. Such opposition stems from the Voices' pacifist background.

> We oppose the development, storage and use—in any country—of any weapons of mass destruction, be they nuclear, chemical, biological or economic. We advocate active development of the effective nonviolence methods of social change.[77]

In order to examine how this perspective has led to opposition to U.S. policy, it is first necessary to briefly describe the background of the current situation in Iraq and to provide a brief history of Voices in the Wilderness. We then shall discuss the measures used by Voices to accomplish its goals and the degree to which it has been successful.

The Situation in Iraq

In response to the Iraqi invasion of Kuwait, the United Nations established an embargo on the importation of all food by Iraq as of August 1990. The embargo was not successful in persuading Iraq to withdraw from Kuwait, thus in 1991 the allied coalition launched an attack upon Iraq (Desert Storm). During the Gulf War, the allied coalition, led by the

United States and the United Kingdom, caused widespread damage in Iraq through its extensive bombing campaign. Much of the infrastructure, including hospitals, power plants, sewage treatment systems, food storage and processing, schools and university facilities, and agricultural and oil production, was destroyed. There are even reports that the allied forces deliberately destroyed Iraq's water supply.[78] After the war, the sanctions against Iraq were expanded to include the creation of no-fly zones in northern and southern Iraq, and the allies continue to bomb Iraq to destroy what they see as potential threats. These sanctions are to remain in place until inspectors certify that Iraq is free of weapons of mass destruction. The embargo was modified in 1996 when the United Nations established the so-called oil-for-food program, which was supposed to alleviate some of the harsher results of the sanctions; however, the improvement has been minimal. In addition to the sanctions, the United States is spending millions of dollars to foster Iraqi groups opposed to the rule of Saddam Hussein. The apparent aim is to help the INC (Iraqi National Congress, an umbrella organization of opposition groups) establish an operation inside the U.S.-protected "safe area" of northern Iraq. After almost eleven years, these measures have still failed to change the regime in Iraq. As Denis Halliday, the former UN humanitarian coordinator in Baghdad, has concluded:

> We have done this in full knowledge of these unacceptable consequences, apparently as a means to punish the government and coerce the President of Iraq to step down. As many members of Congress and Administration officials know full well from the U.S. bilateral experience, economic sanctions targeting a people, are not likely to bring down a head of state or produce the fullest cooperation.[79]

The results of these policies upon the people of Iraq have, however, been increasingly disastrous. Even a report for the UN Subcommission on Human Rights admitted: "The worst case is Iraq, where ten years of UN sanctions driven by the United States and Great Britain has led to 'a humanitarian disaster comparable to the worst catastrophes of the past decades.'"[80] Numerous other international organizations, including the World Health Organization, the World Food Program, the Food and Agriculture Organization, the United Nations Development Program, UNESCO, UNICEF, and the United Nations humanitarian coordinator's office in Baghdad, have made thousands of visits each year to water projects, power plants, farms, warehouses, mills, food distributors, schools, hospitals, and ordinary homes in order to gauge the situation in Iraq. All have found that child malnutrition in particular remains a serious problem. A 2000 UNICEF report found that Iraq had a 160 percent increase in child mortality from 1990 to 1999.[81] In addition to the destruction of the infrastructure, results of the sanctions and bombing span all elements of Iraqi life, including increased mortality rates; widespread malnutrition; increased poverty and unemployment; growing crime; the limiting of educational opportunities and burgeoning illiteracy; the decline in the role of professionals; and the breakdown of the family, which includes increasing divorce and suicide rates, the abandonment of children, and the development of an angry isolated younger generation.[82] Instead of alleviating this situation, supplies to be distributed under the oil-for-food program have been delayed as members of the Security Council, particularly the United States, raise questions about whether items ranging from sprinkler parts to agricultural chemicals could have military uses. As a result, some medicines and basic equipment such as chlorinators to purify drinking water are forbidden by the sanctions. Bad water has created an epidemic of dysentery and infectious diseases, resulting in thousands of children's deaths.[83] It has been estimated that 500,000 children have died due to sanctions. Children are also being born with an increasing number of serious birth defects, which may be tied to the depleted uranium used in allied weapons. As Irishwoman Felicity Arhethnot, a London journalist, concluded: "I am absolutely convinced that when history is written with truth, then this embargo on Iraq will go down with the fire bombing of Dresden, with the Holocaust and with Hiroshima."[84]

Voices in the Wilderness, Background

Voices in the Wilderness (VitW) is a humanitarian organization determined to end the sanctions against the people of Iraq. Voices was created as a result of a social gathering (in Chicago in 1995) of a group of people who had been concerned for a long time about the results of the sanctions against Iraq. One member of this group was Kathy Kelly, a teacher who had been active in the Catholic Worker movement (a worldwide network of hospitality houses that has been a hub of radical activity for years). As Kelly explained, "A number of us had been in Iraq during the Gulf War as part of the peace team on the border between Saudi Arabia and Iraq, others had gone to Iraq before or after the war, and we decided we had to do something."[85] Immediately prior to the outbreak of the Gulf War, the Gulf Peace Team had decided to station peace camps on the Saudi, Iraqi, and Kuwaiti borders. Kelly was at the Iraqi border for fourteen days until the team was evacuated to Baghdad (for four days) and ultimately out to Jordan. The decision to participate in this action reflects the pacifist philosophy that motivates Kelly and the Voices in the Wilderness. It is partially based on the Gandhian idea of trying to deter war by stationing persons of conscience between the combatants. As Kelly explained:

I don't want to lose the idea of actually going into the places where warfare is being declared and having nonviolent peace activists taking the same risks as those required of soldiers, but going unarmed, always unarmed. . . . Nonviolence is something that has given me a life I am very happy with, and if you're not happy, then you really can't stick with these kinds of things.[86]

For Kelly, the Gulf War has never ended, it has only been changed into a different kind of warfare.[87] Her activities in Voices in the Wilderness represent merely a stage in a lifelong commitment to nonviolence.

The first task for Voices was to create a basic document that summarized the philosophy and goals of the group. In this instance, the basic document took the form of "a letter to Attorney General Janet Reno declaring our intent to go to Iraq in open and public violation of the sanctions and bring medicine and medical supplies. . . . The idea was to use nonviolent civil disobedience in order to provoke a confrontation with what we felt was an incredibly wrongful and horrible set of rules."[88] Initially there were three hundred signers on the first document. The group held a press conference to publicize their commitment in Chicago on January 15, 1996, the eve of what was the fifth year since the Gulf War. On January 22, they received a reply from the U.S. Attorney General that warned them that if they persisted with their plan, they risked twelve years in prison, a $1 million fine, and a $250,000 dollar administrative charge.[89] When the signers were notified of the response, their numbers quickly reduced to eighty. Yet Kelly credits the threatening letter from the government as being the impetus that really moved them along to a higher profile and increased level of activity. By March 1996, they had their first delegation ready to go to Iraq.

At this stage, VitW also began to develop an organizational framework, though it was quite limited. Initially in 1996–1997, it was basically a one-person office (Kathy Kelly) with a student from DePaul University who would come up on his bike to help out. Kelly was consistently consulting with the others located around the country who were the key players in getting Voices started. They would periodically come and meet in Chicago, particularly before a delegation would leave for Iraq. As the volume of work increased (including giving lectures as well as organizing the delegations), additional people joined the Chicago office, and an affinity group was established of people who volunteered to help. However, the organization itself remained limited. When Jeff Guntzel joined VitW in 1998, he described Voices as "as punk an operation as anything I've ever seen. Operating independently of large, establishment humanitarian organizations . . . the entire organization is run out of the second floor of a 2-bedroom flat in uptown Chicago."[90] This description is still accurate, with three to four people living and working in Kelly's apartment, which is the headquarters of VitW. As a result of continually increasing levels of activity, the organizational structure has recently been formalized a bit more, though they deliberately do not have a hierarchical administrative structure. There are two basic decision-making groups, which are generally comprised of the people who have been most active in VitW since 1996. Though most basic decisions are made by whoever is working in the Chicago office, important decisions are made by a twelve-person decision-making team. In December 2000, VitW added a three-person committee specifically to make decisions about sending particular delegations to Iraq (based on the potential delegation members). VitW also maintains a list of people who have traveled with them as delegation members, now well over 150, who receive updates on VitW activities. Additionally, Voices has established strong affinity groups (of people who work with them regularly) in eight cities. Much of the actual responsibility for activities is broadly delegated. For instance, they have someone on the west coast who has been drafting a "sign-on letter" to President Bush, while an affiliate in Washington, D.C., will be responsible for its release.

This minimalist organizational structure is very much linked to VitW's vision of nonviolence. As Kelly explained:

> It was never that nonviolence was only a matter of choosing between picking up arms or unarmed struggle. But rather it is the idea that you deliberately try to find your freedom by not having attachments to belongings that could get in the way of it, or attachments to needing to establish prestige, or needing to establish some way that you could be beholden to the system, because then they could take it away from you. So simplicity, not in any kind of sentimental fashion, saying that there is nothing that you can take from us: that is where we find some of our freedom. That, and a serious radical sharing of resources. For me not paying taxes for war is an everyday kind of thing, but it is a definite breaking of the law every single day. So what I see as the heart of nonviolence is simplicity, service, sharing. Service is the idea that our lives are oriented toward serving some cause that is beyond ourselves. "Social Security" is making sure that I am connected to people who share a vision of a world where you would never dream of trying to employ violent tactics or dream of stealing or robbing from other people.[91]

This desire to remain true to the vision leads inevitably to the decision to eschew the trappings of a large organization. There is a fear that becoming too institutionalized would restrict their freedom of action. "If you throw a lot of money at a nonprofit, they will have to hire people and rent space, and keep having to spend more money, and then raising more money, to pay salaries and pay the rent. Your outlook becomes institutionalized, and your effectiveness is really, really reduced. I would never enter an institutionalized peace effort if I were serious about making a difference."[92]

Tactics

In contrast to the minimalist organizational structure, Voices in the Wilderness has adopted a wide array of tactics in pursuit of their goal of eliminating the sanctions. "We try every nonviolent way we can think of to draw attention to this massive loss of life."[93] Similar to the characteristics of pacifist groups in general, VitW's preference is for "outsider" tactics rather than "insider" attempts to directly influence policymakers. VitW sees one of its primary goals as shifting public opinion, and thus many of its tactics focus on ways to educate the public. "Democracy is based on information. We have the information and we're doing our best to get it out to a public that might otherwise never hear about it."[94] Yet educating Americans about Iraq is particularly difficult for a number of reasons. At the most basic level, Americans know relatively little about, and are less interested in, the Middle East. The public finds it easier to relate to nonviolence issues in Central America, for instance, due to its proximity to the United States. Disseminating information about the Middle East is thus much more difficult to accomplish. Second, as mentioned above, in the 1990s the public became less interested in foreign affairs and became particularly disenchanted with the peace movement. They have become more focused on domestic concerns. As Kelly has observed:

> We have so much freedom in this country it is a pity that we don't use it quite a bit more. In order to maintain the lifestyle people are accustomed to here in this country, the United States government uses incredibly brutal and ruthless measures outside of the United States. But people just don't see it, they don't hear it. People are just so very very comfortable, they don't want to rock the boat, which makes me think that so much of the work that needs to be done is the education.[95]

In terms of gathering information and trying to make it widely available, a primary tactic upon which VitW relies is sending delegations to Iraq, despite the possible penalties of fines and imprisonment. These delegations are a valuable tool in that they combine informational activities with the direct action activity of breaking the sanctions by bringing medicine and supplies to Iraq. Before each departure, VitW notifies the U.S. attorney general of the upcoming trip and invites the office to join them in conscientious objection to the policies they contend violate international law and basic human rights. Between January 1996 and February 2002, forty-two delegations from VitW traveled to hospitals and clinics in

Baghdad, Basra, and Mosul, breaking the siege imposed by the sanctions by taking medicine and medical supplies. These delegations included representatives of the media, Voices members from other countries (such as Britain) as well as the United States, and members of other peace movement organizations. After July 1998, VitW was sending one delegation every two and a half weeks (though this pace has since slowed), and the delegations generally stay in Iraq for ten days. "Our aim was to carry medicines to the sick children of Iraq as a gift of peace in a time of war, providing a small measure of relief, and by refusing to apply for an export license, mounting a direct challenge to the sanctions regime which has inflicted 'chronic malnutrition' on 960,000 Iraqi children according to UNICEF."[96] On occasion, some of the antibiotics they carried have been seized by U.S. Customs. In addition, delegates often visit schools and meet with UN officials, representatives of the Iraqi government, religious leaders, and families. Thereby, the delegates have been able to gather information and take pictures and videos of the destruction of what had once been a very prosperous country, filled with well-educated and healthy people. They have seen the hospitals filled with hundreds of children with little hope of survival. Kelly has accompanied fourteen of the VitW delegations to Iraq, leading to her passport being confiscated on one occasion. In December 1998, Kathy was in Iraq during some of the allied bombing raids, and she observed: "We surveyed the area and there could not have possibly been a military target anywhere near the suburban home. People understandably feel that they are the targets of the bombing."[97] As a result of these raids, 144 people living in the very areas that were meant to be protected by the aircraft have died and 446 had been wounded.[98]

One of the lengthier VitW trips to Iraq was the Voices in Basra Project, in the summer of 2000. VitW sent six members to the southern no-fly zone of Iraq to live for seven weeks on the UN food rations in the homes of Iraqi families.

> We tried to understand the effect of economic sanctions against Iraq by learning what it is like to live without electricity for 14 hours per day in 120 degree heat, to share meals made from meager rations, and to be cut off from communication with the rest of the world. . . . While I was there, U.S. and British planes attacked a railway station, a grain storage area, and a decrepit tire store in a rundown area. I visited each of these spots and was bewildered by the show of force. A fraction of the money used to launch the daily sorties that patrol and bomb in the no-fly zones could solve a host of problems for Iraqi civilians.[99]

Despite the often frustrating and disheartening experiences of these trips, VitW considers the delegations to be a good formula: "People go, they see firsthand the tremendous civilian suffering and they come back impassioned to find anything they can do to educate other people about what's happened and to try and bring an end to the sanctions."[100] The trips are also a valuable tactic in generating media coverage. VitW has also produced a number of educational materials, including a video, a CD, a slide show, and a book based on delegation trips.

VitW is also engaged in a number of other educational efforts as well. Through their website (www.nonviolence.org/vitw), Voices makes information available on its activities and provides "talking points," which are informational responses to the statements justifying the sanctions. The site also contains links to other nonviolence websites. During 2000–2001, another educational effort was the Remembering Omran Bus Tour, during which a bus with information and speakers toured the west coast, the east coast, the midwest, and the south Atlantic coast, stopping at 150 campuses. This effort not only served to provide information, but also to encourage student involvement in the anti-sanction effort. Though the bus trip was draining in terms of effort and resources, it was so successful that a repeat is planned for September 2002. Kelly admitted that "I do realize that it was probably the best means of outreach and education that we have had here in the United States. But it was a heck of a lot of work and it costs a lot of money."[101] VitW also sends speakers to address college campuses and local community groups. It also holds training workshops for activists, or potential activists.

In addition to trying to spread its message by educational activities, VitW has also utilized direct nonviolent actions. It has sponsored actions at military bases, particularly Air National Guard installations, because of their frequent roles in Iraq. For instance, activists tried to deliver food and medicine to the Missouri Air National Guard, which was slated to patrol the no-fly zones in northern and southern Iraq in February 2001. Ten members of VitW were arrested for delivering food and medicine to the New York State Air National Guard, which was leaving for Iraq in February 2000. Protests were also staged against the Iowa Air National Guard. These types of direct actions are valuable for a number of reasons, including generating media attention, educating the public, and necessitating a response by the government. Although these protests were unsuccessful in stopping the military deployment, they were particularly successful in initiating public debate over the legality of the patrols. For instance, one of the protesters in Iowa, Michael Sprong, was put on trial. Famed international law scholar Richard Falk served as a witness for Sprong, and he testified that, under the principles of Nuremberg, an individual is allowed to disobey the government if he has knowledge that government itself is engaged in illegal activity. Given that the no-fly zones have never been sanctioned or even approved by the United Nations, the daily bombing runs represent a violation of Iraq's national sovereignty and of the 1991 cease-fire. Although Sprong was found guilty, the trial was one of the first cases wherein the legality of the sanctions and the patrols were openly discussed. It also precipitated a serious debate over this policy at the local level, especially within the editorial sections of the Iowa press.[102]

Other types of direct action utilized by VitW include staging hunger strikes at the United Nations compound in Baghdad; holding peace vigils and hunger strikes at government facilities; and trying to interrupt speeches by political candidates in order to raise questions about the sanctions policy. In an attempt to garner media attention, a member of VitW tried to interrupt the *Oprah* show (also based in Chicago) in order to attempt to ask George Bush about his policy toward Iraq. Audience members were given roses to wear in memory of the children who died in Iraq, but the roses were confiscated upon the audience's entrance into the *Oprah* studio. VitW has also tried to influence politicians directly by such activities as gathering signatures from community leaders for a letter to be sent to the president. VitW has also encouraged its supporters to express their opinions to national and local politicians by letters, phone calls, and e-mails.

Two direct action efforts, collectively referred to as Life Under Siege Encampments, were undertaken during the summer of 2001. The first part of the encampments involved a fast from all solid foods for forty days at the United Nations in New York City, beginning on August 6, which was the eleventh anniversary of the imposition of the sanctions. By the time the UN delegates returned for the UN session, the VitW representatives had survived approximately twenty-one days of ingesting only fruit juice. The activists also linked the UN action to the United States by proceeding once a week to the U.S. mission and offering to share a simple meal of lentils and rice (in solidarity with the people of Iraq) with the American delegation. Each time, not only was their offer refused, but the members of the delegation were arrested. As Kelly conceded, "it was an ordeal, but nothing when compared to eleven years of economic sanctions."[103] The second phase of the encampments was scheduled for the beginning of September, when students, community groups, and religious institutions in twenty-eight cities across the country set up similar "life under siege encampments," where people voluntarily moved into a tent-like dwellings and cut themselves off from computers and refrigeration, cars, and cell phones for three days. The goal was to dramatize the conflict in a way that would make it real for more people. It was hoped that this would both further publicize the ramifications of the sanctions policies and enable activists to have an opportunity to reflect on the meanings of nonviolent resistance. Kelly also saw the encampments as a way to gradually initiate students into nonviolent resistance.

We really are treated with kid gloves over here. I've probably been arrested forty-three times, and I've never been subjected to anything more difficult than going without food for a while or sleeping in uncomfortable conditions. It is the same thing with U.S. prisons. It is a stupid, stupid system, but after spending a year in it I never felt that it was anything close to the kind of brutality and torture that people face in other places. The good thing about people engaging in civil obedience [sic] and getting their feet wet in this country is that the fear of what would happen if I got arrested, what would happen if I went to court, what would happen if I went to jail, can be dampened considerably.[104]

Another tactic that was critical for the success of the Vietnam peace movement was networking and cooperating with similarly concerned organizations; and VitW utilizes this tactic extensively. For example, the Middle East Children's Alliance purchased the bus for the Omran bus tour. Both the VitW brochures and the website provide contact information for other groups that are also concerned with the effects of the sanctions on Iraq. Such groups include EPIC (Education for Peace in Iraq), ADC (American-Arab Anti-Discrimination Committee), FOR (Fellowship of Reconciliation), AFSC (American Friends Service Committee), and Pax Christi USA. Jointly, these groups have staged a number of demonstrations and educational events. Coordinating with such groups gives further visibility to VitW's concern about Iraq among peace movement groups that are primarily concerned with other issues, and the goal of ending the sanctions is becoming an element of more groups' agendas. For instance, the Fellowship of Reconciliation, an interfaith anti-war organization, held a series of events in Washington called the People's Campaign for Nonviolence, which promoted the goals of seeking nuclear disarmament and abolition of the death penalty, as well as the lifting of the sanctions on Iraq.[105]

People and governments around the world are working, for various reasons, to end the war on Iraq. . . . The American Friends Service Committee and Fellowship of Reconciliation have initiated a Campaign of Conscience whereby a person gives money to help rebuild the infrastructure in Iraq and signs a statement that such action may be against the law. The Veterans for Peace is going to build four water treatment plants in the countryside around Basra which, according to Alan Pogue (an Austin, Texas, veteran) "should help save the lives of 75,000 people." LIFE for Relief & Development, a Moslem-American group, is a partner in this worthy project. For economic as well as humanitarian reasons, cities and counties have taken a stand by passing resolutions against the sanctions, breaking the embargo by trading with Iraq, signing contracts in hopes that they will soon be able to trade legally with this beleaguered nation.[106]

VitW also is linked with the new national organization focusing on Iraq that was formed at a meeting in Denver, and VitW has been successful in contributing to the creation of organizations with similar concerns. ARROW (Active Resistance to the Roots of War), which had organized the first British sanctions-breaking trip, decided to set up Voices in the Wilderness UK. Several individuals who had been members of VitW delegations to Iraq subsequently created similar organizations and programs. Erik Gustafson, a veteran of Desert Storm, joined a Voices delegation to Iraq in 1997 and returned to found Education for Peace in Iraq. Another VitW former delegate now conducts yearly trips to Iraq for Physicians for Social Responsibility in Western Washington. Rick McDowell developed ties to the Dominican sisters and priests and has accompanied them on three separate delegations to Iraq. Voices for Veritas II was the second group of Dominican sisters to visit Iraq.

A characteristic of pacifist organizations—the reluctance to focus on "insider" tactics to influence policies—can also be said to be true of VitW. VitW has, however, begun efforts in this arena by extending its educational efforts to governmental decision makers. Two VitW members even accompanied a group of congressional staff members to Iraq in 1999. VitW also encourages its supporters to send informational letters to their governmental officials. However, one general type of tactic that VitW has not really utilized is becoming involved in electoral activities. This is one measure that they do hope to add to their repertoire. VitW plans to develop a more systematic legislative approach of going to each of the people up for election in this off-term and providing a listing of the people pledged to support VitW and oppose sanctions, and indicating that "we won't vote for you if you aren't going to try to end these sanctions."[107]

Recent events have added urgency to VitW's mission to sway public opinion and have prompted VitW to expand its repertoire of tactics. The VitW delegates were on the last three days of the encampment in New York City on September 11, 2001. Though they were horrified by the attacks on the World Trade Center and the Pentagon, the VitW members also felt that they could not remain silent in the face of the calls for revenge.[108] Consequently, VitW, along with several people who had lost loved ones in the attacks, organized a walk from Washington, D.C., to New York City on November 25, 2001, named a Walk for Healing and Peace.[109] Since September, the Bush administration has escalated its threats against Iraq in conjunction with the war on terrorism, going so far as to label Iraq as a component of the "axis of evil." The government has increased its cooperation with Iraqi opposition groups, has proposed tightening the embargo, has taken action against individuals and organizations that had sent funds to families in Iraq, and has been trying to generate international support for efforts to overthrow Saddam Hussein.[110] In the face of such a concerted effort, VitW has intensified its activities, particularly in the areas of direct nonviolent tactics and increased coordination with other factions of the peace movement. In particular, VitW has begun efforts to establish an ongoing presence in Iraq and is planning on taking larger delegations to Iraq for longer periods of time in the future. VitW also encouraged participation in a peace walk from Jordan to Baghdad in May and June 2002 that was sponsored by an affiliated group, the Compassion Iraq Coalition. The growing levels of violence in the war on terrorism and in the Israeli-Palestinian conflict have reenergized a number of justice and peace organizations, and VitW is working within this broader coalition to stage a march on Washington to Stop the War at Home and Abroad. Such collaborations have the potential to increase media coverage and public awareness about the range of peace issues confronting Americans today, including the issue of sanctions against Iraq.

Influence

There is growing opposition to the sanctions policy, both within the United States and worldwide. Though it is impossible to judge how much of this shift can be attributed to the activities of Voices in the Wilderness directly, it is clear that such changes (though glacial) would not have occurred without the activities of peace movement organizations. There are a number of markers by which one can see this transformation. On a general level, there has been evidence of growing activism by other peace groups, applying direct pressure on the government. Ramsey Clark's International Action Center helped pull together the National Emergency Coalition to Stop the War Against Iraq, a coalition of two hundred organizations, which organized mass rallies that took place on February 28, 1998, in San Francisco and in New York. In San Francisco 2,500 people took to the streets and 5,000 rallied in Times Square to demand an end to war threats and sanctions.[111] There has also been growing activism on college campuses, and a particular protest at Ohio State against the United States' plans to bomb Iraq caught the Clinton administration, the media, and even some veteran peace activists by surprise. Protesters confronted Secretary of State Madeleine Albright, Defense Secretary William Cohen, and National Security Advisor Sandy Berger on February 18, 1998, before an international television audience. Consequently, within weeks, the outlines of a new anti-war movement began to appear, which combined seasoned activists and newcomers. "Appalled by the prospect of a U.S. bombing raid, sickened by news of civilian casualties since the 1991 Gulf War, people who had never been politically active before began to organize teach-ins, vigils, demonstrations, and information campaigns—and prepared for civil disobedience. They might not have been striving for systematic political change, but they insisted that U.S. policy toward Iraq is wrong."[112] A distinctive element of this movement is the large turnouts by the Muslim community.

Another of the interesting developments has been the number of former U.S. and UN officials who have now become active in efforts to end the sanctions. In the fall of 1998 Denis Halliday, the coordinator of the UN's oil-for-food program, quit, calling the sanctions a bankrupt concept.[113] His successor, Hans von Sponeck, has also resigned, as has Jutta Burghardt, director of the World Food Program in Iraq. Scott Ritter, the former head of the concealment investigations unit for UNSCOM (the United Nations Special Commission), and Edward Peck, who served as U.S. chief of mission in Iraq, are now both active in opposition to the sanctions.

Similarly, calls to end the sanctions on moral grounds have come from the Vatican and Venezuelan president Hugo Chavez. Several of the former Gulf War coalition partners (such as France) have tried to encourage the United States and the United Kingdom to drop the sanctions. Britain recently proposed a modification of the sanctions to "smart sanctions." Kelly, however, is suspicious of this move. "I think it is more saving face than saving lives. I think the opprobrium that has been heaped on the U.S. and the UK for persisting with policies that so clearly inflict suffering on innocent people is something that no administration wants to continue to shoulder."[114] There has even been some movement within the U.S. Congress, where some are becoming aware that there is another side to the story. In 2000, seventy-two members of Congress signed a letter to President Clinton calling for the delinking of economic from military sanctions and for the lifting of economic sanctions on the people of Iraq. Congressman John Conyers (D-Mich.) was also one of the conveners of a 2000 congressional hearing on U.S.-Iraqi policy, at which Denis Halliday and Hans von Sponeck testified. Von Sponeck warned Congress that the information being dispensed by the administration was not entirely accurate: "disinformation, distortion, misinterpretation, wherever you look you see it on all sides—but the finest example of distorted information is a State Department Report of 17th September last year, where every single figure is either not explained and therefore gives the wrong impression or it is the wrong information."[115]

Though there clearly is not yet a consensus to end the sanctions, progress is being made. In recognition of their efforts in this endeavor, the American Friends Service Committee nominated Kelly and Halliday for the Nobel Peace Prize in 2000. Kelly is aware of the opportunities, as well as the barriers, confronting Voices in the Wilderness. She sees a revived interest in joint action within the U.S. populace, which she sees as quite impressive. Yet, on the other hand she admits that "Most of our efforts to challenge the U.S. policy I think are understood by the U.S. government as something to be dismissed as quickly as possible."[116] The realization that the pace of change is so slow in the United States has actually led VitW to consider the possibility that it might have a better chance of reaching people in other countries, so that they could put pressure on their elective leadership to either unilaterally break the sanctions or put pressure on United States and the United Kingdom. To an extent, this realization fueled the decision to hold the Life under Siege Encampment at the United Nations in order to broaden the audience for their message. Yet VitW is committed to continuing its efforts. As Kelly explains, "The people in the Middle East, knowing how much our lifestyle is affected by being able to take their irreplaceable goods at cut-rate prices, must wonder where are the people of conscience in that country, and why are they doing nothing."[117] VitW does not want to be seen to be doing nothing, though that is very unlikely to be its legacy. Daniel Sinker summarizes his evaluation of the role of VitW this way: "It is also the story of Voices in the Wilderness, an organization that has ignored U.S. law, tight finances and countless other hurdles not for financial gain or even media exposure, but simply because they have a sense of what is right and what is wrong. It is a story that is moving not only because of the horror it exposes, but also because of the hope—however small—it offers."[118]

NOTES

1. Victoria Neufeldt, ed. *Webster's New World Dictionary* (New York: Webster's New World, 1988), 993.

2. Katherine Meerse, "Peace Activism and Social Justice: The Minnesota Branch of the Women's International League for Peace and Freedom, 1939–1940," *Peace & Change* 23, no. 4 (October 1998): 500.

3. Bruce Kent, "Protest and Survive," *History Today* (May 1999): 14.

4. Kent, "Protest," 14.

5. Michael True, "Since 1998: The Concept of Global Nonviolence and Its Implications for Peace Research," *Social Alternatives* 16, no. 2 (April 1997): 9.

6. True, "Since 1998," 8.

7. Thomas Fleming, *Liberty! The American Revolution* (New York: Viking, 1997), 142.

8. Paul Buhle, "Peace Movements," in *Encyclopedia of the American Left*, ed. Mari Jo Buhle, Paul Buhle, and Dan Georgakas (Urbana: University of Illinois Press, 1992), 565–566; Nancy L. Roberts, "'Ten Thousand Tongues' Speaking for Peace: Purposes and Strategies of the Nineteenth Century," *Journalism History* 21, no. 1 (Spring 1995): 16.

9. Roberts, "Ten Thousand," 16–17.

10. Roberts, "Ten Thousand," 16.

11. Eric Foner and John A. Garraty, eds., *The Reader's Companion to American History* (Boston: Houghton Mifflin, 1991), 236.

12. Susan Zeiger, "Finding a Cure for War: Women's Politics and the Peace Movement in the 1920s," *Journal of Social History* 24, no. 1 (Fall 1990): 83.

13. Buhle, "Peace Movements," 567.

14. Buhle, "Peace Movements," 566.

15. Zeiger, "Finding a Cure," 70.

16. Zeiger, "Finding a Cure," 69.

17. Zeiger, "Finding a Cure," 70.

18. Zeiger, "Finding a Cure," 85.

19. Buhle, "Peace Movements," 569.

20. Buhle, "Peace Movements," 570.

21. Stanley Karnow, *Vietnam: A History* (New York: Viking, 1983), 598.

22. Sharon Erickson Nepstad, "School of the Americas Watch," *Peace Review* 12, no. 1 (March 2000): 67–72.

23. Sam Marullo and Alexandra Chute, "Pacifist and Non Pacifist Groups in the U.S. Peace Movement of the 1980s," *Peace & Change* 16, no. 3 (July 1991): 235–260.

24. Bob Edwards and Sam Marullo, "Organizational Mortality in a Declining Social Movement: The Demise of Peace Movement Organizations in the End of the Cold War Era," *American Sociological Review* 60, no. 6 (December 1995): 908.

25. Edwards and Marullo, "Organizational Mortality," 919.

26. Bruce W. Jentleson, *American Foreign Policy: The Dynamics of Choice in the 21st Century* (New York: Norton, 2000), 45.

27. Jentleson, *American*, 50–52.

28. Jentleson, *American*, 47–49.

29. Jentleson, *American*, 60–62.

30. Nancy E. McGlen and Meredith Reid Sarkees, *Women in Foreign Policy: The Insiders* (New York: Routledge, 1993), 104.

31. Ron Pagnucco and Jackie Smith, "The Peace Movement and the Formulation of U.S. Foreign Policy," *Peace & Change* 18, no. 2 (April 1993): 172.

32. Johan Galtung, "The Peace Movement: An Exercise in Micro-Macro Linkages," *International Social Science Journal* 50, no. 3 (September 1988): 402–403.

33. Galtung, "The Peace Movement," 402.

34. Edwards and Marullo, "Organizational Mortality," 915.

35. Edwards and Marullo, "Organizational Mortality," 923.

36. Mary Anna Colwell, "A Peace Research Agenda," *Peace Review* 9, no. 2 (June 1997): 280.

37. Colwell, "A Peace Research," 280.

38. Colwell, "A Peace Research," 281.

39. Marullo and Chute, "Pacifist," 236.

40. Marullo and Chute, "Pacifist," 235.

41. Marullo and Chute, "Pacifist," 247.

42. David S. Meyer, "Peace Movements and National Security Policy," *Peace & Change* 16, no. 2 (April 1991): 131.

43. Meyer, "Peace Movements," 132.

44. Bruce H. Franklin, "The Antiwar Movement We Are Supposed to Forget," *Chronicle of Higher Education* (October 20, 2000): B8.

45. Franklin, "The Antiwar Movement," B8.

46. Franklin, "The Antiwar Movement," B8.

47. Franklin, "The Antiwar Movement," B7.

48. Franklin, "The Antiwar Movement," B9.

49. Melvin Small, *Johnson, Nixon and the Doves* (New Brunswick, N.J.: Rutgers University Press, 1988), 225.

50. Franklin, "The Antiwar Movement," B8.

51. David Cortright, "Assessing Peace Movement Effectiveness in the 1980s," *Peace & Change* 16, no. 1 (January 1991): 46.

52. Kent, "Protest," 15.

53. Cortright, "Assessing Peace Movement, " 55.

54. Jentleson, *American*, 167.

55. Edwards and Marullo, "Organizational Mortality," 922.

56. Buhle, "Peace Movements," 572.

57. Jentleson, *American*, 167.

58. Kent, "Protest," 14.

59. Kent, "Protest," 16.

60. Buhle, "Peace Movements," 572.

61. Stephen Zunes, "The American Peace Movement and the Middle East," *Arab Studies Quarterly* 20, no. 1 (Winter 1998): 39.

62. Zunes, "The American Peace," 44.

63. Zunes, "The American Peace," 34.

64. Susan Rosegrant and Michael D. Watkins, "Power Case Study, The Gulf Crisis: Building a Coalition for War," in *Perspectives on American Foreign Policy: Readings and Cases*, ed. Bruce W. Jentleson (New York: W. W. Norton & Company, 2000), 243.

65. Edwards and Marullo, "Organizational Mortality," 925.

66. Zunes, "The American Peace," 30.

67. Zunes, "The American Peace," 39.

68. Zunes, "The American Peace," 36.

69. George Anderson, "Working to End War: Pax Christi," *America* 177, no. 6 (September 13, 1997): 5.

70. Jackie Smith, "Characteristics of the Modern Transnational Social Movement Sector," in *Transnational Social Movements and Global Politics*, ed. Jackie Smith, Charles Chatfield, and Ron Pagnucco (Syracuse, N.Y.: Syracuse University Press, 1997), 47.

71. Charles Chatfield, "Intergovernmental and Nongovernmental Associations to 1945," in Smith, Chatfield, and Pagnucco, *Transnational Social Movements*, 19–20.

72. Ronald J. Deibert, "International Plug 'n' Play? Citizen Activism, the Internet, and Global Public Policy," *International Studies Perspectives* 1, no. 3 (December 2000): 256.

73. Deibert, "International Plug 'n' Play?" 255.

74. Deibert, "International Plug 'n' Play?" 263.

75. Nat Hentoff, "Where Is the Peace Movement?" *Village Voice* (May 11, 1999): 30.

76. Dirk Oegema and Bert Klandermans, "Why Social Movement Sympathizers Don't Participate: Erosion and Non-Conversion of Support," *American Sociological Review* 59 (October 1994): 704.

77. Voices in the Wilderness, "Who We Are," accessed February 10, 2002, www.nonviolence.org/vitw/vwhoweare.html.

78. "Allies Deliberately Poisoned Iraq Public Water Supply in Gulf War Investigation," *Sunday Herald* (Scotland), September 17, 2000.

79. Denis J. Halliday, "Statement of Denis Halliday for a Congressional Briefing," Washington, May 3, 2000, handout prepared by Voices in the Wilderness.

80. Naomi Koppel, "UN Report: Sanctions Ineffective," *Associated Press*, August 15, 2000.

81. Hans von Sponek, "Iraq: Economic Sanctions and the Humanitarian Exemption: An Example of Failure," February 21, 2002, accessed April 12, 2002, www.nonviolence.org/vitw.

82. Denis J. Halliday, "Ex-UN Humanitarian Chief in Iraq Briefs Canadians on UN Iraq Policy," *Iraq Notebook* 7 (2000): 17.

83. Koppel, "UN Report."

84. Cited in Halliday, "Ex-UN Humanitarian Chief," 17.

85. Kathy Kelly, personal interview, Chicago, May 23, 2001.

86. Kathy Kelly, personal interview, Chicago, February 15, 2001.

87. Kelly, personal interview, February.

88. Daniel Sinker, "The Murder of Iraq," *Punk Planet Magazine*, no. 30 (March/April 1999): 65.

89. Sinker, "The Murder of Iraq," 65.

90. Jeff Guntzel, "Finding My Voice," *Punk Planet Magazine*, no. 30 (March/April 1999): 65–66.

91. Kelly, personal interview, February.

92. Kelly, personal interview, February.

93. Kelly, personal interview, May.

94. Kelly, quoted in Sinker, "The Murder of Iraq," 73.

95. Kelly, personal interview, May.

96. Milan Rai, "Moral Victory for Mil & Martin: Prosecution Dropped," *Voices: Newsletter of Voices in the Wilderness UK*, no. 1 (1998), accessed February 10, 2002, www.nonviolence.org/vitw/vitwuk2.html.

97. Kelly, quoted in Sinker, "The Murder of Iraq," 68.

98. Hans von Sponeck, "Second UN Relief Chief to Resign Says 'Economic Sanctions Must Be Lifted Now! Today, Not Tomorrow!'" *Iraq Notebook* 7 (2000): 3.

99. Kathy Kelly, "Through the Looking Glass," *Common Dreams* (September 18, 2000).

100. Kelly, quoted in Sinker, 65–66.

101. Kelly, personal interview, May.

102. Voices in the Wilderness, "Action Steps for Campaigns at Air National Guard Bases," handout.

103. Kelly, personal interview, November 6, 2001.

104. Kelly, personal interview, May 2001.

105. Gustav Niebuhr, "A Mission to Redirect Money Used for Defense," *New York Times*, October 3, 2000.

106. Lee Loe, "Some Dynamics of the Gulf Conflict," *Iraq Notebook* 7 (2000): 12.

107. Kelly, personal interview, May.

108. Kathy Kelly, "While Hearts Still Ache," Voices in the Wilderness website accessed April 12, 2002, www.nonviolence.org/vitw.

109. Kathy Kelly, "A Brief Reflection on Day One of the Walk," Voices in the Wilderness website accessed November 25, 2001 www.nonviolence.org/vitw.

110. Romesh Ratnesar, "Getting Saddam, Part II," *Time* (March 18, 2002): 54.

111. Annie Decker, "A New Peace Movement," *Progressive* 62, no. 4 (April 1998): 24.

112. Decker, "A New Peace Movement," 21.

113. Shannon Jones, "US Intelligence Officer & UN Arms Inspector Denounce Iraq Sanctions," *Iraq Notebook* 7 (2000): 7.

114. Kelly, personal interview, May.

115. Von Sponeck, "Second UN Relief Chief," 1.

116. Kelly, personal interview, May.

117. Kelly, personal interview, May.

118. Sinker, "The Murder of Iraq," 64.

Index

Note: Italicized page numbers indicate figures or tables.

AARP. *See* American Association of Retired Persons

ABM. *See* Anti-Ballistic Missile Treaty

abortion, 173

ACLU. *See* American Civil Liberties Union

ACORN. *See* Association of Community Organizations for Reform Now

Action for Nuclear Disarmament (AND), 101, 114

Active Resistance to the Roots of War (ARROW), 256

ACT UP. *See* AIDS Coalition to Unleash Power

ADA. *See* Americans with Disabilities Act

ADAPT. *See* American Disabled for Accessible Public Transportation

ADAPT. *See* American Disabled for Attendant Programs Today

Administration on Aging (AoA), 73

African Growth and Opportunities Act, 150

African National Congress (ANC), 37

AGE. *See* Americans for Generational Equity

AI. *See* Amnesty International

AIDS Coalition to Unleash Power (ACT UP), 133–58; and bathhouse closures, 136–38, 139; demonstration at California State House, 134; groups originating from, 148; Lesbian Avengers formed, 147–48; National Gay, Lesbian, and Bisexual March on Washington, D.C., 140; opposition to South African generic drug production sanctions, 150–53; overview, 133–34; and queer politics, 145–47; and sex panics, 135–38; and social justice, 148–49; strategies of, 134–35. *See also* Gay Men's Health Crisis

AIDS Prevention Action League, 149

Air Carrier Access Act, 167

Air National Guard, 253

Alabama v. Garrett, 177

Albright, Madeleine, 257

Alexander, Jane, 114

Alinsky, Saul, 142

Alliance for Quality Nursing Home Care, 75

altruistic movements. *See* Green parties; Human Rights Watch; peace movement

American Association of Retired Persons (AARP), 67, 70, 71–73, 77

American Civil Liberties Union (ACLU), 169, 212

American Council of the Blind, 164

American Disabled for Accessible Public Transportation (ADAPT), 168–69

American Disabled for Attendant Programs Today (ADAPT), 169

American Federation of Labor and

Congress of Industrial Organizations (AFL-CIO), 7, 89–90
American Foundation for the Blind, 163–64
American Friends Service Committee, 243, 255, 258
American Health Care Association, 75
American Hospital Association, 75
American liberal values. *See* Human Rights Watch
American Peace Society, 231
American Revolution, 231
American School for the Deaf (Hartford, Connecticut), 163
Americans for Generational Equity (AGE), 68–69
Americans with Disabilities Act (ADA), 167, 177
Americas Watch, 218
Amnesty International (AI), 217, 221
Amundson, Ron, 163
anarchism, and anti-globalization movements, 25
AND. *See* Action for Nuclear Disarmament
Andrus, Ethel Percy, 67
And the Band Played On (Shilts), 136
anti-apartheid movement, 37–38
Anti-Ballistic Missile Treaty (ABM), 126
anti-capitalism. *See* anti-globalization movements
anti-globalization movements, 17–50; and anarchism, 25; characteristics of, 24; diverse nature of, 24; effect of communications technologies on, 21–22; effect of fissures among capitalists and nation-states on, 22; goals and practices of, 25–28; impacts of, 31–33; Internet use, 21, 44; labor rights, 38, 42; member organizations and constituents, 24–25; other movements joining, 22; overview, 17–19; People's Global Action, 23; principal targets, 18–19, 21, 28–30; reform versus revolution, 34–35;

tactics of, 30–31; third world roots of, 23; violence from, 33, 40–41. *See also* anti-sweatshop movement
anti-imperialism, 231
anti-militarism. *See* peace movement; Women's Action for New Directions
anti-sweatshop movement, 83–98; boycotts, 88; and Clinton administration, 91; living wage campaigns, 92–93; overview, 83–85; point of consumption strategies, 88–89; solidarity, 93–94; strategies of, 90–93; sweatshop production and global power repertoires, 87–89; Union Summer program, 89–90
antiwar movement. *See* peace movement; Women's Action for New Directions
AoA. *See* Administration on Aging
Applebaum, Richard, 89
Arc, 164. *See also* Association for Retarded Citizens; National Association for Retarded Children; National Association for Retarded Citizens
Arhethnot, Felicity, 248
"armchair activism," 245
arms control. *See* peace movement; Women's Action for New Directions
Aronson, Diane, 114, 117, 119
ARROW. *See* Active Resistance to the Roots of War
ASEAN. *See* Association of Southeast Asian Nations
ASGP. *See* Association of State Green Parties
Asia Division, of HRW, 222
"Asian values" argument, 225n4
Aspis, Simone, 174
Assistant Secretary State for Human Rights, 218
Association for Retarded Citizens, 164
Association of Community Organizations for Reform Now (ACORN), 7
Association of Southeast Asian Nations (ASEAN), 224

Association of State Green Parties
(ASGP), 190

Balanced Budget Act (BBA), 75
Barnartt, Sharon N., 170–71
Barresi, Charles, 75
Barshefsky, Charlene, 151
bathhouse closures, 136–38, 139
BBA. *See* Balanced Budget Act
BEAVOTER.org website, 72
Bello, Walden, 45
Benjamin, Medea, 36–37, 40–41
Berg, John C., 1, 171, 172, 175–76, 178,
265
Berger, Sandy, 257
Berkeley Center for Independent Liv-
ing, 166
Bernstein, Robert, 215, 216
Berry, Jeffrey, 105
Bérubé, Allan, 135
Better Budget Resolutions, 123–24
Binstock, Robert H., 68, 71, 74
Biotechnology Industry Organization,
75
Blackmun, Harry, 139
blind persons, 163–64
"Blue-Green" alliance, 200
Bobbio, Norberto, 3
Boston Center for Independent Living,
166
Boulding, Kenneth, 232
Bouvia, Elizabeth, 169
Bowers v. Hardwick, 139
boycotts, of sweatshop products, 88
Bracken, Eric, 89, 93
Branco, Kenneth, 69–70
Braverman, G'Dali, 142
Briggs, John, 137
Brown, Bob, 174
Bryant, Anita, 137
Buchanan, Pat, 191–92
budgetary process, national, 123–24
Bundy, McGeorge, 216
Burghardt, Jutta, 258
Burns, James McGregor, 119
Burns, Joan, 119
Burstein, Paul, 6

Bush administration: and globalization, 50n74; and Gulf War, 241–43

Caldicott, Helen, 101, 106; in early his-
tory and founding of WAND, 108–9;
lessening of role, 116; and scope of
issue definition in WAND, 113
Califia, Pat, 138
California State House demonstration,
134
Campaign for Nuclear Disarmament
(CND), 240
Campaign of Conscience, 255
Campus Codes of Conduct, 90, 91
Capital Blue Cross, 74
capitalism. *See* anti-globalization
movements
Carnegie Endowment, 237
CARP. *See* Collective Action Research
Program
Carter, Jimmy, 218
Catt, Carrie Chapman, 232
CCCW. *See* Committee on the Cause
and Cure of War
Celeste, Dagmar, 118
Center for Ethical Concerns, 88
Chavez, Hugo, 258
Chentex factory, 94
Chevron Corporation, 38
children with disabilities, 163, 164
child seduction scares, 137
Christian movement, 7
Chute, Alexandra, 237
Citizens for Better Medicare, 75
civil rights movement, 2, 212
Civil War, 231
Clark, Ramsey, 257
class, 3, 53–63, 83–84, 103, 202. *See also*
labor movement
class positions, and left and right
movements, 3
Clinton administration, and anti-
sweatshop movement, 32, 91
cloning, human, 162
Cloward, Richard, 87–88, 89
CND. *See* Campaign for Nuclear Disarmament

Coalition for Medicare Choices, 75
coffee retailers, Fair Trade campaign against, 39–40
Cohen, Stanley, 135
Cohen, William, 257
Cold War, and left and right movements, 2, 3
Coleman, Diane, 169
Collective Action Research Program (CARP), 8
Colwell, Mary Anna, 237
Commentaries (Blackstone), 168
Commission on Human Rights, 214
Committee on Economic Security, 67
Committee on the Cause and Cure of War (CCCW), 232
communications technologies, effect on social movements, 21–22
Communication Workers of America (CWA), 55, 58, 64n14
The Communist Manifesto (Marx and Engels), 17
Compassion Iraq Coalition, 257
Conference on Security and Cooperation in Europe, 216, 217
Congressional Aging Committee, 71
"Congressional Presence for Survival," 111
conservative, use of term, 2
constituency-based movements, 10–11
Constitutional Peace Initiative, 120
convergence centers, 30
Conyers, John, 258
Copperheads, 231
Costain, Anne N., 7, 105
Council on Foreign Relations, 237
Crimp, Douglas, 140, 145
cultural feminism, 104
cultural hegemony, 9
culture, distinguishing from politics, 5
Cuomo, Mario, 139
CWA. *See* Communication Workers of America

Danaher, Kevin, 26, 29, 36, 37, 38, 40
Daschle, Tom, 60
The Day After (television movie), 240

deaf persons, 163, 164
Declaration of Human Rights, 33
Deibert, Ronald, 244
Democrats: disability issues, 174–75; and labor movements, 55, 56, 60–61; and senior interest groups, 76
Department of Energy, 123
Department of Health, Education, and Welfare (HEW), 166
Department of Peace and Arbitration, 231
Desert Storm. *See* Gulf War
developing countries. *See* Third World nations
Developmental Disabilities Assistance and Bill of Rights Act, 166
DIA. *See* Disabled in Action
Diaper Campaign, 119
Dickinson, John, 231
disability movement, 159–83; advocacy on state and local levels, 164–65; disability studies, 165; distinction between interest groups, 175–76; distinction between other movements, 178–79; and euthanasia, 169, 173, 178; events, 166–68; future issues, 177; independent living centers, 166; Kaiser Permanente issue, 160; and medical model, 177–78; and mental health care, 178; organizations belonging to, 164; origins of, 163–65; overview, 159; relation to other movements, 165; rights advocates, 159–60; services advocates, 160; today, 168–71
Disability Studies Quarterly (periodical), 165
Disabled in Action (DIA), 164
disabled persons: blind, 163–64; deaf, 163, 164; discrimination against, 161–63, 167–68; paralyzed veterans, 164; retarded, 164; special education for, 162; who qualifies as, 160–61
District of Columbia Housing Authority, 169
DNR (Do Not Resuscitate) orders, 162

Dobbs, Bill, 135, 144–45, 148–49
domestic living wage campaigns,
92–93
Dominguez, Ricardo, 152
Drake, Stephen, 170
Droz, Beverly, 117
Dyke March, 148

Earth Island Institute, 1
ecological movements. *See* Green parties
economic changes, 21
economic issues. *See* anti-globalization;
class; globalization; labor movement
economics, distinguishing from politics, 5
education, for children with disabilities, 162, 166
Education for All Handicapped Children Act, 166
Education for Peace in Iraq, 256
Edwards, Bob, 236
egalitarians, 3
elderly. *See* senior interest groups
"electoral bluff," 76–77
Engels, Frederick, 17
English Common Law, 168
environmental interest groups, 200
environmental movements. *See* Green parties
European Union, 224
euthanasia, 169, 173, 178
Ewing, Keith D., 60
exclusive organizations, 107

Fair Housing Amendments, 167
Fair Labor Association (FLA), 32, 91
Fair Trade Program, 39–40, 42–43
Falk, Richard, 253
FAPE. *See* free, appropriate, public
education
Farabundo Martí para la Liberación
Nacional (FMLN), 25
FARC. *See* Fuerzas Armadas Revolucionarias de Colombia
Federal Employees Pension Act, 67
Fed Up Queers (FUQ), 149

Feinberg, David, 133, 134
Fellowship of Reconciliation, 232, 243,
255
feminist movement, 103–4
Final Act of the Conference on Security
and Cooperation in Europe, 216
FMLN. *See* Farabundo Martí para la
Liberación Nacional
Food First, 37
Ford Foundation, 221, 222, 227n16
foreign policy structure, U.S., 233–34
Franklin, Bruce, 239
Franklin, Roosevelt, 67
free, appropriate, public education
(FAPE), 166
Freedom Fighters, 218
free market system. *See* anti-globalization movements
free riders, 171
Fuerzas Armadas Revolucionarias de
Colombia (FARC), 25
FUQ. *See* Fed Up Queers

G-7/G-8 nations, 33
Galbraith, John K., 119
Galtung, Johan, 235
garment workers. *See* anti-sweatshop
movement
Garner, Roberta Ash, 106, 107, 113, 120
Garrett, Alabama v., 177
Gates, Bill, 27
GATT. *See* General Agreement on Tariffs and Trade
Gay Men's Health Crisis (GMHC),
141–42
gay movements. *See* AIDS Coalition to
Unleash Power (ACT UP)
Gelfand, Donald, 75
Genden, Stephen, 140
General Agreement on Tariffs and
Trade (GATT), 20
General Motors, 88
Georgakas, Dan, 4
Gereffi, Gary, 87, 88
German Greens, 15n25
Giddens, Anthony, 2
Gill, Carol, 169

"Global Alliance for Workers and Communities," 32

global capitalism. *See* anti-globalization movements; globalization

Global Economic Rights Campaigns, 38

Global Exchange, 35–43; and NGOs, 40–43; overview, 36–37; what it is/does, 37–40

globalization: and American labor movement, 58–60; environmental effects, 29; Millennium Summit discussion of, 32; origins of, 20–21. *See also* anti-globalization movements

global justice movement. *See* anti-globalization movements

global nonviolence, 230

Global South, 32, 46n5

GMHC. *See* Gay Men's Health Crisis

Gore, Al, 150, 151, 195

Grassroots Peace Directory, 233

Grassroots Self-Help Project, 39

"Gray Lobby," 65

Gray Panthers, 70, 72, 80n49

Great Kiddy Porn Panic, 137

"Green-Camouflage" coalition, 201

Green parties, 187–209; and racial minority groups, 200–201; diversity within, 189–90, 198; divisions within, 189–90, 201–2; effect of September 11, 2001, terrorist attacks, 201; election 2000, 191–92; future of, 202–3; German Greens, 15n25; growing support for, 193–94; membership, 189; overview, 187–91; and postmaterialism, 194–96, 198; strategic potential, 198–202; Ten Key Values, 189

Greenspan, Alan, 32

"Guidelines for Multinational Enterprises," 32

Gulf Peace Team, 248

Gulf War, 241–44. *See also* Voices in the Wilderness

Guntzel, Jeff, 249

Gustafson, Erik, 256

hacking, computer, 30

Halliday, Denis, 247, 258

Hardwick, Michael, 139

Harvard University, living wage campaign, 92

Haussman, Melissa, 101, 265

Havel, Vaclav, 216

Hayduk, Ronald, 17, 265

health care: and senior interest groups, 75. *See also* disability movement; Medicare/Medicaid

Health Maintenance Organizations (HMOs), 75

Helsinki Accords, 212, 216

Helsinki Watch, 215–16, 218

Hentoff, Nat, 245

HERE. *See* Hotel Employees and Restaurant Employees

HEW. *See* Department of Health, Education, and Welfare

Hildt, Barbara, 121

Hill, Joe, 135

Hispanics, and Green parties, 201

HMOs. *See* Health Maintenance Organizations

Home Depot, 38

homosexuality. *See* AIDS Coalition to Unleash Power

Horne, Ken, 136

Hotel Employees and Restaurant Employees (HERE), 55

hotel workers, 62

House Resolution 195, 126

HRW. *See* Human Rights Watch

human cloning, 162

human rights: conventions on, 214–15; documentation of abuses, 215; emergence as international issue, 213–15; NGOs involvement, 225n4; and Reagan, 218. *See also* anti-sweatshop movement; labor movement

Human Rights Campaigns, 38

Human Rights Watch (HRW), 211–28; as American and international institution, 224; Asia Division, 222; contrast with other organizations, 221; divisions of, 212; focus on accountability and mobilization of shame,

219–20; history of, 215–19; and international financial institutions, 222–23; limitations of, 224; Mission Statement, 211; overview, 211–13; research and reports from, 220–21; stress on advocacy, 220–21; and transnational corporations, 222–23

IDEA. *See* Individuals with Disabilities Education Act
identity-based movements, 10–11, 83
ideology, distinguishing from politics, 5
IFIs. *See* international financial institutions
Illinois Bureau of Labor Statistics, 87
ILO. *See* International Labor Organization
IMF. *See* International Monetary Fund
imperialism, activism against, 231
INC. *See* Iraqi National Congress
inclusive organizations, 107
independent living centers, 166, 171
Individuals with Disabilities Education Act (IDEA), 166
inequality: among elderly, 78; effect of globalization on, 21, 26
INF. *See* Intermediate Nuclear Forces Treaty
Inglehart, Ronald, 3–4, 70, 103, 172–73, 193–94, 204
interest groups: divisions of, 234–35; how peace movement differs from, 235; use of term, 5–6, 175–76, 222
Intermediate Nuclear Forces (INF) Treaty, 241
International Action Center, 257
International Brotherhood of Teamsters, 54
International Campaign to Ban Landmines, 223
International Covenants, 226n9
international financial institutions (IFIs), 222–23
International Labor Organization (ILO), 94, 223

International Monetary Fund (IMF), 19, 29, 32–33, 223
International Speakers Bureau, 39
international trade organizations, 20
International Youth Foundation, 32
Internet: anti-globalization movement use of, 21, 44; disability movement use of, 167; labor movement use of, 57; peace movement use of, 243, 244–45
Iowa Air National Guard, 253
Iraq, U.S. sanctions against, 246–48. *See also* Voices in the Wilderness
Iraqi National Congress (INC), 247

Jackson, Jesse Jr., 33
James, C. L. R., 4
Jones, Cleve, 140, 145, 149–50

Kafka, Bob, 170
Kaiser Permanente, 160
Keck, Margaret E., 220, 222
Kelly, Christine, 83, 265
Kelly, Kathy, 248–49; on "smart sanctions," 258; on conditions in Iraq, 252; on Life Under Siege Encampments, 254; on Omran Bus Tour, 253; on U.S. foreign policy, 251; on VitW's vision of nonviolence, 250
Kennedy, Ted, 92
Kent, Bruce, 230
Kerry, John, 92, 118, 119
Kevorkian, Jack, 170
Kiddy Porn Panic, 137
Kimmeldorf, Howard, 54
Kirkland, Lane, 55
Kirkpatrick, Jeanne, 227n17
Klandermans, Bert, 245
Kohl's (retailer), 89
Korey, William, 215, 219, 224
Kramer, Larry, 142
Kuk-Dong factory, 93
Kuwait, Iraqi invasion of, 246

labor movement, 53–64; AFL-CIO, 54–56; effect of recession on, 60–63; effect of war against Afghanistan on, 60–63; efforts to enforce federal laws, 55; and globalization, 58–60; Internet use and, 57; organizing new economy's labor force, 56–58; overview, 53–54; Republican actions and, 55, 60–61; and unemployment, 63; union density, 55. *See also* anti-sweatshop movement; class

landmines, 223

L.C., Olmstead v., 177

leathermen, 136, 137, 138

Lefever, Ernest, 218

Lefkowitz, Joel, 83, 266

left movements, use of term, 2–5

Legal Defense and Educational Fund, 212

Lesbian Avengers, 147–48

lesbianism: and AIDS activism, 147–48; and Women's Party for Survival, 110

Lewis, Jerry, 164

liberal, use of term, 1–2

liberal feminism, 104

liberal values, American. *See* Human Rights Watch

Lichbach, Mark, 8

LIFE for Relief & Development, 255

Life Under Siege Encampments, 254, 259

Light, Paul, 71

living wage campaigns, 92–93

Los Angeles Times, 30

MacManus, Susan, 76

MAI. *See* Multilateral Agreement on Investment

Mandela, Nelson, 151

Marcuse, Herbert, 144

market system

Marullo, Sam, 236, 237

Marx, Karl, 17, 26, 85

Marxism, 3, 25, 104

Marymount University's Center for Ethical Concerns, 88

materialism, and left and right movements, 3–4. *See also* postmaterialism

material needs, movements based on.

See anti-sweatshop movement; labor movement; senior interest groups

McDowell, Rick, 256

McGroarty, John S., 66

McKinney, Cynthia A., 94

McKnight, John, 140

McKusick, Lwon, 136

McNulty, Jimmy, 151

medical model, 177–78

Medicare Catastrophic Care Act, 77

Medicare Catastrophic Coverage Act, 72–73

Medicare/Medicaid, 65, 69, 72–73, 75, 78

Meerse, Katherine, 230

Meese Commission Report on Pornography, 137

Melucci, Alberto, 86

membership requirements, 107

mental health care, 178

Mental Patients' Liberation Front, 166

Mexico, Zapatista uprising, 23, 152

Mexmode, 93

Middle East, war in. *See* Gulf War

Middle East Children's Alliance, 255

militarism, movements against. *See* peace movement; Women's Action for New Directions

Millennium Summit, 32

minority groups, and cuts in public programs, 78

Moller, Kirsten, 36, 37

Moody, Kim, 92

Moore, Michael, 32

Mothers' Day nuclear disarmament coalitions, 110, 111

The Mouth (periodical), 165

movements, use of term, 5–6, 7

Moynihan, Daniel Patrick, 141

Multilateral Agreement on Investment (MAI), 22

Murray, Stephen O., 136

Muscular Dystrophy Association, 164

Myers, Woodrow, 144

NAACP. *See* National Association for the Advancement of Colored People

Nader, Ralph, 191–93, 194, 195, 196–98, 199–200, 201, 206
NAFTA. *See* North American Free Trade Agreement
Names Quilt, 140
NARFE. *See* National Association of Retired Federal Employees
NASC. *See* National Alliance of Senior Citizens
National Alliance of Senior Citizens (NASC), 69
National Association for Retarded Children, 164
National Association for Retarded Citizens, 164
National Association for the Advancement of Colored People (NAACP), 212
National Association of Retired Federal Employees (NARFE), 67
National Association of the Deaf, 164
national budgetary process, 123–24
National Civil Liberties Bureau, 232
National Committee to Preserve Social Security and Medicare (NCPSSM), 69
National Council of Senior Citizens (NCSC), 67, 70
National Council on Disability, 169–70
National Election Study (NES), 194
National Emergency Coalition to Stop the War against Iraq, 257
National Gay, Lesbian, and Bisexual March on Washington, D.C., 140
National Guard, 253
National Institute on Aging (NIA), 73
National Intelligence Estimates, 126
National Labor Relations Act, 62
National Labor Relations Board, 55
National Retired Teachers Association, 67
Nature Conservancy, 5
NCPSSM. *See* National Committee to Preserve Social Security and Medicare
NCSC. *See* National Council of Senior Citizens

NDY. *See* Not Dead Yet
Neier, Aryeh, 216–17, 219, 227n13
neoliberalism, 20
NES. *See* National Election Study
Ness, Immanuel, 53, 266
New England Non-Resistance Society, 231
New Era, 93
New International Economic Order, 27
New Party, 7
new social movement (NSM) theories, 3–4, 85–87, 102–8
New World Order, 27, 31, 44–45
New York State Air National Guard, 253
New York Times, 152
New York University, living wage campaign, 93
NGOs. *See* nongovernmental organizations
NIA. *See* National Institute on Aging
Niemoller, Martin, 138
Night of Rage, 148
Nike Corporation, 93
1999 Seattle protests. *See* Seattle protests (1999)
1963 Test Ban Treaty. *See* Test Ban Treaty (1963)
Nobel Peace Prize, 217, 258
nongovernmental organizations (NGOs): growing political significance of, 213; and human rights, 225n4; role in anti-globalization movements, 25, 27–28, 41–42. *See also names of specific NGOs*
Non-Nuclear World Weekend, 111
North American Free Trade Agreement (NAFTA), 20, 23
Northrop, Ann, 146, 150
Not Dead Yet (NDY), 169
NSM. *See* new social movement theories
nuclear freeze campaign, 239–41
Nuclear Freeze Petition, 112
nuclear proliferation, movements against. *See* peace movement; Women's Action for New Directions

nuclear utilization targeting strategy
    (NUTS), 240

OAA. *See* Older Americans Act
OECD. *See* Organization for Economic
    Cooperation and Development
Oegema, Dirk, 245
Offe, Claus, 4
Ohio State University, 93–94
oil-for-food program, 247, 248, 258
Older Americans Act (OAA), 78
Olive Branch Petition, 231
Olmstead v. L.C., 177
Olson, Laura Katz, 65, 266
Omran Bus Tour, 253
Oprah (television show), 254
Ordeshook, Peter C., 171
"organizational maintenance," 106–7
Organization for Economic Coopera-
    tion and Development (OECD), 22,
    32
"outside" strategy, 7

pacifist groups, 238. *See also* peace
    movement
Paralyzed Veterans of America, 164
parties, use of term, 5–6, 7
Paul VI, Pope, 230
Pax Christi, 244
peace, defined, 229–30
Peace Democrats, 231
peace movement: current trends,
    244–46; groups comprising, 230;
    and Gulf War, 241–44; history of,
    230–33; Internet use and, 243,
    244–45; limited success of, 238;
    nuclear freeze campaign, 239–41;
    number of groups involved in, 233;
    pacifist groups, 238; public opinion
    use, 235; and strategic defense ini-
    tiative, 240; tactics of, 233–38; and
    Vietnam War, 239. *See also* Voices in
    the Wilderness
Peck, Edward, 258
Pelosi, Nancy, 33
pension movements, 66–67

People's Campaign for Nonviolence,
    255
People's Council of America for Peace
    and Democracy, 231–32
People's Global Action (PGA), 23
Persian Gulf, war in. *See* Gulf War
Peterson, Steven A., 76
Pfeiffer, David, 159, 266
PGA. *See* People's Global Action
Physicians for Social Responsibility,
    106, 108, 256
Piven, Frances Fox, 87–88, 89
Pogue, Alan, 255
"political," use of term, 4–5
Pope Paul VI, 230
Populorum Progressio (Pope Paul VI),
    230
PoR (Professionalization of Reform),
    140–42
Pôrto Alegre, Brazil, 34, 45
postmaterialism, 103; and 2000 elec-
    tion, 194–96, 198; and left and right
    movements, 3–4, 172–73; measure
    of, 203–7
postmaterialist identities, movements
    based on. *See* AIDS Coalition to
    Unleash Power; disability move-
    ment; Women's Action for New
    Directions
postmaterialists, voting tendencies of,
    195
poverty: effect of globalization on, 21;
    of elderly, 65–66; gap between
    wealth and, 27
Powell, Lawrence, 69–70
pragmatism, 86–87
Pratt, Henry, 65
Prisoners of Conscience, 217
Professionalization of Reform (PoR),
    141
progressive movements: effect of Sep-
    tember 11, 2001, terrorist attacks on,
    12–13; use of term, 2. *See also* social
    movements
Proposition 187, 148
Public Citizen, 25

Public Education Program, 39
Public Law 94–142, 166
public opinion, peace movement's use of, 235
public sector workers, 62
pure refusal concept, 144

queer activism. *See* AIDS Coalition to Unleash Power
Queer Nation, 146–47

racial minority groups, and Green parties, 200–201
radicalism, 86–87
The Ragged Edge (periodical), 165
Rainforest Action Network, 33
Randolph, A. Philip, 10
rational choice theory, 8, 86, 171
Reagan administration: arms control, 240, 241; Diaper Campaign directed at, 119; and globalization, 20; and human rights, 218–19; and programs for elderly, 68, 70, 73–74, 77
Reality Tours, 38–39
Reebok Corporation, 93
reform versus revolution, 34–35
Rehabilitation Act, 166, 167
Reich, Robert, 92
Remembering Omran Bus Tour, 253
Reno, Janet, 249
Republicans: and American labor movement, 55, 60–61; and disability issues, 174–75; and senior interest groups, 70, 76
resource mobilization (RM) theory, 8–9, 86, 105–8
Revolution, American, 231
Rhodebeck, Laurie, 73
Rifkin, Jeremy, 32
Riker, William, 168, 171
Ritter, Scott, 258
RM. *See* resource mobilization theory
Rodriguez, Kenia, 84, 85
Rofes, Eric, 137, 140, 149
Rolson, Adam, 140
Roosevelt, Eleanor, 214
Roth, Ken, 216, 219

Rubin, Gayle, 138
Russo, Vito, 139, 139–40, 153

Sakharov, Andrei, 216
San Francisco Department of Health, 136
San Francisco Examiner, 136
SAPs. *See* structural adjustment policies
Sarkees, Meredith Reid, 229, 266
Sawyer, Eric, 150
Schneider, Claudine, 118
School of the Americas (SOA) Watch, 233
Schroeder, Patricia, 118
Schulman, Sara, 147–48
Scotch, Richard, 170–71
SDI. *See* strategic defense initiative
SDS. *See* Society for Disability Studies
Seattle protests (1999), 1, 12, 17, 28, 30
Section 504, 166
Sedgwick, Eve, 139
SEIU. *See* Service Employees International Union
senior interest groups, 65–82; "electoral bluff," 76–77; emergence and growth of, 67–70; health care, 75; historical considerations, 65–67; 1990s and beyond, 77–78; pension movements, 66–67; power over social policy, 73–76; unemployment and poverty among elderly, 65–66. *See also names of specific senior interest groups*
Seniors Coalition, 69
September 11, 2001, terrorist attacks: effect on anti-globalization movements, 44–45; effect on Green mobilization, 201; effect on labor movements, 60–63; effect on social movements, 12–13; Teamsters response to, 64n7; Voices in the Wilderness response to, 256; Women's Action for New Directions response to, 125–27
Service Employees International Union (SEIU), 55

SexPanic!, 149
sex panics, 135–38
Shaer, Susan, 121, 123
Shaw, Randy, 88
Sheldon, Sayre, 114
Shell Oil Corporation, 38
Shepard, Benjamin, 133, 266–67
Shilts, Randy, 136
Sibley, Tom, 60
Sierra Club, 25
Sikkink, Kathryn, 220, 222
Silverman, Merv, 136
Simmons, James R., 187, 267
Simmons, Solon J., 187, 267
Sinker, Daniel, 259
60/Plus Association, 69
Smith, Jackie, 236
SMOs. *See* social movement organizations
SOA. *See* School of the Americas Watch
social capital metaphor, 9
social justice: and AIDS Coalition to Unleash Power, 148–49; use of term, 6
social movement organizations (SMOs), use of term, 6–7. *See also* transnational social movement organizations (TSMOs)
social movements: circumstances resulting in, 102; and cultural hegemony, 9; disagreements between, 10–12; effect of structural changes on, 106; examples of, 102–3; goals of, 11; membership requirements, 107; "organizational maintenance," 106–7; postmaterialist theory, 103; radicalism versus pragmatism, 86–87; resource mobilization theory, 86, 105–8; strategies of, 11–12; and structural determinism, 8–9; theories of, 7–9; use of term, 5–7, 175–76; why rational individuals join, 8. *See also* progressive movements
Social Security, 65–67, 68, 69, 70, 77
Society for Disability Studies (SDS), 165

sodomy law, 139
Solo, Pam, 119
Somit, Albert, 76
South Africa, generic drug production, 150–53
Spannon, Brad, 1
special education, 162
spokescouncils, 30–31
Sponeck, Hans von, 258
Sprong, Michael, 253, 254
SSI. *See* Supplementary Security Income
Starbucks Corporation, 40, 42–43
Star Wars (strategic defense initiative), 240
Stein, Leon, 87
Stocker, Michael, 74
strategic defense initiative (SDI), 240
Strauss, Leo, 5
structural adjustment policies (SAPs), 29
structural determinism, 8–9, 104–5
Students Against Sweatshops. *See* anti-sweatshop movement
Students for Social Equality, 93
Students Taking Action for New Directions (STAND), 122
Supplementary Security Income (SSI), 78
Surkin, Marvin, 4
sweatshops, students against. *See* anti-sweatshop movement
Sweeney, John, 32, 55, 56, 92, 94
syndicalism, 54

"Talking Points on National Missile Defense," 126
Tarrow, Sidney, 6, 15n25, 104, 112
tax breaks, 60
TCs. *See* transnational corporations
Teamsters: response to September 11, 2001, terrorist attacks, 64n7; use of term, 1, 54
terrorist attacks of September 11, 2001. *See* September 11, 2001, terrorist attacks
Test Ban Treaty (1963), 232

Thatcher, Margaret, 20
"There Is No Alternative" (TINA) policy, 20
Third World nations: debt-relief plan, 32; influence on anti-globalization movements, 23; labor rights, 38; Reality Tours, 38–39; use of term, 46n5. *See also* anti-sweatshop movement
Thompson, Mark, 138
TINA. *See* "There Is No Alternative" policy
Title V senior employment, 78
Townsend, Francis E., 66
Townsend movement, 66
trade organizations, and global capitalism, 20
transnational corporations (TCs), 222–23
transnational social movement organizations (TSMOs), *236*, 244
Treaty Bodies, 215
True, Michael, 230
TSMOs. *See* transnational social movement organizations
Turnabout report, 118–19
turtles, use of term, 1, 54
Tutu, Desmond, 152–53
Twin Towers attack. *See* September 11, 2001, terrorist attacks
TWO. *See* Woodlawn Organization, The
"200 Club: A Proposal for Electoral Empowerment," 120

UAW. *See* United Auto Workers
UDHR. *See* Universal Declaration of Human Rights
unemployment, 63, 65–66
Union Cities program, 57
Union of International Associations, 213
unions. *See* labor movement
Union Summer, 89–90
UNITE. *See* United Needletrades, Industrial, and Textile Employees
United Auto Workers (UAW), 58
United Nations Organization: Declara-

tion of Human Rights, 33; embargo on Iraq, 246, 247; Global Compact, 32; and human rights, 212, 214; Subcommission on Human Rights, 247; Voices in the Wilderness at, 254, 259; World Court, 33
United Needletrades, Industrial, and Textile Employees (UNITE), 55
United Seniors Association (USA), 69
United States Department of Health, Education, and Welfare (HEW), 166
United States exceptionalism, 213
United States foreign policy structure, 233–34
United Students against Sweatshops (USAS), 84, 85, 89–90, 92, 95
Universal Declaration of Human Rights (UDHR), 214
University of California, San Diego, living wage campaign, 93
University of Connecticut, living wage campaign, 92–93
University of Kentucky, living wage campaign, 93
University of Wisconsin, living wage campaign, 93
University of Wisconsin at Madison, 91
Urban Mass Transportation Act, 166
USA. *See* United Seniors Association
USAS. *See* United Students against Sweatshops
U.S. Department of Health, Education, and Welfare (HEW), 166
U.S. exceptionalism, 213
user fee, 32–33
U.S. foreign policy structure, 233–34

Vance, Cyrus, 218
Veterans for Peace, 255
Vietnam War, 232–33, 237, 239
violence, from anti-globalization movements, 33, 40–41
VitW. *See* Voices in the Wilderness
Voices in Basra Project, 252
Voices in the Wilderness (VitW), 246–59; background, 248–51; cooperation with other organizations,

255; and educating public, 251; goal of involvement in electoral activities, 256; influence of, 257–59; and Life Under Siege Encampments, 254; overview, 246; response to September 11, 2001, terrorist attacks, 256; sending delegations to Iraq, 251–53; website, 253

voting: by elderly, 76–77; by postmaterialists, 195

Voting Accessibility for the Elderly and Handicapped Act, 167

Walker, Jack, 7
Walk for Healing and Peace, 256
Wallach, Lori, 32, 40–41, 45
WAND. *See* Women's Action for New Directions
Washington, George, 231
Washington Consensus, 20, 31
WCTU. *See* Women's Christian Temperance Union
wealth, gap between poverty and, 27
Welch, Claude E., Jr., 211, 267
Wertz, Dorothy C., 162
Wesleyan University, living wage campaign, 93
Western Hemisphere Institute for Security Cooperation, 233
Western Social Science Association, 165
White House Conference on Handicapped Individuals, 166–67
Wichita Metropolitan Transit Authority, 160
WiLL. *See* Women Legislators' Lobby
Williamson, John, 69–70
WILPF. *See* Women's International League for Peace and Freedom
Wilson, Hank, 144
Wilson, Pete, 134
Wojnarowicz, David, 140
Women's Action for New Directions (WAND), 101–31; affiliate development, 121; broadening of issue focus, 123; budgetary and electoral emphases, 121–24; cultural feminist characteristics, 104; fundraising,

121–22; membership, 121–22; name change to, 121; and national budgetary process, 123–24; 1990–2001, 121–24; opposition to House Resolution 195, 126; overview, 101–2; partner organizations, 122–23; response to September 11, 2001, terrorist attacks, 125–27; social movement events leading up to, 103–5; Women Take Action for Real Security campaign, 125–26. *See also* Women's Action for Nuclear Disarmament; Women's Party for Survival (forerunner of WAND)

Women's Action for Nuclear Disarmament (WAND), 101; Constitutional Peace Initiative, 120; Diaper Campaign, 119; fundraising, 115–17; media campaign, 119–20; membership, 115–16; name change to, 113–14; 1982–1990, 113–20; reconfiguration and institutionalization in, 113–20; Turnabout report, 118–19; 200 Club, 120. *See also* Women's Action for New Directions (WAND); Women's Party for Survival

Women's Christian Temperance Union (WCTU), 231
Women's Equality Summit and Congressional Action Day, 127
Women's International League for Peace and Freedom (WILPF), 229–30, 232
women's movements, general discussion, 103–6
Women's Party for Survival, 101, 106; founding and early history of, 108–13; and lesbianism, 110; racial diversity in, 109–10. *See also* Women's Action for Nuclear Disarmament (WAND)
Women's Peace Party, 232
Women's Peace Union, 232
Women's Strike for Peace, 111
Wo-Men for Survival, 109

Women Legislators' Lobby (WiLL), 122–23, 126
Women Take Action for Real Security campaign, 125–26
Woodlawn Organization, The (TWO), 156n48
Workers' Rights Consortium (WRC), 91–92
Workers Party, 25, 34
Workers Rights Consortium, 90
World Bank, 19, 29, 31–33, 223
World Bank Bond boycott, 43
World Court, 33
World Development Reports, 31
World Economic Forum, 32
World Social Forum, 34, 45
World Trade Center attack. *See* September 11, 2001, terrorist attacks

World Trade Organization (WTO): and American labor movement, 59; changes in policies and practices, 31–32; and human rights, 223; ruling of U.S. laws as barriers to free trade, 29–30; and Seattle meetings, 17
World Values surveys, 172–73
WRC. *See* Workers' Rights Consortium
WTO. *See* World Trade Organization

Yearbook of International Organizations, 244

Zald, Mayer N., 106, 107, 113, 120
Zapatista uprising, 23, 152
Zweig, Michael, 3

About the Contributors

John C. Berg teaches political science at Suffolk University and is the reviews editor for *New Political Science*. His Marxist analysis of Congress, *Unequal Struggle: Class, Gender, Race, and Power in the US Congress*, was published in 1994; he is now working on a book about Ralph Nader, the Greens, and the role of minor parties in political change.

Frank L. Davis is associate professor of political science at Lehigh University. His areas of specialty are interest groups, political parties, and the U.S. Congress. Davis has published in *Political Studies*, *Polity*, *American Politics Quarterly*, *New Political Science*, and *American Review of Politics*.

Melissa Haussman is an associate professor of government at Suffolk University. Her graduate work, in Canadian and U.S. comparative politics, was done at Carleton University, Ottawa, Canada, and Duke University. Her research interests focus on women's movement strategies for legislative and constitutional change in the United States and Canada.

Ronald Hayduk teaches political science at the City University of New York and is a consultant to the Aspen Institute. He was the director of the New York City Voter Assistance Commission from 1993 to 1996 and was a consultant to Demos: A Network for Ideas and Action from 1999 to 2001. Hayduk has written about political participation, race and regionalism, immigration, and social movements including co-editing *From ACT UP to Seattle: Urban Activism and Community Building in the Era of Globalization* (2001). Hayduk is currently finishing a book on election administration and voter participation.

Christine Kelly is assistant professor of political science at William Paterson University and the author of *Tangled Up in Red, White, and Blue* (2001).

Joel Lefkowitz is assistant professor of political science at the State University of New York at New Paltz.

Immanuel Ness is associate professor of political science at Brooklyn College, City University of New York. His research focuses on labor, electoral politics, and union organizing. He is currently working on a book on organizing and union jurisdiction among new immigrant workers.

Laura Katz Olson has been a professor of political science at Lehigh University since 1974. She has published four books: *The Political Economy of Aging: The State, Private Power and Social Welfare*; *Aging and Public Policy: The Politics of Growing Old in America*; *The Graying of the World: Who Will Take Care of the Frail Elderly*; and *Age Through Ethnic Lenses: Caring for the Elderly in a Multicultural Society*. Currently she is working on another book, *The Not So Golden Years*. She has published widely in the field of aging and women's studies on such topics as pensions, Social Security, problems of older women, and long-term care.

David Pfeiffer is resident scholar in the Center on Disability Studies at the University of Hawaii at Manoa and he is also associated with the Department of Urban and Regional Planning and the Department of Pediatrics (John A. Burns School of Medicine). He has a number of publications in the field of disability studies and other policy areas. His Ph.D. is from the University of Rochester and he is a wheelchair user. He is a past president of the Society for Disability Studies and is presently editor of *Disability Studies Quarterly*.

Meredith Reid Sarkees is currently a visiting professor of political science at DePaul University. Her past articles have included examinations of U.S. foreign policy and politics in the Middle East. She has worked for many years with J. David Singer and the Correlates of War Project at the University of Michigan. She has also investigated the role of women in foreign policy formulation and is the author, with Nancy E. McGlen, of *Women in Foreign Policy: The Insiders* (1993).

Benjamin Shepard is a social worker moonlighting as a social historian. From nine to five, he works as program director for a supportive housing program for people with HIV/AIDS and substance abuse histories in the South Bronx. After five, Shepard is involved in campaigns to prevent New York City from becoming one giant shopping mall. He is coeditor of *From ACT UP to the WTO: Urban Protest and Community Building in the Era of Globalization* (2001) and author of *White Nights and Ascending Shadows: An Oral History of the San Francisco AIDS Epidemic* (1997). His work has appeared in *Monthly Review, WorkingUSA: A Journal of Labor, Minnesota Review, Antioch Review,* and David Colbert's *Eyewitness to the American West: 500 Years of Firsthand History* (1999).

James R. Simmons is chair of the political science department at the University of Wisconsin, Oshkosh. Jim teaches and does research in public policy, public administration, American politics, and environmental studies. He has published work extensively in journals ranging from *New Political Science* and the *Policy Studies Journal* to *Extrapolation and Environmental Impact Assessment Review.* He is the coauthor (with Benjamin I. Page) of *What Government Can Do* (2000).

Solon J. Simmons is a graduate student in sociology at the University of Wisconsin, Madison. His research interests are in social stratification, class analysis, political behavior, and quantitative methods. He is currently writing a dissertation on the continuing influence of social class on party identification and presidential voting.

Claude E. Welch, Jr., is distinguished service professor and director of the Human Rights Center/Program in International and Comparative Law, University of Buffalo of the State University of New York.

DATE DUE